Adventures in Mexico
and the Rocky Mountains

Adventures in Mexico and the Rocky Mountains

Experiences of Mexico and the American South West during the 1840's

George F. Ruxton

LEONAUR

Adventures in Mexico and the Rocky Mountains
Experiences of Mexico and the
American South West during the 1840's
by George F. Ruxton

First published under the titles
Adventures in Mexico and the Rocky Mountains

Leonaur is an imprint
of Oakpast Ltd

ISBN: 978-1-84677-790-5 (hardcover)
ISBN: 978-1-84677-789-9 (softcover)

http://www.leonaur.com

Publisher's Notes

In the interests of authenticity, the spellings, grammar and place names
used have been retained from the original editions.

The opinions of the authors represent a view of events in which he
was a participant related from his own perspective,
as such the text is relevant as an historical document.

The views expressed in this book are not necessarily
those of the publisher.

Contents

Preface

Some apology, I am aware, is necessary for offering so meagre an account of Mexico as that which is set before the reader in the following pages. In justice to myself, however, I may state that all the notes and memoranda of the country I passed through, as well as several valuable and interesting documents and MSS. connected with the history of Northern Mexico and its Indian tribes, which I had collected, were unfortunately destroyed (with the exception of my rough notebook) in passing the Pawnee fork of the river Arkansas, as I have mentioned in the body of this narrative; and this loss has left me no alternative but to give a brief outline of my journey, which, bare as it may be, I prefer to lay before the reader in its present shape, rather than draw at hazard from the treacherous notebook of memory, or the less reliable source of a fertile imagination.

It is hardly necessary to explain the cause of my visiting Mexico at such an unsettled period; and I fear that circumstances will prevent my gratifying the curiosity of the reader, should he feel any on that point.

This little work is merely what its title professes it to be, *The Rough Notes of a Journey through Mexico, and a Winter spent among the wild scenes and wilder characters of the Rocky Mountains,* and has no higher aim than to give an idea of the difficulties and hardships a traveller may anticipate, should he venture to pass through it and mix with its semi-barbarous and uncouth people, and to draw a faint picture of the lives of those hardy pioneers of civilization, whose lot is cast upon the boundless prairies and rugged mountains of the Far West.

With a solitary exception, I have avoided touching upon American subjects; not only because much abler pens than mine have done that country and people more or less justice or injustice, and I wished to attempt to describe nothing that other English travellers have written upon before, and to give a rough sketch of a very rough journey through comparatively new ground; but, more than all, for the reason that I have, on this and previous visits to the United States, met with such genuine kindness and unbounded hospitality from all classes of the American people, both the richest and the poorest, that I have not the heart to say one harsh word of them or theirs, even if I could or would.

Faults the Americans have—and who have not? But they are, I maintain, failings of the head and not the heart, which nowhere beats warmer, or in a more genuine spirit of kindness and affection, than in the bosom of a citizen of the United States.

Would that I could say as much of the sister people. From south to north I traversed the whole of the Republic of Mexico, a distance of nearly two thousand miles, and was thrown among the people of every rank, class, and station; and I regret to have to say that I cannot remember to have observed one single commendable trait in the character of the Mexican; always excepting from this sweeping clause the women of the country, who, for kindness of heart and many sterling qualities, are an ornament to their sex, and to any nation.

If the Mexican possesses one single virtue, as I hope he does, he must keep it so closely hidden in some secret fold of his *sarape* as to have escaped my humble sight, although I travelled through his country with eyes wide open, and for conviction ripe and ready. I trust, for his sake, that he will speedily withdraw from the bushel the solitary light of this concealed virtue, lest before long it be absorbed in the more potent flame which the Anglo-Saxon seems just now disposed to shed over benighted Mexico.

CHAPTER 1

Under Weigh

On the 2nd of July, 1846 at one p.m. the Royal Mail-packet steamed out of Southampton Water. For three hours we had been in the usual state of confusion attending the sailing of a packet on a long voyage. Being the first on board, and having no friends with long faces and handkerchiefs to their eyes to distract my attention, I had leisure to look about me, and survey the different passengers who came on board, in every stage of delight and despair. Some there were who possibly had set their feet for the last time on their native shore, and had in perspective a tropical futurity, with sugar-hogsheads, cocoa-nuts and *vomito* in the distance.

Others again were homeward bound, delighted to turn their backs on the suicidal mists of the isle of vapours, and revelling in anticipated enjoyment of the fiery paradise beyond the sea. Red and swelled eyes, however, were in a decided majority; and as the steam hissed and snorted, so did faces become more elongated, and the corners of mouths take a downward angle.

At length the ominous bell gave notice that the moment of parting had arrived. Fathers and mothers, brothers and sisters, and lovers with quivering lip, for the last time embraced; the tender cast off her hawser, and the huge steamer was speeding on her way. And now solitary figures with swelled eyes leaned over the taffrail, gazing intently toward the land, and at the little speck dancing on the waves, which was bearing so quickly away loved objects, seen by many of them for the last time.

Our passengers comprised a motley group: Creoles of the West India islands and the main, Spaniards of Havana, French of Martinique and Guadaloupe, Danes of St. Thomas, Dutch of Caraçao, Portuguese of Madeira, Jamaica Jews, merchants of Costa Rica, military officers, and emigrating Yorkshire farmers, were among the various items of the human freight.

However, forty-eight hours' shaking together amalgamated the mass; and when that number of hours and a southernly course had carried us into a smooth sea and heavenly climate; all sorrows were for the time forgotten. A Jamaica Jew had taken up a position on the cabin skylight, where, with a pack of cards and a pile of gold before him, he every day, and all day long, officiated as *dueño* of a *monté*-table, a little Rabbi, throwing aside his sacerdotal cares, and shining in glossy black, superintending the receipts and disbursements of the bank. The *provideur*, who, by the way, was the life of the ship, was already chalking on the deck a marine billiard-table; and under his direction and tuition, English and French, Spaniards and Dutch, were soon engaged in momentous matches, on which depended many a bottle of iced champagne.

These amusements, combined with a vast deal of eating, drinking, and smoking, fortunately preserved us in good humour for six days; when, just as shovel-board had lost its charms, champagne its flavour, and the *monté* Israelite his customers, the welcome cry of "Land, ho!" at midnight on the 12th, turned out all hands on deck; and there, looming in the hazy distance on our starboard bow, lay Puerto Santo, part and parcel of "soft" Madeira.

When I rose the next morning we were standing into Funchal Roads, and shortly after came to anchor within three quarters of a mile of the shore and opposite the town of Funchal. At this distance the island, rising to a great elevation from the water's edge, with the town, washed by the Atlantic, at its base, and innumerable white houses, with here and there a convent's spires, dotted up the sides, resembles a scene of a gigantic panorama, with every object so clearly displayed to the eye, and fore and background of deep-blue sky and azure-sea.

On landing in one of the country boats, as soon as the keel had touched the beach, a cavalcade of horsemen, mounted on handsome, active ponies, charged to the very water's edge, and, nearly trampling us in their furious onslaught, reined up suddenly, bringing their steeds on their haunches. Our first thought was instant flight; but, finding their object was pacific, we learned that this Arab-like proceeding was for the purpose of displaying the merits of their cattle, and to tempt us to engage in an equestrian expedition up the mountain. Selecting three promising-looking animals, and preceded by their funnel-capped proprietors as guides, we proceeded to the town.

Funchal in no degree differs from any sea or riverside town in Portugal. The Funchalese are Portuguese in form and feature; the women, if possible, more ordinary, and the beggars more importunate and persevering. The beach is covered with plank sleds, to which are yoked most comical little oxen no larger than donkeys. In these sleds the hogsheads of wine are conveyed to the boats, as they are better adapted to the rough shingle than wheeled conveyances. To a stranger the trade of the town appears to be monopolized by vendors of straw hats and canary-birds. These articles of merchandise are thrust into one's face at every step. *Sombreros* are pounded upon your head; showers of canaries and goldfinches, with strings attached to their legs, are fired like rockets into your face; and the stunning roar of the salesmen deafen the ear.

Ascending the precipitous *ruas*, we soon reached the suburbs, our guides holding on by the tails of the horses to facilitate their ascent. Still mounting, we pass where vines are trellised over the road; sweet-smelling geraniums, heliotrope, and fuschias overhang the garden-walls on each side; while, in the beautiful little gardens which every where meet the eye, the graceful banana, the orange-tree and waving maize, the tropical aloe and homely oak, form the most pleasing contrasts and enchant the sight. Winding still up the mountainside, the interminable stone-paved suburb is passed; but even while toiling over the uneven, slippery pavement, and sitting in an almost vertical saddle, hanging on to the mane like grim death, it is impossible even to whisper an imprecation, everything around is so soft and pleasing; and, *malgré lui*, one (even if he be an Englishman) has not the heart to growl or complain.

Here the vivid colourings of a tropical scene blend in harmony with the sober tints of a more temperate landscape. By the orange and leaf-spreading banana grow the oak and apple; the cactus and the daisy bloom together; the luscious pine and humble potato yield their fruit; and, side by side with the golden-coloured canary, the robin redbreast warbles his sweet and well-known song.

The sides of the mountain are clothed with vines, and numerous streamlets trickle along the roadside, cooling the air with their refreshing murmurs; while a mountain torrent here and there forces its impetuous way. The paths which wind along the mountain overhang precipices lined with foliage, and water everywhere glitters through the verdure and relieves the eye. In the valleys are seen delicious nooks, green and cool, shadowed by the lofty rocks, with picturesque cottages and smiling gardens, and scenes of such quiet beauty as one never tires to gaze upon. Turning in your saddle, you see the town of Funchal at your feet, reflected in the smooth and glittering sea. The vessels in the roads appear no larger than fishing-boats; and the huge steamer, lying lazily at her anchor, will be the victim of a malediction, that it is so soon to bear you away from this sweet island.

The sun, too, is not the fireball of the tropics, or even the heat-engendering luminary we have left behind us, but shines faintly bright through a dim, soft mist; and while sweet-smelling flowers dispense their odours around, and the notes of song-birds are heard on every side, the air breathes soft and soothingly.

With no little regret I turned my horse's head down the mountainside, after several hours' ramble in this Elysian spot; and not even a glass of the Messrs. Gordon's Tinta or Malvozia, of a choice vintage, could reconcile me to the idea of again entering the snorting prison-house which puffed impatiently in the roads.

On leaving Madeira we had thirteen days of most monotonous steaming, during which a most universal *ennui* prevailed on board, relieved occasionally by the outbreakings of some wooer of the fickle goddess, whose winnings as losings had been more than usually great, and consequently occasioned a greater or leas amount of self-gratulation or excitement. When every mortal means of amusement was supposed to have been exhausted, it was providentially discovered that the Rabbi was in the habit of slaying with his own hand, and according to the strict letter of the Mosaic Law, the docks, fowls, and sheep which he desired to devour.

The day after the discovery the butcher was seen to approach the Rabbi with some mysterious communication, who immediately tucked up his sleeves, took a knife which was handed to him by the butcher, and accompanied that functionary to the hen-coops.

In an instant the quarter-deck was deserted; every passenger stealthily took up a position where he could witness the mysterious catastrophe. The Rabbi, with upturned wristbands, carefully kneaded the breasts of several fowls which were offered to his knife by the butcher, and at length, selecting one whose condition was undeniable, casting up his eyes and invoking Moses to give him the requisite nerve, he administered the mystic stab, and instantly retreated. As a reward for the excitement he had caused, I noticed that at dinner that day the Rabbi received most friendly offers of ham and roast pork.

On the thirteenth morning after leaving Madeira the low, regular outline of Barbadoes was visible on the horizon. This island exhibits less tropical scenery than any other in the West Indies, being less mountainous, and the plains and hills cultivated in every part, and consequently the bush is cleared off to make way for agricultural improvements. It is not, however, the less beautiful on this account; and every where the snug-looking houses of the planters, with mills and sugar-houses, and all the appliances of thriving plantations, were seen as we hogged the

13

shore.

On landing I found myself, very fortunately and unexpectedly, among many old friends, whose hospitality I enjoyed during my stay at the island.

Among the celebrated of Barbadoes whom I deemed it my duty to visit, was the renowned Betsy Austin, once (in the days when the late King William was a jolly mid) the pride of the 'Badian dignity balls, but now in "the sere and yellow leaf," fat as a turtle, and always very drunk. I found the ancient beauty sitting in the verandah of her house, surrounded by a dozen sable and yellow handmaidens, some of them very pretty girls, who were engaged in pickling and preserving West India fruits. She insisted on my joining her in a *sangaree*, which was prepared in a tumbler holding about half a gallon; and, shaking my hand at parting, being crying drunk, slobbered out a "Gar bless you, sar! Hab notin to do wid Car'line Lee;" which Caroline Lee is own sister to Betsy, but guilty of keeping an opposition house, and hence the warning.

I found nothing striking in Barbadoes but the sun, which is a perpetual furnace, and the pepper-pot—a dish to the mysteries of which I was initiated here for the first time. It is a delicious compound of flesh, fish, and fowl, *piqué* with all the hot peppers and condiments the island produces, and mystified in a rich black sauce. The flavour of this wonderful dish is impossible to be described. Imagine a mass of cockroaches stewed in pitch, and a faint idea may be had of the appearance and smell of the savoury compound.

Of Bridgetown, the capital, the less said the better. It is infested with a most rascally and impudent race of Negroes, who almost resort to violence to wrench unwilling *pistareens* from the stranger's pocket. Just before my arrival half the town had most providentially been destroyed by fire, so that, if rebuilt, hopes are entertained of a more respectable-looking place being erected.

Chapter 2

A Capture

The next island touched at was Grenada, one of the most picturesque of the Antilles. The little harbour is completely land-locked, and, as it were, scooped out of the side of the mountain, which rises from the water's edge. An old green fort, perched upon a crag, commands the anchorage; and the little town, interspersed with palmtrees and aloes, appears to be crawling up the mountain. Here we remained but a few hours, and steered thence to San Domingo, one of the largest of the group. Coasting along, it presented a bold, imposing outline of rugged mountains covered with forests, and but little appearance of cultivation. Staying but a few hours at Jacmel, to receive and deliver mails, we soon came in sight of Jamaica, with its fine bold scenery of mountain and valley; and, threading the intricate and dangerous reefs, and passing the forts and batteries of Port Royal, we anchored, about noon, off Kingston, the chief town of the island.

Here we left the greater part of our fellow-passengers, including the card-playing Jew and the Rabbi. The former left the steamer minus several hundred pounds by his *monté* speculation, the greater part of which had been won by two boys from Birmingham, who were on their way to Havana to set up a cooperage. Elated with their (to them) enormous gains, they, in honour of the occasion, sacrificed too freely to the rosy god, the consequence of which was, that, in a few weeks, both were carried off by the relentless *vomito*.

A couple of days spent among the *killbucra*[1] and *sopilotes*[2] of Uppark rendered my regret at leaving Jamaica anything but poignant; and, taking leave of the dusty, dirty town of Kingston, with its ruinous houses and miserable population, in a few days we were coasting along the south side of Cuba, passing Cape Antonio and the Isle of Pines, once famous, or, rather, infamous, as the resort of pirates, who infested these seas until within a few years, and still the rendezvous of equally nefarious slavers.

La Havana (the Haven) is one of the finest harbours in the world, and capable of holding a thousand vessels. It is completely land-locked, and the entrance so narrow that vessels must pass within musket-shot of the "Morro," whose frowning batteries lock down on the very decks. Besides the Morro, the formidable batteries of the Principe and La Cabaña show their teeth on each side, and numerous detached works crown every eminence.

The Spaniards may well be jealous of Cuba, which, with their usual *fanfaron* (just, however, in this case), they style *La joya mas brillante en la corona de España*—the most brilliant jewel in the crown of Spain. This, the last of their once magnificent dependencies, they may well guard with watchful eye; for not only do the colonists most cordially detest the mother country, and only wait an opportunity to throw off the yoke, but already an unscrupulous and powerful neighbour "of the north" casts a longing eye toward this rich and beautiful island.

The cruel dissensions and bloody revolutions which have so long convulsed unfortunate Spain have seldom extended their influences to this remote colony. Cuba, content in her riches and prosperity, has looked calmly on, indifferent to the throes which have agonised the maternal frame. Her boastful soubriquet, *Siempre fiel isla de Cuba*—the ever-faithful island of Cuba—has thus been: cheaply earned, and passively retained by the ironical Havaneros, who will assuredly one day pluck out from the Spanish crown this "fine jewel," or suffer it to be transferred to a foreign bonnet.

---

1. A yellow flower, which is said to be more abundant during sickly seasons.
2. The *sopilote* is the turkey-buzzard.

The harbour has been so often described that it is needless to dilate upon its beauties. In one corner is a rank mangrove swamp, which exhales a fatal *miasma*, and which, wafted by the land-breeze over the town and shipping, is one great cause of the deplorable mortality which occurs here in the sickly season. Havana is quite a Spanish town, and reminded me of Cadiz more than any other. It is, however, cleaner and better regulated, with a very efficient police. The streets are narrow, as they ought to be in hot countries, and toward the evening thronged with *volantes*, a light, spider-like carriage peculiar to Cuba, freighted with black-eyed beauties, on their way to the *paseo*, shopping, or to Dominica's, the celebrated *neveria* or ice-shop, where they very properly pull up a *refrescar un tantito*—to cool the courage-before "showing" on the excitable *paseo*.

From seven to ten the *Paseo Tacon* is thronged, and a stranger had better pause before he runs the gauntlet of such batteries of eyes and fans as be never before, in his northern philosophy, thought or dreamed of. The ladies dress in white, with their beautiful hair unsacrificed by bonnet, and, if ornamented, by a simple white or red rose, *á la moda Andaluza*, However perfect may be their figures, you see them not. One's gaze is concentrated in their large, lustrous eyes, which, when you get within their reach, swallow you up as the sun swallows a comet when he is rash enough to approach too near, throwing you out again, a burned-up cinder, to be resuscitated and reburned by the next eyes which pass. The Havaneras certainly surpass the Spaniards in the beauty of their eyes, if that be possible.

With their eyes and *abanicos* (fans) the Havaneras have no need of tongues, which, however, they can use on emergencies; whereas every pretty woman can, in some degree, "make the eyes speak," no other than a Spanish beauty can use a fan. This is to them the *idioma de amor*—the language of love. Assisted by the eye it is eloquence itself; and, in the hands of a coquet, like a gun in the hands of a careless boy, is a most dangerous weapon.

To see this language spoken in perfection, visit the theatre Tacon, which, by the way, is the prettiest theatre in the world.

Here, between the acts, nothing is heard but the clicking of fans, while cross-fires of lightning-glances pierce one through and through. The front of the boxes in the Tacon is of light open-work, through which the white dresses of the ladies are seen, and which has a very pretty effect. Unlike the boxes of our opera, which invidiously conceal all but the beauties "above the zone," here the whole figure, simply draped in white, is fully displayed. Foreigners say that an Englishwoman should never be seen but in an opera-box; and the Spaniards affirm that, whereas an "Englishwoman should be seen at a window, and a French-woman promenading, the gods have vouchsafed that a Spaniard may be looked at everywhere: "*La Ynglesa en la ventana, la Francesca paseandose, la Española, por onde se quiere.*"

Three miles from Havana is El Cerro, where the wealthy merchants have their country seats, and resort with their families during the sickly season. The fronts of these houses are completely open, save by light bars, so that at night, when lighted up, the whole interior is perfectly displayed. Night is the fashionable time for visiting; and through this open birdcage-work may be seen a formal row of males in front of the ladies, for here, in this excitable climate, it is deemed imprudent to bring into actual contact such substances as flint and steel, or fire and tow.

After four days' stay in Havana, I again embarked on board the steamer, and in such a storm of thunder and rain as I shall never forget. I engaged a shore-boat manned by two *mulattos*, and before we could reach the steamer the hurricane broke upon us. The lightning appeared actually to rain down, the flashes being incessant, while the rain descended with such violence as nearly to fill and swamp the boat. The boatmen swore and cursed, and crouched under the thwarts; the sail and mast were blown clean away; and for more than an hour we were unable to face the storm. At length, taking advantage of a lull, we managed to reach the vessel, and after a vexatious delay of several hours, got under weigh. On passing the Morro, we were hailed and ordered to bring to, while, at the same moment, a boat, with a corporal and three men, put off from the castle, and boarded us. We had on board a great number of passengers on their way to Mexico, and many were probably leaving Cuba without the necessary passport, so that, on the arrival of the boat, many olive-coloured gentlemen with moustaches dived suddenly below, being seized with a sadden desire to explore the hold and other cavernous portions of the ship. However, in a few minutes all the passengers were mustered on deck by the captain, and their names called.

As one unlucky Spaniard answered to his name, the corporal stepped up to him, laying his finger on his shoulder, with "*En el nombre del gobernador*"—in the name of the governor. "*A su disposicion, amigo*"—at your service, friend—answered the captured one, and, quietly lighting his cigar, descended into the guard-boat with his trunk, *en route* to the dungeons of *the* Morro.

"*Viva!*" exclaimed the Spaniards: "*maldito sea el déspota*"—curse the despot; and, breathing freely, relighted their *puros*, and indulged in a little abuse of their colonial government.

The day after our departure from Havana we overtook a small steamer, under the British flag, which was pronounced to be the *Arab*, having on board the ex-President of Mexico, General Santa Anna. As she signalled to speak, we bore down upon her, and, running alongside, her captain hailed to know if we would take on board four passengers; which was declined, our skipper not wishing to compromise himself with the American blockading squadron at Vera Cruz, by carrying Mexican officers. We had a good view of Santa Anna, and his pretty young wife, who, on hearing our decision, stamped her little foot on the deck, and turned poutingly to some of her suite.

It seemed that the *Arab* had disabled her machinery, and was making such slow progress that Santa Anna was desirous of continuing the trip in the *Medway*. He was provided with a passport from the government of the United States to enable him to pass the blockade; which very questionable policy on the part of that government it is difficult to understand, since they were well aware that Santa Anna was bitterly hostile to them, whatever assurances he may have made to the contrary; and at the same time was, perhaps, the only man whom the Mexican army would suffer to lead them against the American troops.

On the fifth morning after leaving Havana, at six a.m., we made the land, and were soon after boarded by one of the American blockading squadron—the corvet *St. Mary's*. It was expected that Santa Anna was on board, and the officer said that instructions had been received to permit him to enter Vera Cruz.

At seven we passed the castle of San Juan de Ulloa, and anchored off the city of the True Cross, or, as it is often and most aptly called, "*La Ciudad de los Muertos*"—The City of the Dead.

CHAPTER 3

The Fever-Cloud

Vera Cruz derives its name from the first city built on this continent by Cortes, in 1519-20. *La villa rica de la Vera Cruz*— the rich city of the True Cross—was situated a few miles to the north-east of the present city, and was built by the *conquistador* as a garrison on which to fall back, in case his expedition into the interior proved a failure.

From the sea the coast on each side the town presents a dismal view of sand hills, which appear almost to swallow up the walls. The town, however, sparkling in the sun, with its white houses and numerous church-spires, has rather a picturesque appearance; but every object, whether on sea or land, glows unnaturally in the lurid atmosphere. It is painful to look into the sea, where shoals of bright-coloured fish are swimming; and equally painful to turn the eyes to the shore, where the sun, refracted by the sand, actually scorches the sight, as well as pains it by the quivering glare which ever attends refracted light.

The city is well planned, surrounded by an *adobe* wall, with wide streets crossing each other at right angles. There are also several large and handsome buildings fast mouldering to decay. One hundred years ago a flourishing commercial city, like everything in Spanish America, it has suffered from the baneful effects of a corrupt, impotent government. Now, with a scanty population, and under the control of a military despotism, its wealth and influence have passed away.

The aspect of the interior of the town is dreary and desolate beyond description. Grass grows in the streets and squares; the churches and public buildings are falling to ruins; scarcely a human being is to be met, and the few seen are sallow and lank, and skulk through the streets as if fearing to encounter, at every corner, the personification of the dread *vomito*, which at this season (August) is carrying off a tithe of the population. Everywhere stalks the *sopilote* (turkey-buzzard), sole tenant of the streets, feeding on the garbage and carrion which abound in every corner.

The few foreign merchants who reside here remove their families to Jalapa in the season of the *vomito*, and all who have a few dollars in their pockets betake themselves to the temperate regions. The very natives and negroes are a cadaverous, stunted race; and the dogs, which contend in the streets with the *sopilotes* for carrion, are the most miserable of the *genus* cur. Just before my window one of these curs lay expiring in the middle of the street. As the wretched animal quivered in the last gasp, a *sopilote* flew down from the church-spire, and, perching on the body, commenced its feast. It was soon joined by several others, and in five minutes the carcass was devoured. These disgusting birds, are, however, useful scavengers, and, performing the duty of the lazy Mexicans, are, therefore, protected by law.

The town still presents numerous souvenirs of the bombardment by the warlike De Joinville, in 1839. The church-towers are riddled with shot, and the destructive effects of shells still visible in the heaps of ruins which have been left untouched. Since my visit it has also felt the force of American ire, and withstood a fierce bombardment for several days, with what object it is impossible to divine, since a couple of thousand men might have at any time taken it by assault. The castle was not attacked, and was concluded in the capitulation without being asked for—*cosa de Mexico*.

The town was attacked by the American troops under General Scott within ten months after my visit. It suffered a bombardment, as is well known, of several days, an unnecessary act of cruelty in my opinion, since, to my knowledge, there were no defences around the city which could not have been carried, including the city itself, by a couple of battalions of Missouri volunteers. I certainly left Vera Cruz under the impression that it was not a fortified place, with the exception of the paltry wall I have mentioned, which, if my memory serves me, was not even loopholed for musketry.

However, temporary defences might have been thrown up in the interval between my visit and the American attack; still I cannot but think that the bombardment was cruel and unnecessary. The castle could have been carried by a frigate's boarders, having but seven hundred naked Indians to defend it.

At the moment of my arrival there was no little excitement in Vera Cruz. The *siempre heroica*—always heroical city and castle—had pronounced for the immortal saviour of his country, as they styled Santa Anna; forgetting, in their zeal, that twelve months before they had kicked out the same worthy, heaping every opprobrious epithet and abuse that Mexican *facultad de lengus* could devise. Moreover, the hero was hourly expected, and great preparations were on hand for his reception.

With this object the crack regiment of the Mexican army, *el Onze*—the 11th—which happened to be in garrison at the time, cut most prodigious capers in the great *plaza* several times a-day, *disciplinando*—drilling for the occasion. Nothing can, by any possibility, be conceived more unlike a soldier than a Mexican *militar*. The regular army is composed entirely of Indians—miserable-looking pigmies, whose grenadiers are five feet high. Vera Cruz, being a show place, and jealous of its glory, generally contrives to put decent clothing, by subscription, on the regiment detailed to garrison the town; otherwise clothing is not considered indispensable to the Mexican soldier.

The muskets of the infantry are (that is, if they have any) condemned Tower muskets, turned out of the British service years before. I have seen them carrying firelocks without locks, and others with locks without hammers, the lighted end of a cigar being used as a match to ignite the powder in the pan. Discipline they have none. Courage a Mexican does not possess; but still they have that brutish indifference to death, which could be turned to account if they were well led, and officered by men of courage and spirit.

Before delivering my letters I went to a *fonda* or inn kept by a Frenchman, but in Mexico-Spanish style. Here I first made acquaintance with the *frijole*, a small black bean, which is the main food of the lower classes over the whole of Mexico, and is a standing dish on every table, both of the rich and poor. The cuisine, being Spanish, was the best in the world, the wine good, and abundance of ice from Orizaba. Among the company at the *fonda* was a party of Spanish *padres*, a *capellan* of a Mexican regiment, and a Capuchin friar. I was invited one evening to their room, and was rather surprised when I found I was in for a regular punch-drinking bout The Capuchino presided at the bowl, which he concocted with considerable skill; and the jolly priests kept it up until the gray of the morning, when they all sallied out to mass, it being the feast of San Isidro.

The next day I accompanied this clerical party to the castle of San Juan de Ulloa, which we were allowed to inspect in every part. I thought it showed very little caution, for I might have been an American for all they knew to the contrary. The fortress is constructed with considerable skill, but is in very bad repair. It is said to mount three hundred and fifty pieces of artillery, many of heavy calibre, but is deficient in mortars. The garrison did not amount to more than seven hundred men, although they were in hourly expectation of an attack by the American squadron; and such a miserable set of naked objects as they were could scarcely be got together in any other part of the world.

Our party was *ciceroned* by an *aide-de-camp* of the governor, who took us into every hole and corner of the works. The soldiers' barracks were dens unfit for hogs, without air or ventilation, and crowded to suffocation.

In one of the batteries were some fine ninety-eight-pounders, all English manufacture, but badly mounted, and some beautiful Spanish brass guns. Not the slightest discipline was apparent in the garrison, and scarcely a sentinel was on the look-out, although the American squadron was in sight of the castle, and an attack was hourly threatened. On the side facing the island of Sacrificios the defences were very weak; indeed, I saw no obstruction of sufficient magnitude to prevent half a dozen boats' crews making a dash in the dark at the water-batteries, where at this time were neither guns nor men, nor one sentry whose post would command this exposed spot; thence to cross the ditch which had but two or three feet of water in it, blow open the gate of the fortress with a bag of powder, and no organized resistance could be dreaded when once in the castle.

I pointed this out to one of the officers of the garrison. He answered, "*No hay cuidado, no hay cuidado! somos muy valientes,*"- Never fear, never fear! we are very bravo here. "*Si quieren los Americanos, que vengan*"—If the Americans like to try, let them come.

As we returned at night to Vera Cruz, a dull yellowish haze hung over the town. I asked the "patron" of the boat what it was. Taking his cigar from his mouth, he answered quite seriously, "*Señor, es el vomito*"—it's the fever.

There is a very good market at Vera Cruz: the fish department is well worth a visit. At sunrise, the Indian fishermen bring in their basket-loads, which they pile on the ground; and the beautiful and varied tints of the fish, which exhibit all the colours of the rainbow, as well as the fish themselves, of all shapes and sizes, form a very pleasing sight Two hours after sunrise the fish are all sold or removed: indeed, if not immediately cooked they will putrefy in a few hours.

The vegetable-market is well supplied, and exhibits a great variety of tropical fruits. The Indians of the *tierra caliente* are neither picturesque in dress nor comely in appearance. They are short in stature, with thick, clumsy limbs, broad faces without any expression, and a lazy, sullen look of *insouciance*. They are, however, a harmless, inoffensive people, and possess many good traits of character and disposition. In the market devoted to flesh and fowl, parrots form a staple commodity. They are brought in great numbers by the Indians, who lay great store on a talking-

25

bird, *un papagaya que habla*. Peccaries, deer, and huge snakes I also saw exposed for sale.

Chapter 4

Arrival of Santa Anna

On the 16th of August the castle, with a salvo of artillery, announced the approach of the steamer having on board the illustrious ex-president, General Santa Anna. At 9 a.m., *El Onze* marched down to the wharf with colours flying and band playing. Here they marched and counter-marched for two hours before a position was satisfactorily taken up. An officer of rank, followed by a most seedy *aide-de-camp*, both mounted on wretched animals, and dressed in scarlet uniforms of extraordinary cut, caracoled with becoming gravity before the *aduana* or customhouse.

A most discordant band screamed national airs, and a crowd of boys squibbed and crackered on the wharf, supplied with fireworks at the expense of the heroic city. By dint of cuffing, *el Onze* was formed in two lines facing inward, extending from the wharf to the *palacio*, where apartments had been provided for the general. Santa Anna landed under a salute from the castle, and walked, notwithstanding his game leg, preceded by his little wife, who leaned on the arm of an officer, through the lane of troops, who saluted individually and when they pleased, some squibbing off their firelocks, and others, not knowing what to do, did—nothing.

Don Antonio Lopez de Santa Anna is a hale-looking man between fifty and sixty, with an Old Bailey countenance and a very well built wooden leg. The *Señora*, a pretty girl of seventeen, pouted at the cool reception, for not one "*viva*" was heard; and her mother, a fat, vulgar old dame, was rather unceremoniously congeed from the procession, which she took in high dudgeon. The general was dressed in full uniform, and looked anything but pleased at the absence of everything like applause, which he doubtless expected would have greeted him. His countenance completely betrays his character; indeed, I never saw a physiognomy in which the evil passions, which he notoriously possesses, were more strongly marked. Oily duplicity, treachery, avarice, and sensuality are depicted in every feature, and his well-known character bears out the truth of the impress his vices have stamped upon his face. In person he is portly, and not devoid of a certain well-bred bearing which wins for him golden opinions from the surface-seeing fair sex, to whom he ever pays the most courtly attention.

If half the anecdotes are true which I have heard narrated by his moat intimate friends, any office or appointment in his gift can always be obtained on application of a female interceder; and on such an occasion he first saw his present wife, then a girl of fifteen, whom her mother brought to the amorous president, to win the bestowal upon her of a pension for former services, and Santa Anna became so enamoured of the artless beauty, that he soon after signified his gracious intention of honouring her with his august hand, after a vain attempt to secure the young lady in a less legitimate manner, which the politic mamma, however, took care to frustrate.

Aug. 17.—We had an *émeute* among the Vera-Cruzanos. As I was passing through the great *plaza*, a large crowd was assembled before the *casa de ayuntamiento*, or town-hall. Accosting a negro, who, leaning against a pillar, was calmly smoking his paper cigar, a quiet spectator of the affair, I inquired the cause of the riotous proceeding. "*No es mucho, caballero; un pronunciamiento, no mas,*" he answered—nothing, sir, nothing; only a revolution. On further inquiry, however, I learned that the cause of the mob assembling before the *ayuntamiento* was, that the people of Vera Cruz willed that one of that body should, as their representative, proceed to the palace to lay before Santa Anna a statement of certain griev-

28

ances which they required should be removed. Not one of that body relished the idea of bearding the lion in his den, although supposed at this moment to be on his good behaviour, but one Sousa, a native of Vera Cruz, and by trade a tinman, who stepped forth from the crowd and declared himself ready to speak on the part of the people.

They had previously clamoured for Santa Anna to show himself in the balcony of the palace, but he had excused himself on the plea of being unable to stand on account of his bad leg, and said he was ready at any time to receive and confer with one of their body Sousa, the volunteer at once proceeded to the palace, and without ceremony entered the general's room, where Santa Anna was sitting, surrounded by a large staff of general officers, priests, &c. Advancing boldly to his chair, he exclaimed, "*Mi* general, for more than twenty years you have endeavoured to ruin our country. Twice have you been exiled for your misdeeds; beware that this time you think of us, and not of yourself only!"

At this bold language Santa Anna's friends expressed their displeasure by hissing and stamping on the floor; but Sousa, turning to them with a look of contempt, continued: "These, general, are your enemies and ours; *y mas, son traidores*—and more than this, they are traitors. They seek alone to attain their ends, and care not whether they sacrifice you and their country. They will be the first to turn against you. *Para nosotros, Vera-Cruzanos qui somos*—for us, who are of Vera Cruz—what we require is this: remove the soldiers; we do not want to be ruled by armed savages. Give us arms, and we will defend our town and our houses; but we want no soldiers."

Santa Anna, taken aback, remained silent.

"Answer me, general," cried out the sturdy tinman: "I represent the people of Vera Cruz, who brought you back, and will be answered."

"Tomorrow," meekly replied the dreaded tyrant, "I will give orders that the troops be removed, and you shall be supplied with one thousand stand of arms."

"*Está bueno, mi general*"—it is well, general—answered Sousa, and returned to the mob, who, on learning the result of the conference, filled the air with *vivas*.

"*Valgame en Dios!*" exclaimed my friend the negro; "*que hombre tan osado es este!*"—what pluck this man must have to open his lips to the *presidente*!

The next morning Santa Anna left Vera Cruz for his *hacienda* —*Manga del Clavo*—first causing a *manifiésto* to be published, declaring his views and opinions with regard to the present critical state of affairs. This paper was very ably written by Rincon, and exhibited no little cleverness of composition, inasmuch as great tact was required, owing to the numerous tergiversations of Santa Anna, to steer clear of such subjects as would compromise his present declaration in favour of federalism, to which he has hitherto been strenuously opposed. In it he declares his determination to prosecute to the last the war with the United States, and his willingness to sacrifice his life and fortune in defence of his country; deprecates the notion of foreign intervention, and scouts at the idea of the "monarchical question" being introduced into any political discussion. In conclusion, he earnestly besought his countrymen to arm against the common foe.

Two or three days after my arrival in Vera Cruz, suspicious rumours of *vomito* reached my ears, and caused me to pack up my traps; and having determined to ride to Jalapa, instead of travelling by the lumbering *diligencia*, my hospitable entertainers, on learning my intention, immediately made arrangements for a supply of cavalry, and placed me under the charge of a confidential servant of the house, who was to pilot me to Jalapa.

About four p.m. on the 19th of August, Castillo made his appearance, with a couple of horses equipped in Mexican style, himself attired in a correct road costume—black glazed *sombrero* with large brim and steeple crown, ornamented with a band of silver cord and silver knob on the side; blue jacket with rows of silver buttons, and fancifully braided; *calzoneras* or pantaloons of velveteen, very loose, and open from the hip-bone to the bottom of the leg, the outside ornamented with filigree buttons;

under these overalls, the *calzoncillas* or loose drawers of white linen; boots of untanned leather, with enormous spurs, buckled over the instep by a wide, embroidered strap, and with rowels three inches and a half in diameter; a crimson silk sash round his waist, small open waistcoat exhibiting a snow-white shirt, a *puro* in his mouth, and a *quarta,* or whip hanging by a thong from his wrist. Such was Castillo, not forgetting, however, that in person he was comely to look upon, and, living in an English house, was no libel upon its excellent cuisine, carrying a most satisfactory corporation and a fat, good-humoured face.

A common way of travelling in the *tierra caliente* is by *littera,* a litter carried between two mules, in which the traveller luxuriously reclines at full length, sheltered from the rain and sun by curtains which inclose the body, and smokes or reads at his pleasure. In one of these, about to return empty to Jalapa, I dispatched my baggage, consigning a change of linen to Castillo's *alforjas* or saddle-bags. At four p.m. we trotted out of Vera Cruz, and, crossing the sandy plain outside the town, pulled up at an Indian hut, where Castillo informed me it was necessary to imbibe a stirrup-cup, which was—accordingly presented by an Indian Hebe, who gave us a *"buen viage"* in exchange for the *clacos* we paid for the *mezcal.*

The road here left the sandy shore, and turned inland, through a country rank with tropical vegetation, with here and there an Indian hut—a roof of palm-leaves supported on bamboo poles, and open to the wind—peeping out of the dense foliage. We presently came to a part of the road cut up and flooded by the heavy rains which, toward sunset, poured mercilessly upon us, but not before Castillo had thrust his head through the slit in his *sarape,* And, with his shoulders protected by his broad-brimmed *sombrero,* defied the descending waters.

Not so my unlucky self, who, green as yet in the mysteries of Mexican travelling, had not provided against aqueous casualties, and in a few seconds my unfortunate Panama was flapping miserably about my ears, and my clothes as drenched as water could make them. However, there was no remedy, and on we floun-

31

dered, through pools of mud and water full of ducks, and snipe, and white herons; the road becoming worse and worse, and the rain coming down with undeniable vigour. Just before sunset we overtook the rear-guard of the valiant Eleventh, which that day had marched from Vera Cruz en route to the seat of war, for the purpose, as one of the officers informed me, "*dar un golpe à los Norte Americanos*"—to strike a blow at the North Americans.

The marching costume of these heroes, I thought, was peculiarly well adapted to the climate and season—a shako on the head, while coat, shirt, and pantaloons hung suspended in a bundle from the end of the firelock earned over the shoulder, and their *cuerpos* required no other covering than the coatings of mud with which they were caked from head to foot, singing merrily, however, as they marched.

Night now came on, and pitchy dark, and the road was almost impassable from the immense herds of cattle which literally blocked it up. The *ganado*[1] all belonged to Santa Anna, whose estate extends for fifty miles along the road, and bore the well-known brand of A. L. S. A.—*alsa,* or forward, as the Mexicans read it, which are the initials of the General Antonio Lopez de Santa Anna. Finding it utterly impossible to proceed, we stopped at the first Indian hut we came to, where we secured our animals in a shed, and, in company with the rear-guard of the "*Onze,*" who arrived shortly after, made ourselves uncomfortable for the night.

The next morning, before daylight, we were in our saddles, the rain still descending in torrents. "*No hay remedio*—there's no help for it"—said Castillo; "we had better push on:" and on we splashed.

"*Hi esta muy buen coñac*—very good brandy up there"—he remarked, after we had ridden a few miles; and, dashing the spurs into his beast, darted up a hill to a house, and called for a tumbler of brandy and milk, which was not unpalatable after our wet ride. Sitting under the verandah were two sailors—deserters from the *Endymion,* lying at Sacrificios. They told me they had

---

1. *Ganado mayor*—cattle; *ganado menor*—sheep and pigs.

32

been to Jalapa on a spree, and now were on their way back to rejoin their ship.

CHAPTER 5

Arrive at Jalapa

The weather clearing, we resumed our journey, and halted to breakfast at Puente Nacional, once del Rey.

The bridge, built of stone, spans a picturesque torrent, now swelled and muddy with the rains. The village is small and dirty, with a tolerable inn, where the *diligencia* stops. Here we were regaled with *frijoles* and *chile colorado*, and waited upon by a very pretty Indian girl.

The scenery is wild and desolate; the vegetation, although most luxuriant, looks rank and poisonous, and the vapours, which rise from the reeking undergrowth, bear all kinds of malaria over the country. Few villages are met with, and these consist of wretched hovels of unburned brick (adobe), or huts of bamboo and palm-leaf. Each has its little patch of garden, where the plantain, maize, and *chile* are grown. Strings of the latter invariably hang on every house, and with it, fresh or dried, the people season every dish.

The land appears good, but, where everything grows spontaneously, the lazy Indian only cares to cultivate sufficient for the subsistence of his family. The soil is well adapted for the growth of cotton; sugar, and tobacco. I asked a farmer why he did not pay more attention to the cultivation of his land. "*Quien sabe,*" was his answer; "*con maiz y chile, no falta nada*"—who wants more than corn and *chile, vaya*?

"These men are brutes," put in Castillo; "*ni vida saben*"—they don't know even what it is to live; just then a "*biftek à la Ynglesa*" in the kitchen of "*la casa*" in Vera Cruz occurring to his mind's eye.

When we turned out after breakfast we found the heavy, rolling clouds clearing off, and the sun shining brightly from a patch of deep blue.

"*Ya viene buen tiempo*," prophesied our host, as he held my stirrup; and for once he was a true prophet, for we had six or eight hours' magnificent weather, during which the sun dried our clothes, and baked the mud upon them, and we were enabled to keep our cigars alight, which in the morning was an impossibility. The road was wretched, although it has been called by an ingenious traveller "a monument of human industry;" a monument of human ignorance and idleness would be the better term. On each side the scenery was the same—a sea of burning green.

Now, however, the woods were alive with birds of gaudy plumage: cardinals, and catbirds, and parrots, with noisy chatter, hopped from tree to tree; every now and then, the Mexican pheasant—*chachalaca*—a large, noble bird, flew across the road; and *chupamirtos* (humming-birds) darted to and fro. The pools were black with ducks, cranes, and bitterns; the air alive with bugs and beetles; and in the evening *cocuyos* (fire-bugs) illuminated the scene. Mosquitoes were everywhere, and probed with poisonous proboscis every inch of unprotected skin.

At sunset we reached El Plan del Rio, a miserable *venta*, which we found crowded with cavalry soldiers and their horses, so that we had great trouble in finding room for our own animals. This hostelry belonged to the genus meson, a variety of the inn species to be found only in Mexico. It was, however, a paradise compared to the *mesones* north of the city of Mexico; and I remember that I often looked back upon this one, which Castillo and I voted the most absolutely miserable of inns, as a sort of Clarendon or Mivart's. Round the corral, or yard, where were mangers for horses and mules, were several filthily dirty rooms, without windows or furniture.

These were the guests' chambers. Mine host and his family

35

had separate accommodations for themselves, of course; and into this part of the mansion Castillo managed to introduce himself and me, and to procure some supper. The chambermaid—who, unlocking the door of the room apportioned to us, told us to beware of the *mala gente* (the bad people) who were about—was a dried-up old man, with a long, grizzled beard and matted hair, which fell, guiltless of comb or brush, on his shoulders. He was perfectly horrified at our uncomplimentary remarks concerning the cleanliness of the apartment, about the floor of which troops of fleas were caracoling, while flat, odoriferous bugs were sticking in patches to the walls.

My request for some water for the purpose of washing almost knocked him down with the heinousness of the demand; but when he had brought a little earthen-ware saucer, holding about a tablespoonful, and I asked for a towel, he stared at me, open-mouthed, without answering, and then burst out into an immoderate fit of laughter. "*Ay que hombre, Ave Maria Purisslma, quo loco es este!*"—Oh, what a man, what a madman is this! "*Servilleta, pañuela, toalla, que demonio quiere?*"—towel, napkin, handkerchief—what the devil does he want?—repeating the different terms I used to explain that I wanted a towel.

"*Ha, ha, ha! es medio-tonto, es medio-tonto*"—a half-witted fellow, I see. "*Que demonio! quiere agua, quiere toalla!*"—what the d—l! he wants water, towels, everything, "*Adios!*"

El Plan del Rio is situated in a circular valley or basin, surrounded by lofty hills, which are covered with trees. An old fort crowns the summit of a ridge on the left of the road, from whence a beautiful view is had of the valley, which is the exact figure of a cup. We were now constantly ascending, and, leaving behind us the *tierra caliente*, were approaching the more grateful climate of the *tierra templada*, or temperate region.

At Los Dos Rios we had a good view of the Peak of Orizaba, with its cap of perpetual snow; and, still ascending, the scenery became more varied, the air cooler, and the country better cultivated; oaks began to show themselves, and the vegetation became less rank and more beautiful. Presently, cresting a hill, before us lay beautiful Jalapa, embosomed in mountains and veiled by cloud and mist.

Jalapa, the population of which is nearly seventeen thousand, is situated at the foot of Macultepec, at an elevation of four thousand three hundred and thirty-five feet above the level of the sea. Unfortunately this elevation is about that which the strata of clouds reach, when, suspended Over the ocean, they come in contact with the ridge of the Cordillera, and this renders the atmosphere exceedingly humid and disagreeable, particularly in northeasterly winds. In summer, however, the mists disappear, the sun shines brightly, and the sky is clear and serene. At this time the climate is perfectly heavenly; the extremes of heat and cold are never experienced, and an even, genial temperature prevails, highly conducive to health and comfort. Fever is here unknown; the dreaded *vomito* never makes its appearance on the table-land; and, spite of the humid climate, sickness is comparatively rare and seldom fatal. The average temperature is 60° to 65° in summer.

There are seasons, however, when Jalapa presents a direct contrast to such a picture. Heavy, dense clouds envelop, as in a shroud, the entire landscape; a floating mist hangs over the town; and the rolling vapours, which pour through the valley, cause a perpetual *chipi-chipi,* as this drizzling rain is termed. The sun is then for days obscured, and the Jalapeño, muffled in his *sarape,* smokes his *cigarro,* and mutters, "*Ave Maria Purissima, que venga el sol!*"— O for a peep at the sun, Holy Virgin!

On a bright, sunny day the scenery round Jalapa is not to be surpassed: mountains bound the horizon, except on one side, where a distant view of the sea adds to the beauty of the scene. Orizaba, with its snow-capped peak, appears so close that one imagines it is within reach; and rich and evergreen forests clothe the surrounding hills. In the foreground are beautiful gardens, with fruits of every clime—the banana and fig, the orange, cherry, and apple. The town is irregularly built, but picturesque; the houses are in the style of Old Spain, with windows to the ground, and barred, in which sit the Jalapeñas, with their beautifully fair complexions and eyes of fire.

Las Jalapoñas son muy halagueñas is a saying common in Mexico; and bewitching they are, even with their *cigaritos*, which make a good foil to a pretty mouth. Here is still preserved some of the *sangre azul,* the blue blood of Old Castile. Many of the Jalapa women are dazzlingly fair, while others are dark as a Malagueña. In the *fonda* Vera Cruzana, where I put up, and advise all travellers to do the same, were two daughters of mine host—one as fair as Jenny Lind, the other dark as Jephtha's daughter, and both very pretty. Although the proverb says *Ventera hermosa, mal para la bolsa*—a pretty hostess gives no change—here it is an exception; and my friend Don Juan will take good care of man and beast, and charge reasonably.

Near Jalapa are two or three cotton-factories, which I believe pay well. They are under the management of English and Americans. The girls employed in the works are all Indians or Mestizas, healthy and good-looking. They are very apt in learning their work, and soon comprehend the various uses of the machinery. In the town there is but little to see. The church is said to have been founded by Cortez, and there is also a Franciscan convent. However, a stranger is amply interested in walking about the streets and market, where he will see much that is strange and new. The vicinity of Jalapa, although poorly cultivated, produces maize, wheat, grapes, jalap (from which plant it takes its name); and a little lower down the cordillera grow the vanilla, the bean which is so highly esteemed for its aromatic flavour, and the fruits of the temperate and torrid zones.

On inquiry as to the modes of travelling from Jalapa to the city of Mexico, I found that the journey in the *diligencia* to the capital was to be preferred to any other at this season, on account of the rains; although by the former there was almost a certainty of being robbed or attacked. So much a matter of course is this disagreeable proceeding, that the Mexicans invariably calculate a certain sum for the expenses of the road, including the usual fee for *los caballeros del camino.* All baggage is sent by the *arrieros* or muleteers, by which means it is insured from all danger, although a long time on the road. The usual charge is twelve dollars a *carga,* or mule-load of two hundred pounds, from Vera Cruz to the capital, being from ten to twenty days on the road.

The Mexicans never dream of resisting the robbers, and a coach-load of nine is often stopped and plundered by one man. The *ladrones*, however, often catch a Tartar if a party of foreigners should happen to be in the coach; and but the other day, two Englishmen, one an officer of the Guards, the other a resident in Zacatecas. being in a coach which was stopped by nine robbers, near Puebla, on being ordered to alight and *bocabaxo*—throw themselves on their noses—replied to the request by shooting a couple of them, and, quietly resuming their seats, proceeded on their journey.

During my stay two English naval officers arrived in the *diligencia* from Mexico. As they stepped out, bristling with arms, the Mexican bystanders ejaculated, "*Valgame Dios!* What men these English are!" "*Esos son hombres!*"—These are men! The last week the coach was robbed three times, and a poor *Gachupin*, mistaken for an Englishman, was nearly killed, the robbers having vowed vengeance against the palefaces for the slaughter of their two comrades at Puebla; and a few months before, two robbers crawled upon the coach during the night, and, putting a pistol through the leathern panels, shot an unfortunate passenger in the head, who, they had been informed, carried arms and was determined to resist. There is not a travelling Mexican who cannot narrate to you his experiences on "the road;" and scarcely a foreigner in the country, more particularly English and Americans, who has not come to blows with the *ladrones* at some period or other of his life.

Such being the satisfactory state of affairs, before starting on this dangerous expedition, and particularly as I carried all my baggage with me (being too old a soldier ever to part with that), assisted by mine host, Don Juan, I had a minute inspection of arms and ammunition, all of which was put in perfect order. One fine morning, therefore, I took my seat in the *diligencia,* with a formidable battery of a double-barrel rifle, a *ditto* carbine, two brace of pistols, and a blunderbuss. Blank were the faces of my four fellow-passengers when I entered thus equipped. They protested, they besought—everyone's life would be sacrificed were one of the party to resist.

"*Señores*," I said, "here are arms for you all; better for you to fight than be killed like a rat." No, they washed their hands of it; would have nothing to do with gun or pistol. "*Vaya: no es el costumbre*"—it is not the custom, they said.

From Jalapa the road constantly ascends, and we are now leaving the *tierra temptada,* the region of oaks and liquid amber, for the still more elevated regions of the *tierra fria,* called cold, however, merely by comparison, for the temperature is equal to that of Italy, and the lowest range of the thermometer is 62°. The whole tableland of Mexico belongs to this division. The scenery here becomes mountainous and grand; and on the right of the road is a magnificent cascade, which tumbles from the side of a mountain to the depth of several hundred feet. The villages are few, and fifteen or twenty miles apart, and the population scanty and miserable. No signs of cultivation appear, but little patches of maize and *chile,* in the midst of which is an Indian but of reeds and flags.

In the evening we passed through a fine plain in which stands the town and castle of Perote, and near which is the celebrated mountain of basaltic porphyry, which, from the singular figure of a rock on its summit, is called *El Coffre,* the chest. The castle of Perote is the "Tower" of Mexico. In it are confined the unlucky chiefs whom revolutions and counter-revolutions have turned upon their backs. The late President Paredes was at this time confined within its walls, and would have, in a day or two, the pleasure of seeing Santa Anna (who himself has been a resident here) pass in state to resume the reins of government. However, in this country, overturned presidents, *et hoc genus omne,* are always well treated, since it is the common fate of them all to be set up and knocked down like ten-pins, and therefore they have a fellow-feeling for each other in their adversity.

In Perote the houses present to the street a blank wall of stone without windows, and one large portal, which leads to the *patio-corral,* or yard, round which are the rooms. This shows the want of security, where every man's house is indeed his castle. From Perote the dangerous road commences, and it is necessary, as the conductor informed me, *tener mucho cuidado*—to keep a sharp lookout.

We left Perote at four in the morning; consequently, it was quite dark; and, as morning dawned, the first objects that met our view were the numerous little crosses on the roadside, many of them marking the places where unfortunate travellers had been murdered. These crosses, however, have not always so bloody a signification, being placed in the road oftentimes to mark the spot where a coffin has been set down on its way to the burial-ground, in order that the bearers may rest themselves, or be changed for others. Every now and then our driver looked into the window to give notice that we were drawing near a dangerous spot, saying, "*Ahora mal punto, muy mal punto*"—now we are in a very bad place; "look to your arms."

The country appeared rich and fertile, but, as usual, was wretchedly cultivated; and the same miserable population of Indians everywhere. Now and then a Mexican proper would gallop past, armed to the teeth, when our conductor invariably demanded, "*Que novedad hay?*"—is there anything new?—always having reference to the doings of the *ladrones.*

"*No hay nada*"—there is nothing stirring— was generally the answer; which could seldom be relied on, as there is hardly a *ranchero* who is not in league with the robbers, and our informant was, most likely, one of them on the look-out.

At eleven we stopped to breakfast, and were joined by a stout wench of La Puebla, with a nut-brown face, and teeth as white as snow. She informed us that there were *muy mala gente* on the road—very bad people—who had robbed the party with which she was travelling but the day before; and, being *muy sin vergüenza*— shameless rascals—had behaved very rudely to the ladies of the party. Our buxom companion was dressed in true Poblana style. Her long black hair was combed over her ears, from which descended huge silver earrings; the red *enagua,* or short petticoat, fringed with yellow, and fastened round her waist with a silk band; from her shoulders to the waist a *chemisette* was her only covering, if we except the gray *reboso* drawn over her head and neck; and on her small naked foot was a tiny shoe with silver buckle.

However, we reached Puebla safe and sound, and drove into the yard of the *Fonda de las Diligencias,* where the coach and its contents were minutely inspected by a robber-spy, who, after he had counted the passengers and their arms, immediately mounted his horse and galloped away. This is done every day, and in the teeth of the authorities, who wink at the cool proceeding.

In a country where justice is not to be had—where injustice is to be bought—where the law exists but in name, and is despicable and powerless, it is not to be wondered at that such outrages are quietly submitted to by a demoralized people, who prefer any other means of procuring a living than by honest work; and who are ready to resort to the most violent means to gratify their insatiable passion for gambling, which is at the bottom of this national evil.

It is a positive fact that men of all ranks and stations scruple not to resort to the road to relieve their temporary embarrassments, the result of gambling; and numerous instances might be brought forward where such parties have been detected, and in some cases executed for thus offending against the laws. One I may mention, that of Colonel Yanes, *aide-de-camp* to Santa Anna, who was garrotted for the robbery and murder of the Swiss consul in Mexico a few years since.

CHAPTER 6

First View of Mexico

Puebla, the capital of the intendancy of that name, is one of the finest cities in Mexico. Its streets are wide and regular, and the houses and public buildings are substantially built and in good taste. The population, which is estimated at between eighty and one hundred thousand, is the most vicious and demoralized in the republic. It was founded by the Spaniards, in 1531, on the site of a small village of Cholula Indians, and, from its position and the fertility of the surrounding country, was unsurpassed by any other city in the Spanish Mexican dominions. The province is rich in the remains of Mexican antiquities. The fortifications of Tlaxcallan and the pyramids of Cholula are worthy of a visit, and the noble cypress of Atlixo (the *Ahahuete, Cupressus disticha,* Lin.) is seventy-six feet in circumference, and, according to Humboldt, the "oldest vegetable monument" in the world.

At the *posada* at Puebla I was introduced to the most enormous woman I have ever seen, but uniting with this awful magnitude the most perfect symmetry of form and feature. Her manners were perfectly ladylike, and she seemed in no degree disconcerted by her unusual size. I sat next her at supper, and in conversation she very abruptly alluded to her appearance, but with the most perfect good-humour.

"Would you believe, *caballero*," she said to me, "that there is in this very Puebla a girl actually fatter than I am?"

"Many as fat, *señorita*," I answered, "but (perpetrating a preposterously far-fetched compliment) few so fair."

"Ah, *señor*, you are laughing at me," she said: "*ya lo se bien que soy vaca, pero hay otra mas gorda que yo.*"—I know well that I am a cow, but, thank God, there is one other in the world fatter than I am.

I shuddered to see her shovelling huge masses of meat into her really pretty mouth, and thought of what the consequences would be in a few years' time, when her fine figure would subside into a mountain of flesh.

We left Puebla early in the morning, and, as day broke, a scene of surpassing beauty burst upon us. The sun, rising behind the mountains, covered the sky with a cold, silvery light, against which the peaks stood in bold relief, while the bases were still veiled in gloom. The snow-clad peak of Orizaba, the lofty Popocatepetl (the hill that smokes) and Iztaccihuatl (the white woman) lifted their heads now bright with the morning sun. The beautiful plain of Cuitlaxcoapan, covered with golden corn and green waving maize, stretched away to the mountains which rise in a gradual undulating line, from which in the distance shot out isolated peaks and cones, all clear and well defined.

Passing through a beautiful country, we reached Rio-Frio, a small plain in the midst of the mountains, and *muy mal punto* for the robbers, as the road winds through a pine-forest, into which they can escape in case of repulse. The road is lined with crosses, which here are veritable monuments of murders perpetrated on travellers. Here, too, we took an escort, and, when we had passed the *piñol*, the corporal rode up to the windows, saying, "*Ya se retira la escolta,*"—the escort is about to retire; in other words, Please remember the guard.

Each passenger presented him with the customary *dos riales*, and the gallant escort rode off quite contented. Here, too, all the worst *puntos* being passed, my companions drew long breaths, muttered "*Ave Maria Purissima—gracias à Dios ya no hay cuidado,*" and lighted their cigars.

We soon after crested the ridge of the mountain, and, descending a winding road, turned an abrupt hill, and, just as I was settling myself in the corner for a good sleep, my arm was seized convulsively by my opposite neighbour, who, with half his body out of the window, vociferated: "*Hi esta, hi esta, mire, por Dios, mire!*"—Look out, for God's sake! there it is. Thinking a *ladron* was in sight, I seized my gun; but my friend, seeing my mistake, drew in his head, saying, "*No, no, Mejico, Mejico, la ciudad!*"

To stop the coach and jump on the box was the work of a moment; and, looking down from the same spot where probably Cortez stood three hundred years ago, before me lay the city and valley of Mexico, bathed by the soft flooding light of the setting sun.

He must be insensible, indeed, a clod of clay, who does not feel the blood thrill in his veins at the first sight of this beautiful scene. What must have been the feelings of Cortez, when, with his handful of followers, he looked down upon the smiling prospect at his feet, the land of promise which was to repay them for all the toil and dangers they had encountered!

The first impression which struck me on seeing the valley of Mexico was the perfect, almost unnatural, tranquillity of the scene. The valley, which is about sixty miles long by forty in breadth, is on all sides inclosed by mountains, the most elevated of which are on the southern side; in the distance are the volcanoes of Popocatepetl and Iztaccihuatl, and numerous peaks of different elevation. The lakes of Tezcuco and Chalco glitter in the sun like burnished silver, or, shaded by the vapours which often rise from them, lie cold and tranquil on the plain. The distant view of the city, with its white buildings and numerous churches, its regular streets and shaded *paseos*, greatly augments the beauty of the scene, over which floats a solemn, delightful tranquillity.

On entering the town, one is struck with the regularity of the streets, the chaste architecture of the buildings, the miserable appearance of the population, the downcast look of the men, the absence of ostentatious display of wealth, and the prevalence of filth which every where meet the eye. On every side the passenger is importuned for charity. Disgusting lepers whine for *clacos*: maimed and mutilated wretches, mounted on the backs of porters, thrust out their distorted limbs and expose their sores, urging their human steeds to increase their pace as their victim increases his to avoid them. Rows of cripples are brought into the streets the first thing in the morning, and deposited against a wall, whence their infernal whine is heard the livelong day. Cries such as these everywhere salute the ear :

"*Jesus Maria Purissima; una corta caridad, caballero, en el nombre de la santissima madre de Dios: una corta caridad, y Dios, lo pagara a usted.*"—In the name of Jesus, the son of the most pure Mary, bestow a little charity, my lord; for the sake of the most holy mother of God, bestow a trifle, and God will repay you.

Mexico is the headquarters of dirt. The streets are dirty, the houses are dirty, the men are dirty, and the women dirtier, and everything you eat and drink is dirty.

This love of dirt only refers to the Mexicans proper, since the *Gachupines*,[1] and all foreigners in the city, and those Mexicans who have been abroad, keep themselves aloof and clean. The streets are filled with *leperos*, with officers in uniform (pleasing themselves as to the style), with priests, and fat and filthy Capuchinos, friars and monks.

Observe every countenance; with hardly an exception a physiognomist will detect the expression of vice, and crime, and conscious guilt in each. No one looks you in the face, but all slouch past with downcast eyes and hangdog look, intent upon thoughts that will not bear the light. The shops are poor and ill supplied, the markets filthy in the extreme. Let no fastidious stomach look into the *tortillerias*, the shops where pastry is made.

The stranger in Mexico is perpetually annoyed by the religious processions which perambulate the streets at all hours. A coach, with an eye painted on the panels, and drawn by six mules conveys the Host to the houses of dying Catholics who

---

1. The *Gachupin* is the term of contempt which was bestowed upon the Spaniards in the War of Independence, and is now invariably used by the lower classes to distinguish a Spaniard from a Mexican.

are rich enough to pay for the privilege: before this equipage a bell tinkles, which warns the orthodox to fall on their knees; and woe to the unfortunate who neglects this ceremony, either from ignorance or design. On one occasion, being suddenly surprised by the approach of one of these processions, I had but just time to doff my hat and run behind a corner of a building, when I was spied by a fat priest, who, shouldering an image, brought up the rear of the procession. As he was at the head of a vast crowd who were just rising from their knees, he thought it a good opportunity of venting an anathema against a vile *heretico*. Turning first to the crowd, as much as to say, "Just see what a dressing I am going to give this fellow," he, with a most severe frown, addressed me :

"Man," said he, "do you refuse to kneel to your God?"

"*No, mi padre*," I answered, "*pero àl imagen de madéra*"—but to an image of wood.

"*Vaya*," muttered the padre; "*lo te pagara el demonio*"—the devil will pay thee—and marched away.

The cathedral is a fine, large building of incongruous architecture. The interior is rich in silver and gold candlesticks and ornaments of the precious metals. It is far inferior to the churches of Catholic Europe. I visited it during a grand *funcion*, when it was crammed with *leperos* and Indians, the odour from whose water-avoiding skins drove me quickly into the open air. I vainly searched for a Murillo, which is said to hang unnoticed and unhonoured, in some dark corner of the church. After a fruitless search of more than two hours, I gave it up, right glad to think that no production of that great master existed where it would not be appreciated.

It is said the quantity of gold and silver plate and ornaments of precious stones possessed by this church are worth several millions sterling. They are, however, carefully hidden, lest they should excite the cupidity of some unscrupulous president; but the gold and silver, &c., actually displayed, would be well worthy the attention of a sacking party of American volunteers, should the city of the Aztecs be rash enough to stand an assault.

47

The interior is dark and gloomy, with the usual amount of tinsel and tawdry. The view from the top, of the city and valley of Mexico, is very fine; although the old woman who keeps the key of the tower declares that the "*vista mas hermosa*"—the most beautiful view—is into the square, where nothing is to be seen but a stand of hack *carratelas,* and the scaffolding round Santa Anna's statue, which has just been dragged from its corner and re- erected.

There is little or nothing in the shape of sightseeing in Mexico. The national museum is worth a visit, as it contains a good collection of Mexican antiquities, of a light and trivial character however. I have seen no Aztecan remains which impress me with the most distant idea that the ancient Mexicans possessed any of the arts of civilization, or were farther advanced than many other nations of ingenious savages, who work in stones and feathers. In the working of stones they were certainly clever, and the wonder is, with the rude instruments they possessed, how they could fashion into any shape the brittle mate*riales* they made use of. Some masks of the human face, cut out of obsidian, are really well executed, as are also several figures of beasts, insects, and reptiles, in amethyst, agate, porphyry, serpentine, &c.

In the courtyard of the museum is a colossal equestrian statue of Charles the Fourth of Spain. This used to ornament the great square, where Humboldt assisted in its erection in 1803; but after the War of Independence, when kings went out of fashion in Mexico, it was removed to its present site. As a whole it is a work of merit, and the conception good; but it possesses many glaring faults. The legs of the rider and hind quarters of the horse are out of all proportion; nevertheless, the animal is a correct study of a Mexican horse. The drapery is good, and the attitude of the horse gives a good idea of a trotting charger.

One of the lions here is the collection of paintings by old (?) masters, belonging to the Conde de Cortina. They are now removed to the count's *casa de campo,* or country-seat, at Tacubaya, and enjoy the reputation of being the choicest gallery on the continent of America. Among them are two reputed Murillos, and some others attributed to the first masters.

I gladly availed myself of an opportunity to inspect the collection, which, I regret to say, greatly disappointed me. One of the paintings attributed to Murillo, although of considerable merit, does not possess one iota of the style peculiar to that great master; the other is manifestly spurious. Of the remainder I need only say that they have been collected at great expense, but I fear with little judgment. The Conde de Cortina, the head of an old Spanish family, has expended large sums of money in making this collection, but it is to be regretted that the agents to whom he intrusted the purchase of paintings have, either through ignorance or imposition, squandered away such large sums as would, if judiciously spent, have been sufficient to have purchased many of the finest pictures in Europe.

Tacubaya is the Richmond of Mexico: villas and country residences abound, where the aristocracy resort during the hot months. The road passes the great aqueduct which supplies the city with water from a spring in Chapultepec. It is not strongly built, and the arches exhibit many cracks and fissures occasioned by the earthquakes. At this season the valley was partly inundated, and the road almost impassable to carriages.

By this road Cortez retreated from the city on the memorable *noche triste*, the sorrowful night. The fatal causeway, the passage of which was so destructive to the Spaniards, was probably on nearly the same site as the present road, but the latter since that period has entirely changed its character. On returning from Tacubaya, I visited the hill of Chapultepec, celebrated as being the site of Montezuma's palace, on which, toward the close of the seventeenth century, the viceroy Galvez erected a huge castle, the remains of which are now occupied by the military school.

Far more interesting than the apocryphal tradition of the Indians' palace, the viceroy's castle, or the existing eyesore, is the magnificent grove of cypress, which outlives all the puny structures of man, and, still in the prime of strength and beauty, looks with contempt on the mined structures of generation after generation which have passed away.

One of these noble trees is upward of seventeen yards in girth, and the most picturesque, and at the same time most nobly proportioned tree it is possible to conceive. It rises into the sky a perfect pyramid of foliage, and from its sweeping branches hang pendulous, graceful festoons of a mossy parasite. There are many others of equal height and beauty; but this one, which I believe is called Montezuma's cypress, stands more isolated, and is therefore conspicuously grand. From the summit of the hill, to which a path winds through a labyrinth of shrubs, a fine view of the valley and city of Mexico is obtained, and of the surrounding mountains and volcanic peaks.

CHAPTER 7

Preparations to start for the North

The "*Paseo*" is the Hyde Park of Mexico. Here resort, about four in the afternoon, all the gay and fashionable of the city. Coaches, built in the days of our great-grandfathers, rumble along on their ponderous leathern springs, drawn by teams of sleek and handsome mules. Out of the quaint windows peep the lustrous eyes of the *señoritas*, dressed in simple white. The modern European carriages of the foreign ministers dash past; among them, conspicuous for correctness of turnout, the "Clarence" of her Britannic Majesty's representative, with his lady dressed *à la Mexicana*, and drawn by a pair of superb mules. *Caballeros curvet* on their *caballas de paseo*—park hacks—with saddles and bridles worth a Jew's ransom, and all dressed *para la silla*—for the saddle—eschewing everything in the shape of "tail" to their coats; for on horseback the correct thing is the *chaqueta,* an embroidered jacket, alive with buttons and bullion.

The *sombrero Mexicano*, and pantaloons open from the knee and garnished with silver buttons, and silver spurs of enormous size and weight, complete their costume. The horse appointments are still more costly. The saddle, the pommel and cantle of which are of solid silver, is embossed with the same metal in every part; the stirrups, covered by a flap of ornamented leather, and the massive bit, are of silver, and frequently partly of gold; and the reins, and every other portion of the equipment, are in similar style.

After a turn or two in the broad drive, the carriages range up side by side along the road, whence their fair inmates admire the passing dandies as they curvet past on their well-trained steeds. To the eye of an Englishman nothing is more ridiculous than a Mexican's seat on horseback: the form of the saddle compels him to sit bolt upright, or, rather, overhanging the pommel, while the stirrups, placed behind the girth, draw his legs fur behind the centre of gravity, his toes just touching the ponderous stirrup. Every moment you expect him to fall with his nose between the horses' ears, but the high cantle and pommel hold him as in a vice, and render his being spilled anything but an easy matter.

The *Paseo* itself is a very poor affair, and made still more so by two ridiculous fountains, which rival in meanness the equally absurd squirts in our Trafalgar Square.

The private houses in Mexico are well built and commodious. The exteriors of many are chastely and most beautifully decorated, and the rooms are lofty and well proportioned. The entrance is by a large gateway (sometimes double, the exterior one being of open iron-work) into the patio or courtyard, round which are the stables, coach-houses, and servants' offices. The visitor has frequently to thread his way through horses and mules, frisking under the hands of grooms, *mozos de caballo.* The dwelling-rooms are on the first and upper stories.

The hotels are few and wretchedly bad. The best is "La Gran Sociedad," under the same roof with the Theatre Nacional, now rechristened of Santa Anna. This is the grand theatre, and is rather a good house, with a company of Spanish comedians. There is also a smaller one, devoted to light comedy and vaudeville. The performers are generally from the Havana, and occasionally a "star" arrives from Old Spain.

The streets of Mexico at night present a very animated appearance. In the leading thoroughfares the *tortilleras* display their tempting *viands,* illuminated by the blaze from a *brazero,* which serves to keep the *tortillas* and *chile Colorado* in a proper state of heat. To these stalls resort the *arrieros* and loafers of every description, tempted by the shrill invitations of the presiding fair ones to taste their wares. Urchins, with blazing links, run before the lumbering coaches proceeding to the theatres. *Cargadores*—porters—stand at the corners of the flooded streets, to bear across the thin-booted passenger on their backs. The cries of the *pordioseros,* as the beggars are called, from their constant use of "*por Dios,*" redouble as the night advances. The mounted ones urge their two-legged steeds to cut off the crowd thronging toward the theatres, mingling their supplications for alms with objurgations on their lazy hacks.

"*Una limosnita, caballerito, por* (to the *cargador) Malraya! piernas de piedra, anda*—and-a-a—" A small trifle, my little lord, for the sake of—(aside to the unfortunate porter, in a stage whisper) Thunder and fury, thou stony-legged one! get on for the love of mercy: he is going to give me a *claco. Ar-hé—ar-r-hé.*

Red-petticoated *poblanas*[1] *reboso*-wrapped, display their little feet and well-turned ankles as they cross the gutters; and; cigar in mouth, they wend their way to the *fandangoes* of the Barrio de Santa Anna. From every *pulque*-shop is heard the twanging of guitars and the quivering notes of the *cantadores,* who excite the guests to renewed potations by their songs in praise of the grateful liquor. The popular chorus of one of these is:—

Sabe que es pulque?
Licor divino-o!
Lo beben los angeles
En el sereno-o.

Know ye what pulque is?
Liquor divine!
Angels in heaven
Prefer it to wine.

Those philosophical strangers who wish to see "life in Mexico" must be careful what they are about, and keep their eyes skinned, as they say in Missouri. Here there are no detective police from which to select a guide for the back slums—no Sergeant Shackel to initiate one into the mysteries of St. Giles's

---

1. The *Poblana* is the *Manola* of Mexico.

and the Seven Dials. One must depend upon his own nerve and bowie-knife, his presence of mind and Colt's revolver: but, armed even with all these precautions, it is a dangerous experiment, and much better to be left alone. Provided, however, that one speaks the language tolerably well, is judicious in the distribution of his dollars, and steers clear of committing any act of gallantry by which he may provoke the jealousy and *cuchillo* of the susceptible *Mejicano*, the expedition may be undertaken without much danger, and a satisfactory moral drawn therefrom.

One night, equipped from head to foot "*al paisano*," and accompanied by one Jose Maria Canales, a worthy rascal, who, in every capacity, from a colonel of dragoons to a horse-boy, had perambulated the republic from Yucatan to the valley of Taos, and had inhabited apartments in the palace of the viceroys as well as in the Acordada, and nearly every intermediate grade of habitation, I sallied out for the very purpose of perpetrating such an expedition as I have attempted to dissuade others from undertaking.

Our first visit was to the classic neighbourhood of the Acordada, a prison which contains as unique a collection of malefactors as the most civilized cities of Europe could produce. On the same principle as that professed by the philosopher, who, during a naval battle, put his head into a hole through which a cannon-shot had just passed, as the most secure place in the ship, so do the rogues and rascals, the pickpockets, murderers, burglars, highwaymen, coiners, *et hoc genus omne,* choose to reside under the very nose of the gallows.

My companion, who was perfectly at home in this locality, recommended that we should first visit a celebrated *pulqueria*, where he would introduce me to a *caballero*—a gentleman—who knew everything that was going on, and would inform us what amusements were on foot on that particular night. Arrived at the *pulque*-shop, we found it a small, filthy den, crowded with men and women of the lowest class, swilling the popular liquor, and talking unintelligible slang. My *cicerone* led me through the crowd, directly up to a man who, with his head through a species of sack without sleeves, and *sans chemise,* was serving out the *pulque* to his numerous customers. I was introduced as *"un forastero, un caballero Yngles"*—a stranger—an English gentleman, his particular friend. Mine host politely offered his hand, assured me that his house and all in it was mine from that hour, poured us out two large, green tumblers of *pulque,* and requested us to be seated.

It was soon known that a foreigner was in the room. In spite of my dress and common *sarape,* I was soon singled out. Cries of *"Estrangero, Tejano, Yanqué, burro,"* saluted me; I was a Texan, a Yankee, and consequently burro—a jackass. The crowd surrounded me, women pushed through the throng, *à ver el burro*—to look at the jackass; and the threats of summary chastisement and ejection were muttered. Seeing that affairs began to look cloudy. I rose, and, placing my hand on my heart, assured the *caballeros y las señoritas* that they laboured under a slight error: that, although my face was white, I was no Texan, neither was I Yankee or a jackass, but *"Yngles, muy amigo a la republica"*—an Englishman, having the welfare of the republic much at heart; and that my affection for them, and hatred of their enemies, was something too excessive to express; that to prove this, my only hope was that they would do me the kindness to discuss at their leisure half an *arroba* of *pulque,* which I begged then and there to pay for, and present to them in token of my sincere friendship.

The tables were instantly turned: I was saluted with cries of *"Viva el Yngles! Que meueren los Yanqués! Vivan nosotros y pulque!"*—Hurrah for the Englishman! Death to the Yankees! Long live ourselves and *pulque*! The dirty wretches thronged round to shake my hand, and semi-drunken *poblanas* lavished their embraces on *"el güero."* I must here explain that, in Mexico, people with fair hair and complexions are called *güero, güero*; and, from the caprice of human nature, the *güero* is always a favourite of the fair sex: the same as, in our country, the olive-coloured foreigners with black hair and beards are thought "such loves" by our fair countrywomen. The *güero,* however, shares this favouritism with the genuine unadulterated negro, who is also greatly admired by the *Mejicanas*.

After leaving the *pulqueria*, we visited, without suspicion, the dens where these people congregate for the night—filthy cellars, where men, women, and children were sleeping, rolled in *sarapes*, or in groups, playing at cards, furiously smoking, quarrelling, and fighting. In one we were attracted to the corner of a room, whence issued the low sobs of a woman, and, drawing near the spot as well as the almost total darkness would admit. I saw a man, pale and ghastly, stretched on a *sarape*, with the blood streaming from a wound in the right breast, which a half-naked woman was trying in vain to quench.

He had just been stabbed by a *lepero* with whom he had been playing at cards and quarrelled, and who was coolly sitting within a yard of the wounded man, continuing his game with another, the knife lying before him covered with blood.

The wound was evidently mortal; but no one present paid the slightest attention to the dying man, excepting the woman, who, true to her nature, was endeavouring to relieve him.

After seeing everything horrible in this region of crime, we took an opposite direction, and, crossing the city, entered the suburb called the *Barrio de Santa Anna*.

This quarter is inhabited by a more respectable class of villains. The *ladrones à caballo*—knights of the road—make this their rendezvous, and bring here the mules and horses they have stolen. It is also much frequented by the *arrieros*, a class of men who may be trusted with untold gold in the way of trade, but who are, when not *en atajo* (unemployed), as unscrupulous as their neighbours. They are a merry set and the best of companions on the road; make a great deal of money, but, from their devotion to *pulque* and the fair sex, are always poor. "*Gastar dinero como arriero*"—to spend money like an *arriero*—is a common saying.

In a *meson* much frequented by these men we found a *fandango* of the first order in progress. An *atago* having arrived from Durango, the *arrieros* belonging to it were celebrating their safe arrival by entertaining their friends with a *bayle;* and into this my friend, who was "one of them," introduced me as an *amigo particular*—a particular friend.

The entertainment was *al-fresco*, no room in the meson being large enough to hold the company; consequently the dancing took place in the corral, and under the portals, where sat the musicians, three guitars and a tambourine, and where also was good store of *pulque* and *mezcal*.

The women, in their dress and appearance, reminded me of the *manolas* of Madrid. Some wore very picturesque dresses, and all had massive ornaments of gold and silver. The majority, however, had on the usual *poblana enagua*, a red or yellow kind of petticoat, fringed or embroidered, over the simple *chemisette*, which, loose and unconfined, except at their waists, displayed most prodigally their charms. Stockings are never worn by this class, but they are invariably very particular in their *chaussure*, a well-fitting shoe, showing off their small, well-formed feet and ankles.

The men were all dressed in elaborate Mexican finery, and in the costumes of the different provinces of which they were natives.

The dances resembled, in a slight degree, *the fandango* and *arabe* of Spain, but were more clumsy, and the pantomimic action less energetic and striking. Some of the dances were descriptive of the different trades and professions. *El Zapatero*, the shoemaker; *el Sastroncito*, the little tailor; *el Espadero*, the swordsman, &c., were among those in the greatest demand; the guitar-players keeping time and accompanying themselves with their voices in descriptive songs.

The *fandango* had progressed very peacefully, and good-humour had prevailed until the last hour, when, just as the dancers were winding up the evening by renewed exertions in the concluding dance, the musicians, inspired by *pulque*, were twanging with vigour their relaxed catgut, and a general chorus was being roared out by the romping votaries of Terpsichore, above the din and clamour a piercing shriek was heard from a corner of the corral, where was congregated a knot of men and women, who chose to devote themselves to the rosy god for the remainder of the evening, rather than to the exertions of the dance. The ball was abruptly brought to a conclusion, every one hastening to the quarter whence the shriek proceeded.

Two men, with drawn knives in their hands, were struggling in the arms of several women, who strove to prevent their encounter—one of the women having received an ugly wound in the attempt, which had caused the shrink of pain which had alarmed the dancers.

"*Que es eso?*"—What is this?—asked a tall, powerful *Durangueño*, elbowing his way through the crowd. "*Que quieren esos gallos?*"—What do these game-cocks want? "*A'pelear?*"—To fight, eh? "*Vamos, a ver los toros!*"—Come, let us see the fun!—he shouted. In an instant a ring was formed; men and women standing at a respectful distance, out of reach of the knives. Two men held the combatants, who, with *sarapes* rolled round their arms, passion darting out of their fiery eyes, looked like two bulldogs ready for the fray.

At a signal they were loosed at each other, and, with a shout, rushed on with uplifted knives. It was short work with them, for at the first blow the tendons of the right arm of one of them were severed, and his weapon fell to the ground; and as his antagonist was about to plunge his knife into the body of his disarmed foe, the bystanders rushed in and prevented it, at the same moment that the *patrulla* (the patrol) entered the corral with bayonets drawn, and *sauve-qui-peut* was the word; a visit to the Acordada being the certain penalty of being concerned in a brawl where knives have been used, if taken by the guard. For myself, with a couple of soldiers at my heels, I flew out of the gate, and never stopped until I found myself safe under the sheets, just as daybreak was tingeing the top of the cathedral.

Society in Mexico, although good, is not much sought after by the foreign residents, who have that resource among themselves; neither do the Mexicans themselves care to mix with those out of their own circle. The Mexican ladies are totally uneducated, and in the presence of foreigners, conscious of their inferiority, are usually shy and reserved. This, of course, refers only to general society. In their own houses, and among themselves, they are vivacious, and unaffectedly pleasing in their manners and conversation; and in all classes is evinced a warmth of heart and sympathy which wins for the women of Mexico the respect and esteem of all strangers.

As for their personal attractions, I will say, that although not distinguished for beauty, I never once remember to have seen a really ugly woman. Their brilliant eyes make up for any deficiency of feature, and their figures, uninjured by frightful stays, are full and voluptuous. Now and then, moreover, one does meet with a perfectly beautiful creature; and when a Mexican woman does combine such perfection she is "some pumpkins," as the Missourians say when they wish to express something superlative in the female line.

For everything connected with the manners and *mantua-making* of Mexico, the reader is recommended to consult Madame Calderon de la Barca, who, making allowances for the *couleur de rose* with which she tints all her pictures, is a lively painter of men, manners, and millinery.

Great preparations were in progress for the proper reception of the great Santa Anna, who was daily expected to arrive in the city from the Encerro, his country-house, and where, under the pretence that his leg (a never-failing resource) was in such a state of inflammation that he was unable to travel, he had been very wisely waiting the course of events, and until such time as the popular feeling should manifest itself in his favour. His statue, which, on the occasion of his being kicked out of Mexico a year before, had been consigned to a corner, was now restored to light, and in course of erection in the *plaza*. Painters were busy at the corners of the streets printing his name and erasing the new one, which at his last exit had been substituted for the numerous Calles de Santa Anna.

The *Teatro National* was once more the *Teatro de Santa Anna*. Triumphal arches were erected in every direction, with inscriptions laudatory of his achievements. One erected on the spot where they, twelve months before, shut the gates on him, throwing his renowned leg after him, hailed him in enormous letters as "*El benemerito de su patria: el immortal salvador de la republica: el heroe de, Tamaalipas*"—the hero of Tamaalipas: the immortal saviour of the republic: the man who deserved well of his country: the hero of a hundred fights. At night a crowd—hired by the friends of Santa Anna—perambulated the streets carrying torches and long stalks of maize, crying, "*Viva Santa Anna y Mejico: meuren los estrangeros*"—death to the foreigners, &c.

After I had been a few days in Mexico I made preparations for my journey to the north. In my search for horses and mules I paid a visit to the horsedealing establishment of one Smith, a Yankee, and quite a character, who is making a fortune in the trade of horseflesh. His stables were filled with nags of all sorts and sizes, and among them were some of General Taylor's troophorses, belonging to a detachment of dragoons which was captured by the Mexicans on the Rio Grande. Smith, who is a hearty John-Bull-looking man, has the reputation with the Mexicans of being *muy picaro*—up to snuff—as what horse-jockey is not? but he has all the custom of the city, and is, of course, a great authority on all subjects connected with horseflesh.

A deputation had just waited upon him to persuade him to officiate as Jehu to a carriage and four, which was to be dispatched some ten miles out of the city to bring in. Santa Anna. Five hundred dollars was, I believe, the sum offered, which the independent Smith refused, as it was a *sine quâ non* that he should attire himself in a general's uniform, as he called it, but, in plain terms, was nothing more or less than a *chasseur's* livery.

I selected and purchased two horses from his stud, and better animals never felt a saddle: one I rode upward of three thousand miles, and brought it to the end of the journey without flinching; the other, a little blood-horse from the *tierra caliente*, with a coat as fine as silk, I was obliged to part with before entering the intemperate climate of New Mexico, where the cold would have quickly killed it. For mules I visited the Barrio de Santa Anna, the headquarters of the *arriero*, where I soon provided myself with those useful animals.

The greatest difficulty was to procure servants, who were unwilling to undertake a journey of such a length, New Mexico being here a *terra incognita,* and associated with ideas of wild beasts and wilder Indians, and horrors of all sorts. I at length hired a *mozo* to proceed with me as far as Durango, five hundred and fifty miles from Mexico, and considered the Ultima Thule of civilization. He was a tall, shambling Mexican, from Puebla: his name, as usual, Jesus Maria. His certificate of character announced him to be *"muy hombre de bien"*—very respectable, faithful, and a good road-servant. His wages were one dollar a-day and his food—*"un peso diario y la comida"*—or equal to nearly eighty pounds a-year of sterling money.

I was so fortunate as to become acquainted with a young Spaniard who was about to start for the mines of Guadaloupe y Calvo; and as our road as far as Durango was the same, we agreed to travel in company, which was as agreeable on the score of companionship as it was advantageous in point of security against the attacks of robbers, who, in large bands, infest this road.

We had, however, anything but a pleasant prospect before us, as the rainy season was at its height; the valley of Mexico was inundated, and the roads almost impassable. In the city of Mexico an inundation was dreaded. The streets were many of them covered with water, and the black mud was oozing out from between the stones of the pavement in every direction, showing the boggy nature of the foundation on which the city is built.

CHAPTER 8

Miseries of Meson

On the 14th of September, just as a salvo of artillery announced the entrance of Santa Anna into the city, our cavalcade, consisting of upward of twenty horses and mules, packed and loose, sallied out of the north gate, and entered a large common outside the city; and then, once out of the streets, where they were easily managed, each loose horse and mule, throwing up its head with a grunt of pleasure at seeing the open country, betook itself to independent expeditions in search of grass. The *mozos* rushed frantically here and there to collect the scattered *atajo*.

The pack-mules threw up their hind legs and refused to listen to reason. A big beast of a mule, that was carrying my heaviest packs, lay down and rolled, disarranged the *aparejo* or pack-saddle, and off tumbled the baggage into the mud; my rifle-case disappeared in a deep pool, into which my *mozo* dived, head first, to rescue it. By this time the other mules had most of them got rid of their packs and were quietly grazing, but were at length caught and repacked, brought to some degree of order, and we resumed our journey—my *mozo* meeting with an accident which was nearly proving serious; on attempting to remount his horse it plunged and threw him upon his head, and for several minutes, stunned by the fall, he was perfectly insensible. The same horse played me the same trick some days after.

With mules, the first day's start is invariably a scene of the greatest confusion. The animals are wild, the pack-saddles hate always something wanting, and the *mozos* half drunk and helpless. In a few days, however, everything is ship-shape; the mules become as docile as dogs, are packed well and quickly, and proceed along the road in regular order.

After proceeding a few miles we found the country entirely covered with water, and the road almost impassable. Six miles from the city we met some cars floating in the road, and the carriers were swimming the cargoes—cases of *cebo* (grease or lard)— to a dry spot. A little farther on, a *carratela*, full of ladies, was stuck hard and fast in the mud; the mules grazing on the roadside, and the men away seeking assistance. A troop of donkeys carrying charcoal to the city presented the most absurd spectacle. The poor patient animals were literally buried in the mud to their very necks, and unable to move a limb. There they remained, the very picture of patience, while the *arrieros* removed their packs and laid them on the mud.

Our animals, being strong and fresh, got safely through, after a hard struggle, and by dint of the most incessant vociferations on the part of our *mozos,* and with the assistance of a score of invoked saints. About dusk we reached Guatitlan, a small town fifteen miles from Mexico, and put up in the meson, the corral of which was belly-deep in black mud, and round which were half a dozen rooms filthily dirty and destitute of furniture. We procured for supper a *pipkin* of rice-soup and tomatoes and a dish of *frijoles*; after which, drenched to the skin and sleepy, I rolled myself in my wet *sarape*, and rushed into the arms, not of Somnus, but of hundreds of thousands of fleas, and bugs, and mosquitoes, whose merciless attacks continued till two o'clock in the morning, when, swallowing a cup of chocolate, we were in our saddles and on our journey.

Sept. 15th.—To avoid the water-covered plains, we took the mountain-road, passing through a tract of country covered with lava and scoria, with wild and picturesque scenery. At the little village of Tapage we halted to breakfast, for which purpose, as there was no meson or public-house of any description, we took by storm a little mud-built house, where an old Indian woman was making tortillas at the door. Our *mozos* laid the village un-

63

der contribution, and soon returned with a hatful of eggs, which our Indian hostess, with the aid of *chile Colorado* and garlic, converted into a palatable dish.

On crossing the bridge over an *arroyo* outside the village, my attention was drawn to the figure of an Indian who was kneeling before a little cage built in the parapet of the bridge. Looking through the bars, I was surprised to see two exceedingly clever heads of Joseph and Mary in a framed painting. They were executed, the Indian informed me, by an artist who passed through Tapage a short time before.

The country here is very beautiful, but poorly cultivated, and the population squalid and miserable in the extreme. About noon we arrived at the *hacienda* of Canañas, in which is a *meson* of the usual description. I enjoyed a bath in the ice-cold waters of a fierce mountain-stream, which dashes through a wild dell clothed with beautiful shrubs. As I was lying on the ground enjoying a cigar after my bath, a number of Indians approached, and examined me with the greatest curiosity. Many of them had never before seen a foreigner, and, as they stood staring round me, muttered, "*Valgame en Dios; Ave Maria Purissima! que guëro, guëro, y habla como nosostros!*"—How white, how white is this man, and yet speaks as we do!

The day was beautiful; and as we had finished our day's journey of thirty-five miles by one o'clock, the afternoon was devoted to cleaning mules and horses and arranging *aparejos*. Our supper consisted of rice, *chile*, and *frijoles*, after which I rolled myself like a mummy in my *sarape*, and, spite of entomological attacks, was asleep in an instant, and stood the assaults of mosquito, bug, and flea until the *mesonero* roused me at three o'clock with a cup of chocolate, which is the only obtainable breakfast in all the *mesones* on the road.

16th.—We picked our way up a mountain in the dark, through a perfect sea of rocks and stones, and on the summit came suddenly upon the bivouac of a large party of *arrieros*, who were lying snoring in their *sarapes* round a roaring fire, their mules grazing round them. I got off my horse to light a cigar at their fire, when one of them, starting up and seeing a stranger, shouted *"Ladrones!"* which quickly roused the rest, who seized their *escopetos* and shouted, "Where, where?" Seeing their mistake, they rubbed their eyes, and asked the news— the *novedades*—which I found with them related to the state of the roads, and not revolutions, counter-revolutions, and the like, with which, true philosophers, they never trouble their heads. In the first part of this day's journey the country was mountainous, and covered with dwarf-oak and ilex.

We then entered upon a tract of open, undulating downs dotted with thickets, but with no signs of habitation. Every eight or ten miles we passed a miserable Indian village with its patch of maize; but the country is entirely uncultivated with this exception, and not a soul is met on the road. The downs here resemble the rolling prairie of the Far West, are covered with excellent grass, and capable of supporting immense herds of cattle. The plains are singularly destitute of trees, which the Mexicans say were destroyed by the Spanish conquerors, but with what object it is impossible to understand, for the want of fuel is a great drawback to the settlement of this portion of the country.

At two p.m. we arrived at the end of our day's journey, thirty-five miles, halting at the *Hacienda del Rio Sarco*—the farm of the muddy brook. We found here a detachment of cavalry on their way to the seat of war, and three staff-officers requested permission to join our party the next day as a security against robbers. The *meson* was better than usual, being the stopping-place of the *diligencia* to Fresnollo; but of beds we had taken a long leave; at least I had—for my companion, more luxurious, carried a camp-bedstead, which was the load of two mules.

1 do not think I have fully described a *meson*, which, as it is a characteristic discomfort of Mexican travelling, deserves a sketch.

The *meson* is everywhere the same in form; a large corral, or yard, entered by a huge gateway, is surrounded by some half dozen square rooms without windows or furniture. In one corner is generally a stone platform raised about three feet from

65

the floor of clay. This is the bed. A little deal table is sometimes furnished if demanded. In one corner of the corral is the *cocina*, the kitchen, so called—*lucus a non lucendo*—from the fact that nothing is cooked there; and in an outer yard is the *caballriza*, the stable, with a well in the centre. The mules are unpacked and the baggage secured in one of the rooms destined for the masters, while the *aparejos*, the saddles, &c., are placed in another occupied by the servants.

On entering, the *mozo* shouts for the *mesonero*, the landlord, who makes his appearance, armed with the key of the granary, where corn and straw are kept. He condescends to serve out the straw and barley, or maize, as the case may be, all of which is duly weighed. The mules and horses are consigned to the stable and fed, after which the *mozos* forage for themselves and masters. The following conversation then takes place with the landlord:—

Mozo. "*Amigo, que hay a comer?*"—What is there to eat?

Mesonero. "*Ah, señor, aqui no hay nada*"—Ah, my lord, there is nothing here.

Mozo. "*Valgame Dios, que pais es este!*"—Heaven defend me, what a country have we come to!

Mesonero. "*Si, señor es muy povre*"—It's true, my lord, it's a very poor country.

Mozo. "*Pero que vamos hacer? Eatan muriendo de hambre los caballeros*"—But what are we to do? The gentlemen are dying of hunger.

Mesonero. "*Si, aus mercedes lo gustan, hay pollo, hay frijoles, hay chile Colorado, hay tortillas*"—Well, if their worships like it, they can have a fowl and *frijoles*, and red peppers and *tortillas*.

Mozo. "*Esta bueno, amigo!*"—Capital, my friend, and let there be enough for us, too; and then "*Quien sabe*" how much corn the horses eat! Eh, my friend (winking his eye): "*Vaya, que vengan*" —Go to, let them be prepared.—Exit *Mesonero*.

In due course several *pipkins* make their appearance, containing the *pollo*, the *frijoles*, the *chile Colorado*, and a pile of *tortillas*: knives, spoons, and forks are not known in a *meson*.

In the morning, before daylight, the *mesonero* makes his appearance with little cups of coffee, and *biscochos* (a sweet cake), and presents the bill.

17th.—Leave Rio Sarco—the Mexican officers, in company. These worthies amused us vastly by their accounts of what they Were going to do. General Ampudia, they said, was merely waiting for the Americans to advance, when he intended to entrap them, leap upon and annihilate them at once: that hitherto he had had but raw troops, *rancheros* and the like, but when the regular cavalry reached him, then, *à Dios!* he would act.

The country, like that through which we passed yesterday, was undulating, with fine downs and excellent pasture. The villages, consisting of a few huts built of adobes, were few and far between. Before the doors of several were placed small stools spread with a white cloth—a sign that there the hungry traveller might break his fast; and at one of these *mesas puestas* we made it a custom every morning to halt, and discuss the usual fare of eggs, *frijoles*, and *chile*.

On a large level plain, covered with cattle, and better cultivated than is generally the case, stands the *hacienda de la Soledád* (of solitude), well named, since it stands alone in the vast plain, the only object which breaks the monotony of the view for many miles. The plain is surrounded by mountains, and the road passes over a stony *sierra*, thickly covered with the yellow-flowered *nopalo*, a gigantic species of cactus.

As we were slowly traversing the rocky *sierra*, we descried, a few hundred yards ahead of us, a band of seven horsemen drawn up across the road. One of my companion's servants, who had been many years a smuggler on this road, instantly recognized them as a well-known band of robbers; we, therefore, as their object was plain, collected our *mulada* into a compact body, and, distributing our party of six, half on each side, we unslung our carbines, threw the flaps off our bolsters, and steadily advanced, the Spaniard and myself in front, with our pieces cocked and ready for service.

The robbers, however, saw at a glance that two of us were foreigners, for whom and their arms they have a great respect,

67

and, wheeling quickly on one side of the road, they hitched their ready lassos on the horns of their saddles, and, remaining in line, allowed us to pass, saluting us with *"Adios, caballeros, buen viage!"*—a pleasant journey to you—the leader inquiring of one of the *mozos*, as he passed, whether the *diligencia* was on the road and had many passengers?

They were all superbly mounted, and well armed with carbine, sword, and pistols; and each had a lasso hanging on the horn of his high-peaked saddle. *"Adios, amigos,"* we said, as we passed them, *"y buena fortuna"*—and good luck this fine morning.

Crossing the *sierra*, we descended into a level and beautiful *champaign*, through which meandered a rushing stream, the Rio Lerma. The soil seemed everywhere to be rich and fruitful, but no signs of cultivation appeared until we approached San Juan del Rio, a town of considerable size, and here the *milpas* (the maize fields) looked green and beautiful. The town, when seen from the *sierra*, as we descended into the plain, looked exceedingly Spanish and picturesque. Indeed, in crossing those vast and uncultivated tracts, anything in the shape of human abode is grateful to the eye; and even the adobe hut of the Indian, with its *mesa puesta*, is a refreshing oasis in these desert solitudes. San Juan del Rio is very beautifully situated, and surrounded by fine gardens, which are celebrated for grapes and *chirimoyas*.

It is difficult to arrive at anything like a correct estimate of the population of a Mexican town, unless comparing the size with that of another, the number of whose inhabitants is known; and it is almost impossible to obtain anything like correct information on any statistical point from a Mexican, who, for the glory of his town or province, will invariably give an absurdly exaggerated statement. Thus, in asking in San Juan of a respectable merchant what was the number of its inhabitants, he gravely answered, *"Mas que ochenta mil"*—more than eighty thousand; and on another occasion, on asking the same question of a *"rico"* of Taos, a valley of some twelve thousand inhabitants, he answered, without hesitation, "two millions."

At a rough guess I should estimate the population of San Juan del Rio at eight or ten thousand.

The houses are generally of one story, and built of stone, whitewashed, with barred windows,[1] the same as in Old Spain, looking into the streets. No particular trade appears to be carried on in the town, if we except begging, which here, as everywhere else in the country, is in a most flourishing condition.

We arrived at San Juan about noon, although our day's journey was thirty-five miles; but our animals were getting more tractable, and travelled with less disorder, and consequently performed the journey quicker, and with less fatigue.

18th.—The road today was better than usual, although we passed through a broken country, diversified by mountain, rugged sierras, and fertile plains. Our practice was to start before daylight in the morning, by which means we avoided travelling in the very hot part of the day, stopping to breakfast wherever a *mesa puesta* presented itself; our animals, in the mean while, travelling on, performing the whole day's journey without stopping, and which, I believe, is the best plan; for a halt of a few minutes does not rest the animals, and the removal of packsaddles from the heated beasts often produces troublesome wounds.

The district in which we were now travelling is situated on the verge of the volcanic region of Jorullo, where, in 1759, occurred one of the most extraordinary phenomena which has ever been observed. A large tract which had long since been subjected to volcanic action, but for many centuries had been undisturbed, was suddenly the scene of most violent subterraneous commotion.

A succession of earthquakes continued for the space of two months, to the great consternation of the inhabitants, at the end of which time they subsided for a few days, but suddenly recommenced with frightful subterranean noises and continued shocks The frightened Indians fled to the neighbouring mountains, whence they beheld, with horror and alarm, flames issuing from

---

1. The *rejas* of the Moorish houses of Andalusia.

the plain, which heaved and tossed like a raging sea, rocks and stones being hurled high in air; and suddenly the surface of the plain was seen gradually to rise in the shape of a dome, throwing out, at the same time, numerous small cones and masses, which rose to an elevation of twelve and fourteen hundred feet above the original level of the plain.

This is the first of a series of volcanic districts which stretch from the valley of Mexico along the whole of the table-land, at irregular distances from each other.

This morning a village presented itself to us, just as we had given up all hopes of meeting a breakfast, and a promising-looking, whitewashed house augured well for our hungry stomachs. Unfortunately some *arrieros* had been before us, and all we could muster was a *guisado* of well-picked bones and some *chilé'd frijoles*.

Descending from the *sierra*, we entered a magnificent plain inclosed by mountains, and arrived at Queretaro at two in the afternoon, distant from San Juan del Rio forty miles, it being the first town of size or note we had yet seen since leaving Mexico.

CHAPTER 9

Curiosity of Natives

Queretaro, the chief city of the department of that name, is well built, and contains many handsome churches and other buildings. Its population is over forty thousand, twelve thousand of whom are Indians. It is surrounded by beautiful gardens and orchards, which produce a great quantity of fruit for the market of the capital. It has several cloth-factories, which employ a considerable number of Indians, but are not in a very flourishing state. An aqueduct of stone conveys water to the city from some springs in the neighbourhood. Its chief trade is in the manufacture of cigars of the tobacco of the country.

The tobacco, as in France and Spain, is a government monopoly. The privilege of cultivating the plant is limited to a small extent of country in the departments of Vera Cruz, Puebla, and Oajaca; but lately, on account of its isolated position, and the great distance from the capital, with its consequent difficulty of transport, the territory of New Mexico is privileged to grow tobacco for its own consumption. The tobacco grown in the above districts is purchased by the government at a stated price, and its manufacture is committed to individuals in different departments.

This monopoly, together with that of salt and gunpowder, has always been a source of annoyance to the government, and ill feeling on the part of the people. The revenue produced by the tobacco monopoly does not amount to more than a half a million of dollars, owing to the pickings and stealings carried on in this as well as every other government department. If properly managed, it would be the source of a considerable and certain revenue. As it is, little or nothing finds its way into the treasury after the expenses of the concern are paid.—(*Cosas de Mejico.*)

The cigars of Queretaro are of a peculiar shape, about three inches long, and square at both ends. To one accustomed to the tobacco of the Havana the pungent flavour of the Queretaro cigars is at first disagreeable, but in a short time the taste acquired for this peculiar raciness renders all other tobacco insipid and tasteless. Excellent *pulque* is made here; and a beverage called *colinche,* expressed from the juice of the *tuna* (fruit of the prickly pear), I tasted for the first time. It is of a blood-red colour, but of sharp and pleasant flavour.

As we were now in the land (*par excellence*) of *pulque,* the drink of thirsty angels, a short description of this truly national liquor and its manufacture will not be out of place. The *maguey,* American aloe, Agave Americana, is cultivated over an extent of country embracing fifty thousand square miles. In the city of Mexico alone the consumption of *pulque* amounts to the enormous quantity of eleven millions of gallons *per annum,* and a considerable revenue from its sale is derived by government.

The plant attains maturity in a period varying from eight to fourteen years, when it flowers; and it is during the stage of inflorescence only that the saccharine juice is extracted. The central stem which incloses the incipient flower is then cut off near the bottom, and a cavity or basin is discovered, over which the surrounding leaves are drawn close and tied. Into this reservoir the juice distils, which otherwise would have risen to nourish and support the flower. It is removed three or four times during the twenty-four hours, yielding a quantity of liquor varying from a quart to a gallon and a half.

The juice is extracted by means of a siphon made of a species of gourd called *acojote,* one end of which is placed in the liquor, the other in the mouth of a person, who by suction draws up the fluid into the pipe and deposits it in the bowls he has with him for the purpose. It is then placed in earthen jars, and a little old *pulque, madre de pulque,* is added, when it soon ferments, and is immediately ready for use. The fermentation occupies two or three days, and when it ceases the *pulque* is in fine order.

Old *pulque* has a slightly unpleasant odour, which heathens have likened to the smell of putrid meat; but, when fresh, is brisk and sparkling, and the most cooling, refreshing, and delicious drink that ever was invented for thirsty mortal; and when gliding down the dust-dried throat of a way-worn traveller,, who feels the grateful liquor distilling through his veins, is indeed the *"liquor divino,"* which Mexicans assert, is preferred by the angels in heaven to ruby wine.

To return to Queretaro. As we entered the town by the *garita,* in a *desague,* or small canal, which ran by the side of and in the very street, were a bevy of women and girls "in the garb of Eve," and in open day, tumbling and splashing in the water, enjoying themselves like ducks in a puddle. They were in no degree disconcerted by the gaze of the passengers who walked at the edge of the canal, but laughed and joked in perfect innocence, and unconsciousness of perpetrating an impropriety.

The passers-by appeared to take it as a matter of course; but we strangers, struck with the singularity of the scene, involuntarily reined in our horses at the edge of the water and allowed them to drink, during which we were attacked by the swarthy *naiads* with laughing and splashing, and shouts of *"Ay que sin vergüenzas!"*—what shameless rogues! *"Echa-les, muchachas !"*—at them, girls; splash the rascals!—and into our faces came showers of water, until, drenched to the skin, we were glad to beat a retreat.

We found the town full of troops *en route* to San Luis Potosi, mid had great difficulty in finding a corral for our animals: ourselves we were fain to stow away in a loft above the corral, where, among soldiers and *arrieros,* we passed a flea and bug-ridden night.

There was nothing eatable in the house, and we sallied out to the stall of a *tortillera* in the market-place, where we took a standing supper of *frijoles* and *chile* as usual. On presenting a sil-

73

ver dollar in payment, I received eight cakes of soap in change—current coin of Queretaro.

"*Valgame Dios!*" I exclaimed, as the saponaceous medium was piled into my *sombrero*.

"*Virgen Purissima! Ave Maria!*" returned the unmoved *tortillera*; "*y javon el mas blando*"—and the softest of soap too—she added, as I eyed the curious currency. "*Vaya.*"

I had intended to remain a day or two in Queretaro,[1] but the town was so crowded with soldiers of the "liberating army," and the accommodation for man and beast at the *mesones* was so execrable, that I determined to proceed at once.

The next morning, the 19th, our lazy *mozos*, having indulged too freely in *pulque* the night before, did not make their appearance until five a.m.: we therefore made a late start, and were still further delayed by our animals, accustomed to start in the dark, taking it into their heads to explore the town, and persisting-in turning down every street but the right one.

Between Queretaro and Celaya the geological features of the country undergo a change, limestone taking the place of the .primary and volcanic rocks ever which we had till now been passing. We appeared also to be gradually, but perceptibly, descending from the high table-lands, and the climate became warmer and more tropical. The plains are exceedingly beautiful, teeming with fertility, and better cultivated. The gardens and maize-patches of the small Indian villages are inclosed with hedges, or, rather, walls, of *organo,* a species of single, square-stemmed cactus, which grows to the height of forty and fifty feet.

It is called *organo* on account of its resemblance to the pipes of an organ. Planted close together, the walls of *organo* are impervious to pigs and poultry, and form admirable corrals to the Indian huts. Here the houses are built of un-cemented limestones, piled loosely one on the other, and are sometimes roofed with talc. The road was flooded and impassable, and we were obliged to wade for many miles through a *lagune*, which was very distressing to the animals. The mules frequently sunk so deep into the

---

1. Distance from San Juan del Rio to Queretaro, forty miles.

mud that we were obliged to unload the packs before they could extricate themselves.

During the day we passed through "*El Paseo*," a comical little place in the midst of the mud, and surrounded by plantations of *magueyes*. The houses were all without windows, and the inhabitants, mostly Indians, appeared to have no other occupation than making *pulque* and drinking it. At a house where the usual sign of a *maguey*-leaf hung at the door, I had a most delicious draught of *pulque*, fresh from the plant, sparkling and effervescent as champagne, and fifty times more grateful.

Magueyes and *nopalos*[2] now lined the road, the latter loaded with fruit. The Indians gather it with long sticks with a fork at one end, in which they secure the *tuna*.[3] Near every village, and sometimes at great distances, are seen women and girls under a tree, with enormous piles of this refreshing fruit prepared for the mouth by the removal of the prickles. I have seen our *mozos* attack a pyramid of *tunas* three feet high, and demolish it before I smoked out a cigar.

The fruit is full of juice, and is said to be very wholesome and nourishing. I invariably carried a knife and fork in my holsters, and, travelling along, without stopping, would make a thrust with my fork at some tempting tuna which overhung the road, and thus quench my thirst in the absence of *pulque*. The *colinche* made from the juice of the *tuna* is also very agreeable.

We entered Celaya by a handsome bridge over the Lerma. Inscribed on a stone let into the parapet is a notice to travellers that the good people of Celaya erected this bridge "*por el beneficio de los viageros*"—for the benefit of the wayfarer—which fact they take care shall not be forgotten. Like all Mexican towns, Celaya is full of churches and *leperos*, and a conspicuous object is the large *collecturia*, a building where the tithes of corn and fruits belonging to the church are kept. In most villages the *collecturia* stands side by side with the *iglesia*, and is invariably the larger

---

2. On a prickly pear I observed a growth of mistletoe (? *orchis*) with a superb crimson flower.
3. Fruit of the prickly pear.

building of the two.

The Carmelite church is an imposing structure of mixed architecture, with Corinthian and Ionic columns. The interior is sombre and gloomy, but enriched with a great quantity of gold and silver ornaments.

The trade of the town consists in the manufacture of saddles, bridles, and articles of leather required for the road. Population about seven thousand. Grain of all kinds is most prolific and abundant in the plains of Celaya, and horses and mules are bred in considerable numbers. The distance from Queretaro is thirty-seven miles.

20th.—Leaving Celayn, we passed over a wild and but partially cultivated country, leaving Salamanca on the left. Hares of very large size, and tame as dogs, abound on these plains, and our march today was enlivened by an incessant popping of carbines and rifles. In one patch of *mezquit*, a thorny shrub very common on the plains, I counted seventy hares in a little glade not one hundred yards square, and they were jumping out of the grass at every step of our animals. We breakfasted at a little Indian village called La Xuage in the comical-looking church of which a grand *funcion* was in progress, and while our meal was in preparation we strolled to the *iglesia* to see what was going on.

The priest, equipped in full uniform, was engaged before the altar praying with open book, and at particular passages gave a signal with his hand behind his back, when half a score of Indian boys outside immediately exploded a number of squibs and fire-wheels, and a bevy of adult Indians fired off their rusty *escopetos*, the congregation shouting vociferously.

At the time when one of the salvos should had taken place, and a huge *trabuco* fired off, which was fastened for safety to the door of the church, the *padre* rushed out, in the middle of his discourse, and clapped a match to the bunghole, giving a most severe look at the neglectful bombardier, and, banging off the blunderbuss, returned, bock in hand, to the altar, where he resumed his discourse.

The farther we advanced from Mexico the more curious

became the provincials in examining "*los estrangeros*" and their equipments. Our hostess in La Xuage, after she had served the eggs and *frijoles*, rushed to all her female acquaintance with the news that two strangers were in her house, and "*por Dios*" that they should come and see the *guëro*. As a "*guëro*" I was an object of particular attention. I was examined from head to foot, and the hostess took upon herself to show me off as a jockey would a horse. My hair was exposed to their wonder and admiration; and "*mire*," added my exhibitor, taking me by the moustaches, "*mire sus bigotes, son guëros tambien*"—and do look here, if his *bigotes* are not *guëros* too. "*Valgame Dios!*"

Nothing excited the curiosity and admiration of the men so much as the sight of my arms. My double rifle, and servant's double-barrelled short carbine and pistols, were handled, and almost worshiped. "*Armas tan bonitas*" they had never seen. With such weapons, they all agreed, neither Indian or Texan, nor *el demonio* himself, was to be feared. One old Indian, who told me he had served against all the enemies of the republic, was incredulous when they told him that the guns were double. Half blind, he thrust his fingers into the muzzles, and, assured of the fact, muttered, "*Ave Maria! dos-tiros, dos-tiros! Valgame Dios! dos-tiros, dos-tiros; dos-tiros, dos-balas. Jesus Maria! dos-tiros!*"—all which exclamations hinged upon the extraordinary fact of a gun possessing two barrels and two balls.

After a long journey of nearly fifty miles through an uninteresting country, we arrived at the solitary *rancho* of Temascatéo, standing alone in a large, uninhabited plain, which bears the reputation of being infested with robbers, and "*muy mala gente*" from the towns of Celaya, Salamanca, and Silao.

Mine host of Temascatéo was the *beau-ideal* of a *ventero*. Fat and *pulque*-lined, his heavy head, with large fishy eyes, almost sunk into his body, his neck, albeit of stout proportion, being inadequate to support its enormous burden. Concealed from his sight behind the sensible horizon of a capacious paunch, a pair of short and elephantine legs shook beneath their load. The stolid, heavy look of this mountain of meat was inexpressible.

Sitting outside the house in a chair, with a paper cigar in his mouth, he directed the issue of the fodder; his wife, a bustling, busy dame, almost as unwieldly as her spouse, doing the talking part of the business.

The only words which appeared able to force their way through his adipose larynx were "*Si, señor; No, señor*," from the bottom of his stomach. After supper I paid the worthy couple a visit, and, presenting mine host with a real Havana, it threw him into such a state of excitement and delight that I expected to see him either burst, or subside in an apoplectic fit.

"*Dios mio, Dios mio!*" he grunted; "a *puro* all the way from Havana!" turning it in his hands and kissing it with affection. His wife was called to see it. Was there ever such a beauty of a *puro*? He had not smoked such a one for thirty years. Asking me all the news of the war, he remarked that *los Tejanos*, as the Americana are called here, were very bad Indians and cannibals; that it was horrible to think of such people taking the country. Much better, he said, if the English, who, he had heard, were a very strong and rich nation, with "*muy poco desorden en su gobierno*"—very little disorder in its government,—were to take it; and as England was "*poco mas alia de Mejico*"—only a little the other side of Mexico; in fact, a neighbour—it would not be so bad.

A room in the *rancho*, as is often the case, was fitted up as a little chapel, with a figure of San Miguel, "*imagen muy hermosa y bien pintada*"—a very beautiful and well-painted image, they told me; and as this happened to be a "*dia de fiesta*," or feast-day, a *funcion* was to be held at nine o'clock in honour of the saint, to which I was duly invited, but declined on the plea of fatigue and sleepiness.

I was roused at midnight by our host, who came to inform me that a band of robbers had just left the house, where they had stopped for a dram, and, after inquiring about my party, had proceeded on the road to Silao. He said he knew them to be *muy mala gente*, and warned me to be on my guard, even that very night, and in the house, "as who knows," he said, "but they may return and murder us all." However, I was too sleepy to watch, and, merely putting another pair of pistols within my blanket, I was soon in the land of dreams, where not even a *ladron* disturbed me.

The next morning one of my mules was found to be so ill that it was unable to carry its pack; and another, belonging to my friend the Spaniard, had given out entirely, and was lying in the corral, unable to rise. Its shoes were taken off, and it was left in the hands of the *mesonero*. My sick mule (it had a bad fistula in the shoulder, which broke out the day after I left Mexico) was relieved by one which I hired at the *rancho* to carry the pack as far as Silao, where I intended to purchase two or three more.

CHAPTER 10

Communication with the Pacific

21st.—We left the *rancho* late, as we had only twenty-four miles to travel; and, moreover, we wished to have our little affair with the robbers (which was expected) in broad daylight, and, passing through a fertile but uncultivated plain, reached Silao in the middle of the day.

In Silao I spent the greater part of the day in hunting up and down the town for mules; and, although hundreds were brought to me, there was scarcely one that was not more or less wounded by packsaddles. It is no uncommon thing to see mules so lacerated by the chafings of the *aparejos*, that the rib-bones are plainly discernible, and in this state the poor animal is worked without intermission. With proper care an animal may perform the longest journey under a pack without injury.

Although the Mexicans are from childhood conversant with the management of mules, it is astonishing what palpable errors they commit in the care of their beasts. The consequences of their system were very manifest in our journey to Durango. My companion allowed his *mozos* to treat his animals according to their system, whereas mine were subject to an entirely different one, from which I never permitted the servants to deviate.

On coming in after a journey of forty miles, performed for the most part under a burning sun, my companion's animals were immediately stripped of their saddles, and frequently of large portions of their skin at the same time: they were then instantly taken to water, and permitted to fill themselves at discretion. Mine, on the other hand, remained with loosened girths until they were nearly cool, and were allowed to drink but little at first, although on the road they drank when water presented itself.

Before reaching Durango the advantages of the two systems were apparent. The Spaniard lost three mules which died on the road, and all his remaining horses and mules were actually putrefying with sores. My animals arrived at Durango fat and strong, and without a scratch, and performed the journey to Santa Fé in New Mexico, a distance of nearly two thousand miles by the road I took, in fifty-six days, and with ease and comfort.

After rejecting a hundred at least which were brought for my inspection, I purchased a *tronco*—a pair—of Californian mules, than which no better ever carried saddle or *aparejo*. This pair, with the two horses I brought with me from Mexico, were the most perfectly enduring animals I ever travelled with. No day was too long, no work too hard, no food too coarse for them. One of the mules, which from its docility and good temper, I promoted to be my hunting-mule, was a short, stumpy animal, with a very large head and long flapping ears.

Many a deer and antelope I killed off her back; and, when hunting, I had only to dismount and throw down the *lariat* on the ground, and she would remain motionless for hours until I returned. These mules became so attached to my horse Panchito, that it was nearly impossible to separate them; and they would follow me like dogs when mounted on his back. They both crossed the grand prairies with me to the Missouri; and when compelled to part them from poor Panchito, I thought their hearts would have broken.

In the meson of Silao we were literally besieged by representatives from every shop in the town, who poured upon us, offering their wares for sale, and every imaginable article required for "the road." This is the custom in all the towns, and shows the scarcity of regular traffic. No sooner does a stranger enter a *meson* than to it flock vendors of saddles, bridles, bits, spurs, whips, *alforjas*, *sarapes* for yourself, *rebosos* for your lady-love, sashes, *som-*

breros, boots, silks, and velvets (cotton), and goods of every kind that the town affords. Besides these, Indian women and girls arrive with .baskets of fruit—oranges, lemons, grapes, *chirimoyas, batatas, platanos*, plantains, *camotes, granaditas, mamayes, tunas*, pears, apples, and fruit of every description. *Pulque* and *colinche* sellers are not wanting, all extolling their goods and pressing them on the unfortunate traveller at the same moment, while *leperos* whine and pray for alms, and *lavenderas* for your clothes to wash, the whole, uniting in such a Babel-like din as outbeggars description.

Rid yourself of these, and gangs of a more respectable class throng the door for the express purpose of staring; and this is a most ill-bred characteristic of Mexican manners, and one of the greatest of the- many annoyances which beset a traveller. Silao is notorious for its population of thieves and robbers, who, it is the boast of the place, are unequalled in audacity as well as dexterity. I saw a striking instance of this. A man entered the corral of the *meson*, and unblushingly offered for sale a pair of wax candles which he had just stolen from a church, boasting of the deed to his worthy companions, who quite approved the feat.

Silao is on the borders of the departments of Guanaxuato and Jalisco, and contains about five thousand inhabitants. The plains in the vicinity produce abundantly wheat, maize, frijoles, barley, &c., and the soil is admirably adapted for the growth of cotton, tobacco, and cochineal.

We were now perceptibly, but very gradually, decreasing our elevation, and the increased temperature was daily becoming more manifest. Jalisco, which we were now entering, belongs to the *tierra caliente*, where all tropical productions might be cultivated, but are not. It is on the western declivity of the Cordillera of Anahuac, which may be said to connect the Andes of South and Central America with the great chain of the Rocky Mountains.

Jalisco has equal if not greater advantages, in point of soil, climate, and communication with the coast, than any other section of Mexico. The table-land on the western ridge of the Cordillera is exceedingly fertile and enjoys a temperate climate. Here are situated the populous towns of Silao, Leon, Lagos, and Aguas Calientes, in the midst of a most productive *champaign*. The central portion, of a less elevation and consequently more tropical temperature, which produces cotton, cochineal, and vanilla, as well as every variety of cereal produce, contains a population for the most part engaged in mines and manufactures.

This port has a communication with the Pacific coast by means of the Rio de Santiago or Tololotlan, which flows from the great lake of Chapala, and on which the important city of Guadalaxara is situated, with a population of twenty-three or twenty-five thousand. The regions near the coast are teeming with fertility, and covered with magnificent forests; but, unfortunately, the *vomito* here holds its dreaded sway, and the climate is fatal to strangers, and, indeed, to the inhabitants themselves.

22nd. —From Silao to La Villa de Leon the eye looks in vain for signs of cultivation. On these vast plains, day after day, we meet no other travellers than the *arrieros* with their *atajos* of mules from Durango, Zacatecas, and Fresnillo. These picturesque cavalcades we always hailed with pleasure, as they were generally the bearers of news, *novedades,* from Durango, of Indian attacks, and of bands of robbers they had met on the road, which intelligence always put us on the *qui vive,* and made our *mozos* look very blue. Leon is own brother to Silao, and rivals that town in its celebrity as being prolific in robbers and assassins. Grain of every kind is here very abundant and of excellent quality.

I had a little affair at Leon which was nearly proving disagreeable to me, and I have no doubt was anything but pleasant to one of the parties concerned. I had been strolling, about nine o'clock in the evening, through the *plaza*, which at that time presents a lively scene, the stalls of the market-people being lighted by fires which are made for that purpose in the square, and which throw their flickering light on the picturesque dresses of the peasantry who attend the market as buyers or sellers, and the still more lively garb of the idle loungers who, wrapped in showy *sarapes* and *cigarros* in mouth, loaf at that hour along the streets.

Returning from the *plaza* through a dark, narrow street, I was detected as a stranger by a knot of idle rascals standing at the door of a *pulque*-shop, who immediately saluted me with cries of "*Texano, Texano, que meura*"—let's kill him, the Yankee dog. Wishing to avoid a rencounter with such odds, and with no other means of defence than a bowie-knife, I thought on this occasion that discretion would be much the better part of valour, so I turned off into another dark street, but was instantly pursued by the crowd, who followed, yelling at my heels.

Luckily, an opportune and dark doorway offered me a shelter, and I crouched in it as my pursuers passed with loud cries and knives in hand. The instant that they all, as I imagined, had passed me, I emerged from my hiding-place, and ran almost into the very arms of three who were bringing up the rear. "*Hi esta, hi esta!*" they shouted, baring their knives and rushing at me. "*Maten le, maten le!*"—here he is, here he is: kill him, kill the jackass.

The darkness was in my favour. As the foremost one rushed at me with uplifted blade I stepped quickly to one side, and at the same moment thrust at him with my knife. He stumbled forward on his knees with a cry of "*Dios! me ha matado*"—he has killed me—and fell on his face. One of the remaining two ran to his assistance, the other made toward me; but, finding that I was inclined to compare notes with him and waited his attack, he slackened his pace and declined the encounter. I returned to the *meson*, and, without telling the Spaniard what had occurred, gave directions for the animals to be ready at midnight, and shortly after we were in the saddle and on the road.

23rd.—From Leon the road ascends a *sierra*, from the top of which is a magnificent view of the plains of Silao. The mule-path by which we descended is rough and dangerous, and we had to wait on the summit of the *sierra* until the day dawned before we could with safety undertake the descent. The whole country exhibits traces of a volcanic origin; pumice and lava strew the ground, and the *sierras* are broken into tabular masses of a singular regularity of outline.

One isolated mountain rises abruptly from the plain, and resembles the Table-mountain of the .Cape of Good Hope in the general form and regularity of its summit. This tabular form is a characteristic feature in the landscape of these volcanic regions: it is called *mesa,* table, by the Mexicans. Lagos lies at the foot of another *sierra,* with a lake in the distance, and, seen from this elevation, the prospect is very beautiful. Far from any habitation, we came upon an old woman sitting under a rock by the roadside, with numerous *ollas* simmering in the ashes of a fire, containing *frijoles* and *chile,* and here we stopped for our usual breakfast.

It was a "*dia de fiesta,*" and when we entered Lagos we found the population in great excitement, as on the morrow a *funcion de toros,* (a bull-fight), was to take place, and the *feria,* (annual fair), commenced that very night.

The *rancheros,* with their wives and daughters, were pouring into the town from far and near, and we had met on the road many families on their way to the fair, forming a very picturesque cavalcade. First the *ranchero* himself, the *pater familias,* in glossy *sombrero* with its gold or silver rolls, *calzoneras* glittering with many buttons, and snow-white drawers of Turkish dimensions, mounted on a showy horse gaily caparisoned, and bearing on its croup the smiling, smirking dame in span-new *reboso* and red or yellow *enagua.*

Next a horse-load or two of *muchachitas,* their brown faces peeping from the *reboso,* showing their black eyes and white teeth, as, shining with anticipated delight of the morrow's festivities, and in a state of perfect happiness and enjoyment, they return their acknowledgments to the compliments of the passing *caballeros.* These, in all the glory of Mexican dandyism, armed with *scopeta* and *machete* (sword), and the ever-ready lasso hanging from the saddle-bow, escorted the party, caracoling along on their prancing steeds.

The *diques*—streams which run through the streets—were full of women and girls undergoing preparatory ablution, and dressing their long, black hair with various unguents at the side of the water. Pedlars were passing from house to house offering for sale gaudy ornaments to the women, earrings of gold and silver and coloured glass, beads of coral, and shell from California, amulets and love-charms from the capital, indulgence for *peccadilloes* committed on the morrow, and suitable for the occasion, the which were in great demand.

In the *plaza* were numerous gambling-booths, where bunks of gold, silver, and copper suited the pockets of every class. Here resorted the wealthy *haciendado* with his *rouleaus* of *onzas,* the *ranchero,* with his silver *pesos,* and the *lepero* with his copper *clacos.* In one of a middle class, where *pesetas* were the lowest stake, were congregated a mixture of all classes. The table, covered with green cloth, displayed tempting lines of gold and silver, surrounded by eager faces. Six women at one end of the room were singing national songs, and occasionally a winner threw them a silver coin, or a loser, for good luck, chucked a *peseta* over his shoulder to the same destination. Some of the airs were very pretty, although the words were generally pure nonsense. A song which described the courtship of a Mexican beauty by a soldier of Guadalaxara was repeatedly encored. Its chorus was the concluding words of the indignant beauty to the presumptuous suitor, and his meek reply:

Soy Mejicana
De este pais.
Yo, un soldado
Soy infeliz.

A Mexican girl
Of this country am I.
And I a poor soldier—
Woe is me!

In conclusion, after the aspiring *muchacha* had run through a long list of the sacrifices she would make if she listened to the suit of the poor soldier, the lover draws a glowing picture of the delights of a barrack life, the constant change of scene, and its advantages over the monotonous existence of a *rancheria.* He offers her *rebosos* of Puebla and *enaguas* of Potosi, the most retired corner in the *quartel*, and assures her that all his "*bona robas*" shall be discarded for her sake. This part put me in mind of the beautiful ballad of Zorilla, in which the Moorish knight woos the Christian lady with glowing descriptions of the presents he would make her, of his castle in Granada, with its beautiful gardens, &c.

> *Y si mi Sultana eres,*
> *Que desiertos mis salones,*
> *Esta mi harem sin mugeres,*
> *Mis oidos sin canciones.*
> *Yo te daré terciopelos,*
> *Y perfumes orientales.*
> *De Grecia te traeré velos,*
> *De Cachemira chales.*
> *Y te daré blancas plumas*
> *Para que adornes tu frente,*
> *Mas blancas que las espumas*
> *De nuestro mar del oriente.*
> *Y perlas para el cabello;*
> *Y baños para el calor;*
> *Collares para el cuello,*
> *Por tus labios: Amor;*

—and describes his brown fortress in the plains of Xenil which will be queen among a thousand when it incloses the beautiful Christian:

> *Que será reina entre mil,*
> *Cuando encierre tu belleza.*

But with the Mexican *muchacha*, as with the Christian lady, the *rebosos* of Puebla, the *enaguas* of Potosi, or even the retired corner in the barrack-room, have as little effect as the velvets and perfumes of the East, the veils brought from Greece, the Cashmere shawls, and the gray fortress in Granada, had with the fair lady, who valued more her towers of Leon than the Moor's Granada

Que mis torres de Leon
Valen mas que tu Granada:

My Leon towers I doubly prize,
Than all the plains of thy Granada.

24th.—We left Lagos for *La Villa de la Encarnacion* through a barren and uninteresting country, destitute of trees, and the vegetation sparse and burned up. The road was up and down *sierras* the whole day, scattered with *nopalo* and prickly pear; the heat tremendous, and the sun's rays, reverberated from the rocky *sierra*, fiery and scorching. We crossed a river which washes the walls of the town, by a ford on the right of a ruined bridge, destroyed during the War of Independence, and never rebuilt.

This town was the first I saw in which all the houses were of *adobes* (sunburned bricks). It exactly resembled the sketch of Timbuctoo as given in René Caillé's book, and its appearance, as might be expected, was miserable in the extreme. As we passed the quaint-looking church, with its bells swung high in air, the organ was playing a crashing polka—a *funcion* at the time being in progress inside, and groups of *leperos* kneeling in the inclosed space in front.

Among the beggars, who as usual attended our levee on arrival, was a *lepero* without even the rudiments of legs, who dragged himself along the ground on his stomach, like a serpent, and had a breastplate of leather for the purpose of protecting his body from the rough stones over which he crawled. This disgusting wretch took up his position in the corral, and, as it cost him no little labour to crawl thus far, seemed determined to sicken us out of a coin. The night was so hot and close that I placed my blanket in the balcony which ran round the rooms, which in this meson were above the stables, and ascended by wooden steps.

Being very tired, I had turned in early, and was in a pleasant doze, when I imagined I heard a dog which belonged to my companion, and which had on leathern shoes to protect its feet, scraping or scratching near me. Thinking the animal, which was a great favourite, wanted to lie down on my blanket, I called to it to come and lie down, saying, "*Ven aca, povrecito, ven aca*" (Come here, poor fellow, come here). I immediately felt something at my side, and lazily opening my eyes, what was my intense horror and disgust at seeing the legless *lepero* crawling on my bed!

Human nature could not stand it. "*Maldito!*" I roared out, "*afuera!*" and gathering up my leg, kicked him from me. I did not recover from my disgust until I saw the wretch crawling across the corral and out of the gate. He had come to beg or steal; and, of course imagining from my words that I was charitably inviting him to share my blanket, was thus unceremoniously ejected from the balcony.[1]

---

1. From Lagos to La Encarnacion, forty miles.

CHAPTER 11

Massacre of the *Rancheros*

25th—To Aguas Calientes, a very pretty town, with some handsome buildings. We met a gipsying or picnic party on the road, mounted on *borricos*, with a mule packed with comestibles. A bevy of very pretty girls brought up the rear, under the escort of half a dozen exquisites of the town, got up in the latest fashion of the capital. Their monopoly of such a fair troop was not to be borne, and with tolerable impudence we stopped the party.

The dandies, from our sunburned and road-stained appearance and bristling arms, at once set us down as robbers, and without more ado turned their donkeys and retreated, leaving us masters of the field and the fair. With them our peace was soon made, and we received a pressing invitation to join the party, which, however, we were fain to decline, as our horses were sorely tired. They laughed heartily at the panic of their gallant escort, who were huddled together at a little distance, not knowing whether to advance or retreat. I sent my *mozo* to them to say that the ladies required their presence; and we rode on to the town, where we found our *mulada* arrived and waiting our approach.

In Aguas Calientes I was accosted by a negro, a runaway slave from the United States. He informed me he was cook at the house where the *diligencia* stopped, and that if I chose he would prepare a dinner for us—roast-beef, &c., and all the "fixings" of an American feed. I gladly made the bargain, and proceeded to the house at the time appointed, but found the rascal had never been there, and dinner there was none.

In the *plaza* is a column erected to some patriot or another, which is pointed out to the stranger as being *muy fino*. The pedestal is surmounted by geese with long claws like an eagle's, and hairy heads of dogs stick out of the sides—the most absurd thing I ever saw.

25th.—To the *hacienda* of La Punta, in a large plain where are several other plantations, and two *rancherias* celebrated as being the abode of a band of robbers called "*picos largos*," long bills. In this day's journey of forty miles one of the horses died from fatigue and heat, and two others were scarcely able, from the same cause, to continue it to its close.

26th.—To Zacatecas, through wild uncultivated plains and *sierras*. On the road we passed some abandoned copper-mines, where an old Indian was picking for stray pieces of ore, of which a dream had promised the discovery.

Zacatecas, a populous city of between thirty and forty thousand inhabitants, is in the midst of one of the most valuable mining districts in Mexico. The country round it is wild and barren, but the rugged *sierras* teem with the precious metals. Near the town are several lakes or *lagunes*, which abound in *muriate* and carbonate of soda. The town itself is mean and badly built, the streets narrow and dirty, and the population bear a very bad character; which, indeed, is the case in all the mining towns in the country, and is but natural from the very nature of their employment.[1]

From this point the *novedades* poured upon us daily: "*Los Indios! los Indios!*" was the theme of every conversation. Thus early (it was a very early Indian season this year and the last) they had made their appearance in the immediate vicinity of Durango killing the *paisanos*, and laying waste the *haciendas* and *ranchos*, and it was supposed they would penetrate even farther into the interior. What a "*cosa de Mejico*" is this fact! Five hundred savages

---

1. From Hacienda de la Punta to Zacatecas, fifty miles.

depopulating a *soi-disant* civilized country, and with impunity!

27th.—The road from Zacatecas to Fresnillo lies through a wild, uncultivated country without inhabitants. We met a *conducta* from the mines of Fresnillo, bearing bars of silver to the mint at Zacatecas. The wagon in which it was carried was drawn by six mules galloping at their utmost speed. Eight or ten men, with muskets between their knees, sat in the wagon, facing outward, and as many more galloped alongside, armed to the teeth. Bands of robbers, three or four hundred strong, have been known to attack *conductas* from the mines, even when escorted by soldiers, engaging them in a regular stand-up fight.

Fresnillo is a paltry, dirty town, with the neighbouring *sierra* honeycombed with mines, which are rich and yield considerable profits. A share which the government had in these mines yielded an annual revenue of nearly half a million of dollars; but that short-sighted vampire, which sucks the blood of poor Mexico, eager to possess all the golden eggs at once, sold its interest for less than one year's income. *Cosa de Mejico*, here as everywhere !

We were .here very kindly invited to take up our abode, during our stay, in the *hacienda* of the mines, the *administrador* of which is an American, and the officers mostly Spaniards. Enjoying their hospitality, we spent two or-three days very pleasantly, and were initiated into all the mysteries of mining. The process of extracting the metal from the ore is curious in the extreme, but its description would require more science than I possess, and more space than I am able to afford. Two thousand mules are at work daily in the *hacienda de beneficios,* and two thousand five hundred men are employed in the mines.

From this an idea may be formed of the magnitude of the works. The main shaft is twelve hundred feet in depth, and a huge engine is constantly employed in removing water from the mines. This vast mass of machinery appeared to take care of itself, for I saw neither engineers nor others in the engine-house. There are many Cornishmen employed in the mines, who drink and fight considerably, but withal find time to perform double as much work as the Mexicans. The patio or yard of the *hacienda de beneficios*, where the porphyritic crushing-mills are at work, contains thirty-two thousand square yards. In undergoing one process, the crushed ore, mixed with copper and salt, is made into enormous mud puddings, and trodden out by mules, which are back deep in the paste; indeed, the whole process of the *beneficio*, a purely chemical one, is most curious and worthy of attention.

The miners are a most dissolute and vicious class of men, and frequently give great trouble to the officers of the hacienda. But for the firmness and presence of mind of the *administrador*, the American gentleman before alluded to, the miners on more than one occasion would probably have sacked the *hacienda*.

The Cornishmen, however, can always be relied on, their only fault being the love of fighting and whisky; and a depot of arms is kept in the *hacienda* ready for any emergency.

On a bare rock, which was entirely destitute of soil, the miners have formed a most beautiful and productive garden, the soil with which it is made having been conveyed to the spot on the backs of mules and donkeys; it is now luxuriant and thriving, although, I believe, but two years old, and is full of fruit-bearing trees of every description. In the centre is a fountain and ornamental summer-house, and, curiously enough, this garden is the resort of flocks of humming-birds, which are but rarely found on the neighbouring plains.

On the road between Zacatecas and Fresnillo, as I was jogging gently on, a Mexican, mounted on a handsome horse, dashed up and reined in suddenly, doffing his sombrero and saluting me with a *"Buenos dias, caballero."* He had ridden from Zacatecas for the purpose of trading with me for my sword, which he said he had heard of in that town as being something *muy fino*. Riding up to my left side, and saying, *"Con su licencia caballero"*—by your leave, my lord—he drew the sword from its scabbard, and, flourishing it over his head, executed a neat *demivolte* to one side, and performed some most complicated manoeuvres.

At first I thought it not unlikely that my friend might take it into his head to make off with the sword, as his fresh and powerful animal could easily have distanced my poor tired steed, so I just slipped the cover from the lock of my carbine, to be ready in case of need. But the Mexican, after concluding his exercise, and having tried the temper of the blade on a *nepalo*, rode up and returned the sword to its scabbard with a low bow, offering me at the same time his horse in exchange for it, and, when that was of no avail, another and another—horses, he assured me, "*de la mejor sangre*"—of the best blood of the country, and of great speed and strength.

On the 30th we left Fresnillo, having a journey of fifty-five miles before us to Zaina. The country is desolate and totally un-cultivated, excepting here and there where a solitary hacienda or rancho is seen; these are all fortified, for we were now entering the districts which are annually laid waste by the Comanches. The *haciendas* are all surrounded by walls, and flanked with towers loopholed for musketry. A man is always stationed on an eminence in the vicinity, mounted on a fleet horse, on the lookout for Indians; and on their approach a signal is given, and the *peones*, the labourers employed in the *milpas*, run with their families to the *hacienda*, and the gates are then closed and preparations made for defence.

This morning I gave my horse Panchito a run, *suelto,* among the mules and loose animals, mounting Bayou Lobo, the *tierra caliente horse* which gave my *mozo* so severe a fall the day we left the capital. I had dismounted to tighten the girths a short time after leaving Fresnillo, and before daylight, when, on remounting, the animal, as usual, set off full gallop, and, being almost imprisoned in my *sarape*, which confined my arms and legs, in endeavouring to throw my right leg over the saddle I pitched over on the other side and fell upon the top of my head, at the same moment that the horse kicked out and struck with great force on my left ear.

I lay in the road several hours perfectly insensible; my servant imagined I was dead, and, dragging me on one side, rode on to overtake the Spaniard. However, showing signs of life, they placed me again in the saddle, and I rode on for several hours in a state of unconsciousness. My jaw was knocked on one side, and when I recovered I had hard work to pull it into its former position; for days, however, I was unable to open it farther than to admit a fork or a spoon; and as I had to ride forty-five miles the same day that I met with the accident, and under a burning sun, I thought myself fortunate in not being disabled altogether.

Zaina is a very pretty little town, surrounded with beautiful gardens. It is an isolated spot, and has little or no communication with other towns.

Oct. 1st.—To Sombrerete, distance thirty-four miles. The country became wilder, with less fertile soil, and entirely depopulated, as much from fear of Indians as from its natural unproductiveness. Sombrerete was once a mining-place of some importance, and the *Casa de la Diputadon de Mineria,* a large, handsome building, is conspicuous in the town. The *sierra* is still worked, but the veins are not productive. The *veta negra de Sombrerete,* the famous black vein of Sombrerete, yielded the greatest *bonanzas*[2] of any mine on the continent of America. It is now exhausted.

2nd.—We left the usual road, and struck across the country to the *hacienda de San Nicolas,* as I was desirous of passing through the tract of country known as the *Mai Pais,* a most interesting volcanic region, a perfect *terra incognita* even to Mexicans; and as to travellers, such *raræ aves* are as little known in these parts as in Timbuctoo. We journeyed through a perfect wilderness of *sierra,* and *chaparral* thickly covered with *nopalos* and *mezquite,* which now became the characteristic tree. The high, rank grass was up to our horses' bellies, and, matted with the bushes of *mezquite* and prickly pear, was difficult to make our way through. Hares and rabbits, and *javali,* a species of wild hog, abounded, with quail and partridge, and many varieties of pigeons and doves. We passed, on our left hand, a curiously-formed ridge, and a py-

---

2. When a rich vein or lode is struck in a mine yielding a large quantity of ore, such a fortunate event is termed "*bonanza.*"

ramidal hill which stood isolated in the plain, such as the ancient Mexicans made use of as pedestals for their temples, and which have been ingenuously described as artificial structures by writers on Mexican antiquities. This day's journey was long and fatiguing, as we had to make our way for the most part across a trackless country, striking a mule-path only within about fifteen miles of the *hacienda*. Our animals were completely exhausted when we reached it, having performed nearly sixty miles during the day.

The *hacienda de San Nicolas* is one of those enormous estates which abound in every part of Mexico, and which sometimes contain sixty and eighty square miles of land. Of course not a hundredth part is under cultivation; but on some, immense herds of horses, mules, and cattle roam almost wild, or, rather, did roam, for the Indians have carried off incredible numbers. The *hacienda* itself is generally surrounded by the huts of the *peones*. The labourers who are employed on the plantation exist in a kind of serfdom to the owners, and their collection of adobe hovels forms almost a town of itself. The *haciendados* live in almost feudal state, having their hundreds of retainers, and their houses fortified to repel the attacks of Indians or other enemies.

On riding up to the gate of the *hacienda* we surprised two of the *señoritas* in *dishabil*, smoking their *cigarros* of *hoja*—cornshucks—on a stone bench in front of the house; they instantly ran off like startled hares, so unexpected was the apparition of strange *caballeros* with a retinue of *mozos*, and, banging to the gate, reconnoitred us through the chinks. Nothing would induce them to reappear, go we withdrew, and sent one of the *mozos* on the forlorn hope of procuring admittance.

With him they parleyed through the gate, and informed us, through him, that, as their *padre* was from home, they were unable to receive us within the castle, but that a stable was *à la disposition de los caballeros,* and a *quarto,* used sometimes as a henhouse, and at others as a calf-pen, should be cleaned for their reception. With this we were fain to be content, and, as there was ample provision for our tired beasts, and a good corral, had no reason to complain, as sleeping in the air was no hardship in this climate.

Presently, with the compliments of the ladies, an excellent supper made its appearance, comprising a *guisado* of hare, *frijoles*, eggs, &c., and a delicious salad prepared by the fair hands of the *señoritas*, and their regrets at the same time that the absence of their *señor* prevented them from having the pleasure of affording better accommodation.

3rd.—Our road laid through the *Mai Pais*—the evil land (as volcanic regions are called by the Mexicans), which has the appearance of having been, at a comparatively recent period, the theatre of volcanic convulsions of an extraordinary nature. The convexity of the disturbed region enables one to judge of the extent of the convulsion, which reaches from the central crater to a distance of twelve or fourteen miles.

The valley, between two ridges or *sierras*, is completely filled up to nearly a level with the sierra itself; it is, therefore, impossible to judge of the height of the tract of ground raised by the volcano. The crater is about five or six hundred yards in circumference, and filled with a species of dwarf oak, *mezquite*, and cocoa-trees, which grow out of the crevices of the lava. In it is a small, stagnant lake, the water of which is green and brackish; huge blocks of lava and scoria surround the lake, which is fringed with rank shrubs and cactus.

It is a dismal, lonely spot, and the ground rumbles under the tread of the passing horse. A large crane stood, with upraised leg, on a rock in the pool, and a *javali* was wallowing near it in the mud. Not a breath of air ruffled the inky surface of the lake, which lay as undisturbed as a sheet of glass, save where here and there a huge water-snake glided across with uplifted head, or a duck swam slowly out from the shadow of the shrub-covered margin, followed by its downy progeny.

I led my horse down to the edge of the water, but he refused to drink the slimy liquid, in which frogs, efts, and reptiles of every kind were darting and diving. Many new and curious water-plants floated near the margin, and one, lotus-leaved, with small, delicate tendrils, formed a kind of net-work on the water, with a superb crimson flower, which exhibited a beautiful contrast with the inky blackness of the pool.

The Mexicans, as they passed this spot, crossed themselves reverently, and muttered an *Ave Maria*; for in the lonely regions of the *Mai Pais*, the superstitious Indian believes that demons and gnomes, and spirits of evil purposes have their dwelling-places, whence they not unfrequently pounce upon the solitary traveller, and bear him into the cavernous bowels of the earth; the arched roof of the prison-house resounding to the tread of their horses as they pass the dreaded spot, muttering rapidly their prayers, and handling their amulets and charms to keep off the treacherous *bogles* who invisibly beset the path.

The surrounding country is curiously disturbed, and the flow of the molten lava can easily be traced, with its undulations, and even retaining the exact form of the ripple as it flowed down from the crater. Hollow cones appear at intervals like gigantic petrified bubbles, and extend far into the plain. Some of these, in shape like an inverted cup, are rent, and present large fissures while others are broken in two, one half only remaining, which exhibit the thickness of the shell of basaltic lava to be only from one to three feet.

We arrived at the rancho of La Punta in the afternoon, in time to witness the truly national sport of the *coléa de toros*— in English, bull-tailing—for which some two or three hundred *rancheros* were assembled from the neighbouring plantations.

This *rancho*, in the fall of last year, was visited by the Comanches, who killed several of the unfortunate *peones*, whom they caught in the road and at work in the *milpas*, and carried off all the stock belonging to the farm. On the spot where the *rancheros* were killed and scalped, crosses are erected, and the little piles of stones, which almost bury them, testify to the numerous *Ave Marias* and *Pater Nosters* which their friends have uttered when passing, in prayer for their souls in purgatory, and for each prayer have deposited at the foot of the cross the customary stone.

Without warning, the Indians one day suddenly appeared on the *sierra*, and swooped down upon the *rancho*. The men immediately fled and concealed themselves, leaving the women and children to their fate. Those who were not carried away were violated, and some pierced with arrows and lances, and left for dead. The *ranchero's* wife described to me the whole scene, and bitterly accused the men of cowardice in not defending the place.

This woman, with two grown daughters and several smaller children, fled from the *rancho* before the Indians approached, and concealed themselves under a wooden bridge which crossed a stream near at hand. Here they remained for some hours, half dead with terror: presently some Indians approached their place of concealment: a young chief stood on the bridge and spoke some words to the others. All this time he had his piercing eyes bent upon their hiding-place, and had, no doubt, discovered them, but concealed his satisfaction under an appearance of indifference.

He played with his victims. In broken Spanish they heard him express his hope "that he would be able to discover where the women were concealed—that he wanted a Mexican wife and some scalps." Suddenly he jumped from the bridge and thrust his lance under it with a savage whoop; the blade pierced the woman's arm and she shrieked with pain. One by one they were drawn from their retreat.

"*Dios de mi alma!*"—what a moment was this !—said the poor creature. Her children were surrounded by the savages, brandishing their tomahawks, and she thought their last hour was come. But they all escaped with life, and returned to find their house plundered, and the corpses of friends and relations strewing the ground.

"*Ay de mi!*"—what a day was this! "*Y los hombres,*" she continued, "*qui no son hombres?*"—And the men—who are not men—where are they? "*Escondidos como los ratones*"—hidden in holes like the rats. "*Mire!*" she said, suddenly, and with great excitement: "look at these two hundred men, well mounted and armed, who are now so brave and fierce, running after the poor bulls; if twenty Indians were to make their appearance, where would they be? "*Vaya, Vaya!*" she exclaimed; "*son cobardes*"—they are cowards all of them."

The daughter, who sat at her mother's feet during the recital, as the scenes of that day were recalled to her memory, buried her face in her mother's lap, and wept with excitement.

To return to the *toros*. In a large corral, at one end of which was a little building, erected for the accommodation of the lady spectators, were inclosed upward of a hundred bulls. Round the corral were the horsemen, all dressed in the picturesque Mexican costume, examining the animals as they were driven to and fro in the inclosure, in order to make them wild for the sport—*alzar el corage*. The *ranchero* himself, and his sons, were riding among them, armed with long lances, separating from the herd, and driving into another inclosure, the most active bulls.

When all was ready, the bars were withdrawn from the entrance of the corral, and a bull driven out, who, seeing the wide level plain before him, dashed off at the top of his speed. With a shout, the horsemen pursued the flying animal, who, hearing the uproar behind him, redoubled his speed. Each urges his horse to the utmost, and strives to take the lead and be the first to reach the bull. In such a crowd, of course, first-rate horsemanship is required to avoid accidents and secure a safe lead. For some minutes the troop ran on in a compact mass—a sheet could have covered the lot.

Enveloped in a cloud of dust, nothing could be seen but the bull, some hundred yards ahead, and the rolling cloud. Presently, with a shout, a horseman emerged from the front rank; the women cried "*viva!*" as, passing close to the stage, he was recognized to be the son of the *ranchera*, a boy of twelve years of age, sitting his horse like a bird, and swaying from side to side as the bull doubled, and the cloud of dust concealed the animal from his view.

"*Viva Pepito! viva!*" shouted his mother, as she waved her *reboso*, to encourage the boy; and the little fellow struck his spurs

100

into his horse, and doubled down to his work manfully. But now two others are running neck and neck with him, and the race for the lead, and the first throw, is most exciting. The men shout, the women wave their *rebosos*, and cry out their names: "*Alza— Bernardo—por mi amor, Juan Maria—Viva Pepito!*" they scream in intense excitement.

The boy at length loses the lead to a tall, fine-looking Mexican, mounted on a fleet and powerful roan stallion, who gradually, but surely, forges ahead. At this moment the sharp eyes of little Pepe observed the bull to turn at an angle from his former course, which movement was hidden by the dust from the leading horseman. In an instant the boy took advantage of it, and, wheeling his horse at a right angle from his original course, cut off the bull. Shouts and *vivas* rent the air at sight of this skilful manoeuvre, and the boy, urging his horse with whip and spur, ranged up to the left quarter of the bull, bending down to seize the tail, and secure it under his right leg, for the purpose of throwing the animal to the ground.

But here Pepe's strength failed him in a feat which requires great power of muscle, and in endeavouring to perform it he was jerked out of his saddle, and fell violently to the ground, stunned and senseless. At least a dozen horsemen were now striving hard for the post of honour, but the roan distanced them all, and its rider, stronger than Pepe, dashed up to the bull, threw his right leg over the tail, which he had seized in his right hand, and, wheeling his horse suddenly outward, upset the bull in the midst of his career, and the huge animal rolled over and over in the dust, bellowing with pain and fright.

This exciting but dangerous sport exhibits the perfect horsemanship of the Mexicans to great advantage. Their firm yet graceful seat excels everything I have seen in the shape of riding, and the perfect command which they have over their horses renders them almost a part of the animals they ride. Their seat is quite different from the "park-riding" of Mexico.

The sport of *coléa* lasts as long as a bull remains in the corral, so that at the conclusion, as may be imagined, the horses are perfectly exhausted.

Another equestrian game is "*el gallo*"—the cock. In this cruel sport, an unfortunate rooster is tied by the legs to a tree, or to a picket driven in the ground, with its head or neck well greased. The horsemen, starting together, strive to be the first to reach the bird, and, seizing it by the neck, to burst the thongs which secure it, and ride off with the prize. The well-greased neck generally slips through the fingers of the first who lay hold of it; but, as soon as one is in possession, he rides off pursued by the rest, whose object is to rescue the fowl. Of course in the contest which ensues the poor bird is torn to pieces; the scraps of the body being presented by the fortunate possessors as a *gâge d'amour* to their mistresses.

The people in the *rancho* were so poor in comestibles, that we supped that night on beans and bread, and made our beds afterward outside the door, where all night long continued such a clatter of women's tongues, such grunting of pigs, barking of curs, braying of *borricos*, &c., that I was unable to sleep until near morning, when, before daylight, we were again in our saddles. :

Oct. 4th.—At daybreak we came to a river, which, in the absence of a ferry, we swam with all our animals, both packed, and loose. We passed through a flat country, entirely inundated, and alive with geese and *gruyas*. The latter bird, of the crane species, is a characteristic feature in the landscape of this part of Mexico. The corn-fields are visited by large flocks, and, as they fly high in the air, their peculiar melancholy note is constantly heard, both in the day and night, booming over the plains.

Durango, the metropolis of northern Mexico, is situated near the root of the Sierra Madre, at the northwestern corner of a large plain, poorly cultivated and sparsely inhabited. It is a picturesque city, with two or three large churches and some government buildings, "fair to the eye but foul within," with a population of eighteen thousand, seventeen thousand of whom are rogues and rascals.

Like all other Mexican cities, it is extremely dirty in the exterior, but the houses are clean and tidy within, always excepting government buildings. It is celebrated for its scorpions and bad *pulque*, and the enormous mass of malleable iron which rises isolated in the plain, about three miles from the town. This rock is supposed to be an aërolite, as its composition and physical character are identical with certain aërolites which fell in 1751 in some part of Hungary, and analogous to the general character of others of the same nature, of which the aërolitic origin is equally certain and authenticated. It contains seventy-five *per cent*, of pure iron, according to the analysis of a Mexican chemist; and some specimens, which Humboldt procured, were analyzed by the celebrated Klaproth, with, I believe, the same result.

Durango is distant from the city of Mexico five hundred miles in a due course, or as the bird flies, but by the road must be upward of six hundred and fifty; my reckoning makes it six hundred and sixty-five—many miles, I have no doubt, too much or too little. Its elevation, according to Humboldt, is six thousand eight hundred and forty-five feet above the level of the sea, while that of Mexico is seven thousand four hundred and seventy, and La Villa de Leon six thousand and twenty-seven feet; thus showing that the tableland of Mexico does not decline so suddenly as is imagined. Indeed, excepting in the plains of Salamanca and Silao, there is no perceptible difference in the temperature, and I believe, in reality, but little of elevation, in the vast region between the capital and Chihuahua.

Snow falls here occasionally, and the mercury is sometimes seen below the freezing point. For the greater part of the year, however, the heat is excessive, when a low intermittent fever is prevalent, but rarely fatal.

Durango is the seat of a bishopric, and the worthy prelate lately undertook a journey to Santa Fé, in New Mexico, which progress created a furore among the devout; and the good old man was glad to return with any hem to his garment, so great was the respect paid to him. That he escaped the Apaches and Comanches is attributed to a miracle: the unfaithful assign the glory to his numerous escort. *Quien sabe* ?

The City of Scorpions (as it is called) was in dread and expectation of an Indian invasion during my stay. Some five hundred Comanches were known to be in the vicinity toward the *northeast;* so, after a *fanfarron* of several days, and high mass in the church for the repose of those who were going to be killed, &c., the troops and *valientes* of the city, with beating drums and flying colours, marched out to the southwest, and happened to miss "*los barbaros.*"

However, it saved them a sound drubbing, and the country the *valientes* who would have been killed; so the fatality was not much regretted, at least by the military, and the people by this time are accustomed to these "chances." *Cosas de Mejico.*

There is an English merchant in Durango, and one or two Germans and Americans. Their hospitality is unbounded. There is also a mint, the *administrador* of which is a German gentleman, who has likewise established a cotton-factory near the city, which is a profitable concern: *y de mas* (and moreover), *las Durangueñas son muy balagüenas* (the ladies of Durango are very pretty).

I stayed in the house of the widow of a Gachupin, whose motherly kindness to me, and excellent cooking taught, her by her defunct *sposo,* is one of the most pleasurable *memorias* I bear with me from Mexico, where a bastard and miserable imitation of the inimitable Spanish cuisine exists in all its deformity.

CHAPTER 12

Dangers of Travelling

Travelling in Mexico may be divided into two heads, *viz.*, *en grande* (or *en prince,* as they say in France), or in the style of the *hombre de jaqueta,* which, however, although considered *infra dig.* in Spain, is, as far the garment is concerned, the only correct costume for the road in Mexico. The wealthy *haciendado* of the *tierra caliente* rolls along in his *carretela* drawn by half a dozen mules, his lady in more luxurious *littera,* while the gentlemen and *solteros* of the family—the bachelors—prance at the sides of the litter, mounted on their Puebla hacks, and arrayed in all the glory of buttons and embroidery.

If the object be to see the country, and become acquainted with the people and their manners and customs, the traveller should, in the first place, leave in charge of the steward of the royal mail steam-ship, at Vera Cruz or Tampico, his English reserve and prejudice in the pocket of his Tweed shooting-jacket; all of which, together with his Lincoln and Bennet and cockney notions, he must at once discard before leaving the steamer. Then, having donned a broad-brimmed Panama and white linen roundabout, he may forthwith deliver his letter to his consignee, and make up his mind to the enjoyment of unbounded hospitality for as long as he pleases; and the longer, the better pleased his entertainers: for here, it may be remarked, among the foreigners, the most genuine hospitality makes the stranger immediately at home, even m the city of the dreaded *vomito.*

Here, if he has the good fortune to possess, at the bottom of en introductory epistle, the talismanic "open *sesame*" of Messrs. Coutts and Co., he will find that he has fallen on his legs indeed; and at the *casa* of *los señores* M—— and M—— he will be put in the way of equipping himself for any mode of travelling, whether *par diligencia*, by *dilly*; *à caballo*, on horseback; or by lazy *littera*: in which last luxurious conveyance he can travel to Jalapa, and smoke and dream away his time, through the most picturesque scenery of the *tierra caliente*, which, of course, through the pendent curtains, he cannot get a glimpse of.

If, too, Castillo, that prince of *mozos*, should happen, at the time of his departure, to have an inclination to visit his soft-eyed *Jalapeña*, he may be as lucky as I was in securing his *ciceroneship* as far as the "City of the Mist;" whence to the capital the coach is the safest and surest mode of transit.

From Mexico to the north, a large escort is necessary to. protect the traveller from the exactions of *los caballeros del camino*— the highwaymen; and if the journey is continued still farther— toward the pole, a respectable force is absolutely indispensable, if he wish to arrive at his journey's end with the hair on the top of his head; for my passage, *sin novedad*, through that turbulous country is to be attributed alone to extraordinary good fortune, and so sharp a lookout as to render the journey anything but a mere pleasure trip.

Indeed, the traveller in any part of Mexico must ever bear in mind the wholesome Yankee saying, "Keep your primin' dry, and your eyes skinned." It is not even saying too much to advise those who have never served an apprenticeship of hard knocks, and who would find no little difficulty in adapting their fastidious *cuerpos* to the rough-and-tumble life they must necessarily lead, to confine their rambles to the well-steamered Rhine, or within the radius of the *Messageries* Royales and Lafitte's.

It must be some time after the termination of the present war before the country will be fit to travel over; for woe to the luckless wight whose turnip complexion and hair of the carrot's hue proclaim him to be of Anglo-Saxon race, should he fall into the hands of a marauding party of disbanded soldiers! and the present bitter feeling of hostility to foreigners must pass away before it will be safe to show one's nose outside the gates of the larger cities.

The usual mode of travelling long distances by even the wealthiest of the male class, is invariably on horse or mule back, several sumpter-mules being packed with the *catre* (bedstead), *alforjas* (saddlebags), *cantin* (a portable canteen), bed, blankets, provisions, &c.; while half a dozen servants—*mozos*—well mounted and armed, escort their lords and masters. The usual pay of these is one dollar a-day each, four shillings and a fraction of our money, with board wages of two *riales*—*dos riales diarios par la comida*—for which they always stipulate, saying that not even a *lepero* could live for less, a *rial* being equivalent to about sixpence. One of these is appointed captain, and to him is intrusted the payment of the road expenses, out of which, if he be "*hombre de bien*," *i. e.*, an approved rascal, he manages to pouch another dollar daily, as perquisite for the confidence which he is supposed not to abuse.

This *capitan*, or *major-domo*, if allowed to rob his master quietly and genteelly, is worthy of every trust, and will take especial care that his privilege is not trespassed upon by others; therefore, says the proverb-loving Mexican, "*Mas vale un ladron que viente picaros*"—give me one honest robber before twenty, rogues—a distinction finely drawn upon the meaning of the terms.

"*Que comedor de maiz es aquel macho! valgame Dios, que cabe mas que tres almudas!*" "What a corn-eater is that little mule," said my *mozo* to me one day; "Heaven save me, but he holds three *almudas* (about six pecks) at a bout! He is the one to eat. Every day he eats the same. Oh! what a *macho* is that!"

Every traveller has his *macho*, who eats treble allowance, or, rather, who eats one ration, while the price of the two imaginary ones finds its way into the pocket of the *mozo*.

The *capitan* is also invariably in league with the *mesonero* of the Hostelry where you put up for the night; and his recommendations of extra feeds rouse you, rolled in *sarape*, as, hat in hand, he stands at the door of the *quarto*, with mine host looking over his shoulder, saying—

"*Valgame, Don Jorge, que tengan mucha hambre las bestias! ya se acabo la cena; quiere su merced que les echo mas maiz?*"—God save me, Mr. George, what hungry bellies the animals have tonight! they have already gobbled up their suppers: will your worship please that I give them some more corn? "*Mañana tenemos jornada muy largita, es preciso que comen bien*"—Tomorrow we have a long little journey before us, and they had better eat plenty tonight.

"*Vaya! maldito,*" cries the tormented *amo*; "*que comen mil fanegas si pueden!*"—Go to the devil, and let them eat a thousand sacks if they can!—and, covering his head with his *sarape*, soon snores, while his trustworthy *mozo* puts the price of two *almudas* in his pocket, and mine host the third for his share of the transaction.

Thus it may be supposed that here the old adage is carried out which says that "*con el ojo del amo se engorda el buey*"—with the master's eye the steer is fattened; and the traveller who loves to see the his well-worked animals in good case, and dislikes to draw his pursestrings every three or four days to pay for another and another fresh horse or mule, had better follow my practice, which was to put a *puro* in my mouth, take up a position on the manger, and watch that every measure was well filled, and eaten, before I paid attention to the wants of my own proper carcass, taking care to give but half the compliment of corn at first, reserving the remainder for night, and in the interval seeing that all the beasts were led to water for the second time.

Heaven help the wight who trusts a Mexican! The following is the bill presented to me by my *mozo* the first and only time I ever trusted him with the office of paymaster; and beneath is the amended or taxed bill, or, rather, the account of the night's expenditure as wrung from the unwilling *mesonero* after I had accused my worthy steward of peculation, and threatened summary chastisement. The copy is *verbatim* :—

"*Pago José Maria en el meson de la santisma vergen de guadalaxara dos dias de comida para el 4 riales dos fanegas de mais cuatro pesos yotras dos 4 pesos entrada de nueve bestias dos por una tres riales tres comidas per mi cabayero dos pesos por mi cabayero otra 3 riales tres riales otra otra tres por mi cabayero cinco quartios pulque por mi cabayero paja nueve riales un medio por pulque otro mismo quarto tres dias 6 riales quarto un dia 2 riales otro 2 otro 2.*   todo   dies *yocho pesos cinco riales."*

TRANSLATION.

Joseph the son of Maria paid in the *meson* of the holiest virgin of Guadalaxara two days board for himself 4 *riales* two *fanegas* of corn four dollars and another 4 dollars entrance of nine beasts two for one three *riales* three dinners for my lord two dollars for my lord another three *riales* 3 *riales* for another for my lord five quarts of *pulque* for my lord straw nine *riales* a *medio* for *pulque* another *rial* room three days 6 *riales* room one day 2 *riales* other 2 other 2 Total eighteen dollars five *riales*. 18p. 5r."

	$	r.
Servant's board for two days	0	4
1½ *fanegas* of corn	1	2
My lordship's chocolate and dinners for two days	1	0
Pulque	0	3
Straw for animals	0	4
Hire of room	0	4
Servant's *ditto*	0	4
	4	5

Showing a difference of fourteen dollars on a bill of four, or eighteen shillings instead of £3 12s. 6d. So much for the honesty of "*un hombre de bien!*"

Either from ignorance of their duties or carelessness, Mexican officials seldom trouble the traveller with demanding his passport. It is as well, however, to adhere to the law. and invariably to present it in the larger towns, where it may be presumed the *alcalde* can decipher the name and *rubrica* of the "*ministro de las relaciones interiores.*" From the fact of so many English mining companies being dispersed throughout the country, whose wealth and respectable way of doing business are so apparent to the Mexicans, an Englishman is pretty sure to receive attention from the authorities wherever he goes, and a British passport is a sure and certain safeguard from the insolence and rapacity of Jacks-in-office, who have a wholesome dread of the far-reaching power of the "lion and unicorn" which head those vouchsafing documents.

A *carta, de seguridad*—letter of security—is also indispensable, by which the traveller's transit through the territory of the republic is sanctioned for the space of one year, at the termination of which period it has to be renewed, on presentation to the governor of the state in which he may happen to be. With custom-house regulations there is no inconvenience, a mere form being gone through of opening one package in entering the capitals of the different states, and an opportunely applied dollar will invariably smooth over any difficulty with regard to foreign tobacco, &c., or any of the creature-comforts in the shape of cognac or comestible luxuries, which the traveller will do well to carry with him.

There is one axiom to be never lost sight of in journeying through Mexico. Carry everything with you that you can possibly require on the road, the only limit being the length of your purse, on which will depend your means of conveyance. A European stomach should hardly trust to the country cuisine.

In Northern Mexico and California a custom exists with both sexes of choosing a particular friend, seldom a relation, .to whom the person attaches himself in a bond of strict friendship, confiding to his or her care all his hopes and fears, secrets, &c., and seldom severing the tie, which generally binds them together as long as life lasts.

The *compadre* and *commadre*—literally godfather, godmother —are consulted on every occasion, when advice on the important subject of love is required, and a nice sense of honour restrains them from all betrayal of trust and confidence. They are likewise inseparable companions, and their purses and property are ever at each other's service. Ask a man to lend you his horse; if not mounted on it himself, the chances are that he answers,

"*Lo tiene mi compadre*"—my godfather has it. It must be confessed, however, that many *peccadilloes* are fathered on the *compadre* and *commadre*. To vouch for the correctness of some story a New Mexican is telling you, he adds, "*Pues, si no cree su merced, pregunta a mi compadre*"—Well, since your worship does not believe it, only ask my godfather.

"*Me dixo mi commadre*"—my godmother told me so—says a girl to guaranty a bit of scandal. Thus *compadres* and *commadres* become a species of Mexican Mrs. Harris, who is appealed to on every occasion, and whose imaginary sagacity, profound wisdom, and personal beauty are on every occasion held up to the admiration of the credulous stranger.

I mention this, here, because it very often happens that when, on hiring a servant, credentials or reference as to his character are demanded of him, he immediately requests you to apply to his *compadre*, who of course swears that his friend is everything that is good and honest: "*Muy buen mozo, y hombre de bien.*"

CHAPTER 13

Comanche Attacks

Some of the tales which were narrated to me of the Woody deeds of the Comanches were so affecting and tragical, that they would form admirable themes for the composition of a romance. I may mention one, which was of very recent occurrence, and particularly interested me, as I passed the very spot where the tragical catastrophe occurred. I give the outlines of the tale as it was told to me; and any one in want of *materiales* to work up an exciting melodrama may help themselves to it *con mucha franqueza*.

In a rancho situated in the valley of the Rio Florido, and nearly halfway between the cities of Durango and Chihuahua, lived a family of hardy *vaqueros*, or cattle-herders, the head of which was a sturdy old sexagenarian, known as *El Coxo* (the Game Leg). He rejoiced in a "quiver well filled with arrows," since eight fine, strapping sons hailed him *padre*; than any one of whom not a *ranchero* in the *tierra afuera* could more dextrously *colear* a bull, or at the game of "*gallo*" tear from its stake the unhappy fowl, and bear it safe from the pursuit of competitors, but piecemeal, to the feet of his admiring lady-love.

Of these eight *mozos*, he who bore away the palm of *rancheral* superiority, but still in a very slight degree, was the third son, and the handsomest (no little praise, where each and all laid claim to the title of "*buen mozo y guapo*"), by name Escamilla, a proper lad of twenty, five feet ten out of his *zapatos*, straight as an *organo*, and lithesome as a reed. He was, moreover, more polished

112

than the others, having been schooled at Queretaro—a city, in the estimation of the people of the *tierra afuera*, second only to *Mejico* itself.

With his city breeding, he had of course imbibed a taste for dress, and quite dazzled the eyes of the neighbouring *rancheras* when, on his return to his paternal home, he made his first appearance at a grand *funcion de toro"* in all the elabourate finery of a Queretaro dandy. In this first passage of arms he greatly distinguished himself, having thrown three bulls by the tail with consummate adroitness, and won enthusiastic *"vivas"* from the *muchachas*, who graced with their presence the exciting sport.

Close at the heels of Escamilla, and almost rivalling him in good looks and dexterity, came Juan Maria, his next and elder brother, who, indeed, in the eyes of the more practical vaqueros, far surpassed his brother in manliness of appearance, and equalled him in horsemanship, wanting alone that "brilliancy of execution" which the other had acquired in the inner provinces, and in practice against the wilder and more active bulls of the *tierra caliente*.

Now, Juan Maria, hitherto the first at *el gallo* and bull-tailing, had always laid the trophies of the sport at the feet of one Ysabel Mora, called, from the *hacienda* where she resided, Ysabel de la Cadena, a pretty black-eyed girl of sixteen, the toast of the valleys of Nazos and Rio Florido, and celebrated even by the *cantadores* at the last fair of *el Valle de San Bartolomo* as "*la moza mas guapa de la tierra afuera*." It so happened that the last year, Ysabel had made her first appearance at a public *funcion*; and at this *gallo* she was wooed, and in a measure won, by the presentation of the remains of the gallant rooster at the hands of Juan Maria; who, his offering being well received, from that moment looked upon the pretty Ysabel as his *corteja*, or sweetheart; and she, nothing loath at having the properest lad of the valley at her feet, permitted his attentions, and apparently returned his love.

To make, however, a long story short, the dandy Escamilla, who, too fine to work, had more time on his hands for courting, dishonourably supplanted his brother in the affections of Ysabel;

and as Juan Maria, too frank and noble-hearted to force his suit, at once gave way to his more favoured brother, the affair was concluded between the girl and Escamilla, and a day named for the marriage ceremony, which was to take place at the *hacienda* of the bride, where, in honour of the occasion, a grand *funcion de toros* was to be held, at which all the neighbours (the nearest of whom was forty miles distant) were to be present, including, of course, the stalwart sons of *El Coxo*, the brothers of the bridegroom.

Two or three days before the one appointed for the marriage, the father with his eight sons made their appearance, their gallant figures, as mounted on stout Californian horses they entered the *hacienda*, exacting a buzz of admiration from the collected *rancheros*.

The next day, *El Coxo*, with all his sons excepting Escamilla, attended the master of the *hacienda* into the plains, for the purpose of driving in the bulls which were required for the morrow's sport, while the other *rancheros*; remained to complete a large corral which was destined to secure them; *El Coxo* and his sons being selected for the more arduous work of driving in the bulls, being the most expert and best-mounted horsemen of the whole neighbourhood.

It was toward the close of day, and the sun was fast sinking behind the rugged crest of the "Bolson," tingeing the serrated ridge of that isolated mountain-chain with a golden flood of light, while the *mesquite*-covered plain beneath lay cold and gray under the deep shadow of the sierra. The shrill pipe of the quail was heard, as it called together the bevy for the night; hares limped out of the thick cover and sought their feeding-grounds; overhead the melancholy cry of the *gruyas* sounded feebly in the aerial distance of their flight; the lowing of cattle resounded from the banks of the *arroyo*, where the herdsmen were driving them to water; the *peones*, or labourers of the farm, were quitting the *milpas*, and already seeking their homes, where, at the doors, the women with naked arms were pounding the *tortillas* on the stone *metate,* in preparation for the evening meal; and the universal quiet, and the soft and subdued beams of the sinking sun, which shed a chastened light over the whole landscape, proclaimed that the day was drawing to a close, and that man and beast were seeking their well-earned rest after their daily toil.

The two lovers were sauntering along, careless of the beauty of the scene and hour, and conscious of nothing save their own enraptured thoughts, and the aerial castles, which probably both were building, of future happiness and love.

As they strolled onward; a little cloud of dust arose from the *chapparal* in front of them; and in the distance, but seemingly in another direction, they heard the shouts of the returning cowherds, and the thundering tread of the bulls they were driving to the corral. In advance of these was seen one horseman, trotting quickly on toward the *hacienda*.

Nevertheless, the cloud of dust before them rolled rapidly onward, and presently several horsemen emerged from it, galloping toward them in the road.

"Here come the bull-fighters," exclaimed the girl, withdrawing her waist from the encircling arm of Escamilia; "let us return."

"Perhaps they are my brothers," answered he; and continued, "Yes, they are eight, look."

But what saw the poor girl, as, with eyes almost starting from her head, and motionless with sudden fear, she directs her gaze at the approaching horsemen, who now, turning a bend in the *chapparal*, are within a few hundred yards of them!

Escamilia follows the direction of the gaze, and one look congeals the trembling coward. A band of Indians are upon them. Naked to the waist, and painted horribly for war, with brandished spears they rush on. Heedless of the helpless maid, and leaving her to her fate, the coward turned and fled, shouting as he ran the dreaded signal of "*Los barbaros! los barbarous!*"

A horseman met him—it was Juan Maria, who, having lassoed a little antelope on the plains, had ridden in advance of his brothers to present it to the false but unfortunate Ysabel. The exclamations of the frightened Escamilia, and one glance down the road, showed him the peril of the poor girl. Throwing down the animal he was carefully carrying in his arms, he dashed the spurs furiously into the sides of his horse, and rushed like the wind to the rescue. But already the savages were upon her, with a whoop of bloodthirsty joy.

She, covering her face with her hands, shrieks to her old lover to save her:—"*Salva me, Juan Maria, por Dios, salva me!*" 'At that moment the lance of the foremost Indian pierced her heart, and in another her reeking scalp was brandished exultingly aloft by the murderous savage.

Shortlived, however, was his triumph; the clatter of a galloping horse thunders over the ground, and causes him to turn his head. Almost bounding through the air, and in a cloud of dust, with ready lasso swinging round his head, Juan Maria flies, alas! too late, to the rescue of the unhappy maiden. Straight upon the foremost Indian he charged, regardless of the flight of arrows with which he was received. The savage, terrified at the wild and fierce look of his antagonist, turns to fly; but the open coil of the lasso whirls from the expert hand of the Mexican, and the noose falls over the Indian's head, and, as the thrower passes in his horse's stride, drags him heavily to the ground.

But Juan Maria had fearful odds to contend against, and was unarmed, save by a small *machete,* or rusty sword. But with this he attacks the nearest Indian, and, succeeding in bringing him within reach of his arm, cleaves his head by a sturdy stroke, and the savage dropped dead from his horse. The others, keeping at a distance, assailed him with arrows, and already he was pierced with many bleeding wounds.

Still the gallant fellow fights bravely against the odds, and is encouraged by the shouts of his father and brothers, who are galloping, with loud cries, to the rescue. At that moment an arrow discharged at but a few paces' distance, buried itself to the feathers in his breast, and the brothers reach the spot but in time to see Juan Maria fall from his horse, and his bloody scalp borne away in triumph by a naked savage.

The Indians at that moment were re-enforced by a body of

some thirty or forty others, and a fierce combat ensued between them and *Coxo* and his sons, who fought with desperate courage to avenge the murder of Juan Maria and the poor Ysabel. Half a dozen of the Comanches bit the dust, and two of the Mexicans lay bleeding on the ground; but the *rancheros*, coming up from the *hacienda* in force, compelled the Indians to retreat, and, as night was coming on, they were not pursued.

On the ground lay the still quivering body of the girl, and the two Indians near her who were killed by Juan Maria. One of them had his neck broken and his brains dashed out by being dragged over the sharp stones by the horse of the latter, the lasso being fast to the high pommel of the saddle. This Indian still held the long, raven scalp-lock of the girl in his hand.

Juan Maria was quite dead, and pierced with upward of twenty bleeding wounds; two of his brothers were lying dangerously wounded; and six Indians, besides the two killed by Juan Maria, fell by the avenging arms of *El Coxo* and his sons. The bodies of Ysabel and Juan Maria were borne by the *rancheros* to the *hacienda*, and both were buried the next day, side by side, at the very hour when the marriage was to have been performed. Escamilla, ashamed of his base cowardice, disappeared, and was not seen for some days, when he returned to his father's *rancho*, packed up his things, and returned to Queretaro, where he married shortly after.

Just twelve months after the above tragical event occurred, I passed the spot. About three hundred yards from the gate of the *hacienda* were erected, side by side, two wooden crosses, roughly hewn out of a log of pine. On one, a rudely-cut inscription, in Mexico-Castilian, invites the passer-by to bestow

Un Ave Maria y un Pater Noster
Por el alma de Ysabel Mora,
Qui à los manos de los barbaros cayo muerta,
El dia 11 de Octubre, el año 1845,
En la flor de su juventud y hermosúra.

One Ave Maria and a Pater Noster for the repose of the

soul of Ysabel Mora, who fell by the hands of the barbarians on the 11th of October of the year 1845, and in the flower of her youth and beauty.

On the other—

Aqui yace Juan Maria Orteza,
Vecino de ——
Matado por los barbaros, el dia 11 de Octubre,
del año 1845.
Ora por el, Christiano, por Dios.

Here lies Juan Maria Orteza, native of , killed by the barbarians on the 11th of October, 1845.
Christian, for the sake of God, pray for his soul.

The goodly pile of stones, to which I added my offering, at the feet of both crosses, testify that the invocation has not been neglected, and that many an *Ave Maria* and *Pater Noster* have been breathed, to release from purgatory the souls of Ysabel and Juan Maria.

CHAPTER 14

Causes of Revolutions

The city of Durango[1] may be considered as the Ultima Thule
of the civilized portion of Mexico. Beyond it, to the north and
northwest, stretch away the vast uncultivated and unpeopled
plains of Chihuahua, the Bolson de Mapimi, and the arid deserts
of the Gila. In the oases of these, wild and hostile tribes of Indians have their dwelling-places, from which they continually
descend upon the border settlements and *haciendas*, sweeping
off the herds of horses and mules, and barbarously killing the
unarmed peasantry.

This warfare—if warfare it can be called, where the aggression and bloodshed are on one side only, and passive endurance
on the other—has existed from immemorial time; and the wonder is, that the country has not long since been abandoned by
the persecuted inhabitants, who at all seasons are subject to their
attacks. The Apaches, whoso country borders upon the department of Durango, are untiring and incessant in their hostility
against the whites; and, being near neighbours, are enabled to
act with great rapidity and unawares against the haciendas and
ranchos on the frontier.

They are a treacherous and cowardly race of Indians, and seldom attack even the Mexicans save by treachery and ambuscade.
When they have carried off a number of horses and mules suf-

---

1. The city was founded in 1559, by Velasco el Primero, Viceroy of New Spain,
previous to which it was a *presidio*, or fortified post, to protect the frontier from the
incursions of the Indians (Chichimees).

119

ficient for their present wants, they send a deputation to the governors of Durango and Chihuahua to express their anxiety for peace. This is invariably granted them, and when *en paz* they resort to the frontier villages,- and even the capital of the department, for the purpose of trade and amusement. The animals they have stolen in Durango and Chihuahua they find a ready market for in New Mexico and Sonora; and this traffic is most unblushingly carried on, and countenanced by the authorities of the respective states.

But the most formidable enemy, and most feared and dreaded by the inhabitants of Durango and Chihuahua, are the warlike Comanches, who, from their distant prairie country beyond the Del Norte and Rio Pecos, at certain seasons of the year, and annually, undertake regularly organized expeditions into these states, and frequently far into the interior (as last year to the vicinity of Sombrerete), for the purpose of procuring animals and slaves, carrying off the young boys and girls, and massacring the adults in the most wholesale and barbarous manner.

So regular are these expeditions, that in the Comanche calendar the month of September is known as the *Mexico moon,* as the other months are designated the buffalo moon, the young bear moon, the corn moon, &c. They generally invade the country in three different divisions, of from two to five hundred warriors in each. One, the most southern, passes the Rio Grande between the old *presidios* of San Juan and the mouth of ,the Pecos, and harries the fertile plains and wealthy *haciendas* of *el Valle de San Bartolomo*, the Rio Florido, San José del Parral, and the Rio Nasas. Every year their incursions extend farther into the interior, as the frontier *haciendas* become depopulated by their ravages, and the villages deserted and laid waste. For days together, in the Bolson de Mapimi, I traversed a country completely deserted on this account, passing through ruined villages, untrodden for years by the foot of man.

The central division enters between the *Presidio del Norte* and Monclova, where they join the party coming in from the north, and, passing the mountains of Mapimi and traversing a desert country destitute of water, where they suffer the greatest privations, ravage the valleys of Mapimi, Guajoquilla, and Chihuahua, and even the haciendas at the foot of the Sierra Madre. It appears incredible that no steps are taken to protect the country from this invasion, which does not take the inhabitants on a sudden or unawares, but at certain and regular seasons and from known points. Troops are certainly employed nominally to check the Indians, but very rarely attack them, although the Comanches give every opportunity; and thoroughly despising them, meet them on the open field, and with equal numbers almost invariably defeat the regular troops. The people themselves are unable to offer any resistance, however well inclined they may be to do so, as it has always been the policy of the government to keep them unarmed; and, being unacquainted with the use of weapons, when placed in their hands they have no confidence, and offer but a feeble resistance. So perfectly aware of this fact are the Comanches, that they never hesitate to attack superior numbers. When in small parties the Mexicans never resist, even if armed, but fall upon their knees and cry for mercy. Sometimes, however, goaded by the murder of their families and friends, the rancheros collect together, and, armed with bows and arrows, and slings and stones, go out to meet the Indians (as occurred when I was passing), and are slaughtered like sheep.

In the fall of last year, 1845, and at the present moment, 1846, the Indians have been more audacious than ever was known in previous years. It may be, that, in the present instance, they are rendered more daring by the knowledge of the war between the United States and Mexico, and the supposition that the troops would, consequently, be withdrawn from the scene of their operations. They are now (September) overrunning the whole department of Durango and Chihuahua, have cut off all communication, and defeated, in two pitched battles, the regular troops sent against them. Upward of ten thousand head of horses and mules have already been carried off, and scarcely has a *hacienda* or *rancho* on the frontier been unvisited, and every where the people have been killed or captured. The roads are impassable, all traffic is stopped, the *ranchos* barricaded, and the inhabitants afraid to venture out of their doors. The posts and expresses travel at night, avoiding the roads, and intelligence is brought in daily of massacres and harryings.

My servants refused to proceed farther; nor will money induce a Durnngueño to risk his scalp. Every one predicts certain destruction if I venture to cross the plains to Chihuahua, as the road lies in the very midst of the scenes of the Indian ravages. My hostess, with tears in her eyes, implored me not to attempt the journey; but my mind was made up to proceed, and alone, if I could not induce a *mozo* to accompany me. I had resolved to reach New Mexico by a certain time, and, in travelling through a dangerous country, lay it down as a principle not to be deterred by risks, but to "go ahead," and trust to fortune and a sharp lookout.

I had made preparations for my departure, and had given up any hope of procuring a *mozo*, when, at the eleventh hour, one presented himself, in the person of one of the most rascally-looking natives that ever stuck knife into his master. Asking him what induced him to run the risk of accompanying me, he answered that being "*muy pobre*" and unable to procure a living (the road was shut to him), and hearing that "*su merced*"—my worship—had offered high wages, he had determined to volunteer; being, moreover, as he assured me, "*muy valiente y aficionado a manejar las armas*"—very valiant and accustomed to the use of arms.

The end of it was that I engaged him, although the man bore a notoriously bad character, and was more than suspected of being a *ladron* of the worst description. But it was Hobson's choice at the time, and I did not hesitate to take him, trusting to myself to take care that he did not play me false. I was, however, a little shaken when, the same evening, a man accosted me as I was walking in the streets with an English gentleman, a resident in Durango, and informed me that my new *mozo* was at that moment in a *pulque*-shop, where, after imbibing more than was good for him, he had confided to a friend, and in the hearing of the man who now gave the information, his intention to ease me of my goods and chattels and animals, premising that, as he had heard from my late servants that I intrusted my *mozo* with arms, and generally rode in advance, it would be an easy matter some fine morning to administer *un pistoletazo en la espalda*—a pistol-ball in my back—and make off with the property to Chihuahua, or Sonora, where he would have no difficulty in disposing of the plunder. However, I paid no attention to this story, thinking that, if true, it was merely a drunken boast.

As Durango may be called the limit of Mexico proper and its *soi-disant* civilization, it may not be out of place to take a hasty glance at the general features of the country, the social and moral condition of the people, and the impressions conveyed to my mind in my journey through it.

There are many causes, physical and moral, which prevent Mexico from progressing in prosperity and civilization. Although possessing a vast territory, which embraces all the varieties of climate of the temperate and torrid zones, with a rich and prolific soil capable of yielding every natural production of the known world, yet these natural advantages are counter-balanced by obstacles, which prevent their being as profitable to the inhabitants as might naturally be expected, and in a great measure render them negative and of no avail.

A glance at the physical geography of Mexico will show that the extensive and fertile table-lands of the central region are isolated, and, as it were, cut off from communication with the coast, by their position on the ridge of the Cordilleras, and the insurmountable obstacles to a practicable traffic presented by the escarpments of the *terraces,* the steps, as it were, from the elevated table-lands to the maritime districts, and the tropical regions of the interior.

The country is also destitute of navigable rivers, and possesses but two of even moderate size—the Rio Grande del Norte, which runs into the Gulf of Mexico, and the Rio Grande, or Colorado of the west, which falls into the Pacific Ocean. Its eastern coast is swept at certain seasons by fearful tempests, and presents not one sheltering harbour or secure roadstead. The tropical region, subject to fatal malaria, is almost excluded to the settlement of the white population, and consequently its natural riches are almost entirely neglected and unappropriated. Moreover, when we look at the component parts of the population of this vast country, we are at no loss to account for the existing evils—the total absence of government, and the universal demoralization and want of energy, moral and physical, which is everywhere apparent.

The entire population is about eight millions, of which three fifths are Indians, or of Indian origin, and Indios Bravos, or barbarous tribes; the remainder of Spanish descent. This population is scattered over an area of one million three hundred and twelve thousand eight hundred and fifty square miles, in departments widely separated, and having various and distinct interests, the intercommunication insecure, and a large proportion in remote regions beyond the care or thought of an impotent government.

The vast table-land which stretches along the ridge of the Cordillera of Anahuac, although possessing tracts of great fertility, is not, in itself the rich and productive region it is generally represented to be. The want of fuel and water must always prevent its being otherwise than thinly inhabited, and these great drawbacks to the population and cultivation of these districts would appear to be insurmountable. I believe the capabilities of the whole country to be much overrated, although its mineral wealth alone must always render it of great importance; but it is a question whether the possession of mineral wealth conduces to the wellbeing of a country.

The working of mines of the precious metal in Mexico, however, has certainly caused many spots to be cultivated and inhabited, which would otherwise have been left sterile and unproductive, and has been the means of giving employment to the Indians, and in some degree has partially civilized them, where otherwise they would have remained in their original state of barbarism and ignorance,

The Mexicans, as a people, rank decidedly low in the scale of humanity. They are deficient in moral as well as physical organization: by the latter I do not mean to assert that they are wanting in corporeal qualities, although certainly inferior to most races in bodily strength; but there is a deficiency in that respect which is invariably found attendant upon a low state of moral or intellectual organization. They are treacherous, cunning, indolent, and without energy, and cowardly by nature. Inherent, instinctive cowardice is rarely met with in any race of men, yet I affirm that in this instance it certainly exists, and is most conspicuous; they possess at the same time that amount of brutish indifference to death which can be turned to good account in soldiers, and I believe if properly led, that the Mexicans would on this account behave tolerably well in the field, but no more than tolerably.

It is a matter of little astonishment to me that the country is in the state it is. It can never progress or become civilized until its present population is supplanted by a more energetic one. The present would-be republican form of government is not adapted to such a population as exists in Mexico, as is plainly evident in the effects of the constantly-recurring revolutions. Until a people can appreciate the great principles of civil and religious liberty, the advantages of free institutions are thrown away upon them.

A long minority has to be passed through before this can be effected; and, in this instance, before the requisite fitness can be attained, the country will probably have passed from the hands of its present owners to a more able and energetic race. On the subject of government I will not touch: I maintain that the Mexicans are incapable of self-government, and will always be so until regenerated. The separation from Spain has been the ruin of the country, which, by the by, is quite ready to revert to its former owners; and the prevailing feeling over the whole country inclines to the re-establishment of a monarchical system.

The miserable anarchy which has existed since its separation has sufficiently and bitterly proved to the people the inadequacy of the present one; and the wonder is, that, with, the large and aristocratic party which so greatly preponderates in Mexico (the army and the church), this much-to-be-desired event has not been brought about.

The cause of the two hundred and thirty-seven revolutions, which, since the declaration of its independence, have that number of times turned the country upside down, has been individual ambition and lust of power. The intellectual power is in the hands of a few, and by this minority all the revolutions are effected. The army once gained over (which, by the aid of bribes and the priesthood, is an easy matter), the wished-for consummation is at once brought about. It thus happens that, instead of a free, republican form of government, the country is ruled by a most perfect military despotism.

The population is divided into but two classes—the high and the low: there is no intermediate rank to connect the two extremes, and consequently the *hiatus* between them is deep and strongly marked. The relation subsisting between the peasantry and the wealthy *haciendados*, or land-owners, is a species of serfdom, little better than slavery itself. Money, in advance of wages, is generally lent to the peon or labourer, who is by law bound to serve the lender, if required, until such time as the debt is repaid; and as care is taken that this shall never happen, the debtor remains a bondsman to the day of his death.

Law or justice hardly exists in name even, and the ignorant peasantry, under the priestly thraldom which holds them in physical as well as moral bondage, have neither the energy nor courage to stand up for the amelioration of their condition, or the enjoyment of that liberty, which it is the theoretical boast of republican governments their system so largely deals in, but which, in reality, is a practical falsehood and delusion.

CHAPTER 15

A Scalp lost

On the 10th I left Durango for Chihuahua and New Mexico, taking with me the *mozo* I have before mentioned as bearing anything but a good character. The first day's march led through a wild, uncultivated country, with large plains of excellent pasture, but not a symptom of cultivation. We stopped at night at the hacienda of El Chorro, a little hamlet of adobe huts surrounding the *casa grande* of the plantation. As we arrived, the *rancheros* were driving in an immense cavalcade or herd of horses from the pastures, to be secured during the night in the corrals and near the *hacienda, par las novedades que hay*—on account of the novelties *(i. e.,* Indians) which are abroad—as the proprietor informed me. The vicinity of the *hacienda* abounds in salitrose springs and deposits of *muriate* of soda, to which the horses and mules were constantly breaking away, and drinking the water, and licking the earth with the greatest avidity. Distance from Durango twenty-eight miles.

11th.—To the *rancho* of Los Sauces—the willows. The plains today were covered with cattle, and horses and mules. In the morning I was riding slowly ahead of my *cavallada*, passing at the time through a lonely *mesquite*-grove, when the sudden report of firearms, and the whistling of a bullet passed my head at rather unpleasantly close quarters, caused me to turn sharply round, when I saw my amiable *mozo* with a pistol in his hand, some fifteen yards behind me, looking very guilty and foolish. To whip a pistol out of my holsters and ride up to him was the work of an instant; and I was on the point of blowing out his brains, when

127

his terrified and absurdly guilty-looking face turned my ire into an immoderate fit of laughter,

"*Amigo,*" I said to him, "do you call this being skilled in the use of arms, to miss my head at fifteen yards?"

"*Ah, cabellero!* in the name of all the saints I did not fire at you, but at a duck which was flying over the road. *No lo cree su merced* —your worship can not believe I would do such a thing."

Now it so happened, that the pistols which I had given him to carry were secured in a pair of holsters tightly buckled and strapped round his waist. It was a difficult matter to unbuckle them at any time; and as to having had time to get one out to fire at a duck flying over the road, it was impossible, even if such an idea had occurred to him.

I was certain that the duck was a fable, invented when he had missed me, and, in order to save my ammunition, and my head from another sportsmanlike display, I halted and took from him everything in the shape of offensive weapon, not excepting his knife; and wound up a sermon, which I deemed it necessary to give him, by administering a couple of dozen, well laid on with the buckle-end of my *surcingle*, at the same time giving him to understand, that if, hereafter, I had reason to suspect that he had even dreamed of another attempt upon my life, I would pistol him without a moment's hesitation. Distance from El Chorro thirty-six miles.

12th.—To the *rancho* of Yerbaniz, through the same unculti-vated plains, surrounded by sierras, and passing by a ridge from one into another, each being as like the other as twins. For a thousand miles the aspect of these plains never varied, and the sketch of the plain of Los Sauces would answer for the plain of El Paso, and every intermediate one between Durango and New Mexico. At daybreak this morning I descried three figures, evidently armed and mounted men, descending a ridge and ad-vancing toward me.

As in this country to meet a living soul on the road is per-haps to meet an enemy thirsting for your property or your life, I stopped my animals, and, uncovering my rifle, rode on to reconnoitre. The strangers also halted on seeing me, and, again moving on when they saw me alone, we advanced, cautiously and prepared, toward each other. As they drew near I at once saw by the heavy rifle which each carried across his saddle-bow that they were from New Mexico, and that one was a white man.

He proved to be a German named Spiers, who was on his way to the fair of San Juan with a caravan of nearly forty wagons loaded with merchandise from the United States. He had left the frontier of Missouri in May, crossing the grand prairies to Santa Fé; and, learning that his American teamsters would not be permitted to enter Durango, he had ridden on in advance to obtain permission for their admittance. His wagons had been nearly six months' on the road, travelling the whole time, and were now a few miles behind them.

He gave a dismal account of the state of the country through which I was about to pass. The Comanches were everywhere, and two days before had killed two of his men; and not a soul ventured out of his house in that part of the country. He likewise said it was impossible that I could reach Chihuahua alone, and urged me strongly to return. The runaway Governor of New Mexico, General Armijo, was travelling in company with his caravan, on his way to Mexico, to give an account of his shameful cowardice in surrendering Santa Fé to the Americans without a show of resistance.

A little farther on I saw the long line of wagons, like ships at sea, crossing a plain before me. They were all drawn by teams of eight fine mules, and under the charge and escort of some thirty strapping young Missourians, each with a long, heavy rifle across his saddle. I stopped and had a long chat with Armijo, who, a mountain of fat, rolled out of his American dearborn, and inquired the price of cotton goods in Durango, he having some seven wagon-loads with him, and also what they said, in Mexico, of the doings in Santa Fé, alluding to its capture by the Americans without any resistance.

I told him that there was but one opinion respecting it expressed all over the country—that General Armijo Find the New

Mexicans were a pack of arrant cowards; to which be answered, "*Adios!* They don't know that I had but seventy-five men to fight three thousand. What could I do?" Twenty-one of the teamsters belonging to this caravan had left it a few days previously, with the intention of returning to the. United States by the way of Texas. What became of them will be presently, narrated.

After leaving the caravan I saw a herd of *berendos* (antelope) in the plain, but was unable to get within shot, the ground being destitute of cover, and the animals very wild. We are now in the country of large game, deer and antelope being abundant in the plains, and bears occasionally met with in the *sierras*.

This night I encamped near a *rancho*, being refused admittance into the building, and picketed my animals around the camp. I had also a disagreement with an *arriero*, whom I had hired at Los Sauces, with his mule, to carry one of my packs, one of the mules being lame. He had agreed, for a certain sum, to travel with me two *jornadas,* or days' journeys. In Mexican travelling there are two distinct *jornadas*—one of *atajo,* or the usual distance performed by *arrieros;* the other *de cabailo,* or journey performed on horseback, or with light packs.

To prevent all misunderstanding, I had explicitly agreed with him for two of my own *jornadas,* or days' travel, of twelve leagues, or thirty-five miles, each day; but when he heard that the Indians were so near at hand, he wanted to give up his contract, and claimed the full pay of two *jornadas* for the distance he had already come, which was thirty-six miles, affirming that it was two regular days' journeys of *atajo.* This I refused to pay him, offering the half of the stipulated sum, as he had performed but one day's journey.

Blustering and threatening, off he went to the *alcalde,* for in all ranches the head man is chief magistrate, who sent me a peremptory order to pay the demand in full; to which I sent back an answer more energetic than polite, together with the sum I had originally offered, saying at the same time that if it was not accepted I would not pay a. farthing. Presently I saw the *alcalde,* attended by a posse, sally from the gate of the *rancho* and approach my camp, where I was very busily engaged in cleaning my arms. No sooner was the worthy near enough to observe my employment, than he wheeled off suddenly and returned to the rancho, and I saw no more of him or the *arriero*.

The *ranchos* and *haciendas* in Durango and Chihuahua are all inclosed by a high wall, flanked at the corners by circular bastions loopholed for musketry. The entrance is by a large gate, which is closed at night; and on the *azotea*, or flat roof of the building, a sentry is constantly posted day and night. Round the corral are the dwellings of the *peones*; the *casa grande*, or proprietor's house, being generally at one end, and occupying one or more sides of the square. In this instance I was refused admittance into the inclosure—for what reason I do not know—and obliged to encamp about two hundred yards from it, having to pay for two or three logs of wood, with which I made a fire.

The *rancheria*, however, bears a very bad character, as I afterward learned; and this night I had as much to dread from them and my rascally *mozo* as from the sudden attack of the Indians. My blanket was a little arsenal, as I had not only my own, but my servant's arms, to take care of. That worthy begged hard for a pistol or gun, saying that, if the Indians came, he would be killed like a dog. I told him to go into the *rancho* among his countrymen, which I believe he did, for I saw or heard nothing more of him during the night.

13th.—To La Noria Perdizenia, forty miles; the country getting more wild and desolate, and entirely destitute of water. Not a sign of habitation, or a human being on the road. We passed a gap between two *sierras*, called *El Passage*—the passage—which is wild and picturesque, the plains covered with *mezquite*, and a species of palm, called *palma*. We were approaching the village of La Perdizenia a little before sunset, through a broken country, with hills and bluffs rising on each side of the road, when suddenly, as I was riding in advance, I saw on one of these, which was some five hundred or six hundred yards from the road, a party of Indians, on horseback and on foot.

I instantly stopped, and without saying a word, or pointing

out the cause to the *mozo*, dismounted, and, catching the wildest mule, immediately tied its logs together with a *riata*, and covered the eyes of all with their *tapojos* or blinders. I then pointed with my finger to the hill, saying, "*Mire, los Indios.*"

"*Ave Maria Purissima! estamos perdidos*"—we are lost!—;exclaimed the Mexican, and made toward his horse, from which he had also dismounted; but this I prevented, telling him that he had to fight, and not run. Half dead with fright, he threw himself on his knees, beseeching all the saints in the calendar to save him, and vowing offerings of all kinds if his life were spared. By this time the Indians, perceiving that there were but two of us, commenced descending the hill, leaving one or two of the party on the top as *videttes*.

Seeing a fight was inevitable, I stuck my cleaning-rod into the ground as a rest for my rifle, and, placing my carbine and pistols at my side, sat down to my work, intending to open upon them with my rifle as soon as they came within reach. However, this they did not seem inclined to do; but, striking their shields, and brandishing their bows, shouted to me to give up my animals and pass on. I kept my position for some time, but, finding they were not inclined to attack me, and not wishing to remain there when night was coming on, I unloosed the mules, and sent them forward with the *mozo*, remaining in rear myself to cover their retreat. Once in his saddle, invoking "*todos los suntos*," off he galloped toward the village, driving the mules pell-mell before him; nor did he stop until he was in the midst of the *plaza*, narrating to shrieking women, and all the population of the village, his miraculous escape.

The reason of the Indians not charging upon us was, that they saw a party of Mexicans on their way to the village, from a mine in the *sierra*, who were concealed from our view, and thought, no doubt, that we might be able to defend ourselves until the noise of the firing would bring them to our assistance.

When I arrived at La Noria I rode into the square, and found the inhabitants in the greatest alarm and dismay. They had been expecting the Indians for some days, as they had already committed several atrocities in the neighbouring ranches. The women were weeping and flying about in every direction, hiding their children and valuables, barricading the houses, and putting what few arms they could collect in the hands of the reluctant men.

As I rode through the village seeking a corral for my animals, a woman ran out of a house and begged me to enter, offering her stable, and corn, and straw for the beasts, and the best her house afforded for myself. I gladly accepted her hospitality, and followed her into a neat, clean little house, with a corral full of fig-trees and grape-vines, and a large yard with a pond of water in the centre, and a stack of *hoja* at one end, promising well for the comfort of the tired animals.

"Ah!" she exclaimed, on my entering; "*gracios à Dios*, I have someone to protect the lone widow and her fatherless children. If the savages come now, I don't care, since we have good arms in the house, and those '*qui saben manejarlos*'—who know how to use them."

After supper I visited the *alcalde*, and advised him to take some measures to oppose the Indians in case they attacked the place, as I had no doubt that the party which I had seen was but the advanced guard of a large body.

"Ah, *caballero*," he answered, "*que podemos hacer?*—what can we do? We have no arms, and our people have no courage to use them if we had; but, thank God! the *barbaros* are ignorant of this, and will not attack the town; for how do they know but what we have *escopetas* in every window? These savages are very ignorant."

The next morning I resumed my journey, much to the surprise of the people of La Noria, who looked upon us as lost; and, crossing the Nasas beyond the *hacienda* of El Conejo (the rabbit), intended to go on some leagues farther, when I met some wagons belonging to a Frenchman of Chihuahua, and, as he was brimful of *novedades*, I returned and camped with them near the *hacienda*, to hear the news. The Comanches, he said, were in great force beyond the village of El Gallo, and were killing and slaying in every direction. They had, a few days before, attacked a company of bull-fighters under a *Gachupin* named Bernardo, on their way to the fair of El Valle de San Bartolomo, killing seven of them and wounding all the others. They had also had a fight with the troops at the Rio Florido, killing seventeen and wounding many more.

On the 16th I reached El Gallo (the cock), where the Indians, three days before, had killed two men belonging to Spiers's caravan, within a hundred yards of the village. The road from El Conejo for forty miles passes through a most dismal country, and was crossed several times by the Indian trail. I had now to keep a sharp lookout, as there was no doubt that they were in the neighbourhood, and presently I had ocular proof of their recent presence. We were passing through a *chapparal* of *mezquite*, where the road pusses near a point of rocks, on which were seated hundreds of *sopilotes*.

About a dozen of these birds flew up from the side of the road, and, turning my horse to the spot, I found they had been collected on the dead body of a Mexican, partly stripped, and the breast displaying several ghastly wounds. The head had been scalped, and a broken arrow still remained buried in the face, or, rather, of what remained of it, for the eyes and part of the brain had been already picked out by the *sopilotes*, and a great part of the body devoured. Life did not appear to have been extinct many hours; probably he had been killed the night before, as the birds had but that morning discovered the body. We had no means of digging a grave, and therefore were obliged to leave it as we found it; and as soon as I had left the spot the *sopilotes* recommenced their revolting feast.

I stayed, at El Gallo, in the house of a farmer who had lost three sons by the Indians within a few years. Two of their widows, young and handsome, were in the house, and he himself had been severely wounded by them on several occasions. Their corn was now ready for cutting, but they were afraid to venture outside the village, and procured enough for their daily consumption by collecting together all the villagers and proceeding to the fields in a body to bring in a supply. I remained here for two days, as one of my mules was seriously lame, during which time my chief occupation was sitting with the family, shelling corn, and *platicando* (chatting).

In the evening a guitar was brought, and a fandango was got up for my especial amusement. Some of the dances of the country people are not without grace, and with tolerable pantomimic action; but the greatest charms are the extempore songs which accompany the music, and, being chanted to a low, broken measure, are at the same time novel and pleasing to the ear. In a *rancho* the time is occupied in the following way. At daybreak the females of the family rise and prepare the chocolate or *atole*, which is eaten the first thing in the morning.

Breakfast is usually taken about nine o'clock, consisting of meat prepared with *chile Colorado, frijoles,* and *tortillas*: dinner and supper, at midday and sunset, are likewise substantial meals. The gourd or pumpkin (*calabaza*) is much used in this part of Mexico, and is an excellent and wholesome vegetable. Between the meals the men employ themselves in the *milpas*, or attending to the animals; the women busy themselves about the house, making clothes, &c., &c., as with us; but severe labour is unknown to either men or women. While here I assisted in the erection of two wooden crosses on the spot where Spiers's men were killed by the Comanches three days before. They had remained behind the caravan to bring some bread that was baking for the party, when just outside the town they were set upon by the Indians and killed.

In Durango and the neighbouring state of Chihuahua, the *rancherias* are supplied with such simple goods as they require by small traders, resident in the capitals of these states, who trade from one village to another with two or three wagons, which, when their goods are sold, they freight with supplies for the cities or the mines. These traders are all foreigners—French, Germans, English, and Americans; and their adventures and hairbreadth escapes, while passing through the country overrun by Indians, are often most singular and exciting. Their arrivals in the villages are always welcome, as then the *muchachas* make their purchases of *rebosos* and gay *enaguas*, and the "*majos*" their *sarapes* and sashes.

The night before my departure from El Gallo, I was sitting in the corral "*platicando*," while all the family were busy, as usual, corn-shelling, when a loud voice was heard, a cracking of whips, and cries of "Wo-ha, wo-ha-a, wo-o-h-ha!"

"*Estrangeros!*" exclaimed one of the girls.

"*Los Tejanos!*" exclaimed another.

"*Los carros*" (the wagons), said Don José, and I threw my *sarape* over my shoulder, and proceeding to the open space in the centre of the village, dignified by the name of *plaza*, found four wagons just arrived, and the teamsters unhitching the mules. They proved to be the caravan of one Davy Workman, an Englishman by birth, but long resident in, and a citizen of, the United States, a tall, hard-featured man, and most determined in look, as he was known to be in character—un *hombre muy bien conocido*, as my *patron* informed me. By this arrival more *novedades* were brought, and *los Indios! los Indios!* were on every body's tongue.

Señor Angel, my *mozo*, here openly rebelled, and refused to proceed farther; but a promise of a few extra dollars at length induced him to agree to accompany me as far as Mapimi, sixty-five miles from El Gallo, and situated on what is called the frontier.

CHAPTER 16

Long Ride

From El Gallo to Mapimi a mule-track leads the traveller through a most wild and broken country, perfectly deserted; rugged *sierras* rising from the *mezquite*-covered plains, which are sterile and entirely destitute of water. A little out of the direct route is the *hacienda de la Cadena*, a solitary plantation standing in a dismal plain, the scene of constantly-recurring Indian attacks; for an *arroyo* or water-course which runs through it, and in which that necessary element is found at intervals in deep holes, is resorted to by the Indians, when on their way to the *haciendas* of the interior.

I had resolved to pass through this part of the country, although far out of the beaten track, in order to visit El Real de Mapimi, a little town, near a *sierra* which is said to be very rich in ore; and also for the purpose of travelling through a tract of country laid waste by the Comanches, and but little known, and which is designated, *par excellence,"los desiertos de la frontera"*—the deserts of the frontier; not so much from its sterility, as on account of its having been abandoned by its inhabitants, from the fear of the perpetual Indian attacks, as it lay in their direct route to the interior.

As sixty-five miles was rather a long journey for one day, I resolved to start late, and proceed some twenty or thirty miles and then encamp, although it would be necessary to remain that night without water. Leaving El Gallo about midday, I stopped at some cattle-wells a short distance from the village, to water the animals the last thing, and fill my own *huages* (a canteen made out of a gourd). The mules and horses, however, which unfortunately did not anticipate a scarcity at the end of their day's journey, refused to drink, and we continued our journey under a hot and burning sun.

The *ranchero's* family here took leave of me with tears, and prayers to all. the saints for my safe journey. The old grand-mother, after blessing me, told me that she had, by dint of I don't know how many *Ave Marias*, interested the patron saint of the family in my behalf, one San Ysidro of Guadalaxara, who, she was assured, would take me under his especial keeping. She likewise hung round my neck a copper coin with a miraculous hole in it, which would preserve me from the arrows of the Comanches, and the still more dangerous weapons of "*el enimigo del mundo,*" who, she said, was ever *cazando* (hunting) after the souls of heretics.

The plains were still covered with *mezquite*, and a species of palm which grows to the height of five or six feet, a bunch of long, narrow leaves issuing from the top of the stem, which is frequently as thick as a man's body. From a distance it is exactly like an Indian with a headdress of feathers, and Angel was con-tinually calling my attention to these vegetable savages. Between the plains an elevated ridge presents itself, generally a spur from the *sierras* which run parallel to them on the eastern and western flanks, and this formation is everywhere the same. Where the ground is covered with *mezquite*-thickets or *chapparals*, a high but coarse grass is found; but on the bluffs is an excellent species, known in Mexico as *gramma*, and on the prairies as a variety of the buffalo-grass, on which cattle and horses thrive and fatten equally as well as on grain.

As I was riding close to a bunch of *mezquite* the whiz of a rattlesnake's tail caused my horse to spring on one side and tremble with affright. I dismounted, and, drawing the wiping-stick from my rifle, approached the reptile to kill it. The snake, as thick as my wrist, and about three feet long, was curled up. with its flat, vicious-looking head and neck erected, .and its tail rattling violently. A blow on the head soon destroyed it, but, as I was remounting, my rifle slipped out of my hand, and crack went the stock. A thong of buckskin, however, soon made it as secure as ever.

After travelling about twenty-five miles I selected a camping-ground, and, unloading the mules, made a kind of breastwork of the packs and saddles, behind which to retreat in case of an Indian attack, which was more than probable, as we had discovered plenty of recent signs in the plains. It was about sunset when we had completed our little fort, and, spreading a *petate,* or mat, the animals were soon at their suppers of corn, which I had brought for the purpose. They had all their *cabrestas* or ropes round their necks, and trailing on the ground, in order that they might be easily caught and tied when they had finished their corn; and, giving the *mozo* strict orders to this effect, I rolled myself in my blanket and was soon asleep, as I intended to be on the watch myself from midnight, to prevent surprise.

In about two or three hours I awoke, and, jumping up, found Angel asleep, and that all the animals had disappeared. It was pitchy dark, and not a trace of them could be distinguished. After an hour's ineffectual search I returned to camp, and waited until daybreak, when it would be light enough to track the animals. This there was no difficulty in doing, and I at once found that, after hunting for some time for water, they had taken the track back to El Gallo, whither I had no doubt they had returned for water.

It was certainly a great relief to me to find that they had not been taken by the Indians, which at first I thought was the case; but their course was perfectly plain where they had trodden down the high grass, wet with dew, in their search for water. Not finding it, they had returned at once, and in a direct course, to our yesterday's trail, and made off toward El Gallo, without stopping to eat, or even pick the tempting *gramma* on their way. The only fear now was, that a wandering party of Indians should fall in with them on the road, when they would not only seize the animals, but discover our present retreat by following their trail.

When I returned to camp I immediately dispatched Angel to El Gallo, ordering him to come back instantly, and without delaying a moment, when he had found the beasts, remaining myself to take charge of the camp and baggage. On examining a pair of saddlebags which my kind hostess at El Gallo had filled with *tortillas*, *quesos*, &c., I found that Mr. Angel had, either during the night, or when I was hunting for the missing animals, discussed all its contents, not leaving as much as a crumb; and as the fresh morning air had given me a sharp appetite, I took my rifle and slung a double-barrel carbine on my back, placed a pair of pistols in my belt, and thus armed, started off to the *sierra* to kill an antelope and broil a *collop* for breakfast.

While hunting I crossed the *sierra*, which was rocky and very precipitous, and from the top looked down into a neighbouring plain, where I fancied I could discern an *arroyo* will, running water. Half suffocated at the time with thirst, I immediately descended, although the place was six or seven miles out in the plain, and thought of nothing but assuaging my thirst. I had nearly completed the descent when a band of antelope passed me, and stopped to feed in a little plateau near which ran a *cañon* or hollow, which would enable me to approach them within shot.

Down the *cañon* I accordingly crept, carefully concealing myself in the long grass and bushes, and occasionally raising my head to judge the distance. In this manner I had approached, as I thought, to within rifle-shot, and, creeping between two rocks at the edge of the hollow, I raised my head to reconnoitre, and met a sight which caused me to drop it again behind the cover, like a turtle drawing into its shell. About two hundred yards from the *cañon*, and hardly twice that distance from the spot where I lay concealed, were riding quietly along, in Indian file, eleven Comanches, painted and armed for war.

Each had a lance and bow and arrows, and the chief, who was in advance, had a rifle, in a gaily-ornamented case of buckskin, hanging at his side. They were naked to the waist, their buffalo robes being thrown off their shoulders and lying on their hips, and across the saddle, which was a mere pad of buffalo-skin. They were making toward the *cañon*, which I imagined they would cross by a deer-path near where I stood. I certainly thought my time was come, but was undecided whether to fire upon them as soon as they were near enough, or trust to the chance of their passing me undiscovered.

Although the odds were great, I certainly had the advantage, being in an excellent position, and having six shots in readiness, even if they charged, when they could only attack me one at a time. I took in at once the advantages of my position, and determined, if they showed an intention of crossing the canon by the deer-path, to attack them, but not otherwise. As they approached, laughing and talking, I raised my rifle, and, resting it in the fork of a bush which completely hid me, I covered the chief, his brawny breast actually shining (oily as it was) at the end of my sight. His life, and probably mine, hung on a thread.

Once he turned his horse, when he arrived at the deer-track which crossed the *cañon*, and thinking that they were about to approach by that path, my finger even pressed the trigger; but an Indian behind him said a few words, and pointed along the plain, when he resumed his former course and passed on. I certainly breathed more freely, although (such is human nature) no sooner had they turned off than I regretted not having fired. If an unnecessary, it would not have been a rash act, for in my position, and armed as I was, I was more than a match for the whole party.

However, antelope and water went unscathed, and as soon as the Indians were out of sight I again crossed the *sierra*, and reached the camp about two hours before sunset, where, to my disappointment, the animals had not yet arrived, and no signs of their approach were visible on the plain. I determined, if they did not make their appearance by sundown, to return at once to El Gallo, as I suspected my *mozo* might commit some foul play, and perhaps abscond with the horses and mules.

Sun went down, but no Angel; and darkness set in and found me, almost dead with thirst, on my way to El Gallo. It was with no little difficulty I could make my way, now stumbling over rocks, and now impaling myself on the sharp prickles of the *palma* or *nopalo*. Several times I was in the act of attacking one of the former, so ridiculously like feathered Indians did they .appear in the dim starlight.

However, all was hushed and dark—not even a skulking Comanche would risk his neck on such a night; now and then an owl would hoot over head, and the mournful and long-continued howl of the coyote swept across the plain, or a snake rattled as it heard my approaching footstep. When the clouds swept away, and allowed the stars to emit their feeble light, the palms waved in the night air, and raised their nodding heads against the sky, the cry of coyote became louder, as it was now enabled to pursue its prey, *cocuyos* flitted among the grass like winged sparks of fire, and deer or antelope bounded across my path.

The trail indeed was in many parts invisible, and I had to trust to points of rocks and ridges, and trees which I remembered to have passed the day before, to point out my course. Once, choked with thirst and utterly exhausted—for I had been travelling since sunrise without food or water—I sunk down on the damp ground and slept for a couple of hours, and when I awoke the stars were obscured by heavy clouds, and the darkness prevented me distinguishing an object even a few feet distant. I had lost my bearings, and was completely confused, not knowing which course to follow.

Trusting to instinct, I took what I considered the proper direction, and shortly after, when it again became light enough to see, I regained the path and pushed rapidly on; and at length the welcome lowing of cattle satisfied me that I was near the wells where I had stopped the previous day. I soon arrived at the spot, and, lowering the goatskin bucket, buried my head in the cold water, and drank a delicious draught.

At about three in the morning, just as the first dawn was appearing, I knocked at the door of the *rancho*, and the first voice I heard was that of my *mozo*, asking, lazily, "*Quien llama?*"—who calls?

Everyone was soon up, and congratulating me upon being still alive; for when Angel had told them of the loss of the animals, and that I was remaining alone, they gave me up for lost, as the spot where we had encamped was a notorious stopping-place of the Indians when en route for the haciendas. I was so fortunate as to find all the animals safe; they were quietly feeding near the cattle-wells when the *mozo* arrived there. He made some lame excuse for not returning, but I have no doubt his intention had been to make off with them, which, if I had not suspected something of the sort, and followed him, he would probably have effected.

At daylight I mounted a mule, bare-backed, and Angel another; and, leading the remainder, we rode back to the camp, whence we immediately started for Mapimi.

As a punishment for his carelessness and meditated treachery, I obliged the *mozo* to ride bare-backed the whole distance of nearly sixty miles, and at a round trot. This feat of equitation, which on the straight and razor-like back of an ill-conditioned mule is anything but an easy or comfortable process, elicited from Angel, during his ride, a series of the most pathetic laments on his miserable fate in serving so merciless a master, accompanied by supplications to be allowed to mount the horse which carried his saddle and ran loose. But I was obdurate. He was the undoubted cause, by not having watched the animals, as was his duty, of the delay and loss of time I had suffered, and therefore, as a warning, and as a matter of justice, I administered this salutary dose of "Lynch law," which I have no doubt he remembers to the present moment.

About midday we reached the *hacienda de la Cadena*, first passing a *vidette* stationed on a neighbouring hill, on the lookout for the Indians. The *hacienda* itself was closed, and men were ready on the *azoteas* with guns and bows and arrows, when the approach of strangers was announced by signal from the *ranchero* on the hill. Just outside of the gates were erected several crosses, with their little piles of stones, on which were roughly-cut inscriptions; they were all to the memory of those who had been

143

killed on the spot by Indians.

We stayed at La Cadena merely to water our beasts, the people shouting from the housetop, and asking if we were mad, to travel alone. Angel, to whom I had again intrusted a carbine, answered by striking his hand on the butt of his piece, and vociferating, *"Miren ustedes: somos valientes, que importan los carajos Comanches. Que vengan, y yo los mataré."*—Look here: we are brave men, and don't care a straw for the rascally Comanches. Only let them come, and I will kill them myself. And the *muchachas* waved their *rebosos*, and saluted the *"valiente,"* shouting, *"Adios, buen mozo! mate a los barbaros!"* God keep you, brave lad! kill the savages. At which Angel waved his gun, in a state of great excitement and present valour, which cooled amazingly when we were out of sight of the *hacienda* and among the dreary *chaparrals*.

It was ten at night when we reached Mapimi; and, losing the track, we got bewildered in the darkness, and wandered into a marsh outside of the town, the lights of which were apparently quite close at hand: but all our shouting and cries for assistance and a guide were in vain, and caused the inhabitants to barricade their doors, as they thought the Indians were upon them; which panic was probably increased, when at last guessing at the cause, and almost losing my temper, I gave a succession of most correct war-whoops as I floundered through the mud, and fired a volley at the same moment.

When, therefore, I at length extricated myself and entered the town, not a living soul was visible, and the lights nil extinguished; so, groping my way to the *plaza*, at one side of which trickled a little stream, I unpacked my mules and encamped, sending the *mozo* with a *costal* for a supply of corn for the animals, with which he presently returned, reporting at the same time that the people were half dead with terror. The mules and horses properly cared for, I rolled myself in my blanket in the middle of the street, and went supperless to sleep, after a ride of sixty-five miles.

El Real de Mapimi is situated on a plain at the foot of a mountain called, from its supposed resemblance to a purse, the

144

Bolson de Mapimi. The *sierras*, which surround the plain, teem with the precious metals; but for some reason, probably from its situation near the frontier, and its exposure to Indian attacks, they have never been properly worked.

The mine near the town, and *the hacienda de beneficios*, belong to an inhabitant of Mapimi, who, without capital or machinery, derives a considerable income even from the primitive method employed in working the mine, which produces gold, silver, lead, and sulphur from the same *sierra*. My impression is, that the mines of Mapimi, if properly worked, would be the most productive in the country; and the transportation of machinery, by way of the Rio Grande and Monclova, would be practicable, and attended with comparatively little expense.

The town of itself is merely a collection of adobe houses, and, with the exception of a cotton-factory,[1] the superintendent of which is in Englishman, possesses no trade of any description. The population, of between two and three thousand, live in constant dread of the Indians, who lately entered the town and carried off the *mulada* belonging to the *hacienda de beneficios* out of the very corrals. The surrounding country is sterile and uninhabited; the villages and *ranchos* have been deserted, and the fields laid waste by the savages.

Between Mapirai and Chihuahua is a large, unpeopled tract of country called the *travesia:* it once possessed several thriving villages and ranchos, now deserted and in ruins, where the Indiana resort during their incursions, and leave their tired animals to be recruited in the pastures which have sprung up on the once cultivated fields, removing them on their return. A road from Mapimi, now disused for years and overgrown with grass, leads to Chihuahua through these deserted villages, and I determined to follow it, in spite of the bad character assigned to it by the Mexicans on account of its being so much frequented by the Comanches.

1. In the gardens of the factory at Mapimi I noticed several tea-plants, which thrive in this climate and soil, and the leaves of which, I was informed, are of very tolerable flavour.

Here I gave my *mozo*, Angel, his *congé*, and picked up, much to my astonishment, a little Irishman, who had been eighteen years in Mexico, during which time he had passed over nearly life whole republic, excepting New Mexico. He had lost all traces of his Milesian descent, being in character, manners, and appearance a perfect Mexican, and had almost forgotten his own language. Indians moreover had no terrors for him, and he at once agreed to accompany me to Chihuahua, even by the way of the travesia, "for," said he, "the Indian isn't born who will take my scalp."

During my stay in Mapimi I encamped in the middle of the *plaza*, much to the gratification of the *pelados*[2] of the town, who constantly surrounded me, pilfering everything which lay exposed. My reason for preferring the open air, even of a street, was the absence of vermin, which in the houses actually devour the full-blooded *Europeo*. The evening before our departure a deputation waited upon, me to dissuade me from attempting to cross the *travesia* to Chihuahua. The *alcalde* even went as far as to say that my new *mozo*, who was a Mexican citizen, should not be allowed to leave the town; but this I at once overcame by exhibiting my formidable-looking passports and *cartas de securidad*, or letters of security. They asked how I could expect to escape the Indians. I pointed to my rifle. "*Valgame en Dios!*" was the rejoinder, "*que loco es este Yngles!*"—What a madman this Englishman is!

One event occurred in Mapimi which annoyed me excessively. The night of my arrival, my animals, I fear, were rather scantily supplied with corn; and, to revenge the slight, the mules ate the tail of my beautiful Panchito to the very dock—a tail which I had tied, and combed, and tended with the greatest care and affection. In the morning I hardly recognized the animal; his once ornamental appendage looked as if it had been gnawed by rats, and his whole appearance was disfigured. I got a pair of shears, and clipped and cut, but only made matters worse, and

---

2. *Pelado*, literally skinless, meaning, in Mexico, the ragged, coatless vagabonds who loaf about the towns and villages.

was fain to desist after an hour's attempt. The tails of the mules were at the end of my journey picked like a bone, for, whenever their supper was poor, they immediately fell to work on each other's tails.

A perfect levee was held round my camp, which, being in the open square, of course was exposed enough. In this obtrusion, and the pertinacity with which they maintain it, the Mexicans are infinitely more annoying than the Indians themselves. Wrapped in their *sarapes*, they used to surround my fire, even when I was eating my meals, staring at my every action, and without saying a word. A *pelàdo* would remain thus motionless for two or three hours, when he would retire for the purpose of eating his dinner, returning after it, and taking up the same position. No hints were strong enough, and no rebuffs had any effect in abating the nuisance: but, frequently losing all temper and patience, I rattled out at them in pretty hearty abuse. Then they would move off, muttering, "*Que sin vergüenza!*"—What a shameless, unmannered fellow is this!

When eating, I found that the most efficacious way of getting rid of them was by making use of the "invitation" which Spaniards invariably proffer to strangers of any class before commencing a meal: "*Ustedes gustan?*" I would ask; and, strangely enough, nothing seemed to insult them more than this. Without the usual answer of "*Mil gracias; buen provecho tenga usted*" (a thousand thanks; may your worship have a good appetite), they invariably slunk away without answering.

CHAPTER 17

Dangerous Camp

On the 23rd I left Mapimi, the whole population, I do believe, turning out to see me put my head in the lion's mouth. For thirty-six miles we travelled through an arid *chapparal*; when, toward sunset, we entered into a more open plain, where we saw the ruined houses of Jarral Grande. The houses had been built round a large open space covered with grass, each one standing in a garden. At the entrance of the village, and scattered along the road, was a perfect forest of crosses, many of them thrown down or mutilated by the Indians.

The houses were most of them tumbling to pieces, but some were still entire. The gardens, overrun with a wilderness of weeds, still contained flowers, and melon-vines crept from" the inclosures out into the green. In one house that I entered a hare was sitting on the threshold, and some leverets were inside; and on the flat *azotea* of another sat a large cat. The walls, too, of the ruined houses were covered with creepers, which hung from the broken roofs and about the floors.

I entered another house, which, from its size and appearance, had evidently been the abode of the priest or chief personage of the village. The remains of a recent fire were scattered about the floor, on which were strewed several Indian *xuages* or drinking-gourds, an arrow, and a human scalp. The Indians had very lately visited the village, and some of them had doubtless taken up their abode in this house, and perhaps, departing before daylight, had left these articles behind them.

There were several cats about the ruins; and, as I entered, four or five enormous ones jumped off a wall where they lay basking in the sun, and concealed themselves in the tangled weeds.

The sun set beauteously on this lonely scene. In the distance, the ragged outlines of the *sierra* was golden with its declining rays, which shed a soft light on the ruins of the village; and everything looked so calm and beautiful, that it was difficult to call to mind that this was once the scene of horrid barbarities.

We took the animals down to the *arroyo* near the village, and, rifle in hand, watched them as they drank. In the sand at the edge of the stream were numerous marks of horses' feet and moccasin tracks fresh and recent. The Indians had been there that morning, and might very probably return, so it behooved us to be on the watch. We therefore picketed the mules and horses in the open space in the middle of the village, while we ourselves retreated to the shelter and shadow of a house within pistol-shot, whence we could command all the approaches to the green without being ourselves seen; one standing sentry while the other slept. In the night a number of perfectly wild cattle entered the village, and nearly caused our animals to stampede. One fat young heifer approached to within a few feet of where I was lying watching tinder a wall, and very nearly tempted me to a shot. Little rest we had that night; and long before daylight, that being the hour when Indians make their attacks, we were up and on the alert.

We were in our saddles before sunrise, and with great difficulty made our way in the dark through the thick chapparal. On approaching a stream called *Arroyo de los Indios*, or Indian River, I had been warned to be on the lookout, as that stream was a favourite stopping-place of the Indians. We crossed near where a broad and freshly-used Indian trail entered it, and halted some distance up the stream from the ford. There were deep holes of the clearest and coldest water in the *arroyo*, and I enjoyed a most delicious bathe. My animals were picketed and fared badly, the grass being coarse and sparsely scattered among the bushes.

We had another night of watchfulness, or, rather, half a night, for shortly after midnight we again packed the mules and started. This I did on account of the greater security of travelling at night, and in order to reach Jarral Chiquito, if possible, before sunrise, when, if Indians had been encamped there, as was more than probable, we might escape before we were observed.

The distance from Jarral Grande to Arroyo de los Indios was forty miles, and from that river to Jarral Chiquito, or Little Jarral, the same. The latter place was also a noted stopping-place of the Indians, and my servant had made up his mind that there we should have some work. To do him justice, however, he was nothing loath, and behaved remarkably well all through this dangerous journey. The sun rose magnificently behind us just before we reached Jarral; and, turning in my saddle, I saw Harry looking hard at it with shaded eyes.

"What's the matter ?" I sang out.

"Look, sir—look at the sunrise," he answered; perhaps we may never have another chance, Don Jorge. I never saw it look so beautiful before."

The plains here abounded in deer, and a bird of the pheasant species called *faisan,* and corrupted into *paisano* by the lower classes.

We reached Jarral Chiquito shortly after sunrise, and I rode on to reconnoitre. No Indians were there, but plenty of "sign." The village was situated on a hill, near a small spring of salitrose water, round which grows a clump of cotton-woods, a species of poplar (*alamo*). The village had been entirely burned by the Indians, with the exception of one house which was still standing, the roof of which they had torn off, and from the upper walls had shot down with arrows all the inmates. Inside were the skeleton of a dog, and several human bones.

A dreary stillness reigned over the whole place, unbroken by any sound, save the croaking of a bullfrog in the spring, round which we encamped for a few hours. At noon we again started, and travelled on till nearly dark, when we encamped in the middle of a bare plain, without water for the animals, or wood with which to make a fire. The grass, also, was thin, and the poor beasts fared badly, after a journey of more than sixty miles within twenty-four hours. In the night I saw a fire some distance from us, but apparently on the same plain. It was, doubtless, an encampment of a large, party of Indians who passed Guajoquilla the very day after my arrival there.

On the 26th at daybreak we were packed and off, and, after a journey of forty miles, to our great satisfaction we struck the settlements of Guajoquilla. Before entering the town we crossed a large *milpa*, where the people were busy cutting and carrying the maize. My sudden appearance put them to flight, and men, women, and children rushed like rabbits to the cover of the maize-canes. They mistook me for an Indian, as I was dressed in a hunting-shirt and fringed leggings; and as the Comanches had passed that very morning, killing some of the labourers in the field, they were justified in their alarm.

Guajoquilla[1] is a pretty, quaint little town, with its white-washed adobe houses, and looking clean and neat. The arrival of strangers, and in such an extraordinary garb, and, moreover, evidently from the travesia and Mapimi, created no little sensation.

The people flocked around me, inquiring the *novedades*, and how I escaped the Indians. Hundreds of houses were placed at my disposal, but as few of them contained stables or corrals, I rode into a street near the *plaza*, and seeing a respectable old dame sitting at a large gate which led to a corral, I invited myself to take up my abode with her, which, with a thousand protestations, she instantly agreed to. I had hardly dismounted when a tall, gaunt figure elbowed his way through the admiring crowd, and, seizing my hand, exclaimed, "Thank God, here's a country-man at last!" and burst into tears.

Regarding him with astonishment, I perceived at once that he was an American, and, by his dress of well-worn homespun, evidently, a Missourian, and one of the teamsters who accompanied the Santa Fé caravans from the United States. He quickly told me his story. He was one of the twenty-one Americans who,

---

1. Cotton is cultivated here, and thrives exceedingly well, as also in the valley of the Nazas.

as I have before mentioned, left Mr. Spiers's caravan some thirty or forty days before, intending to proceed across the country to the United States, by way of Texas. They had purchased horses and mules at the *hacienda* of La Sarca; and, without a guide, and knowing nothing of the nature of the country they had to traverse, had entered a tract between the Bolson of Mapimi and the *sierras* of El Diablo, which is entirely destitute of game and water.

Here the animals had nearly all died; and themselves, separating in small parties, had vainly searched for water, remaining for eight days with no other sustenance than the blood of mules, and reduced to the most revolting extremities to assuage their burning thirst. The man before me and another had found their way to a hole of water after several day's travel, near which some *pastors* (shepherds) were tending a large flock of sheep, and these men had brought them into Gunjoquilla. According to his account, the others must long ere this have perished, for when he left them they were prostrate on the ground, unable to rise, and praying for death.

In the hope of recovering some of their effects, his companion after recruiting his strength, had started back to the spot with some Mexicans, but meeting a party of Comanches, they had returned without reaching the place. The next day, however, some *vaqueros* entered the town, bearing six or seven Americans behind their saddles, and toward the evening two more were brought in, making eleven in all who had arrived.

Such miserable, emaciated creatures it has never been my lot to see. With long hair and beards, and thin, cadaverous faces, with the cheek-bones projecting almost through the skin, and their mouths cracked with the drought, they dismounted before my door, weak and scarcely able to stand; most of them had entirely lost their voices, and some were giddy and light-headed with the sufferings they had endured.

From their account I had no doubt that ten of their party were perishing in the *sierra*, or most probably had expired; for they were entirely exhausted when the last of those who had arrived left the spot where they had been lying. After ordering my servant to make a large quantity of strong soup for the poor fellows, and providing for their immediate wants, I proceeded to the *alcalde* of the place, and told him the story.

He at once agreed with me that some steps must be taken to rescue the sufferers if still alive, but he doubted if the people in the town would undertake the expedition, as it was known that the Indians were in the *sierras*, and in fact in every part, and it was a perfect miracle how the men had reached the town in safety. He also promised me that the men should not be confined, but allowed to go at large on *parole*, until he had communicated with the Governor of Chihuahua, and that a large room should be provided for them, where they would be at perfect liberty.

One of these men, a lean and lank Kentuckian, who, raw-boned at any time, was now a perfect skeleton, came up to me, and in a whisper, for his voice was lost for a time, requested to consult me on an important matter. The appearance of the poor fellow was comical in the extreme. His long black hair was combed over his face and forehead, and hung down his back and over his shoulders; and his features, with cheek-bones almost protruding from the skin, Wore an indescribably serio-comic expression. He was, in fact, what his appearance indicated, a "Puritan," and his words drawled out of his threat like fathoms of cable, or the sermon of a Methodist preacher.

"Stranger," said he to me, "you have been about the world, I guess, and are likely to know. What," he asked, putting his face close to mine, "might be the worth, in your country, of a camlet cloak? I never see sich a cloak as that ar one in no parts," he continued, looking up into the sky as if the specter of the camlet cloak was there. "I've worn that ar cloak more nor ten year, lined right away through with the best kind of bleachin. Stranger," he continued, "its a bad fix them poor boys is in, away out thar in them darned dried-up hills, and it jist doubles me to think on it. Now I want to know what's the worth of sich a fixin as that ar camlet cloak."

I answered that I could not possibly tell, knowing nothing

about such matters. "Well, stranger, nil I ar got to say is this— thar aint sich another cloak as that between this and Louisville, any how you can fix it, and I want to know if the govner here will send out to them hills to bring in that ar camlet cloak. It lays jest whar we left them poor boys."

I told him that, although I did not think the "governor" would exactly send out a detachment in search of his cloak, yet I had no doubt that some steps would be taken to rescue the unfortunate men who were left in the *sierras*, and that if I went myself I would endeavour to recover it for him. This calmed him considerably, and taking me by the arm, he said, solemnly, "Stranger, I'll thank you for that;" and, turning away, I heard him soliloquizing— "Sich a cloak as that ar aint nowhere between this and Louisville."

The owner of the lost garment volunteered to accompany me in search of the missing men, for whose recovery he said he would give all he had, even the "camlet cloak;" and I found him the best man of the party. During the journey he rode by my side, the whole subject of his discourse being the merits, of the wonderful garment. As we drew near the spot where he had left it, his excitement became intense. He speculated as to how it was lying—was it folded up?—had the rain injured it? &c.; and at last (he had been riding for some time with his head bent forward, and his eyes almost starting from his head) he darted suddenly on, jumped from his horse, and seized upon something lying on the ground. Holding up to my view an old tattered benjamin, with a catskin collar, and its original blue stained to a hundred different hues, he exultingly exclaimed, "Stranger, h'yar's the darned old cloak; hurraw for my old camlet cloak!— but, darn it, whar's them poor bhoys?"

Determined to go myself in search of the Americans, I beat up for volunteers, and soon got four or five *rancheros*, who were mounted and armed by the prefect, to agree to accompany me. Eight of the Americans were also sufficiently recovered the next day to be off the party; and about noon we started, sixteen in number, well armed and mounted. The *alcalde*, before we left, informed the Americans that, although prisoners, he did not hesitate to allow them to proceed under my command, as I had made myself answerable for their return.

Taking an easterly course, we crossed a *sierra*, and entered upon a broken country dotted with groves of *mezquite* and palms, and intersected by numerous ravines and canons. About ten at night we halted for an hour, to allow our horses to feed on the damp grass, as there was no water, and afterward continued our journey at as rapid a rate as the nature of the country would admit. All night we passed through a wild and perfectly desert tract, crossing rough *sierras* and deep ravines. A large and recent Indian trail crossed the country from north to south, which my Mexican guide said was the main road of the Comanches into the interior.

At sunrise we reached a little hole of water, and a few feet beyond it lay the body of a mule which two of the Americans had killed for its blood, not knowing that water was within a few feet of them. No sooner had they gorged themselves with the hot blood than they discovered the pool, but were so sickened with their previous draught as to be unable to drink. Here we allowed our animals to fill themselves, and immediately rode on without resting. The country became still more broken, and deer were very plentiful. I tumbled over one splendid buck, as he jumped out of a *cañon* through which we were passing, but we were in too great a hurry to stop to take any of the meat.

Toward evening, after travelling rapidly all the day, we approached the spot where the Americans had left their companions, and I caused the party to separate and spread out, to look for tracks of. men or horses. Shortly after one of them stopped and called me to his side. He had discovered the body of a horse which they had left alive when they had last seen their companions. Its swelled tongue and body showed that the poor animal had died from excessive thirst, and was a bad omen of our finding the man alive. A few yards farther on lay another, which had died from the same cause.

Presently we reached the spot, and found guns, and blankets,

155

and ammunition, but no signs of the lost men. The ground, hard and rocky, afforded no clew to the course they had followed, but it was evident that they must have taken an opposite course to that from which we had just come, or we must have seen their tracks in the plains. The horses had been dead at least three days, and had evidently been turned loose to shift for themselves, us they were without ropes.

No doubt remained in my mind as to their fate. The *sierra*, with the exception of the hole where we watered our animals, was destitute of water, and in the direction we imagined them to have taken the country was still more arid, where, if they escaped a miserable death from starvation, they would, in all probability, encounter an equally certain one at the hands of the Indians.

I learned afterward, from a Mexican woman who had been carried a prisoner through this very *sierra* by the Comanches, and afterward purchased from them by an Indian trader, that, in passing through this desert track, the Indians are four days and nights without water for their animals, hundreds of which perish on the road.

After an ineffectual search we were obliged to turn, back, as our animals had been nearly thirty hours without eating, and were almost exhausted; and here there was no grass or herbage of any description. Our guide now recommended that we should strike a new course, and, instead of returning by the way we came, should cross the *sierra* by a gap known as the Puerta del Jabali—the gate of the wild boar; and by this route we might that night reach an old deserted *rancho*, where was good grass, and water for the tired animals.

Striking off to the gap, we passed a wide *cañon*, full of high grass, and literally swarming with deer. As all our provisions were exhausted, I rode ahead and killed a fine doe, which one of the Mexicans threw over his saddle. It was not till late in the night that we reached the old rancho; and at the spring we found several Indian horses, with their backs still wet from the saddle, drinking, while others were feeding around.

From the sign I knew that the Indians had been about since

sundown, that they had probably left their tired animals here, and would return in the morning, or, perhaps, during the night. It was necessary, therefore, to be watchful. The *alamos* round the spring of water were black with ravens and crows, which were roosting in the branches, and one of the Americans thoughtlessly discharged his rifle at them, which set all the Indian horses scampering off, and greatly annoyed me, as I had intended to have secured them.

It might also have had the effect of bringing the Indians upon us, if they were in the neighbourhood, as probably they were. I remained "*alerto*" all night, having two Mexicans on sentry at the same time. The Americans lay snoring round a huge fire, and, being very tired, I did not require them to stand guard. As I was going my rounds I saw a figure crawling on the ground between me and the ruined walls of a house some two hundred yards distant. Assured that it could be no other than an Indian, I threw myself on the ground, and "approached" it, as the hunters say, cautiously and without noise.

The figure was also "approaching" me, and we gradually drew near each other; and I then perceived what I imagined to be an Indian in the very act of drawing his bow upon me. My rifle was instantly at my shoulder, and in another moment would have discharged its contents, when the figure rose on its legs and cried out, "*No tire, no tire, por dios; soy amigo*" don't fire; I'm a friend; and I saw, sure enough, that it was one of the Mexicans, but, dressed in a brown *sarape*, and with his long black hair and dark face, and armed with bow and arrow, he might easily be mistaken for an Indian.

About four in the afternoon next day we rode into Guajoquilla, and, before I had dismounted, Don Augustin Garcia, the prefect, followed by a crowd, accosted me:

"*Que novedades?*" he asked. "Nothing," I answered. "*Pues aqui tiene usted muchas*—well, here we have plenty of bad news for you. The robbers have broken into your room, and stolen all your baggage."

"*Pues*," I answered, "*si no hay remedio*—if it can't be helped, it. can't."

My servant now made his appearance, with a face as white as a sheet; I had given him strict orders, when I started, on do account to leave the house until my return. The night before, however, he had been induced, by the robbers to go to a *fandango*, where they locked him in a room for several hours with a party of men and women drinking and dancing. When he returned to the house he found the door of my room, which was entered from the street, open, and, thinking that I had returned, he went into the house, and, awakening the women, asked them when I had come back. They told him that I was not yet returned, and he replied, "He must be, for his door was wide open."

At this out jumped the *patrona* from her bed: "*Ladrones! ladrones!*" she cried out, instantly guessing what had happened. Striking a light, the whole household entered my room, and found it stripped of everything. They had actually carried off the matting of my packsaddles; trunks and saddles, guns, pistols, sword, and all were gone; and in one of the packs were some three thousand dollars, so they had made a good night's work of it.

My servant was in despair; his first idea was to run, for I would kill him, he said, as soon as I arrived. The old *patrona* did not lose her presence of mind; she rushed to her *sala*, and snatched from the wall a little image of el Niño de Atocha, a juvenile saint of extraordinary virtue. Seizing my distracted *mozo* by the shoulders, she forced him on his knees, and, surrounded by all the women of the family, vowed to the uplifted saint three musses, the cook on her part a penance, and my servant a mass likewise, if the stolen goods were recovered, besides scores of *Pater Nosters*, dozens of *Ave Marias*, &c., &c.

Having done this, as she told me when giving a history of the affair, her heart became calm; the blessed child of Atocha had never deserted her, a lone widow, with on, a *buellada* of two hundred cattle to depend upon, and her husband killed by the *barbaros*; and she felt assured that, by the saint's means, the things would be recovered.

"The scandal," she said, "the '*infamia*' of the robbery taking place in her house!" and a stranger, too, to be plundered, "*lejos de su patria y sus amigos; ay que lastima, que infamia!*"—far from his country and his friends; what an atrocity !

The prefect, Don Augustin, was soon on the scent; one man was already suspected, who had been seen in front of the house late on the night of the robbery, and, passing by frequently,, had attracted the attention of my *patrona*. My *mozo*, pistol in hand, went to the house of this man and collared him, and when I arrived had already lodged him in the *calaboza*. Two others were shortly after taken on suspicion of being accomplices.

"*No hay cuidado*—there is no fear," said Don Augustin; "we'll get everything back; I have put them to the torture, and they have already confessed to the robbery."

My servant, who witnessed the operation, said it was beautiful to see the prefect screwing a confession out of them. Their necks and feet were placed in two different holes, which, by means of a screw, were brought together until every muscle of the body and limbs was in a frightful state of tension, and the bones almost dislocated. At length they divulged where one trunk was concealed, and then another, and after two or three faintings, one article after another was brought to light. In the intervals the prefect rushed to me, wiping the perspiration from his forehead.

"*No hay cuidado, no hay cuidado*; we'll have everything out of them. They have just now fainted off, but when they recover they shall be popped in again."

At last everything was recovered but a small dirk-knife-with a mother-of-pearl handle, which defied screwing, and I begged Don Augustin not to trouble himself about it, as everything else was safe.

But, "*No*," he said, "*No hay cuidado, no hay cuidado*; we'll have everything out of them; strangers must not be robbed with impunity in my prefecture." However, it took another violent screw, and the poor wretch, with eyes starting out of his head, cried out at last to stop, and pulled out of his pocket the missing knife, which he had doubtless determined to keep, on the principle of having "something for his money."

The chief delinquent was the priest's nephew, and most of the stolen property was concealed in the reverend gentleman's garden. To do him justice, however, the *padre* was very active in his attempts to recover my property, and stood by his nephew when under the process of the screw, to exhort him to confession, or administer extreme unction if it was necessary.

When everything had been brought back, my good old *patrona* rushed to me with *el Santo Niño de Atocha*, which she begged of me to kiss, at the same time hanging it in my room to protect it from another spoliation. That evening I was sitting at the door, enjoying a chat with the *señoritas de la casa*, and a *cigarro*, when I saw a figure, or, rather, the trunk, of a woman, moving along on what appeared to be the stumps of legs, enveloped in a cloud of dust, as she slowly crept along the road. She passed three or four times, going and returning upward of a hundred yards, and earnestly praying the while. "*Por Dios*," I asked of one of the girls—"for God's sake, what's this?"

"*Es Dolores, la concinera*"—it's Dolores, the cook—performing penance, was the answer; and her vow instantly recurred to me. The poor old body had vowed to walk so many hundred yards on her knees in the public streets, repeating at the same time a certain number of *Ave Marias*, if the credit of the family was restored by the discovery of the thief and the recovery of my property.

I had a large pot of soup kept always on the fire, to which the half-starved Americans had access whenever they felt inclined, and, as I was sitting at the door, several of them passed into the house, brushing by the *muchachas* without the usual "*con su licencia*," much to the indignation of the ladies.

It is a general impression among the lower classes in Mexico, that the Americans are half savages, and perfectly uncivilized. The specimens they see in Northern Mexico are certainly not remarkably polished in manners or appearance, being generally rough backwoodsmen from Missouri. They go by the name of "*burros*"—jackasses; and have the reputation of being infidels who worship the devil, &c. I was trying to explain to my female friends that the Americans were a very civilized people, and a great portion of them of the same religion as their own, but they scouted the idea; the priests had told them the contrary, and now they saw with their own eyes that they were *burros*.

"*Ni saludan las mugeres!*" indignantly exclaimed a dark beauty, as a conclusive argument—they do not even salute the women when they pass—as, just at that moment, a Missourian, six feet high in his moccasins, stepped over her head as she sat on the sill of the gate.

"*Ni saludan las mugeres,*" she repeated; "you see it yourself. Ah, no, *por Dios, son burros, y muy sin vergüenzas*"—they are jack-asses, and entirely without shame. "*Valgame Dios, que hombres tan fieros!*"—what wild men they are!

In the northern part of Mexico beds are unknown in the *ranchos,* and even in the houses of respectable people. A species of mattress is spread upon the floor at night, on which the sheets and *mantas* are laid, and in the daytime is rolled up against the wall, and, neatly folded and covered with a gay *manta,* forms a settee or sofa. Chairs are not used, and at meals the dishes are placed on the ground, and the guests sit round in Indian fashion, and dip their *tortillas* into the dish. A triangular piece of *tortilla* is converted into a spoon, and soup even is eaten in this way. Spoons are seldom met with even in the houses of the *ricos,* the use of the *tortilla* being universal.

161

CHAPTER 18

Taken for a Spy

On the 3rd of November I left Guajoquilla, under the escort of ten thousand blessings heaped upon me by my kind-hearted hostess and her family, and under the especial protection of the "holy infant of Atocha." We left after dark, as, on account of the *novedades*, it was deemed not only prudent, but indispensable to safety, to travel in the night. About two in the morning I was riding along muffled in my *sarape*, for it was piercingly cold, and half asleep at the time, when I descried ahead of me several campfires a little off the road.

I at once set them down as Indians, as they had been seen the previous day between Guajoquilla and La Remada, and instantly stopped the *cavallada*. Dismounting, I took my rifle, and approached to reconnoitre, creeping up to within a few yards of the fire, where lay snoring a picket of soldiers, while a large body lay bivouacked around. I now remembered that a detachment was out, under the command of one Colonel Amendares, a noted *matador de Indios*, for the purpose of surprising a body of Indians which had passed the Conchos, and would probably return by this route.

Their anxiety to surprise the Indians was evident by the position they had chosen for their ambuscade, being bivouacked in the very middle of the Indian road, and under a high ridge of hills, over which the Indians had to pass, and from whence they could not fail to discover their position. When I regained my horse, and passed close to their fires, I saluted them with a war-hoop which threw the whole camp into a ferment. A little after sunrise we reached the *rancho* of La Remada, where was a detachment of troops to protect the people from the Indians; and we halted here to feed the animals, for two or three hours, after which we resumed our journey to Santa Rosalia. Just before entering the town I killed an antelope in the road. The animal ran to within a hundred yards of my horse, when it stopped and looked at me, giving me time to knock it over from my saddle.

Santa Rosalia is a little dirty place, and has been selected by the Governor of Chihuahua as a point to be defended against the anticipated advance of the Americans. With this object they were busily engaged throwing up walls and parapets, and cutting ditches; but all their work could not convert it into a tenable position.

I put up in the house of an American who has a little "dry-goods" store in the town, and in the middle of the night was called up by a violent knocking at the gate. As the mob had been talking of revenging themselves for the defeat sustained by the Mexican troops at Monterey the other day, by sacking the two unfortunate little stores belonging to Americans, my host thought his time was come, but resolving to die game, came to me to assist in defending the house. We therefore carried all the arms into the store, and placed them on the counter, which served as a parapet for our bodies. The door of the shop opened into the street, and behind it we could hear the clanking of swords and other warlike noises. Presently a loud knock, and a voice exclaimed, loudly, "*Abra la puerta.*"

"*Quien es?*" I asked—Who is it? No answer; but "*Abra la puerta!*"—open the door—was repeated. However, finding that we paid no attention to the request, another summons was tried, with the addition of "*En el nombre del general*—in the name of the general—who has sent me, his *ayudante*, to speak with the master of this house." With this "open *sesame*" we unbarred the door to the general's *aide-de-camp*, a ferocious-looking individual with enormous moustaches and clattering sabre.

"Where," he asked, in an authoritative voice, "is this Ameri-

163

can spy who entered the town today and concealed himself in this house?" No answer. Question repeated with like effect.

The moustached hero grinned with rage, and turned to his followers, saying, "You see this;" and then, turning to us, said, "It is the general's order that every foreigner in this house immediately attend at his quarters, where you will answer for harbouring a spy," turning to the master of the house.

We speedily donned our clothes, and appeared at the house of the general, who was sitting in a room waiting our arrival. Without waiting for any explanation, I immediately presented my credentials saying, "*Hi tiene usted, mi general, mis pasapuertas y carta de seguridad*," which, to the dissatisfaction of the *ayudante*, after glancing at, he returned with a low bow, and many apologies for disturbing me at so late an hour.

It happened to be the feast of Las Animas, when money is collected by the priests for the purpose of praying souls out of purgatory, which on this day is done by wholesale. If money is not to be had, the collectors, usually children, with little boxes which have holes in which the coin is dropped, receive corn or beans; the contribution of my landlord being a couple of tallow candles, which, no doubt, were efficacious in getting some unhappy soul out of several years' pawn, and, perhaps, were useful in greasing the way, as the donor remarked, to the exit of some orthodox *peládo*.

Leaving Santa Rosalia on the 5th, we proceeded to Los Saucillos, a small Indian village, the population of which is entirely employed in mining on their own account. It is situated on the Conchos, here a broad but shallow stream, which runs into the Del Norte above the *presidio* of that name: this village is thirty-six miles from Santa Rosalia. The *gambucinos*, or independent miners, are a class *sui generis*. Their gains depend entirely upon the *bonanza*, or the chance of striking a rich vein, which, with their system of grubbing and pickaxing at random, is a rare event.

Still they work on, year after year, with the golden vision of a *bonanza* ever before their eyes, which will at once raise them to comparative wealth, and, stimulated by the hope, abandon all other labour for the speculative toil of mining. Thus, in these petty *reales*,[1] a scarcity of provisions, and even the necessaries of life, is very apparent. The *gambucinos* are glad to sell their pieces of ore. and even pure metal, for coin considerably less than their value; and the traveller is frequently offered little dumps of silver, and even gold, in exchange for money or articles of clothing.

In this village there was a large, empty *hacienda de beneficios*, full of *scoriae* and *dross*, which covered the floor in heaps, with tumble-down furnaces and moulding apparatus long disused. Here I took up my abode, with the permission of an old Indian, who, perfectly naked save by a small piece of leather round his loins, was superintending some smelting process in a furnace in one corner of the building.

There was abundance of room for myself and animals, who ate their corn out of the washing-troughs, and my supper was cooked on a little fire of charcoal made on the ground, the old Indian joining me in the repast, and telling me long stories of the former riches of the mine, and the hundred times that he had been on the point of securing *bonanzas*. He was, he told me, the most scientific man in the place, knew the probable value of a *lode* at first sight, and was *muy aficionado a los beneficios*—very expert in the process of extracting metal from ore.

There had been a time when he made his two and three dollars a-day, and ore was plentiful; but now the *sierras* were full of "*mala gente*"—demons and bad spirits—who snatched out of their fingers all the metal. He knew a mountain, where one had only to strike his pickaxe and grub up virgin silver at every blow; but it was presided over by a "*demonio*," whose heart was as hard as granite, and who changed the silver into lead when a *gambucino* make his appearance. Other *sierras* there were, he said, *muy lejos*—very far off—where he had been with his father when a boy, and procured much silver; but, shortly after, the Indians made their appearance in that country and killed all they found at work, and they had never been revisited. *Tierra muy rica*

---

1. Mines were, and are still called *reales*—royal—being, in the time of the Spaniards, the property of the crown.

y llena de plata—a very rich country it was, and full of silver.

He had, he told me, in his youth worked in the mine of Sombrerete, and had earned many a dollar in the *bonanzas* of the celebrated Veta Negra, the black vein (a *lode* of metal which yielded an extraordinary quantity of silver). He stayed at Sombrerete until this lode was worked out, and the cause of its failure he narrated to me in the following wonderful story, which he related with the utmost gravity and most perfect seriousness.

His gesticulations, and the solemn asseverations of the truth of the story with which he frequently interrupted it, greatly amused me; and perhaps no more appropriate locale for the narration of such a tale could be found than the spot in which we then were sitting. In the large vaulted building, with its earthen walls covered with mould, and deep recesses, into which the blaze from the fire scarcely penetrated, the old Indian sat cowering over the fire, his sharp, attenuated features lighted up with animation as he narrated his story, stopping occasionally to put from his mouth and nose a cloud of tobacco-smoke, and drawing round his naked figure a tattered blanket, as a cold blast of wind rushed through chinks in the dilapidated wall. In nearly these words he repeated

THE LEGEND OF THE BLACK VEIJT OR SOMBRERETE
(*LA VETA NEGRA DE SOMBRERET"*).

"*Ojala por los dias de oro!*"—oh for the days of gold—sighed the old *gambucino:* "*pero ya se acabó todo eso*—but that is all over now; *ni oro, ni plata hay*—neither gold nor silver is to be had nowadays for picking or digging. *Pedazitos, no mas*—little bits one grubs up here and there; *pero se acabó la veta negra*—but the black vein, the black vein; *onde esta?*—where is it? Worked out long ago.

"I was no older than your worship in those days, and my back was strong. *Valgame madre santissima!* but I could pack the ore nimbly in the mine and up the shaft. Ay, and then all worked with a will, for it was all *bonanza:* day after day, month after month, year after year, there we were at the same old vein; and the more we cut into it the richer it grew. *Ay que plata!* Oh what silver came out of that old vein! *bianco, rico, pesado*—white, rich, and heavy it was—all silver, all silver. Five hundred *pesos fuertes* I made in one week. *Que hermosita era aquella veta negra!*—what a beautiful little vein was that black one!

"But your worship yawns, and my poor old head turns round, when it thinks of that time. *Pues, señor.* All the miners (for there were no *gambucinos* then) were making dollars as fast as they could, but the more they got the more they wanted, although not one of the laziest but had more than he ever before had dreamed of possessing. However, they were not satisfied, and all complained because they did not strike a richer vein than the old *veta negra* —as if that was possible !

"The most dissatisfied of all the miners was a little deformed man called Pepito, who did nothing but swear at and curse his bad luck, although he had made enough money to last three of his lives; and the miserly style in which he lived was the by-word' of everybody.

"However, whether it was from a bitterness of spirit caused by his deformity, or from genuine badness of heart, Pepito was continually grumbling at the old vein, calling it by every op-probrious epithet which he could summon to the end of his tongue, and which was enough to break the heart of any vein, even of iron.

"One night—it was the *fiesta* of San Lorenzo—all the miners were away in the town, for they had agreed to give themselves a holyday; but Pepito took his basket and pick, and declared his intention of remaining to work: 'for,' said he, 'what time have I for holyday, when, with all my work, work, work, I only get enough out of that stony old vein to keep me in *frijolitos*, with-out a taste of *pulque*, since—*quien sabe?*—how long ago? *Maldita sea la veta, digo yo*—curse such a vein, say I!'

"*Valgame Dios!*—this to the black vein, the black vein of Sombrerete!" apostrophized the old *gambucino*.

"Now your worship knows, of course (but *quien sabe?* for foreigners are great fools), that every mine has its metal-king, its *mina-padre,* to whom all the ore belongs. He is, your worship

167

knows, not a man, nor a woman, but a spirit—and a very good one, if he is not crossed or annoyed; and when the miners curse or quarrel at their work, he often cuts off the vein, or changes it to heavy lead or iron; but when they work well and hard, and bring him a good stock of *cigarros*, or leave him in the gallery, when they quit the mine, a little bottle of *pulque* or

, then he often sends *bonanzas*, and plenty of rich ore.

"Well, every one said, when they heard Pepito's determination to remain alone in the mine, and after he had so foully abused the celebrated *veta negra*, '*Valgame!* if Pepito doesn't get a visit from *padre-mina* tonight, it's because he has borrowed holy water or a *rosarioncito* from Father José, the *cura* of Sombrerete.'

"We were all going to work again at midnight, but the *mezcal* was so good that none stirred from the *pulqueria* long after that hour. I, however, shouldered my pick and trudged up the hill to the shaft, first waking up the watchman, who lay snoring at the gate of the *hacienda*, wrapped in his *sarape*. I took him with me to the mouth of the shaft, that he might lower me down in the basket; and down I went.

"When I got to the bottom I called to Pepito, for, knowing he was working there, I had not brought a lantern, but heard nothing save the echo of my own voice, sounding hollow and loud, as it vibrated through the passages and galleries of the mine. Thinking he might be asleep, I groped my way to where we had been working the great lode in the morning, thinking to find him in that direction, and hallooing as I crept, but still no answer; and when I shouted '*Pepito, Pepito, onde esta?*'—where are you?—the echo cried, jeeringly, '*Onde esta?*'

"At length I began to get frightened. Mines, everybody knows, are full of devils, and gnomes, and bad spirits of every kind; and here was I, at midnight, alone, and touching the ' black vein' which had been so abused. I did not like to call again to Pepito, for the echo frightened me, and I felt assured that the answer was made by some unearthly voice, and came direct from the *lode* of the *veta negra*, that we were working. I crept back to the bottom of the shaft, and, looking up to the top, where the sky showed no bigger than a *tortilla*, with one bright star looking straight down, I shouted for the watchman to lower the basket and draw me up; but, holy mother! my voice seemed to knock itself to pieces on the sides of the shaft as it struggled up, and when it reached the top must have been a whisper. I sat down and fairly cried, when a loud shout of laughter rattled along the galleries, and broke as it were up the shaft; I trembled like quicksilver, and heavy drops of perspiration dropped from my forehead to the ground. There was another shout of laughter, and a voice cried out—;

"'Come here, Mattias, come here.'

"'Where, most wonderful *señor*?' I asked, thinking it as well to be respectful.

"'Here, here to the black vein, the old leaden, useless vein,' cried the voice, mockingly; and I thought with horror of the abuse it had that day received.

"Half dead with fear, I crept along the gallery, and, turning an abrupt angle,.came upon the *lode* we had been working. *Ave Maria purissima!* what a sight met my eyes! The gallery seemed a mass of fire, yet there was no blaze and no heat. The rock which contained the vein of ore, and the ore itself, were like solid fire; and yet it wasn't fire, for there was no heat, as I said, but a glare so bright that one could see away into the rock, which seemed to extend miles and miles; and every grain of quartz, and even the smallest particle of sand, of which it was composed, was blazing with light, and shone separately like a million diamonds knocked in one; and yet the eye saw miles into the bowels of the earth, and every grain of sand was thus lighted up.

"But if the stone, and the grit, and the sand were thus fiery bright, and the eye scorched to look upon it, what words can describe, the glitter of the vein, now of sparkling silver, and white, as it were, with flame, but over which a black blush now and then shot, and instantaneously disappeared? It wanted not this, however, to tell me that I was looking at the endless *veta*,

169

negra, the scorned, abused black vein, which throbbed, miles and miles away into the earth, with virgin silver, enough to supply the world for worlds to come.

"'Ha, ha, ha." roared the voice; 'the old leaden, useless vein Where's the man that can eat all this silver's worth of *frijolitos?* Bring him here, bring him here.' And forthwith a thousand little sparkling figures jumped out of the scintillating rock, and, springing to the ground, ringing like new-coined *pesos,* they seized upon the body of Pepito, which I had not till now observed, who lay, blue with fear, in a corner of the gallery, and, lifting him on their shoulders, brought him in front of the silver vein. The brightness of the metal scorched his eyes, which still could not, even in his fear, resist feasting on the richness of the glittering *lode.*

"'*Bonanza, una bonanza!*' shouted the enraptured miner, forgetting his situation, and the presence he was in, for the figure (if figure it can be called, which was like a mist of silver fire) of the *padre-mina*—the mine-king—was now seen sitting in state on the top of the vein.

"'*Bonanza!*' shouted the same voice, derisively; '*bonanza,* from an *old* leaden, useless vein!' repeating the terms which Pepito had used in abusing it. 'Where's the man can eat this silver's worth of *frijolitos?*'

"'What does he deserve who has thus slighted the silver-king?'

"' Turn him to lead, lead, lead!' answered the voice.

"'Away with him then.'

"The thousand sparkling silverines seized the struggling miner. 'Not lead, not lead,' he shouted; 'anything but lead!' But they held him fast by the legs, and bore him opposite the *lode.*

"The rock sparkled up into a thousand times more brilliant coruscations than before, and for an instant I thought my eyes would have 'burned' with looking at the silver vein, so heavenly bright it shone. An instant after a void remained in the rock; a horrid black void. The vein had disappeared, but the rock itself was still as bright as ever, all but the black opening which yawned from out the brightness; and opposite this stood the thousand silverines, bearing the body of the luckless *gambucino*.

"'*Uno, dos, tres,*' shouted the mine-king; and at the word '*tros*'—with a hop, skip, and a jump—right into the gaping hollow sprung the thousand silverines, with the luckless miner on their shoulders, whose body, the instant that his heels disappeared into the opening, with these very eyes, I saw turned to lead.

"*Santa Maria*! then all became dark, and I fell senseless to the ground.

"When I recovered a little, I thought to myself, now will come my turn; but, hoping to conciliate the angry mine-king, I sought, in the breast of my shirt, for a bottle of *mezcal*, which I remembered I had brought with me. There was the bottle, but without a single drop of liquor. This puzzled me: but when I called to mind the fiery spectacle I had just witnessed, I felt no doubt but that the liquor had been dried up in the bottle by the great heat.

"However, I was not molested, and in a short time the miners returned to the work, and, finding me pale and trembling, called me *tonto, boracho*—drunk and mad. We proceeded to the *lode* and grubbed away, but all we succeeded in picking out were a few lumps of poor lead-ore; and from that day not a dollar's worth of silver was ever drawn from the famous 'black vein of Sombrerete.'"

On the 6th we made a short day's journey to San Pablo, a little town on a confluent of the Conchos, in the midst of a marshy plain. Arrived in the *plaza*, I had dispatched my servant in search of a corral, and was myself taking care of the animals, when a *caballero* came out of a house in the square, and very politely invited me to take up my quarters with him for the night, and place the *mulada* in his stables. This offer I gladly accepted, and was presently shown into a large, comfortable room, and, moreover, invited to dinner with my entertainer and his friends. The dinner was served on a table—an unusual luxury; but knife, fork, or spoon, there was none.

Before commencing, at a signal from his master, the *mozo* in

171

attendance said a long grace, at the conclusion of which every one crossed himself devoutly and fell to. One large tumbler of water was placed in the centre of the table, but the custom is not to drink until the meal is finished; so that, if a stranger lays hold of the glass, during dinner, he is instantly stopped by the host, who tells him *"que viene otra cosa,"* that something else is coming.

The next morning I was in the act of making a very long entry in my notebook, to the effect that at last I had met with hospitality in Mexico, when the *mozo* presented himself with a bill of yesterday's entertainment: *seis reales por la comida*—dinner, six *riales*—and out came the leaf of my memorandum-book, *al instante*.

In Guajoquilla I had been tempted to purchase a very beautiful *entero*, an *alazan*, or a blood chestnut stallion, with long, flowing tail and mane, and a perfect specimen of a Mexican caballo de paseo; the most showy and spirited, and at the same time most perfectly good-tempered animal I ever mounted, and so well trained, that I frequently fired at game, resting the rifle on its back, without its moving a muscle. It had travelled, without shoes, and over a flinty road, from Guajoquilla, and had become so sore-footed that I feared I should be compelled to leave it behind me; but hearing that there was an American blacksmith in San Pablo, I paid him a visit for the purpose of getting him to shoe the *alazan*; but unluckily he had no shoes by him, nor the wherewithal to make a set.

Strange to say, that although at this time the horse was so lame that I feared he had foundered altogether, before reaching Chihuahua, and over a very hard road, his feet entirely recovered their soundness, and the next day he travelled without the slightest difficulty.

On the 7th, leaving San Pablo, I met a caravan of wagons from Chihuahua, with a number of officers and families, who were leaving that city from fear of the Americans, who were reported to be on their way to attack it. Among the party was the celebrated Andalucian *matador* Bernardo, who with his troop of bull-fighters had been lately attacked by the Indians, and nearly all of them killed—himself escaping after a desperate sword-fight and many severe wounds. We passed the Cañada, a deep ravine, through which runs a small stream, and where are the ruins of an Indian fort. It is dreaded by travellers, as here the Indians attack them from behind rocks, without exposure to themselves.

In the Cañada we met a couple of priests, with several pupils, on their way to Durango college: they were all well mounted and armed. Shortly after passing the deserted *rancho* of Bachim-ba, we met a general with his escort, "making himself scarce" from Chihuahua; and as they were in the act of encamping, and not wishing to remain in the neighbourhood of the pilfering *soldados*, I rode on, although it was then sunset, and encamped several miles beyond, where, unluckily, the stream was dry, and no water procurable.

The next morning, at sunrise, we started for Chihuahua, crossing a plain abounding with antelope, and reached that city about two o'clock. The first appearance of the town from a neighbouring hill is extremely picturesque, its white houses, church-spires, and the surrounding gardens, affording a pleasing contrast to the barren plain which surrounds it. I was most hos-pitably received by an English family resident in the town, who had the exclusive management of the mint and the numerous mines in the neighbourhood.

In this remote and but semi-civilized city, I was surprised to find that they had surrounded themselves with all the comforts, and many of the luxuries, of an English home; and the kindness I here experienced almost spoiled me for the hardships and pri-vations I met with in my subsequent journey.

CHAPTER 19

Invasion of Americans

Chihuahua, the capital city of the state or department of that name was built toward the close of the seventeenth century, and therefore cannot boast of such antiquity even as the more remote city of Santa Fé. Its population is between eight and ten thousand permanent inhabitants; although it is the resort of many strangers from New Mexico, California, and Sonora. The cathedral, which is considered by the American traders one of the finest structures in the world, is a large building in no style of architecture, but with rather a handsome, *façade*, embellished with statues of the twelve apostles.

Opposite the principal entrance, over the portals which form one side of the square, were dangling the grim scalps of one hundred and seventy Apaches, who had lately been most treacherously and inhumanly butchered by the Indian hunters in the pay of the state. The scalps of men, women, and children were brought into the town in procession, and hung as trophies, in this conspicuous situation, of Mexican valour and humanity!

The unfinished convent of San Francisco, commenced by the Jesuits prior to their expulsion from the country, is also a conspicuous mass of masonry and bad taste. It is celebrated as having been the place of confinement of the patriot Hidalgo, the Mexican Hampden, who was executed in a yard behind the building in 1811. A monument to his memory has been erected in the Plaza de Armas, a pyramid of stone, with an inscription eulogistic of that one honest Mexican.

The town also boasts a *Casa de Moncda,* or mint, under the management of an English gentleman, where silver, gold, and copper are coined, and an aduana, or custom-house. An aqueduct conveys water to the city from the neighbouring stream, the work of the former Spanish government: it is small, and badly constructed.

The shops are filled with goods of the most paltry description, brought mostly from the United States by way of Santa Fé. The cotton goods called "domestics" in the United States are, however, of good quality, and in great demand. Traders arriving in Chihuahua either sell their goods in bulk to resident merchants, or, opening a store, retail them on their own account; but the latter method occasions great delay and inconvenience, the payments being made in copper and small coins, which it is difficult to exchange for gold, and are not current out of the state.

The trade between the United States and Santa Fé and Chihuahua presents a curious feature in international commerce. The capital embarked in it must exceed a million of dollars, which, however, is subject to great risks, not only on account of the dangers to be apprehended in passing the vast prairies, both from Indian attacks and the loss of animals by the severity of the climate, but from the uncertainty of the laws in force in the remote departments of Mexico with regard to the admission of goods and the duties exacted on them.

It appears that in the "port" of Santa Fé the ordinary *derechos de arancel,* or customs duties have been laid aside, and a new tariff substituted, by the late Governor Armijo, who, instead of levying the usual *ad valourem* duties on goods imported from the United States, established the system of exacting duties on "*wagonloads,*" without reference to the nature of the goods contained in them, each wagon paying five hundred dollars, whether large or small.

The injustice of such an impost was apparent, since the merchant, who carried an assortment of rich and valuable goods into the interior of the country for the fair of San Juan and the markets of the capital and larger cities, paid the same duty as the

175

petty trader on his wagon-load of trumpery for the Santa Fé market.

Moreover, the revenue of the customs must have suffered in an equal ratio, for the traders, to avoid the duties, crowded two or more ordinary wagon-loads into one huge one, and thus saved the duties on two wagons. Notwithstanding this, however, the system still prevails, much to the dissatisfaction of those who, in the former state of things, could, by the skilful application of a bribe, pass any amount of goods at almost nominal expense.

The state of Chihuahua produces gold, silver, copper, iron, saltpetre, &c.; indeed, it is productive in mineral wealth alone, for the soil is thin and poor, and there is every where a great scarcity of water. It is, moreover, infested with hostile Indians, who ravage the whole country, and prevent many of its most valuable mines from being worked. These Indians are the Apaches, who inhabit the ridges and plains of the Cordillera, the Sierra Madre on the west, and the tracts between the Conchos and Del Norte on the east, while scattered tribes roam over all parts of the state, committing devastations on the *ranchos* and *haciendas*, and depopulating the remote villages.

For the purpose of carrying on a war against the daring savages, a species of company was formed by the Chihuahuerios, with a capital raised by subscription. The company, under the *auspicea* of the government, offered a bounty of fifty dollars a scalp, as an inducement to people to undertake a war of extermination against the Apaches. One Don Santiago Kirker, an Irishman, long resident in Mexico, and for many years a trapper and Indian trader in the Far West, whose exploits in Indian-killing would fill a volume, was placed at the head of a band of some hundred and fifty men, including several Shawnee and Delaware Indians, and sent *en campaña* against the Apaches. The fruits of the campaign were the trophies I saw dangling in front of the cathedral.

In the month of August, the Apaches being then "*en paz*" with the state, entered, unarmed, the village of Galeana, for the purpose of trading. This band, which consisted of a hundred and seventy, including women and children, was under the command of a celebrated chief, and had, no doubt, committed many atrocities on the Mexicans; but at this time they had signified their desire for peace to the government of Chihuahua, and were now trading in good faith, and under protection of the faith of treaty.

News of their arrival having been sent to Kirker, he immediately forwarded several kegs of spirits, with which they were to be regaled, and detained in the village until he could arrive with his band. On a certain day, about ten in the morning, the Indians being at the time drinking, dancing, and amusing themselves, and unarmed, Kirker sent forward a messenger to say that at such an hour he would be there.

The Mexicans, when they saw him approach with his party, suddenly seized their arms and set upon the unfortunate Indians, who, without even their knives, attempted no resistance, but, throwing themselves on the ground when they saw Kirker's men surrounding them, submitted to their fate. The infuriated Mexicans spared neither age nor sex: with fiendish shouts they massacred their unresisting victims, glutting their long pentup revenge of many years of persecution. One woman, big with child, rushed into the church, clasping the altar and crying for mercy for herself and unborn babe. She was followed, and fell pierced with a dozen lances; and then (it is almost impossible to conceive such an atrocity, but I had it from an eye-witness on the spot not two months after the tragedy) the child was torn alive from the yet palpitating body of its mother, first plunged into the holy water to be baptized, and immediately its brains were dashed out against a wall.

A hundred and sixty men, women, and children were slaughtered, and, with the scalps carried on poles, Kirker's party entered Chihuahua—in procession, headed by the governor and priests, with bauds of music escorting them in triumph to the town.

Nor is this a solitary instance of similar barbarity, for on two previous occasions parties of American traders and trappers perpetrated most treacherous atrocities on tribes of the same nation on the river Gila. The Indians, on their part, equal their more civilized enemies in barbarity; and such is the war of extermination carried on between the Mexicans and Apaches.

But to return to Chihuahua. The state, which comprises an area of one hundred and seven thousand five hundred and eighty-four square miles, contains only one hundred and eighty thousand inhabitants (and this is probably an exaggerated estimate), or not two inhabitants to the square mile. Of this vast territory not twenty square miles are under cultivation, and at least three fifths is utterly sterile and unproductive. The city of Chihuahua is distant from Mexico, in a direct line, one thousand two hundred and fifty miles, and from the nearest sea-port, Guaymas, in the Gulf of California, over an almost impracticable country, six hundred miles. Thus its isolated position, and comparative worthlessness to Mexico are apparent.

Chihuahua is a paradise for sportsmen. In the *sierras* and mountains are found two species of bears—the common black or American bear, and the grizzly bear of the Rocky Mountains. The last are the most numerous, and are abundant in the *sierras* in the neighbourhood of Chihuahua. The *carnero cimarron*—the bighorn, or Rocky Mountain sheep—is also common on the Cordillera. Elk, black-tailed deer, *cola-prieta* (a large species of the fallow deer), the common red deer of America, and antelope, abound on all the plains and *sierras*.

Of smaller game, *peccaries* (*javali*), also called *cojamete*, hares, and rabbits are everywhere numerous; and beavers are still found in the Gila, the Pecos, the Del Norte, and their tributary streams. Of birds—the *faisan*, commonly called *paisano*, a species of pheasant; the quail, or, rather, a bird between a quail and a partridge, is abundant: while every variety of snipe and plover is found on the plains, not forgetting the *gruya,* of the crane kind, whose meat is excellent. There are also two varieties of wolf—the white, or mountain wolf; and the coyote, or small wolf of the plains, whose long-continued and melancholy howl is an invariable adjunct to a Mexican night-encampment.

But, perhaps, in all departments of natural history the ento-

178

mologist would find the plains of Chihuahua most prolific in specimens. I have counted seventy-five varieties of grasshoppers and locusts, some of enormous size and most brilliant and fantastic colours. There is also an insect peculiar to this part of Mexico—at least I have not met with it excepting on the plains of Durango and Chihuahua, neither have I met with more than one traveller who has observed it, although it is most curious and worthy of attention.

This insect is from four to six inches in length, and has four long and slender legs. The body appears to the naked eye to be nothing more than a blade of grass, without the slightest muscular action or appearance of vitality, excepting in the antennae, which are two in number, and about half an inch in length. They move very slowly on their long legs, and resemble a blade of grass being carried by ants. I saw them several times before examining them minutely, thinking that they were, in fact, bits of grass. I heard of no other name for them than the local one of *zacateros,* from *zacate* (grass); and the Mexicans assert that, if horses or mules swallow these insects, they invariably die.[1]

Of bugs and beetles there is endless variety—including the *cocuyo* or lantern-bug, and the tarantula.

Of reptiles, those most frequently met with are the rattlesnake and copperhead, both of which are poisonous. The scorpion is common all over the republic, and its sting is sometimes fatal to children or persons of inflammable temperament. The chameleon abounds in the plains, a grotesque, but harmless and inoffensive animal. It always assimilates its colour to that of the soil where it is found. The chameleon is the "horned frog" of the prairies of America.

The characteristic shrub on the plains of Chihuahua is the *mezquite*—a species of *acacia*, which grows to the height of ten or twelve feet. The seeds, contained in a small pod, resemble those of the laburnum, and are used by the Apaches to make a kind

---

1. Since writing the above, I find that this insect is noticed in Clavigero, who calls it, on the authority of Hernandez, *quauhmecatl*, a Mexican name; therefore it is probable that it is also found in Southern Mexico.

of bread or cake, which is sweet and pleasant to the taste. The wood is exceedingly hard and heavy.[2] This constantly-recurring and ugly shrub becomes quite an eyesore to the traveller passing the *mezquite*-covered plains, as it is the only thing in the shape of a tree seen for hundreds of miles, excepting here and there a solitary *alamo* or willow, which overhangs a spring, and which invariably gives a name to the *rancho* or *hacienda* which may generally be found in the vicinity of water.

Thus, day after day I passed the *ranchos* of El Sauz, Los Sauzes, Los Sauzillos—the willow, the willows, the little willows—or El Alamo, Los Alamitos—the poplar, the little poplars. The last is the only timber found on the streams in Northern Mexico, and on the Del Norte and the Arkansas it grows to a great size.

Chihuahua at this time was in a state of considerable ferment, on account of the anticipated advance of the Americans upon the city from New Mexico. That department had been occupied by them without opposition, Governor Armijo and his three thousand heroes scattering before the barbarians of the north, as they please to call the Americans, without firing a shot. A body of troops had now advanced to the borders of the department, and were known to be encamped on the Rio del Norte, at the entrance of the *"Jornada del Muerto"*—the dead man's journey—a tract of desert, without wood or water, which extends nearly one hundred miles across a bend of the river; and a journey across which is dreaded by the Mexicans, not only on account of these natural difficulties, but from the fact of its being the haunt of numerous bands of Apaches, who swoop down from the *sierras* upon travellers, who, with their exhausted animals, have but little chance of escape.

In rear of the American troops was the long-expected *cara vana* of upward of two hundred wagons, destined for Chihuahua and the fair of San Juan. These, entering Santa Fé with the troops, had, of course, paid no duty in that port of entry, and it was a great object with the Governor of Chihuahua that they should proceed to that city and pay the usual duties to him,

---

2. From the *mezquite* exudes gum Arabic.

which otherwise would have been payable to the custom-house of Santa Fé. The government being entirely without funds, and anxious to raise and equip a body of troops to oppose the advance of the Americans, the arrival of the caravan would have been most opportune, since, at the usual rate of duties, *viz.*, five hundred dollars for each wagon, the amount to be received by the government would exceed one hundred thousand dollars.

However, the merchants, particularly the Americans, were reluctant to trust their property to the chances of Mexican honour, not knowing how they might be treated under the present circumstances of war; and having neglected to profit by the permission of General Kearney, who then commanded the United States troops, to proceed to their destination, now, that that officer had advanced to California, and the command had devolved on another, they were ordered to remain in rear of the troops, and not to advance excepting under their escort.

The commanding officer deemed it imprudent to allow such an amount of the sinews of war to be placed in the hands of the enemy, to be used against the Americans. That this was very proper under the circumstances there could be no gainsaying, but at the same time there was a very large amount of property belonging to English merchants and others of neutral nations, who were suffering enormous losses by the detention of their goods; and as no official notification had been given of the blockade of the frontier town of Santa Fé, this prohibition to proceed was considered unjust and arbitrary. My opinion, however, is, that the officer in command of the United States troops was perfectly justified in the course he pursued, knowing well the uses to which the money thus obtained would have been applied.

In order to keep the enemy in ignorance of the state of affairs in Chihuahua, no one had been permitted to leave the state for some months; and when it was known that I had received a *carte blanche* from Don Angel Trias, the governor, to proceed where I pleased, I was from this circumstance invested with all kinds of official dignities by the population. As it was known that I was the bearer of sundry dispatches from the governor to the Americans, I was immediately voted to be *commissionado* on the part of the Mexican Government to treat for peace, or I was *un coronel Yngles*, bound to Oregon to settle the difference respecting that disputed territory.

The mysterious fact of an Englishman travelling through the country at such a time, and being permitted to proceed "*al norte*," which permission their most influential citizens had been unable to obtain, was sufficient to put the curious on the *qui-vive*: and when on the morning of my departure an escort of soldiers was seen drawn up at my door, I was immediately promoted to be "somebody."

This escort—save the mark!—consisted of two or three dragoons of the regiment of Vera Cruz, which had been several years in Santa Fé, but had run away with the governor on the approach of the Americans, and were now stationed at Chihuahua. Their horses—wretched, half-starved animals—were borrowed for the occasion; and the men, refusing to march without some provision for the road, were advanced their "*sueldo*" by a patriotic merchant of the town, who gave each a handful of copper coins, which they carefully tied up in the corners of their *sarapes*. Their dress was original and uniform (in rags).

One had on a dirty broad-brimmed straw hat, another a handkerchief tied round his head. One had a portion of a jacket, another was in his shirt-sleeves, with overalls, open to the winds, reaching a little below the knees. All were bootless and unspurred. One had a rusty sword and lance, another a gun without a hammer, the third a bow and arrows. Although the nights were piercingly cold, they had but one wretched, tattered *sarape* of the commonest kind between them, and no rations of any description.

These were regulars of the regiment of Vera Cruz. I may as well here mention that, two or three months after, Colonel Douiphan, with nine hundred volunteers, marched through the state of Chihuahua, defeating on one occasion three thousand Mexicans with great slaughter, and taking the city itself, without losing one man in the campaign.

At Sacramento the Mexicans intrenched themselves behind formidable breastworks, having ten or twelve pieces of artillery in battery, and numbering at least three thousand. Will it be believed that these miserable creatures were driven from their position, and slaughtered like sheep, by nine hundred raw backwoodsmen, who did not lose one single man in the encounter?

CHAPTER 20

Arrive at El Paso

On the 10th of November I left Chihuahua, bound for the capital of New Mexico. Passing the Rancho del Sacramento, where a few months after the Missourians slaughtered a host of Mexicans, we entered a large plain well covered with grass, on which were immense flocks of sheep A coyote lazily crossed the road, and, stopping within a few yards, sat down upon its haunches, and coolly regarded us as we passed. Panchito had had a four day's rest, and was in fine condition and spirits, and I determined to try the mettle of the wolf; the level plain, with the springy turf, offering a fine field for a course.

Cantering gently at first, the coyote allowed me to approach within a hundred yards before he loped lazily away; but finding I was on his traces, he looked round, and, gathering himself up, bowled away at full speed. Then I gave Panchito the spur, and, answering it with a bound, we were soon at the stern of the wolf. Then, for the first time, the animal saw we were in earnest, and, with a sweep of his bushy tail, pushed for his life across the plain. At the distance of two or three miles a rocky ridge was in sight, where he evidently sought to secure a retreat, but Panchito bounded along like the wind itself, and soon proved to the wolf that his race was run.

After trying in vain to double, he made one desperate rush, upon which, lifting Panchito with rein and leg, we came up and passed the panting beast, when, seeing that escape was impossible, he lay down, and, with sullen and cowardly resignation, curled up for the expected blow, as, pistol in hand, I reined up Panchito at his side. However, I was merciful, and allowed the animal to escape.

At ten at night I arrived at the *hacienda* of El Sauz, belonging to the Governor of Chihuahua, Don Angel Trias. It was inclosed with a high wall, as a protection from the Indians, who, a short time before, had destroyed the cattle of the *hacienda*, filling a well in the middle of the corral with the carcasses of slaughtered sheep and oxen. It was still bricked up.

The next day we proceeded to another *hacienda*, likewise called after the willows, Los Sauzillos. Passing a large plain, in the midst of which stood a lone poplar, wolves were continually crossing the road, both the coyote and the large gray variety. I was this day mounted upon the *alazan* which I had purchased at Guajoquilla. We were within sight of our halting-place for the night, when the horse, which had carried me all day without my having had recourse to whip or spur, suddenly began to flag, and I noticed that a profuse perspiration had broken out on its ears and neck. I instantly dismounted, and perceived a quivering in the flank and a swelling of the belly. Before I could remove the saddle the poor beast fell down, and, although I opened a vein and made every attempt to relieve it, it once more rose to its legs, and, spinning round in the greatest apparent agony, fell dead to the ground.

The cause of its death was, that my servant, contrary to my orders, had given the animals young corn the night before, which food is often fatal to horses not accustomed to feed on grain.

This *rancho* is situated on the margin of a lake of brackish water, and we found the people actual prisoners within its walls, the gates being closed, and a man stationed on the *azotea* with a large wall-piece, looking out for Indians. At night a large fire was kindled on the roof, the blaze of which illuminated the country far and near. Not a soul would venture after sunset outside the gate, which the *major-domo*, a *Gachupin*, refused to open to allow my servant to procure some wood for a fire to cook my supper, and we had to content ourselves with one of corn cobs, which lay scattered about the corral.

On the 12th, passing Encinillas, a large *hacienda* belonging to Don Angel Trias, we encamped on the banks of an *arroyo*, running through the middle of a plain, walled by sierras, where the Apaches have several villages. This being very dangerous ground, we put out the fire at sunset, and took all precautions against surprise. The animals fared badly, the grass being thin and burned up by the sun, and what little there was being of bad quality.

The next day we reached the small village of El Carmen, and, camping by a little thread of a rivulet outside of the town, were surrounded by all the loafers of the village. The night was very cold, and our fire, the fuel for which we purchased, was completely surrounded by these idle vagabonds.

At last, my temper being frozen out of me, I went up to the fire, and said, "*Señores*, allow me to present you with three *riales*, which will enable you to purchase wood for two fires; this fire I will be obliged to you if you will allow myself and fellow-travellers to warm ourselves by, as we are very cold; and also, with your kind permission, wish to cook our suppers by it." This was enough for them: a Mexican, like a Spaniard, is very sensitive, and the hint went through them. They immediately dispersed, and I saw no more of them the remainder of the evening.

Near El Carmen is a pretty little stream, fringed with *alamos*, which runs through a wild and broken country of *sierras*. The plains, generally about ten to twenty miles in length, are divided from each other by an elevated ridge, but there is no perceptible difference in the elevation of them from Chihuahua to El Paso. The road is level excepting in crossing these ridges, and hard everywhere, except on the marshy plain of Encinillas, which is often inundated.

This lake has no outlet, and is fed by numerous small streams from the sierras; its length is ten miles by three in breadth. The marshy ground around the lake is covered with an alkaline efflorescence called *tezquite*, a substance of considerable value. The water, impregnated with salts, is brackish and unpleasant to the taste, but in the rainy season loses its disagreeable properties.

On the 14th we travelled sixty miles, and camped on a bare plain, without wood or water, the night being so dark that we were unable to reach Carrizal, although it was but a few miles distant from our encampment. The next morning we reached the village, where I stopped the whole day, during an extraordinary hurricane of wind, which rendered travelling impossible.

We had been on short commons for two days, as the hungry escort had devoured my provisions, but here I resolved to have a feast, and, setting all hands to forage, on return we found our combined efforts had produced an imposing pile of several yards of beef (for here the meat is cut into long strips and dried), onions, *chiles*, *frijoles*, sweet corn, eggs, &c. An enormous *olla* was procured, and everything was bundled pell-mell into it, seasoned with pepper and salt and chile.

To protect the fire from the hurricane that was blowing, all the packs and saddles were piled round it, and my servant and the soldiers relieved each other in their vigilant watch of the precious compound, myself superintending the process of cooking. Our appetites, ravenous with a fast of twenty-four hours, were in first-rate order, but we determined that the pot should be left on the fire until the savoury mess was perfectly cooked. It was within an hour or two of sunset, and we had not yet broken our fast. The *olla* simmered, and a savoury steam pervaded the air.

The dragoons licked their lips, and their eyes watered—never had they had such a feast in perspective; for myself, I never removed my eyes from the pot, and had just resolved that, when the *puro* in my mouth was smoked out, the *puchero* would have attained perfection. At length the moment arrived: my *mozo*, with a blazing smile, approached the fire, and with guarded hands seized the top of the *olla*, and lifted it from the ashes.

"*Ave Maria Purissima! Santissima Virgen!*" broke from the lips of the dragoons; "*Mil carajos!*" burst from the heart of the mozo; and I sunk almost senseless to the ground. On lifting the pot the bottom fell out, and splash went everything into the blazing fire. *Valgame Dios!* what a moment was that! Stupefied, and hardly crediting our senses, we gazed at the burning, frizzling, hissing remnants, as they were consuming before our eyes. Nothing was rescued, and our elabourate feast was simplified into a supper of *frijoles* and *chile Colorado,* which, after some difficulty, we procured from the village.

The next morning we started before daylight, and at sunrise watered our animals at the little lake called Laguna de Patos, from the ducks which frequent it; and at midday we halted at another spring, the Ojo de la Estrella—star spring—where we again watered them, as we should be obliged to camp that night without water. We chose a camping-ground in a large plain covered with mezquite, which afforded us a little fuel—now become very necessary, as the nights were piercingly cold. As we had been unable to procure provisions in Carrizal, we went to bed supperless, which was now a very usual occurrence. My animals suffered from the cold, which, coming as they did from the *tierra caliente,* they felt excessively, particularly a little blood horse with an exceedingly fine coat. I was obliged to share my blankets with this poor animal, or I believe it would have died in the night.

Just at daybreak the next morning I was riding in advance of the party when I met a cavalcade of horsemen, whose wild costume, painted faces, and arms consisting of bows and arrows, made me think at first that they were Indians. On their part, they evidently did not know what to make of me, and halted, while two of them rode forward to reconnoitre. I quickly slipped the cover off my rifle, and advanced. Seeing my escort following, they saw we were *amigos;* but the nearer they approached me, the more certain was I that they were Apaches, for they were all in Indian dress, and frightfully painted.

I was as nearly as possible shooting the foremost, when he exclaimed in Spanish, "*Adios, amigo! que novedades hay?*" and I then saw a number of mules, packed with bales and barrels, behind him. They were *Paseños,* on their way to Chihuahua, with *aguardiente,* raisins, and fruit; and. shortly after passing them, I found in the road a large bag of *pazas* or raisins, which I pounced upon as a great prize, and, waiting until the escort came up, we dismounted, and, sitting at the roadside, devoured the fruit with great gusto, as this was our second day of *banyan*. This bag lasted for many days. I found the raisins a great improvement to stews. &c., and we popped a handful or two into every dish.

At ten o'clock we reached a muddy hole of water, entirely frozen—my animals refusing to drink, being afraid of the ice after we had broken it. The water was as thick as pea-soup; nevertheless we filled our *huages* with it, as we should probably meet with none so good that day.

Toward sunset we passed a most extraordinary mountain of loose, shifting sand, three miles in breadth, and, according to the *Paseños*, sixty in length. The huge rolling mass of sand is nearly destitute of vegetation, save here and there a bunch of grease wood half buried in the sand. Road there is none, but a track across is marked by the skeletons and dead bodies of oxen, and of mules and horses, which every where meet the eye.

On one ridge the upper half of a human skeleton protruded from the sand, and bones of animals and carcasses in every stage of decay. The sand is knee-deep, and constantly shifting, and pack-animals have great difficulty in passing. After sunset we reached a dirty, stagnant pool, known as the "Ojo de Malaynca;" but, as there was not a blade of grass in the vicinity, we were compelled to turn out of the road and search over the arid plain for a patch to camp in.

At last we succeeded in finding a spot, and encamped, without wood, water, or supper, being the second day's fast. The next day, passing a broken country, perfectly barren, we struck into the valley of El Paso, and for the first time I saw the well-timbered bottom of the Rio Bravo del Norte. Descending a ridge covered with grease wood and mezquite, we entered the little village of El Paso, with its vineyards, and orchards, and well-cultivated gardens lying along the right bank of the river.

On entering the *plaza* I was immediately surrounded by a crowd, for my escort had ridden before me and mystified them with wonderful accounts of my importance. However, as I did not choose to enlighten them as to my destination or the object of my journey, they were fain to rest satisfied with the egregious lies of the dragoons. In the *plaza* was a little guard-house, where a ferocious captain was in command of a dirty dozen or two *soldados*.

This worthy, to show his importance, sent a sergeant to order my instant attendance at the guard-room. In as many words I told the astonished messenger to tell his officer "to go to the devil," to his horror, and the delight of the surrounding crowd. The answer was delivered word for word, but I heard no more from the military hero. My next visitor was the *prefecto*, who is an important personage in a small place. That worthy, with a dignified air, asked, in a determined tone, as much as to say to the crowd "See how soon I will learn his business,"

"*Por onde pasa usted, caballero?*"—Where are you bound?

"*Por Santa Fé y Nuevo Mejico,*" I answered.

"*No, señor,*" he immediately rejoined, "this cannot be permitted: by the order of the governor no one is allowed to go to the north; and I must request, moreover, that you exhibit your passport and other *documentos.*"

"*Hi lo tiene usted*"—here you have it—I answered, producing a credential which at once caused the hat to fly from his head, and an offer of himself, *su casa, y todo lo que tiene, a mi disposicion*—his house, and all in it, at my disposal. However, all his munificent offers were declined, as I had letters to the *cura*, a young priest named Ortiz whose unbounded hospitality I enjoyed during my stay.

CHAPTER 21

Scarcity of Provisions

El Paso del Norte, so called from the ford of that river, which is here first struck and crossed on the way to New Mexico, is the oldest settlement in Northern Mexico, a mission having been established there by *el padre* Fray Augustin Ruiz, one of the Franciscan monks who first visited New Mexico, as early as the close of the sixteenth century (about the year 1535). Fray Ruiz, in company with two others, named Venabides and Marcos, discovering in the natives a laudable disposition to receive the word of God and embrace *"la santa fé Catolica,"* remained here a considerable time, preaching by signs to the Indians, and making many miraculous conversions.

Eventually, Venabides having returned to Spain and given a glowing account of the riches of the country, and the *muy buen indole*—the very proper disposition of the aborigines—Don Juan Oñate was dispatched to conquer, take possession of, and govern the remote colony, and on his way to Santa Fé established a permanent settlement at El Paso. Twelve families from Old Castile accompanied Oñate to Nuevo Mejico to form a colony, and their descendants still remain scattered over the province.

Several years after, when the Spanish colonists were driven out of New Mexico, they retreated to El Paso, where they erected a fortification, and maintained themselves until the arrival of re-enforcements from Mexico. The present settlement is scattered for about fifteen miles along the right bank of Del Norte, and contains five or six thousand inhabitants. The *plaza*, or village, of El Paso, is situated at the head of the valley, and at the other extremity is the *presidio* of San Eleazario. Between the two is a continued line of adobe houses, with their plots of garden and vineyard.

The farms seldom contain more than twenty acres, each family having a separate house and plot of land.

The Del Norte is dammed about a mile above the ford, and water is conveyed by an *acequia madre*—main canal—to irrigate the valley. From this *acequia*, other smaller ones branch out in every direction, until the land is intersected in every part with dikes, and is thus rendered fertile and productive.

The soil produces wheat, maize, and other grains, and is admirably adapted to the growth of the vine, which is cultivated here and yields abundantly; and a wine of excellent flavour is made from the grapes. Brandy of a tolerable quality is also manufactured, and, under the name of *aguardiente del Paso*, is highly esteemed in Durango and Chihuahua.

Under proper management wine-making here might become a very profitable branch of trade, as the interior of Mexico is now supplied with French wines, the coast of which, owing to the long land-carriage from the sea-ports, is enormous, and wine might be made from the Paso grape equal to the best growths of France or Spain. Fruits of all kinds, common to temperate regions, and vegetables, are abundant and of good quality.

The river bottom is timbered with cotton-woods, which extend a few hundred yards on each side the banks. The river itself is here a small, turbid stream, with the water of a muddy red, but in the season of the rains it is swelled to six times its present breadth, and frequently overflows the banks. It is of fordable depth in almost any part; but from the constantly shifting quicksands and bars, is always difficult, and often dangerous, to cross with loaded wagons. It abounds with fish and eels of large size.

The houses of the *Paseños* are built of the adobe, and are small, but clean and neatly kept. Here, as everywhere else in Northern Mexico, the people are in constant fear of Indian attacks, and, from the frequent devastations of the Apaches, the valley has been almost swept of horses, mules, and cattle. The New Mexicans, too, disguised as Indians, often plunder these settlements (as occurred during my visit, when two were captured), and frequently accompanied the Apaches in their raids on the state of Chihuahua. "Cosas de Mejico."

At this time the *Paseños* had enrolled themselves into a body of troops termed *"auxiliares"* seven hundred strong; but in spite of them the Apaches attacked a *mulada* at the outskirts of the town, and, but for the bravery of two negroes, runaway slaves from the Cherokee nation, would have succeeded in carrying off the whole herd; this was during my stay in this part of the country. One of the herders was killed, but the negroes, when the animals were already in the hands of the Indians, seized their rifles and came to the rescue, succeeding in recapturing the *mulada*.

At El Paso I found four Americans, prisoners, at large. They had arrived here on their way to California, with a mountain trapper as their guide, who, from some disagreement respecting the amount of pay he was to receive, thought proper to revenge himself by denouncing them as spies, and they were consequently thrown into prison. It being subsequently discovered that the informer had committed the most barefaced perjury, these men were released, and the denouncer confined in their stead—quite an un-Mexican act of justice.

However, as they had arrived unprovided with passports, they were detained as prisoners, although permitted to go at large about the place, living, or, rather, existing, on charity. Their baggage had been taken from them, their animals sold, and they were left to shift for themselves. I endeavoured to procure their liberty, by offering to take them with me, and guaranty their good conduct while in the country, and also that they would not take up arms against the Mexicans; but this having no effect, and as the poor fellows were in a wretched condition, I advised them to run for it, promising to pick them up on the road and supply them with the necessary provision, and cautioning them at the same time to conceal themselves in the daytime, travelling at night, and on no account to enter the settlements. They disappeared from El Paso the same night, and what became of them will be presently shown.

On the 19th I left the Paso with an escort of fifteen *auxiliares,* a ragged troop, with whom to have marched through Coventry would have broken the heart of Sir John Falstaff. Armed with bows and arrows, lances, and old rusty *escopetas,* and mounted on miserable horses, their appearance was anything but warlike, and far from formidable. I did my best to escape the honour, knowing that they would only be in my way, and of not the slightest use in case of Indian attack; but all my protestations were attributed to modesty, and were overruled, and I was fain to put myself at the head of the band of valiant *Paseños,* who were to escort me to the borders of the state of Chihuahua.

One of them, a very old man, with a long lance which he carried across his saddle-bow, and an old rusty bell-mouthed *escopeta,* attached himself particularly to me, riding by my side, and pointing out the points—the *mal puntos*—whence the Apaches usually made their attacks. He had, he told me, served all through the War of Independence, "*y por el Rey*"—for the king—he added, reverently doffing his hat at the mention of the king.

He was a loyalist, heart and soul. "*Ojala por los dias felices del reyno!*"—alas for the happy time when Mexico was ruled by a king!—was his constant sighing exclamation. A *doubloon,* with the head of Carlos Tercero, hung round his neck, and was ever in his hand, being reverently kissed every few miles. He was, he said, *media tonto*—half crazy—and made verses, very sorry ones, but he would repeat them to me when we arrived in camp.

Leaving El Paso, we travelled along the rugged, precipitous bank of the river, crossing it about three miles above the village, and, striking into a wild, barren-looking country, again made the river about sunset, and encamped in the bottom, under some very large cotton-woods, at a point called Los Alamitos— the little poplars—although they are enormous trees. We had here a very picturesque camp. Several fires gleamed under the trees, and round them lay the savage-looking *Paseños,* while the animals were picketed round about. Several deer jumped out of the bottom when we entered, and on the banks of the river I saw some fresh beaver "sign."

The next day, halting an hour at the Brazitos, an encamping-ground so called, and a short time afterward passing the battle-ground where Doniphan's Missourians routed the Mexicans, we saw Indian sign on the banks of the river, where a considerable body had just crossed. A little farther on we met a party of seven soldiers returning from a successful hunt after the Americans who had escaped from the Paso. These unfortunates were sitting quietly behind their captors, who had overtaken them at the little settlement of Doñana, which they foolishly entered to obtain provisions.

Doñana is a very recent settlement of ten or fifteen families, who, tempted by the richness of the soil, abandoned their farms in the valley of El Paso, and have here attempted to cultivate a small tract in the very midst of the Apaches, who have already paid them several visits and carried off or destroyed their stock of cattle. The huts are built of logs and mud, and situated on the top of a tabular bluff which looks down upon the river-bottom.

The soil along this bottom, from El Paso to the settlements of New Mexico, is amazingly rich, and admirably adapted for the growth of all kinds of grain. The timber upon it is cotton-wood, dwarf oak, and mezquite, under which is a thick undergrowth of bushes. Several attempts have been made to settle this productive tract, but have all of them failed from the hostility of the Apaches. Should this department full into the hands of the Americans, it will soon become a thriving settlement; for the hardy backwoodsman, with his axe on one shoulder and rifle on the other, will not be deterred by the savage, like the present pusillanimous owners of the soil, from turning it to account.

The next day we encamped at San Diego, the point where the traveller leaves the river and enters upon the dreaded Jornada del Muerto—the journey of the dead man. All the camping and watering-places on the river are named, but there are no settlements, with the exception of Doñana, between El Paso and Socorro, the first settlement in New Mexico, a distance of two hundred and fifty miles. ,

At San Diego we saw more Indian signs, the consequence of which was, that my escort reported their horses to be exhausted and unable to proceed; so, nothing loath, I gave them their *congé*, and the next morning they retraced their steps to El Paso, leaving me with my two servants to pass the *jornada*. I was now at the edge of this formidable desert, where along the road the bleaching bones of mules and horses testify to the dangers to be apprehended from the want of water and pasture, and many human bones likewise tell their tale of Indian slaughter and assault.

I remained in camp until noon, when for the last time we led the animals to the water and allowed them to drink their fill: we then mounted, and at a sharp pace struck at once into the Jornada. The road is perfectly level and hard, and over plains bounded by *sierras*. *Palmillas* and bushes of sage (*artemisia*) are scattered here and there, but the *mezquite* is now becoming scarce, the *tornilla* or screw-wood taking its place: farther on, this wood ceases, and there is then no fuel to be met with of any description.

Large herds of antelope bounded past, and coyotes skulked along on their trail, and prairie-dog towns were met every few miles, but their inmates were snug in their winter-quarters, and only made their appearance to bask in the meridian sun. Shortly after leaving San Diego we found water in a little hole called El Perillo (the little dog), but our animals, having so lately drank, would not profit by the discovery, and we hurried on, keeping the pack-animals in a sharp trot. Near the Perillo is a point of rocks which abuts upon the road, and from which a large body of Apaches a few years since pounced upon a band of American trappers and entirely defeated them, killing several and carrying off all their animals.

Behind these rocks they frequently lie in ambush, shooting down the unwary traveller, whose first intimation of their presence is the puff of smoke from the rocks, or the whiz of an arrow through the air. One of my *mozos*, who was a New Mexican and knew the country well, warned me of the dangers of this spot, and before passing it, I halted the mules and rode on to reconnoitre; but no Apache lurked behind it, and we passed unmolested.

About midnight we stopped at the Laguna del Muerto—the dead man's lake—a depression in the plain, which in the rainy season is covered with water, but was now hard and dry. We rested the animals here for half an hour, and, collecting a few armfuls of *artemisia* attempted to make a fire, for we were all benumbed with cold; but the dry twigs blazed brightly for a minute, and were instantly consumed.

By the temporary light it afforded us we discovered that a large party of Indians had passed the very spot but a few hours, and were probably not far off that moment, and, if so, they would certainly be attracted by our fire, so we desisted in our attempts. The mules and horses, which had travelled at a very quick pace, were suffering, even thus early, from want of water, and my horse bit of the neck off a *huage*, or gourd, which I had placed on the ground, and which the poor beast by his nose knew to contain water.

However, as there was not a vestige of grass on the spot, after a halt of half an hour, we again mounted and proceeded on our journey, continuing at a rapid pace all night. .At sunrise we halted for a couple of hours on a patch of grass which afforded a bite to the tired animals, and about three in the afternoon, had the satisfaction of reaching the river at the watering-place called Fray Cristoval, having performed the whole distance of the Jornada, of ninety-five, or, as some say, one hundred miles, in a little more than twenty hours.

The plain through which the dead man's journey passes is one of a system, or series, which stretch along the table-land between the Sierra Madre, or main chain of the Cordillera, on the west, and the small mountain-chain of the Sierra Blanca and the Organos, which form the dividing ridge between the waters of the Del Norte and the Rio Pecos. Through this valley, fed by but few streams, runs the Del Norte. Its water, from the constant abrasion of the banks of alluvial soil, is very muddy and discoloured, but, nevertheless, of excellent quality, and has the reputation at El Paso of possessing chemical properties which prevent diseases of the kidneys, stone, &c., &c.

The White Mountain and the Organos are singularly destitute of streams, but on the latter is said to be a small lake, in the waters of which may be seen the phenomenon of a daily rise and fall similar to a tide. They are also reported to abound in minerals, but, from the fact of these *sierras* being the hiding-places of Apaches, they are never visited excepting during a hostile expedition against these Indians, and consequently in these excursions but little opportunity is afforded for an examination of the country. The *sierras* are also celebrated for medicinal herbs of great value, which the Apaches, when at peace with the *Paseños*, sometimes bring in for sale.

Indeed, from the accounts which I received from the people of these mountains, I should judge them to be well worthy of a visit, which, however, would be extremely hazardous on account of the hostility of the Indians and the scarcity of water. Their formation is apparently volcanic, and, judging from the nature of the plains, which in many places are strewed with volcanic substances, and exhibit the bluffs of tabular form, composed of basaltic lava, known by the name of *mesas* (tables), the valley must at one time have been subjected to volcanic agency.

Staying at Fray Cristoval but one night, I pushed on to the ruins of Valverde, a long-deserted *rancheria*, a few miles beyond which was the advanced post of the American troops. Here, encamped on the banks of the river in the heavy timber, I found a great portion of the caravan which I have before mentioned ns being en route to Chihuahua, and also a surveying party under the command of Lieutenant Abert, of the United States Topographical Engineers.

Being entirely out of provisions, and my camp hungry, the next morning I mounted my hunting-mule, and crossed the river, which was partially frozen, to look for deer in the bottom.

Thanks to my mule, as I was passing through a thicket I saw it prick its ears and look on one side, and, following its gaze, descried three deer standing under a tree with their heads turned toward me. My rifle was quickly up to my shoulder, and a fine large doe dropped to the report, shot through the heart. Being in a hurry, I did not wait to cut it up, but threw it upon my mule, which I drove before me to the river.

Large blocks of ice were floating down, which rendered the passage difficult, but I mounted behind the deer and pushed the mute into the stream. Just as we had got into the middle of the current a large piece of ice struck the mule, and, to prevent itself being carried down the stream, it threw itself on its haunches, and I slipped over the tail, and head over ears into the water. Rid of the extra load, the mule carried the deer safely over and trotted off to camp, where it quietly stood to be unpacked, leaving me, drenched to the skin, to follow after it.

The traders had been lying here many weeks, and the bottom where they were encamped presented quite a picturesque appearance. The timber extends half a mile from the river, and the cotton-wood trees are of large size, without any undergrowth of bushes. Among the trees, in open spaces, were drawn up the wagons, formed into a corral or square, and close together, so that the whole made a most formidable fort, and, when filled with some hundred rifles, could defy the attacks of Indiana or Mexicans. Scattered about were tents and shanties of logs and branches of every conceivable form, round which lounged wild-looking Missourians, some cooking at the campfires, some cleaning their rifles or firing at targets—blazes cut in the trees, with a bull's-eye made with wet powder on the white bark.

From morning till night the camp rebounded with the popping of rifles, firing at marks for prizes of tobacco, or at any living creature which presented itself. The oxen, horses, and mules were sent out at daylight to pasture on the grass of the prairie, and at sunset made their appearance, driven in by the Mexican herders, and were secured for the night in the corrals. My own animals roamed at will, but every evening came to the river to drink, and made their way to my camp, where they would frequently stay round the fire all night. They never required herding, for they made their appearance as regularly as the day closed, and would come to my whistle whenever I required my hunting–mule.

The poor beasts were getting very poor, not having had corn since leaving El Paso, and having subsisted during the journey from that place on very little of the coarsest kind of grass. They felt it the more as they were all accustomed to be fed on grain; and the severe cold was very trying to them, coming, as they did, from a tropical climate. My favourite horse, Panchito, had lost all his good looks; his once full and arched neck was now a perfect "ewe," and his ribs and hip–bones were almost protruding through the skin; but he was as game as ever, and had never once flinched in his work.

Provisions of all kinds were very scarce in the camp, and the game, being constantly hunted, soon disappeared. Having been invited to join the hospitable mess of the officers of the Engineers, I fortunately did not suffer, although even they were living on their rations, and on the produce of our guns. The traders, mostly young men from the eastern cities, were fine, hearty fellows, who employ their capital in this trade because it combines pleasure with profit, and the excitement and danger of the journey through the Indian country are more agreeable than the monotonous life of a city merchant.

The volunteers' camp was some three miles up the river on the other side. Colonel Doniphan, who commanded, had just returned from an expedition into the Navajo country for the purpose of making a treaty with the chiefs of that nation, who have hitherto been bitter enemies of the New Mexicans. From appearances no one would have imagined this to be a military encampment. The tents were in a line, but there all uniformity ceased. There were no regulations in force with regard to cleanliness.

The camp was strewed with bones and offal of the cattle slaughtered for its supply, and not the slightest attention was paid to keeping it clear from other accumulations of filth. The men, unwashed and unshaven, were ragged and dirty, without uniforms, and dressed as, and how, they pleased. They wandered about, listless and sickly-looking, or were sitting in groups playing at cards, and swearing and cursing, even at the officers if they interfered to stop it (as I witnessed).

The greatest irregularities constantly took place. Sentries, or a guard, although in an enemy's country, were voted unnecessary; and one fine day, during the time I was here, three Navajo Indians ran off with a flock of eight hundred sheep belonging to the camp, killing the two volunteers in charge of them, and reaching the mountains in safety with their booty. Their mules and horses were straying over the country; in fact, the most total want of discipline was apparent in everything. These very men, however, were as full of fight as game-cocks, and shortly after defeated four times their number of Mexicans at Sacramento, near Chihuahua.

The American can never be made a soldier; his constitution will not bear the restraint of discipline, neither will his very mistaken notions about liberty allow him to subject himself to its necessary control. In a country abounding with all the necessaries of life, and where any one of physical ability is at no loss for profitable employment; moreover, where, from the nature of the country, the lower classes lead a life free from all the restraint of society, and almost its conventional laws, it is easy to conceive that it would require great inducements for a man to enter the army and subject himself to discipline for the sake of the trifling remuneration, when so many other sources of profitable employment are open to him. For these reasons the service is unpopular, and only resorted to by men who are either too indolent to work, or whose bad characters prevent them seeking other employment.

The volunteering service, on the other hand, is eagerly sought, on occasions such as the present war with Mexico affords, by young men even of the most respectable classes, as, in this, discipline exists but in name, and they have privileges and rights, such as electing their own officers, &c., which they consider to be more consonant to their ideas of liberty and equality. The system is palpably bad, as they have sufficiently proved in this war. The election of officers is made entirely a political question, and quite irrespective of their military qualities, and, knowing the footing on which they stand with the men, they, if even they know how, are afraid to exact of them either order or discipline.

Of drill or manoeuvring the volunteers have little or no idea. "Every man on his own hook" is their system in action; and trusting to, and confident in, their undeniable bravery, they "go ahead," and overcome all obstacles. No people know better the advantages of discipline than do the officers of the regular service; and it is greatly to their credit that they can keep the standing army in the state it is. As it is mostly composed of foreigners—Germans, English, and Irish, and deserters from the British army—they might be brought to as perfect a state of discipline as any of the armies of Europe; but the feeling of the people will not permit it; the public would at once cry out against it as contrary to republican notions and the liberty of the citizen.

There is a vast disparity between the officers of the regular army and the men they command. Receiving at West Point (an admirable institution) a military education by which they acquire a practical as well as theoretical knowledge of the science of war, as a class they are probably more distinguished for military knowledge than the officers of any European army. Uniting with this a high chivalrous feeling and most conspicuous gallantry, they have all the essentials of the officer and soldier.

Notwithstanding this, they have been hitherto an unpopular class in the United States, being accused of having a tendency to aristocratic feeling, but rather, I do believe, from the marked distinction in education and character which divides them from the mass, than any other reason.

However, the late operations in Mexico have sufficiently proved that to their regular officers alone, and more particularly to those who have been educated at the much-decried West

Point, are to be attributed the successes which have every where attended the American arms; and it is notorious that on more than one occasion the steadiness of the small regular force, and particularly of the artillery, under their command, has saved the army from most serious disasters.

I remained at Valverde encampment several days in order to recruit my animals before proceeding farther to the north, passing the time in hunting; game, although driven from the vicinity of the camp, being still plentiful at a little distance. Besides deer and antelope, turkeys were very abundant in the river-bottom; and, of lesser game, hares, rabbits, and quail were met with on the plain, and geese and ducks in the river.

One day I got a shot at a panther (*painter*), but did not kill it, as my old mule was so disturbed at the sight of the beast, that it refused to remain quiet. The prairie between the Del Norte and the mountain, a distance of twelve or fourteen miles, is broken into gullies and ravines, which intersect it in every direction. At the bottom of these is a thick growth of coarse grass and grease-bushes, where the deer love to resort in the middle of the day.

I was riding slowly up one of these *cañons*, with my rifle across the saddle-bow, and the reins thrown on the mule's neck, being at that moment engaged in lighting my pipe, when the mole pricked its ears and turned its head to one side very suddenly, giving a cant round at the same time. I looked to the right, and saw a large panther, with its tail sweeping the ground, trotting leisurely up the side of the ravine, which rose abruptly from the dry bed of a water-course, up which I was proceeding.

The animal, when it reached the top, turned round and looked at me, its tiger-like ears erect, and its tail quivering with anger. The mule snorted and backed, but, fearing to dismount, lest the animal should run off, I raised my rifle and fired both barrels at the beast, which, giving a hissing growl, bounded away unhurt.

It was, however, dangerous to go far from the camp, as Apaches and Navajos were continually prowling round, and, as I have mentioned, had killed two of the volunteers, and stolen eight hundred sheep. One day, while hunting, I came upon a fire which they had just left, and, as several oxen were lost that night, this party, which, from the tracks, consisted of a man, woman, and boy, had doubtless run them off.

I was that day hunting in company with a French Canadian and an American, both trappers and old mountain-men, when, at sundown, just as we had built a fire and were cooking our suppers under some trees near the river, we heard the gobble-gobble of an old turkey-cock, as he called his flock to roost. Lying motionless on the ground, we watched the whole flock, one after another, fly up to the trees over our heads, to the number of upward of thirty. There was still light enough to shoot, and the whole flock was within reach of our rifles, but, as we judged that we could not hope for more than one shot apiece, which would only give three birds, we agreed to wait till the moon rose, when we might bag the whole family.

Hardly daring to move, we remained quiet for several hours, as the moon rose late, consoling ourselves with our anticipations of a triumphal entry into camp, on the morrow, with twenty or thirty fine turkeys for a Christmas feast.

At length the moon rose, but, unfortunately, clouded: nevertheless we thought there was sufficient light for our purpose, and, rifle in hand, approached the trees where the unconscious birds were roosting. Creeping close along the ground, we stopped under the first tree we came to, and, looking up, on one of the topmost naked limbs was a round black object. The *pas* was given to me, and, raising my rifle, I endeavoured to obtain a sight, but the light was too obscure to draw "a bead," although there appeared no difficulty in getting a level. I fired, expecting to hear the crash of the falling bird follow the report, but the black object on the tree never moved. My companions chuckled, and I fired my second barrel with similar result, the bird still remaining perfectly quiet. The Canadian then stepped forth, and, taking a deliberate aim, bang he went.

"*Sacré enfant de Gârce!*" he exclaimed, finding he too had missed the bird; "I aim straight, *mais light très bad, sacré!*"

Bang went the other's rifle, and bang-bang went my two barrels immediately after, cutting the branch in two on which the bird was sitting, who, thinking this a hint to be off, and that he had sufficiently amused us, flew screaming away. The same compliments were paid to every individual, one bird standing nine shots before it flew off: and, to end the story, we fired away every ball in our pouches without as much as touching a feather; the fact of the matter being, that the light was not sufficient to see an object through the fine sight of the rifles.

At Valverde my Mexican servant deserted, why or therefore I could not understand, as he did not even wait for his pay, and carried off no equivalent. I also left here the Mexico-Irishman who had accompanied me from Mapimi. He was already suffering from the severities of the climate, and, being very delicate, I did not think him able to stand a winter journey over the Rocky Mountains.

He therefore returned to Chihuahua with one of the traders. From this point to my winter-quarters in the mountains I was entirely on my own resources, being unable to hire a servant in whom I could place the least confidence, and preferring to shift for myself, rather than be harassed with being always on the watch to prevent my *fidus* Achates from robbing or murdering me. My animals gave me little or no trouble, and I now had reduced my *requa* to five, having left at El Paso the *tierra caliente* horse, another having died on the road, and a mule having been lost or strayed on the Del Norte.

In travelling I had no difficulty with the pack and loose mules. I rode in front on Panchito, and the mules followed like dogs, never giving me occasion even to turn round to see if they were there; for if, by any accident, they lost sight of the horse, and other animals were near, they would gallop about smelling at each, and often, starting off to horses or mules feeding at a distance, would return at full gallop, crying with terror until they found their old friend.

Panchito, on his part showed equal signs of perturbation if they remained too far behind, as sometimes they would stop for a mouthful of grass, and, turning his head, would recall them by a loud neigh, which invariably had the effect of bringing them up at a hand-gallop.

The greatest difficulty I experienced was in packing the mules, which operation, when on an *aparejo*, or Mexican pack-saddle, is the work of two men, and I may as well describe the process.

The equipment of a pack-mule—*mula de carga*—consists, first and foremost, of the *aparejo*, which is a square pad of stuffed leather. An idea of the shape may be formed by taking a book and placing it saddle-fashion on any object, the leaves being equally divided, and each half forming a flap of the saddle. This is placed on the mule's back on a *xerga,* or saddle-cloth, which has under it a *salea,* raw sheep-skin softened by the hand, which prevents the saddle chafing the back. The *aparejo* is then secured by a broad grass-band, which is drawn so tight, that the animal appears cut in two, and groans and grunts most awfully under the operation, which to a greenhorn seems most unnecessary and cruel. It is in this, however, that the secret of packing a mule consists; the firmer the pack-saddle, the more comfortably the mule travels, and with less risk of being *"matada,"* literally killed, but meaning chafed and cut.

The *carga* is then placed on the top, if a single pack; or if two of equal size and weight, one on each side, being coupled together by a rope, which balances them on the mule's back; a stout pack-rope is then thrown over all, drawn as tight as possible under the belly, and laced round the packs, securing the load firmly in its place. A square piece of matting—*petate*—is then thrown over the pack to protect it from rain, the tapojos is removed from the mule's eyes, and the operation is complete.

The *tapojos*—blinker—is a piece of thin, embroidered leather, which is placed over the mule's eyes before being packed, and thus blinded, the animal remains perfectly quiet. The *cargador* stands on the near side of the pack, his assistant on the other, hauling on the slack of the rope, with his knee against the side of the mule for a purchase; when the rope is taut, he cries *"Adios."*

and the packer, rejoining "*Vaya!*" makes fast the rope on the top of the *carga*, sings out "*Anda!*" and the mule trots off to her companions, who feed round until all the mules of the *atajo* are packed.

Muleteering is the natural occupation of the Mexican. He is in all his glory when travelling as one of the *mozos* of a large *atajo*—a caravan of pack-mules; but the height of his ambition is to attain the rank of *mayor-domo* or *capitan*—(the *brigadero* of Castile). The atajos, numbering from fifty to two hundred mules, travel a daily distance—*Jornada*—of twelve or fifteen miles, each mule carrying a pack weighing from two to four hundred pounds. To a large *atajo* eight or ten muleteers are attached, and the dexterity and quickness with which they will saddle and pack an *atajo* of a hundred mules is surprising.

The animals being driven to the spot, the lasso whirls round the head of the muleteer, and falls over the head of a particular mule. The *tapojos* is placed over the eyes, the heavy *aparejo* adjusted, and the pack secured, in three minutes. On reaching the place where they purpose to encamp, the pack-saddles are all ranged in regular order, with the pack, between, and covered with the *petates*, a trench being cut round them in wet weather to carry off She rain. One mule is always packed with the *metate*—the stone block upon which the maize is ground to make *tortillas*, and the office of cook is undertaken in turn by each of the muleteers. *Frijoles* and *chile Colorado* comprise their daily bill of fare, with a drink of *pulque* when passing through the land of the *maguey*.

CHAPTER 22

British Deserter

On the 14th of December the camp was broken up, the traders proceeding to Fray Cristoval, at the entrance of the *jornada*, to wait the arrival of the troops, which were about to advance on Chihuahua; and myself, in company with Lieutenant Abort's party, *en route* to Santa Fé. Crossing the Del Norte, we proceeded on its right bank ten or twelve miles, encamping in the bottom near the new settlement of San Antonio, a little hamlet of ten or twelve log-huts, inhabited by *pastores* and *vaqueros*—shepherds and cattle-herders. The river is but thinly timbered here, the soil being arid and sterile; on the bluffs, however, the grass is very good, being the *gramma* or feathered-grass, and numerous flocks of sheep are sent hither to pasture from the settlements higher up the stream.

The next day we passed through Socorro, a small, wretched place, the first settlement of New Mexico on the river. The houses are all of adobe, inside and out, one story high, and with the usual *azotea* or flat roof. They have generally a small window, with thin sheets of talc (which here abounds) as a substitute for glass. They are, however, kept clean inside, the mud-floors being watered and swept many times during the day.

The faces of the women were all stained with the fiery red juice of a plant called *alegria,* from the forehead to the chin. This is for the purpose of protecting their skin from the effects of the sun, and preserving them in untanned beauty to be exposed in the *fandangos.* Of all people in the world the Mexicans have the greatest antipathy to water, hot or cold, for ablutionary purposes. The men never touch their faces with that element, except in their bi-monthly shave; and the women besmear themselves with fresh coats of *alegria* when their faces become dirty; thus their countenances are covered with alternate strata of paint and dirt, caked, and cracked in fissures.

My first impressions of New Mexico were anything but favourable, either to the country or the people. The population of Socorro was wretched-looking, and every countenance seemed marked by vice and debauchery. The men appear to have no other employment than smoking and basking in the sun, wrapped in their *sarapes*; the women in dancing and intrigue. The appearance of Socorro is that of a dilapidated brick-kiln, or a prairie-dog town; indeed, from these animals the New Mexicans appear to have derived their style of architecture. In every village we entered, the women flocked round us begging for tobacco or money, the men loafing about, pilfering everything they could lay their hands on.

As in other parts of Mexico, the women wore the *enagua*, or red petticoat, and *reboso*, and were all bare-legged. The men were some of them clad in buckskin shirts, made by the Indians. Near Socorro is a mining *sierra*, where gold and silver have been extracted in small quantities. All along the road we met straggling parties of the volunteers, on horse or mule-back, and on foot. In every camp they usually lost some of their animals, one or two of which our party secured. The five hundred men who were on the march covered an extent of road of more than a hundred miles—the ammunition and provision-wagons travelling through an enemy's country without escort!

On the 16th we passed through Limitar, another wretched village, and a sandy, desert country, quite uninhabited, camping again on the Del Norte; and next day, stopping an hour or two at Sabanal, we reached Bosque Redondo, the *hacienda* of one of the Chaves family, and one of the *ricos* of New Mexico.

The churches in the villages of New Mexico are quaint little buildings, looking, with their adobe walls, like turf-stacks. At each corner of the *façade* half a dozen bricks are erected in the form of a tower, and a centre ornament of the same kind supports a wooden cross. They are really the most extraordinary and primitive specimens of architecture I ever met with, and the decoration's of the interior are equal to the promises held out by the imposing outside.

The houses are entered by doors which barely admit a full-grown man; and the largest of New Mexican windows is but little bigger than the ventilator of a summer hat. However, in his rabbit-burrow, and with his *tortillas* and his *chile*, his *ponche*[1] and cigar of *hoja*,[2] the New-Mexican is content; and with an occasional traveller to pilfer, or the excitement of a stray Texan or two to massacre now and then, is tolerably happy; his only care being, that the river rise high enough to fill his *aceguia,* or irrigating ditch, that sufficient maize may grow to furnish him *tortillas* for the winter, and shucks for his half-starved horse or mule, which the Navajos have left, out of charity, after killing half his sons and daughters, and bearing into captivity the wife of his bosom.

We encamped behind the house at Bosque Redondo, for which privilege I asked permission of the proprietor, who doled us out six pennyworth of wood for our fires, never inviting us into his house, or offering the slightest civility. *Cosas de Mejico.*

On the 17th we reached Albuquerque, next to Santa Fé the most important town in the province, and the residence of the ex-Governor Armijo. We found here a squadron of the United States dragoons, the remainder of the regiment having accompanied General Kearney to California. We encamped near a large building where the men were quartered; and in the evening a number of them came round the fire, asking the news from the lower country. I saw that some of them had once worn a different-coloured uniform from the sky-blue of the United States army; and in the evening, as I was walking with some of the officers of the regiment, I was accosted by one, whom I im-

---

1. A pungent tobacco grown in New Mexico.
2. *Hoja*, corn-shuck, leaves of Indian com.

mediately recognized as a man named Herbert, a deserter from the regiment to which I had once belonged. He had imagined that, as several years had elapsed since I had seen him, his face would not have been familiar to me, and inquired for a brother of his who was still in the regiment, denying at first that he had been in the British service.

The settled portion of the province of New Mexico is divided into two sections, which, from their being situated on the Rio del Norte, are designated Rio Arriba and Rio Abajo, or up the river and down the river. Albuquerque is the chief town of the latter, as Santa Fé is of the former as well as the capital of the province.

The town and the estates in the neighbourhood belong to the Armijo family; and the general of that name, and ex-governor, has here a *palacio;* and has also built a barrack, in which to accommodate the numerous escort which always attends him in his progresses to and from his country-seat.

The families of Armijo, Chaves, Peréa, and Ortiz are *par excellence* the *ricos* of New Mexico—indeed, all the wealth of the province is concentrated in their hands; and a more grasping set of people, and more hard-hearted oppressors of the poor, it would be difficult to find in any other part of Mexico, where the rights or condition of the lower classes are no more considered than in civilized countries is the welfare of dogs and pigs.

I had letters to the Señora Armijo, the wife of the runaway governor: but, as it was late at night when we arrived, and as I intended to leave the next morning, I did not think it worthwhile to present them, merely delivering to the *major-domo* some private letters which had been intrusted to my care from Chihuahua. However, as I passed the windows of the sala, I had a good view of the lady, who was once celebrated as the belle of New Mexico. She is now a fat, comely dame of forty, with the remains of considerable beauty, but quite *passée.*

Our halting-place next day was at Bernalillo, a more miserable place than usual; but as I had brought letters to a wealthy haciendado, one Julian Peréa, I anticipated an unusual degree

211

of hospitality. On presenting the letter, everything Don Julian possessed was instantly thrown at my feet; but out of the magnificent gift I only selected an armful of wood, from a large yardfull, for our fire, and for which he charged me three *riales*, as well as three more for the use of an empty corral for the animals; we ourselves encamping outside his gate on the damp, thawing snow, without receiving the ghost of an invitation to enter his house.

We this day got a first glimpse of one of the spurs of the Rocky Mountains, appearing, far in the distance, white with snow.

On the 20th we encamped in a pretty valley on the Rio Grande, under a high tabular bluff which overhangs the river on the western bank, and on the summit of which are the ruins of an old Indian village. About two miles from our camp was the Pueblo of San Felipe, a village of the tribe of Indians known as Pueblos, or Indios Manzos—half-civilized Indians.

During the night our *mulada*, which was grazing at large in the prairie, was stampeded by the Indians. I was lying out some distance from the fire, when the noise of their thundering tread roused me, and, as they passed the fire at full gallop, I at once divined the cause. Luckily for me, Panchito, my horse, wheeled out of the crowd, and, followed by his mules, galloped up to the fire, and came to me when I whistled, the remainder of the *mulada* continuing their flight. The next morning two fine horses and three mules were missing, and, of course, were not recovered.

The next day we encamped on Galistéo, a small stream coming from the mountains. We had now entered a wild, broken country, covered with pine and cedar. A curious ridge runs from east to west, broken here and there by abrupt chasms, which exhibit its formation in alternate strata of shale and old red sandstone. There are here indications of coal, which are met along the whole of this ridge. We encamped on a bleak bluff, without timber or grass, which overlooked the stream. Late in the evening we heard the creaking of a wagon's wheels, and the wo-ha of the driver, as he urged his oxen up the sandy bluff. A wagon, drawn by six yoke of oxen, soon made its appearance, under the charge of a tall, raw-boned Yankee.

As soon as he had unyoked his cattle, he approached our fire, and, seating himself almost in the blaze, stretching his long legs at the same time into the ashes, he broke out with, "Cuss sich a darned country, I say! Wall, strangers, an ugly camp this, I swar; and what my cattle ull do I don't know, for they have not eat since we put out of Santa Fé, and are darned near giv out, that's a fact; and thar's nothin' here for 'em to eat, surely. Wall, they must just hold on till tomorrow, for I have only got a pint of corn apiece for 'em tonight anyhow, so there's no two ways about that. Strangers, I guess now you'll have a skillet among ye; if yer a mind to trade, I'll just have it right off; anyhow, I'll just borrow it tonight to bake my bread, and, if yer wish to trade, name your price. Cuss sich a darned country, say I! Jist look at them oxen, wull ye !—they've nigh upon two hundred miles to go, for I'm bound to catch up the sogers afore they reach the Pass, and there's not a go in 'em."

"Well," I ventured to put in, feeling for the poor beasts, which were still yoked and standing in the river completely done up, "would it not be as well for you to feed them at once and let them, rest?"

"Wall, I guess if you'll some of you lend ,me a hand, I'll fix 'em right off; tho', darn em! they've give me a pretty darned lot of trouble, they have, darn 'em! but the critters will have to eat, I b'lieve."

I willingly lent him the aid he required, and also added to their rations some corn which my animals, already full, were turning up their noses at, and which the oxen greedily devoured. This done, he returned to the fire and baked his cake, fried his bacon, and made his coffee, his tongue all the while keeping up an incessant clack. This man was by himself, having a journey of two hundred miles before him, and twelve oxen and his wagon to look after; but dollars, dollars, dollars was all he thought of.

Everything he saw lying about he instantly seized, wondered

213

what it cost, what it was worth, offered to trade for it or any-thing else by which he might turn a penny, never waiting for an answer, and rattling on, eating, drinking, and talking without intermission; and at last, gathering himself up, said, "Wall, I guess, I'll turn into my wagon now, and some of you will, may be, give a look round at the cattle every now and then, and I'll thank you;" and, saying this, with a hop, step, and a jump, was inside his wagon and snoring in a couple of minutes.

We broke up camp at daybreak, leaving our friend wo-ha-ing his cattle through the sandy bottom, and "cussing the darned country" at every step. We crossed several ridges clothed with cedars, but destitute of grass or other vegetation; and, passing over a dismal plain, descended into a hollow, where lay, at the bottom of a pine-covered mountain, the miserable mud-built Santa Fe; and, shortly after, way-worn and travel-stained, and my poor animals in a condition which plainly showed that they had seen some hard service, we entered the city, after a journey of not much less than two thousand miles.

CHAPTER 23

Arrive at Taos

Santa Fé, the capital of the province of Nuevo Mejico, contains about three thousand inhabitants, and is situated about fourteen miles from the left bank of the Del Norte, at the foot of a mountain forming one of the eastern chain of the Rocky Mountains. The town is a wretched collection of mud-houses, without a single building of stone, although it boasts a *palacio*—as the adobe residence of the governor is called—a long, low building, taking up the greater part of one side of the *plaza* or public square, round which runs a portal or colonnade supported by pillars of rough pine.

The appearance of the town defies description, and I can compare it to nothing but a dilapidated brick-kiln or a prairie-dog town. The inhabitants are worthy of their city, and a more miserable, vicious-looking population it would be impossible to imagine. Neither was the town improved, at the time of my visit, by the addition to the population of some three thousand Americans, the dirtiest, rowdiest crew I have ever seen collected together.

Crowds of drunken volunteers filled the streets, brawling and boasting, but never fighting; Mexicans, wrapped in *sarape*, scowled upon them as they passed; donkey-loads of *hoja*—corn-shucks—were hawking about for sale; and Pueblo Indians and priests jostled the rude crowds of brawlers at every step. Under the *portales* were numerous *monté*-tables, surrounded by Mexicans and Americans. Every other house was a grocery, as they call a gin or whisky shop, continually disgorging, reeling, drunken men, and every where filth and dirt reigned triumphant.

The extent of the province of New Mexico is difficult to define, as the survey of the northern sections of the republic has never been undertaken,[1] and a great portion of the country is still in the hands of the aborigines, who are at constant war with the Mexicans. It has been roughly estimated at six thousand square miles, with a population of seventy thousand, including the three castes of descendants of the original settlers, Mestizos, and Indies Manzos or Pueblos; the Mestizos, as is the case throughout the country, bearing a large proportion to the Mexico-Spanish portion of the population— in this case as fifty to one.

The Pueblos, who are the original inhabitants of New Mexico, and, living in villages, are partially civilized, are the most industrious portion of the population, and cultivate the soil in a higher degree than the New Mexicans themselves. In these Indians, in their dwellings, their manners, customs, and physical character, may be traced a striking analogy to the Aztecans or ancient Mexicans. Their houses and villages are constructed in the same manner as, from existing ruins, we may infer that the Aztecans constructed theirs. These buildings are of two, three, and even five stories, without doors or any external communication, the entrance being at the top by means of ladders through a trap-door in the *azotea* or flat roof. The population of the different Pueblos scattered along the Del Norte and to the westward of it is estimated at twelve thousand, without including the Moquis, who have preserved their independence since the year 1680.

The general character of the department is extreme aridity of soil, and the consequent deficiency of water, which must ever prevent its being thickly settled. The valley of the Del Norte is fertile, but of very limited extent; and other portions of the province are utterly valueless in an agricultural point of view,

---

1. Lieutenant Abert, of the U. S. T. Engineers, surveyed the greater portion of New Mexico in 1846.

and their metallic wealth is greatly exaggerated. From association with the hardy trappers and pioneers of the Far West, the New Mexicans have in some degree imbibed a portion of their enterprise and hardihood; for settlements have been pushed far into the Rocky Mountains, whose inhabitants are many of them expert buffalo-hunters and successful trappers of beaver. The most northern of these is on the Rio Colorado, or Red-River Creek, an affluent of the Del Norte, rising in the eastern chain of the Rocky Mountains, one hundred miles north of Santa Fé.

Of the many so-called gold-mines in New Mexico there is but one which has in any degree repaid the labour of working. This is El Real de Dolores, more commonly known as El Placer, situated eight leagues from Santa Fé, on the ridge of the *Sierra Obscura*. The gold is mostly found in what is technically called "dust," in very small quantities and with considerable labour. It has perhaps produced, since its discovery in 1828, two hundred thousand dollars; but it is very doubtful if any of these *placeres* would repay the working on a large scale.

It is a favourite idea with the New Mexicans that the Pueblo Indians are acquainted with the existence and localities of some prodigiously rich mines, which in the early times of the conquest were worked, by the Spaniards, at the expense of infinite toil and slavery on the part of the Indians; and that, fearing that such tyranny would be repeated if they were to disclose their secret, they have ever since steadily refused to point them out.

It is remarkable that, although existing from the earliest times of the colonization of New Mexico, a period of two centuries, in a state of continual hostility with the numerous savage tribes of Indians who surround their territory, and in constant insecurity of life and property from their attacks—being also far removed from the enervating influences of large cities, and, in their isolated situation, entirely dependent upon their own resources—the inhabitants are totally destitute of those qualities which, for the above reasons, we might naturally have expected to distinguish them, and are as deficient in energy of character and physical courage as they are in all the moral and intellectual

217

qualities.

In their social state but one degree removed from the veriest savages, they might take a lesson even from these in morality and the conventional decencies of life. Imposing no restraint on their passions, a shameless and universal concubinage exists, and a total disregard of moral laws, to which it would be impossible to find a parallel in any country calling itself civilized. A want of honourable principle, and consummate duplicity and treachery, characterize all their dealings. Liars by nature, they are treacherous and faithless to their friends, cowardly and cringing to their enemies: cruel, as all cowards are, they unite savage ferocity with their want of animal courage; as an example of which, their recent massacre of Governor Bent and other Americans may be given—one of a hundred instances.

I have before observed that a portion of the population of New Mexico consists of Indians, called Pueblos, from the fact of their living in towns, who are in a semi-civilized state, and in whose condition may be traced an analogy to the much exaggerated civilization of the ancient Mexicans. It is well known that, in the traditions of that people, the Aztecs migrated from the north, from regions beyond the Gila, where they made the first of their three great halts; but it is generally supposed that no traces of their course, or former habitation, existed to the northward of this river.

In the country of the Navajoses, as well as in the territories of the independent Moqui, are still discoverable traces of their residence, and, as I have before remarked, the Pueblo Indians construct and inhabit houses and villages of the same form and material as the "*casas grandes*" of the ancient Mexicans; retain many of their customs and domestic arts, as they have been handed down to us, and numerous traces of a common origin.

Among many of the religious forms still retained by these people, perhaps the most interesting is the perpetuation of the holy fire, by the side of which the Aztecan kept a continual watch for the return to earth of Quetzalcoatl—the god of air—who, according to their tradition, visited the earth, and instructed the inhabitants in agriculture and other useful arts. During his *sojourn* he caused the earth to yield tenfold productions, without the necessity of human labour; everywhere corn, fruit, and flowers delighted the eye; the cotton plant produced its woof already dyed by nature with various hues; aromatic odours pervaded the air; and on all sides resounded the melodious notes of singing-birds.

The lazy Mexican naturally looks back to this period as the "golden age;" and as this popular and beneficent deity, on his departure from earth, promised faithfully to return and revisit the people he loved so well, this event is confidently expected to the present day. Quetzalcoatl embarked, in his boat of rattlesnake-skins, on the Gulf of Mexico; and as he was seen to steer to the eastward, his arrival is consequently looked for from that quarter. When the Spaniards arrived from the east, as they resembled the god in the colour of their skin, they were at first generally supposed to be messengers from, or descendants of, the god of air.

This tradition is common to the nations even of the far-off north, and in New Mexico the belief is still clung to by the. Pueblo Indians, who, in a solitary cave of the mountains, have for centuries continued their patient vigils by the undying fire; and its dim light may still be seen by the wandering hunter glimmering from the recesses of a cave, when led by the chase, he passes in the vicinity of this humble and lonely temple.

Far to the north, in the country of the Moquis. the hunters have passed, wonderingly, ruins of large cities, and towns inhabited by Indians, of the same construction as those of the Pueblos, and identical with the *casas grandes* on the Gila and elsewhere.

In the absence of any evidence, traditionary or otherwise, on which to found an hypothesis as to the probable cause of the migration of the Mexicans from the north, I have surmised that it is just possible that they may have abandoned that region on account of the violent volcanic convulsions which, from the testimony of people who have visited these regions, I have no doubt have at a comparatively recent period agitated that portion of the country; and from my own knowledge the volcanic formations become gradually more recent as they advance to the north along the whole table-land from Mexico to Santa Fé. These disturbances may have led to their frequent changes of residence, and ultimate arrival in the south.

If their object was to fly from such constantly-recurring commotions, their course would naturally be to the south, where they might expect a genial soil and climate, in a direction in which they might also avoid the numerous and warlike nations who inhabited the regions south of their abandoned country. Thus we find the remains of the towns built in the course of their migration, generally in insulated spots of fertility, oases in the vast and barren tracts they were obliged to traverse, which spread from the shores of the great salt-lake of the north toward the valley of the Gila, still southward along the ridges of the Cordillera, which, a continuation of the Andes chain, stretch far away to the southern portion of the country.

The Indians of Northern Mexico, including the Pueblos, belong to the same family—the Apache; from which branch the Navajos, Apaches, Coyoteros, Mescaleros, Moquis, Yubipias, Maricopas, Chiricaquis, Chemeguabas, Yumayas (the last two tribes of the Moqui), and the Nijoras, a small tribe on the Gila. All these speak dialects of the same language, more or less approximating to the Apache, and of all of which the idiomatic structure is the same. They likewise all understand each other's tongue. What relation this language bears to the Mexican is unknown, but my impression is that it will be found to assimilate greatly, if not to be identical.

The Pueblo Indians of Taos, Pecuris, and Acoma speak a language of which a dialect is used by those of the Rio Abajo, including the Pueblos of San Felipe, Sandia, Ysleta, and Xeméz. They are eminently distinguished from the New Mexicans in their social and moral character, being industrious, sober, honest, brave, and at the same time peaceably inclined if their rights are not infringed. Although the Pueblos are nominally Cristianos, and have embraced the outward forms of *la santa fé Catolica*, they yet, in fact, still cling to the belief of their fathers, and celebrate in secret the ancient rites of their religion.

The aged and devout of both sexes may still be often seen on their flat house-tops, with their faces turned to the rising sun, and their gaze fixed in that direction from whence they expect, sooner or later, the god of air will make his appearance. They are careful, however, not to practice any of their rites before strangers, and ostensibly conform to the ceremonies of the Roman church.'

In the country of the Moquis are the remains of five cities of considerable extent, the foundations and some of the walls of which (of stone) are still standing, and on the sites of some they still inhabit villages, the houses of which are frequently built of the mate*riales* found among the ruins. A great quantity of broken pottery is found wherever these remains exist, the same in form and material as the relics of the same kind preserved in the city of Mexico. The ruins on the Gila, in particular, abound in these remains, and I have been assured that for many miles the plain is strewed with them. There are also remains of *acequias*, or irrigating canals, of great length and depth.

The five *pueblos* in the Moqui are Orayxa, Masanais, Jongoapi, Gualpa, and another, the name of which is not known. This tribe is, curiously enough, known to the trappers and hunters of the mountains as the Welsh Indians. They are, they say, much fairer in complexion than other tribes, and have several individuals among them perfectly white, with light hair. The latter circumstance is accounted for by the frequent occurrence among the Navajos, and probably the Moquis also, of albinos, with the Indian feature, but light complexions, eyes, and hair.

In connection with this, I may mention a curious circumstance which happened to me, and tends to show that there is some little foundation for the belief of the trappers, that the Moqui Indians are descendants of the followers of Prince Madoc.

I happened, on my arrival at the frontier of the United States (at Fort Leavenworth), to enter the log hut of an old negro woman, being at the time in my mountain attire of buckskins, over which was thrown a Moqui or Navajo blanket, as it was wet weather. The old dame's attention was called to it by its varied and gaudy colours, and, examining it carefully for some time, she exclaimed, "That's a Welsh blanket; I know it by the woof!"

She had, she told me, in her youth, lived for many years in a Welsh family and in a Welsh settlement in Virginia, or one of the southern states, and had learned their method of working, which was the same as that displayed in my blanket. The blankets and *tilmas* manufactured by the Navajos, Moquis, and the Pueblos, are of excellent quality, and dyed in durable and bright colours: the warp is of cotton filled with wool, the texture close and impervious to rain.

Their pottery is, as I have before remarked, the same as that manufactured by the Aztecs, painted in bright patterns by coloured earths and the juice of several plants. The dress of the Pueblos is a mixture of their ancient costume with that introduced by the Spaniards. A *tilma*, or small blanket without sleeves, is worn over the shoulder, and their legs and feet are protected by moccasins and leggings of deerskin or woollen stuff. Their heads are uncovered, and their hair long and unconfined, save the centre or scalp-lock, which is usually bound with gay-coloured ribbon. The women's dress is the same as that of the squaws of the wild Indians of the prairies, generally covered with a bright-coloured blanket, or a mantle of cloth.

The Pueblo Indians have been more than once the chief actors in the many insurrections which have disturbed this remote province. In 1837 they overturned the government, killing the incapable man at the head of it, as they had done his predecessor, and placing one of their own party at the head of affairs. Recently they rose upon the Americans, who have taken possession of the country, and, in conjunction with the Mexicans, massacred Governor Bent and many others.

They were defeated by the American troops in a pitched battle at La Cañada, but defended most gallantly their chief *pueblo* (of Taos), which was taken and destroyed after a desperate resistance.

Although I had determined to remain some time in Santa Fé to recruit my animals, I was so disgusted with the filth of the town, and the disreputable society a stranger was forced into, that in a very few days I once more packed my mules, and proceeded to the north, through the valley of Taos.

It was a cold, snowy day on which I left Santa Fé, and the mountain, although here of inconsiderable elevation, was difficult to cross on account of the drifts. My mules, too, were for the first time introduced to snow on a large scale, and, by their careful, mincing steps and cautious movements, testified their doubts, as to the security of such a road.

The mountain is covered with pine and cedar, and the road winds through the bed of an *arroyo*, between high banks now buried in the snow. Not a living thing was visible, but once a large gray wolf was surprised on our turning a corner of rock, and in his hurry to escape plunged into a snowdrift, where I could easily have dispatched the animal with a pistol, but Panchito was in such a state of affright that nothing would induce him to stand still or approach the spot.

Over ridges and through mountain-gorges we passed into a small valley, where the *pueblo* of Ohuaqui afforded me shelter for the night, and a warm stable with plenty of corn for my animals, a luxury they had long been unaccustomed to.

I was here made welcome by the Indian family, who prepared my supper of *frijoles* and *atole*, the last the dish of New Mexico. It is made of the Indian meal, mixed with water into a thick gruel, and thus eaten—an insipid compound. Far more agreeable is the *pinele* of the *tierra afuera*, which is the meal of parched maize, mixed with sugar and spices, and of which a handful in a pint of water makes a most cooling and agreeable drink, and is the great stand-by of the *arrieros* and road travellers in that starving country.

The *patrona* of the family seemed rather shy of me at first, until, in the course of conversation, she discovered that I was an Englishman. "*Gracias à Dios*," she exclaimed, "a Christian will

223

sleep with us tonight, and not an American!"

I found over all New Mexico that the most bitter feeling and most determined hostility existed against the Americans, who certainly in Santa Fé and elsewhere have not been very anxious to conciliate the people, but by their bullying and overbearing demeanour toward them, have in a great measure been the cause of this hatred, which shortly after broke out in an organized rising of the northern part of the province, and occasioned great loss of life to both parties.

After supper the women of the family spread the floor with blankets, and every one, myself included, cigar in mouth, lay down—to the number of fifteen—in a space of less than that number of square feet; men, women, and children, all smoking and chattering. Just over my head were roosting several fowls; and one venerable cock every five minutes saluted us with a shrill crow, to the infinite satisfaction of the old Indian, who at every fresh one exclaimed, "*Ay, como canta mi gallo, tan claro!*"— how clear sings my cock, the fine fellow!

"*Valgame Dios! que paxarito tan hermoso!*"—what a lovely little bird is this !

The next day, passing the miserable village of La Cañada, and the Indian *pueblo* of San Juan, both situated in a wretched, sterile-looking country, we reached El Embudo—the funnel— where I put up in the house of an old Canadian trapper, who had taken to himself a Mexican wife, and was ending his days as a quiet *ranchero*. He appeared to have forgotten the plenty of the mountains, for his pretty daughter set before us for supper a plate containing six small pieces of fat pork, like dice, floating in a sea of grease, hot and red with *chile colorado*.

We crossed, next day, a range of mountains covered with pine and cedar: on the latter grew great quantities of mistletoe, and the contrast of its bright green and the sombre hue of the cedars was very striking. The snow was melting on the ascent, which was exposed to the sun, and made the road exceedingly slippery and tiring to the animals.

On reaching the summit a fine prospect presented itself. The

Rocky Mountains, stretching away on each side of me, here divided into several branches, whose isolated peaks stood out in bold relief against the clear, cold sky. Valleys and plains lay between them, through which the river wound its way in deep *cañons*. In the distance was the snowy summit of the Sierra Nevada, bright with the rays of the setting sun, and at my feet lay the smiling vale of Taos, with its numerous villages and the curiously constructed pueblos of the Indians. Snow-covered, mountains surrounded it, whose ridges were flooded with light, while the valley was almost shrouded in gloom and darkness.

On descending I was obliged to dismount and lead my horse, whose feet, balled with snow, were continually slipping from under him. After sunset the cold was intense, and wading through the snow, my moccasins became frozen, so that I was obliged to travel quickly to prevent my feet from being frost-bitten.

It was quite dark when I reached the plain, and the night was so obscure that the track was perfectly hidden, and my only guide was the distant lights of the villages. Coming to a frozen brook, the mules refused to cross the ice, and I spent an hour in fruitless attempts to induce them. I could find nothing at hand with which to break the ice, and at length, half frozen, was obliged to turn back and retrace my steps to a *rancho*, which the Indian boy who was my guide said was about a mile distant.

This I at length reached, though not before one of my feet was frost-bitten, and my hands so completely numbed by the excessive cold that I was unable to unpack the mules when I got in. To protect the poor animals from the cold, as there was no stable to place them in, I devoted the whole of my bedding to cover them, reserving to myself only a *sarape*, which, however, by the side of a blazing wood fire, was sufficient to keep me warm. The good lady of the house sent me a huge bowl of *atole* as I was engaged in clothing the animals, which I offered to Panchito as soon as the messenger's back was turned, and he swallowed it, boiling hot as it was, with great gusto.

The next morning, with the assistance of some *rancheros*, I crossed the stream, and arrived at Fernandez, which is the most considerable village in the valley.

CHAPTER 24

Adios Mejico!

El Valle de Taos is situated about eighty miles to the north-ward of Santa Fé, on the eastern side of the Del Norte. It contains several villages or *rancherias*, the largest of which are Fernandez and El Rancho. The population of the valley may be estimated at eight thousand, including the Pueblo Indians. The soil is exceedingly fertile, and produces excellent wheat and other grain. The climate being rigorous, and the summers short, fruit does not ripen to perfection, but vegetables of all kinds are good and abundant, onions in particular growing to great size and of excellent flavour.

The climate is colder than at Santa Fé, the thermometer sometimes falling to zero in winter, and seldom rising above 75° in summer; the nights in summer being delightfully cool, but in winter piercingly cold. Although generally healthy, infectious disorders are sometimes prevalent and fatal; and periodical epidemics have on several occasions nearly decimated the inhabitants.

In all maps the valley of Taos is confounded with a city which under that name appears in them, but which does not exist, Fernandez being the chief town of the valley, and no such town as Taos to be found. The valley derives its name from the Taoses, a tribe of Indians who once inhabited it, and the remains of which inhabit a *pueblo* under the mountain, about seven miles from Fernandez. Humboldt mentions Taos as a city containing eight thousand nine hundred inhabitants. Its latitude is about 36°

30', longitude between 105° 30' and 106° west of Greenwich, but its exact position has never been accurately determined. The extent of the valley from El Rancho to Arroyo Hondo is seventeen miles, the breadth from the Del Norte to the mountains about the same.

Several distilleries are worked both at Fernandez and El Rancho, the latter better known to the Americans as The Ranch. Most of them belong to Americans, who are generally trappers and hunters, who, having married Taos women, have settled here. The Taos whisky, a raw, fiery spirit which they manufacture, has a ready market in the mountains among the trappers and hunters, and the Indian traders, who find the "fire water" the most profitable article of trade with the aborigines, who exchange for it their buffalo robes and other peltries at a "tremendous sacrifice."

In Fernandez I was hospitably entertained in the house of an American named Lee, who had for many years traded and trapped in the mountains, but who now, having married a Mexican woman, had set up a distillery and was amassing a considerable fortune. He gave me a pressing invitation to stop the winter with him, which I was well inclined to accept, if I could have obtained good pasture for my animals; that, however, was not to be had, and I continued my journey.

A few days after my departure, Lee's house was attacked by the Mexicans, at the time when they massacred Governor Bent in the same village, and himself killed, with every foreigner in the place, excepting the brother of Lee, who was protected by the priest and saved by him from the savage fury of the mob.

Bent, as well as Lee, had resided many years in New Mexico, both having wives and children in the country, and were supposed to have been much esteemed by the people. The former was an old trader among the Indians, and the owner of Bent's Fort, or Fort William, a trading-post on the Arkansas, well known for its hospitality to travellers in the Far West.

From his knowledge of the country and the Mexican character, Mr. Bent had been appointed governor of New Mexico by

General Kearney, and it was during a temporary visit to his family at Fernandez that he was killed in their presence, and scalped and mutilated, by a mob of Pueblos and the people of Taos.

William Bent was one of those hardy sons of enterprise with whom America abounds, who, from love of dangerous adventure, forsake the quiet, monotonous life of the civilized world for the excitement of a *sojourn* in the Far West. For many years he traded with Indians on the Platte and Arkansas, winning golden opinions from the poor Indians for his honesty and fair dealing, and the greatest popularity from the hardy trappers and mountaineers for his firmness of character and personal bravery.

Notwithstanding the advice I received not to attempt such a journey at this season, I determined to cross the mountains and winter on the other side, either at the head of Arkansas or Platte, or in some of the mountain-valleys, which are the wintering-places of many of the trappers and mountain-men. I therefore hired a half breed Pueblo as a guide, who, by the by, was one of the most rascally-looking of rascally Mexicans, and on the first of January was once more on my way.

I left Fernandez late in the day, as I intended to proceed only twelve miles to Arroyo Hondo, and there remain for the night. After proceeding a mile or two, we came to a stream about thirty feet in breadth and completely frozen. Here the mules came to a stop, rind nothing would induce them to attempt to cross. Even the last resource, that of crossing myself on Panchito, and pretending to ride away with their favourite, entirely failed, although they ran up and down bellowing with affright, smelling the ice, feeling it with their forefeet, and, throwing up their beads, would gallop to another point, and up and down, in great commotion.

At length I had to take a pole, which was opportunely lying near, and break the ice away, having to remove the broken blocks entirely before they would attempt it. With all this, however, my old hunting-mule still refused; but, as I knew it would not be left behind, I proceeded on with the rest. At this the hunting-mule became frantic, galloped away from the river, returned, bellowed and cried, and at last, driven to desperation, it made a jump right into the air, but not near the broken place, and came down like a lump of lead on the top of the ice, which, of course, smashed under its weight, and down it went into a deep hole, its head just appearing out of the water, which was "mush" with ice.

In this "fix" the mule remained perfectly still, apparently conscious that its own exertions would be unavailing; and I therefore had to return, and, up to my middle in water, break it out of the ice, expecting every moment to see it drop, frozen to death. At last, and with great labour, I extricated it, when it at once ran up to the horse and hinnied its delight at the meeting.

By this time it was pitchy dark, and the cold had become intense; my moccasins and deerskin leggings were frozen hard and stiff, and my feet and legs in a fair way of becoming in the same state. There was no road or track, the snow everywhere covering the country, and my guide had evidently lost his way. However, I asked him in which direction he thought Arroyo Hondo to be, and pushed straight on for it, floundering through the snow, and falling into holes and ravines, and at length was brought to a dead halt, my horse throwing himself on his haunches, and just saving his master and himself a fall down a precipice some five hundred feet in depth, which formed one side of the Arroyo Hondo.

The lights of the *rancho* to which we were bound twinkled at the bottom, but to attempt to reach it, without knowing the road down the ravine, was like jumping from the top of the Monument. However, as I felt I was on the point of freezing to death, I became desperate and charged the precipice, intending to roll down with Panchito, if we could not do better; but the horse refused to move, and presently, starting to one side as I spurred him, fell headlong into a snow-drift some twenty feet in depth, where I lay under him; and, satisfied in my mind that I was "*in extremis*," wished myself farther from Arroyo Hondo and deplored my evil destiny.

Panchito, however, managed to kick himself out; and I, half smothered and with one of my ribs disabled, soon followed his example, and again mounted. We presently came to a little adobe house, and a man, hearing our cries to each other in the dark, came out with a light.

To my request for a night's lodging he replied, "*No se puede, no habia mas que un quartito*"—that there was no room, but one little chamber, but that at the *rancho* I would be well accommodated. With this hint 1 moved on, freezing in my saddle, and again attempted to descend, but the darkness was pitchy, and the road a wall. While attempting the descent once more, a light appeared on the bank above us, and a female voice crying out, "*Vuelvase, amigo, por Dios! que no se baja*"—return, friend, for God's sake! and don't attempt to go down.

"*Que vengan, pobrecitos, para calentarse*"—come, poor fellows, and warm yourselves.

"*Por hi se sube, por hi*"—this way; this is the way up—she cried to us, holding up the light to direct our steps.

"*Ay de mi, como suffren los pobres viageros!*"—alas, what poor travellers suffer!—she exclaimed, eying our frozen appearance, and clothes white with snow; and, still holding up the light, she led the way to her house, where now, lectured by his wife for his inhospitality, the man who had sent us away from his door bestirred himself to unpack the mules, which, with our numbed hands, it was impossible for us to do.

A little shed full of corn-shucks (the leaf of the maize, of which animals are very fond) provided a warm shelter for the shivering beasts; and having attended to their wants, and piled before them enough hoja for a regiment of cavalry, I entered the house where half a dozen women were soon rubbing life into my hands and feet, which were badly frost-bitten, while others were busy preparing *atole* and *chile*, and making tortillas on the hearth.

A white stone marks this day of my journey, when, for the first time, I met with native hospitality on Arroyo Hondo. In this family, which consisted of about fifteen souls, six were on their beds, suffering from *sarampion*—the measles—which was at the time of my journey carrying off many victims in Santa Fé and

231

Taos Valley. An old crone was busy decocting simples in a large *olla* over the fire. She asked me to taste it, giving it the name of *aciete de vivoras*—rattlesnake-oil; and as I expressed my disgust by word and deed at the intimation, which just saved my taking a gulp, the old lady was convulsed with laughter, giving me to understand that it was not really viper-oil, but was so called—*no mas.*

This pot, when cooked, was set on one side, and all the patients, one after the other, crawled from their blankets and imbibed the decoction from a gourd. One of the sick was the mother of the family, who had run after us to bring us back when her husband had told her of our situation—one instance of the many which I have met of the kindness of heart of Mexican women.

The next morning we descended into the Arroyo, and even in daylight the track down was exceedingly dangerous, and to have attempted it in the dark would have been an act of no little temerity. On the other bank of the stream was situated a mill and distillery belonging to an American by the name of Turley, who had quite a thriving establishment. Sheep and goats, and innumerable hogs, ran about the corral; his barns were filled with grain of all kinds, his mill with flour, and his cellars with whisky "in galore."

Everything about the place betokened prosperity. Rosy children, uniting the fair complexions of the Anglo-Saxon with the dark tint of the Mexican, gambolled before the door. The Mexicans and Indians at work in the yard were stout, well-fed fellows, looking happy and contented; as well they might, for no one in the country paid so well, and fed so well, as Turley, who bore the reputation, far and near, of being as generous and kind-hearted as he was reported to be rich. In times of scarcity no Mexican ever besought his assistance and went away empty-handed. His granaries were always open to the hungry, and his purse to the poor.

Three days after I was there they attacked his house, burned his mill, destroyed his grain and his live stock, and inhumanly butchered himself and the foreigners with him, after a gallant defence of twenty-four hours—nine men against five hundred. Such is Mexican gratitude.

I here laid in a small supply of provisions, flour and dried buffalo meat, and got, besides, a good breakfast—rather a memorable occurrence. Just as I arrived, a party of Mormons, who had left Colonel Cooke's command on their way to California, and were now about to cross the mountains to join a large body of their people who were wintering on the Arkansas, intending to proceed to California in the ensuing spring, were on the point of starting.

There were some twelve or fifteen of them, raw-boned fanatics, with four or five pack-mules carrying their provisions, themselves on foot: They started several hours before me; but I overtook them before they had crossed the mountain, straggling along, some seated on the top of the mules' packs, some sitting down every few hundred yards, and all looking tired and miserable. One of the party was an Englishman, from Biddenden, in Kent, and an old Peninsular soldier. I asked what could have induced him to have undertaken such an expedition. He looked at me, and, without answering the question, said, "Dang it, if I only once get hoam!"

Arroyo Hondo runs along the base of a ridge of mountain of moderate elevation, which divides the valley of Taos from that of Rio Colorado, or Red River, both running into, the Del Norte. The trail from one to the other runs through and over the mountain, a distance of about twelve miles. It is covered with pine and cedar, and a species of dwarf oak; and numerous small streamlets run through the cañons and gorges. Near these grows plentifully a shrub which produces a fruit called by the mountaineers service-berries, of a dark blue, the size of a small grape, and of very pleasant flavour.

My animals, unused to mountain travelling, proceeded very slowly. Every little stream of frozen water was the cause of delay. The mules, on reaching the brink, always held a council of war, smelled and tried it with their forefeet, and bellowed forth their

233

dislike of the slippery bridge. Coronela, my hunting-mule, since its mishap at Fernandez, was always the first to cross, but I had first to strew the ice with branches, or throw a blanket over it, before I could induce them to pass; and at last, tired of the delays thus occasioned, I passed with the horse, and left the mules to use their own discretion, although not unfrequently half an hour or more would elapse before they overtook me.

All this day I marched on foot through the snow, as Panchito made sad work of ascending and descending the mountain, and it was several hours after sunset when I arrived at Rio Colorado, with one of my feet badly frozen. In the settlement, which boasted about twenty houses, on inquiry as to where I could procure a corral and *hoja* for the animals, I was directed to the house of a French Canadian—an old trapper named Laforey— one of the many who are found in these remote settlements, with Mexican wives, and passing the close of their adventurous lives in what to them is a state of ease and plenty; that is, they grow sufficient maize to support them, their faithful and well-tried rifles furnishing them with meat in abundance, to be had in all the mountains for the labour of hunting.

I was obliged to remain here two days, for my foot was so badly frozen that I was quite unable to put it to the ground. In this place I found that the Americans were in bad odour; and as I was equipped as a mountaineer, I came in for a tolerable share of abuse whenever I limped through the village. As my lameness prevented me from pursuing my tormentors, they were unusually daring, saluting me, every time I passed to the shed where my animals were corralled, with cries of "*Burro, burro, ven a comer hoja*" (Jackass, jackass, come here and eat shucks), "*Anda coxo, a ver los burros, sus hermanos*" (Hallo, game-leg, go and see your brothers, the donkeys); and at last, words not being found heavy enough, pieces of adobe rattled at my ears.

This, however, was a joke rather too practical to be pleasant; so, the next time I limped to the stable, I carried my rifle on my shoulder, which was a hint never to be mistaken by a Mexican, and hereafter I passed with impunity. However, I was obliged to watch my animals day and night, for, as soon as I fed them, either the corn was bodily stolen, or a herd of hogs was driven in to feed at my expense. The latter aggression I put a stop to by administering to one persevering porker a pill from my rifle, and promised the threatening crowd that I would have as little compunction in letting the same amount of daylight into them if I caught them thieving the provender; and they seemed to think me in earnest, for I missed no more corn or shucks.

I saw plainly enough however, that my remaining here, with such a perfectly lawless and ruffianly crew, was likely to lead me into some trouble, if, indeed, my life was not in absolute danger, which, from what occurred shortly after, I have no doubt it was; and therefore I only waited until my foot was sufficiently recovered to enable me to resume my journey across the mountains.

The fare in Laforey's house was what might be expected in a hunter's establishment: venison, antelope, and the meat of the *carnero cimarron*, the Rocky Mountain sheep, furnished his larder; and such meat (poor and tough at this season of the year), with cakes of Indian meal, either *tortillas* or *gorditas*,[1] furnished the daily bill of fare. The absence of coffee he made the theme of regret at—every meal, bewailing his misfortune in not having, at that particular moment, a supply of this article, which he never before was without, and which, I may here observe, among the hunters and trappers, when in camp or rendezvous, is considered as an indispensable necessary.

Coffee, being very cheap in the states, is the universal beverage of the western people, and finds its way to the mountains in the packs of the Indian traders, who retail it to the mountain-men at the moderate price of from two to six dollars the half-pint cup. However, my friend, Laforey, was never known to possess any, and his lamentations were only intended to soften my heart, as he thought (erroneously) that I must certainly carry a supply with me.

"*Sacré enfant de Gârce,*" he would exclaim, mixing English,

---

1. The *tortilla* is a round, flat pancake, made of the Indian corn-meal; the *gordita* is of the same material, but thicker.

French, and Spanish into a *puchero*-like" jumble, "*voyez-vous* dat I vas *nevare tan pauvre* as dis time; *mais* before I vas *siempre avec* plenty *café*, plenty *sucre; mais* now, God dam, I not go à Santa Fé, God dam, and mountain-men dey come *aqui* from *autre côté*, drink all my *café*. *Sacré enfant de Gârce, nevare* I vas *tan pauvre* as dis time, God dam. I not care *comer* meat, *ni frijole, ni* corn, *mais* widout *café* I no live. I hunt may be two, three day, may be one week, *mais* I eat notin; *mais sin café, enfant de Gârce*, I no live, *parceque* me not *sacré Espagñol, mais* one Frenchman."

Rio Colorado is the last and most northern settlement of Mexico, and is distant from Vera Cruz two thousand miles. It contains, perhaps, fifteen families, or a population of fifty souls, including one or two Yuta Indians, by sufferance of whom the New Mexicans have settled this valley, thus insuring to the politic savages a supply of corn or cattle without the necessity of undertaking a raid on Taos or Santa Fé whenever they require a remount. This was the reason given me by a Yuta for allowing the encroachment on their territory.

The soil of the valley is fertile, the little strip of land which comprises it yielding grain in abundance, and being easily irrigated from the stream, the banks of which are low. The plain abounds with alegria, the plant from which the juice is extracted with which the belles of Nuevo Mejico cosmetically preserve their complexions. The neighbouring mountains afford plenty of large game—deer, bears, mountain-sheep, and elk; and the plains are covered with countless herds of antelope, which, in the winter, hang about the foot of the *sierras*, which shield them from the icy winds.

No state of society can be more wretched or degrading than the social and moral condition of the inhabitants of New Mexico; but in this remote settlement, anything I had formerly imagined to be the *ne plus ultra* of misery fell far short of the reality—such is the degradation of the people of the Rio Colorado. Growing a bare sufficiency for their own support, they hold the little land they cultivate, and their wretched hovels, on sufferance from the barbarous Yutas, who actually tolerate their presence in their country for the sole purpose of having at their command a stock of grain and a herd of mules and horses, which they make no scruple of helping themselves to, whenever they require a remount or a supply of farinaceous food.

Moreover, when a war expedition against a hostile tribe has failed, and no scalps have been secured to insure the returning warriors a welcome to their village, the Rio Colorado is a kind of game-preserve, where the Yutas have a certainty of filling their bag if their other covers draw blank. Here they can always depend upon procuring a few brace of Mexican scalps, when such trophies are required for a war-dance or other festivity, without danger to themselves, and merely for the trouble of fetching them.

Thus, half the year, the settlers fear to leave their houses, and their corn and grain often remain uncut, the Indians- being near; thus the valiant Mexicans refuse to leave the shelter of their burrows even to secure their only food. At these times their sufferings are extreme, being reduced to the verge of starvation; and the old Canadian hunter told me that he and his son entirely supported the people on several occasions by the produce of their rifles, while the maize was lying rotting in the fields. There are sufficient men in the settlement to exterminate the Yutas, were they not entirely devoid of courage; but, as it is, they allow themselves to be bullied and ill treated with the most perfect impunity.

Against these same Indians a party of a dozen Shawnee and Delaware trappers waged a long and most destructive war, until at last the Yutas were fain to beg for peace, after losing many of their most famous warriors and chiefs. The cowardly Mexicans, however, have seldom summoned courage to strike a blow in their own defence, and are so thoroughly despised by their savage enemies, that they never scruple to attack them, however large the party, or in spite of the greatest disparity in numbers between them.

On the third day, the inflammation in my frost-bitten foot having in some measure subsided, I again packed my mules, and, under a fusillade of very hard names from the *pelados*, turned my back on Mexico and the Mexicans.

Laforey escorted me out of the settlement to point out the trail (for roads now had long ceased), and, bewailing his hard fate in not having "plenty *café avec sucre*, God dam," with a concluding *enfant de Gârce*, bid me goodbye, and recommended me to mind my hair—in other words, look out for my scalp. Cresting a bluff which rose from the valley, I turned in my saddle, took a last look at the adobes, and, without one regret, cried "*Adios, Mejico!*"

I had now turned my back on the last settlement, and felt a thrill of pleasure as I looked at the wild expanse of snow which lay before me, and the towering mountains which frowned on all sides, and knew that now I had seen the last (for some time at least) of civilized man under the garb of a Mexican *sarape*.

CHAPTER 25

Sufferings from Cold

Our course, on leaving Red River, was due north, my object being to strike the Arkansas near its head-waters on the other side of the Rocky Mountains, and follow as near as possible the Yuta trail, which these Indians use in passing from the Del Norte to the Bayou Salado, on their annual buffalo-hunts to that elevated valley.

Skirting a low range of mountains, the trail passes a valley upward of fifty miles in length, intersected by numerous streams (called creeks by the mountain-men), which rise in the neighbouring highlands, and fall into the Del Norte, near its upper waters. Our first day's journey, of about twenty-five miles, led through the uplands at the southern extremity of the valley. These are covered with pine and cedar, and the more open plains with bushes of wild sage, which is the characteristic plant in all the elevated plains of the Rocky Mountains.

On emerging from the uplands, we entered a level prairie, covered with innumerable herds of antelope. These graceful animals, in bands containing several thousands, trotted up to us, and, with pointed ears and their beautiful eyes staring with eager, curiosity, accompanied us for miles, running parallel to our trail within fifty or sixty yards.

The cold in these regions is more intense than I ever remember to have experienced, not even excepting in Lower Canada; and when a northerly wind sweeps over the bleak and barren plains, charged as it is with its icy re-enforcements from the snow-clad mountains, it assails the unfortunate traveller, exposed to all its violence, with blood-freezing blasts, piercing to his very heart and bones.

Such was the state of congelation I was in on this day, that even the shot-tempting antelope bounded past unscathed. My hands, with fingers of stone, refused even to hold the reins of my horse, who travelled as he pleased, sometimes sluing round his stern to the wind, which was "dead ahead." Mattias, the half-breed, who was my guide, enveloped from head to foot in blanket, occasionally cast a longing glance from out its folds at the provoking venison as it galloped past, muttering at intervals, "Jesus, Jesus, *que carne*"—what meat we're losing!

At length, as a band of some three thousand almost ran over us, human nature, although at freezing-point, could no longer stand it. I jumped off Panchito, and, kneeling down, sent a ball from my rifle right into the "thick" of the band. At the report two antelopes sprung into the air, their forms being distinct against the horizon above the backs of the rest; and when the herd had passed, they were lying kicking in the dust, one shot in the neck, through which the ball had passed into the body of another. We packed a mule with the choice pieces of the meat, which was a great addition to our slender stock of dried provisions.

As I was "butchering" the antelope, half a dozen wolves hung round the spot, attracted by the smell of blood; they were so tame, and hungry at the same time, that I thought they would actually have torn the meat from under my knife. Two of them loped round and round, gradually decreasing their distance, occasionally squatting on their haunches, and licking their impatient lips, in anxious expectation of a coming feast. I threw a large piece of meat toward them, when the whole gang jumped upon it, fighting and growling, and tearing each other in the furious *mêlée*.

I am sure I might have approached near enough to have seized one by the tail, so entirely regardless of my vicinity did they appear. They were doubtless rendered more ravenous than usual by the uncommon severity of the weather, and, from the fact of the antelope congregating in large bands, were unable to prey upon these animals, which are their favourite food. Although rarely attacking a man, yet in such seasons as the present I have no doubt that they would not hesitate to charge upon a solitary traveller in the night, particularly as in winter they congregate in troops of from ten to fifty. They are so abundant in the mountains, that the hunter takes no notice of them, and seldom throws away upon the skulking beasts a charge of powder and lead.

This night we camped on Rib Creek, the Costilla of the New Mexican hunters, where there was no grass for our poor animals, and the creek was frozen to such a depth, that, after the greatest exertions in breaking a hole through the ice, which was nearly a foot thick, they were unable to reach the water. It is a singular fact that during intense cold horses and mules suffer more from want of water than in the hottest weather, and often perish in the mountains when unable to procure it for two or three days in the frozen creeks.

Although they made every attempt to drink, the mules actually kneeling in their endeavours to reach the water, I was obliged to give it them, one after the other, from a small tin cup which held half a pint, and from which the thirsty animals greedily drank. This tedious process occupied me more than an hour, after winch there was another hour's work in hunting for wood, and packing it on our backs into camp. Before we had a fire going it was late in the night, and almost midnight before we had found a little grass and picketed the animals; all of which duties at last being effected, we cooked our collops of antelope-meat, smoked a pipe, and rolled ourselves in our blankets before the fire. All night long the camp was surrounded by wolves, which approached within a few feet of the fire, and their eyes shone like coals as they hovered in the bushes, attracted by the savoury smell of the roasting venison.

The next day we struck La Culebra, or Snake Creek, where we saw that the party of Mormons had encamped, and apparently halted a day, for more than ordinary pains had been taken to make their camp comfortable, and several piles of twigs, of the sage-bush and rushes, remained, of which they had made teds. However, we were obliged to go farther down the creek, as there was no firewood near the point where the trail crosses it, and there found a sheltered place with tolerable grass, and near an air-hole in the ice where the animals could drink.

I remarked that in the vicinity of the Mormon camp no watering-place had been made for their animals, and, as we had seen no holes broken in the ice of the creeks we had passed, I concluded that these people had allowed their animals to shift for themselves, the consequences of which negligence were soon apparent in our farther advance.

The cold was so intense that I blanketed all my animals, and even then expected that some of the mules would have perished; for it snowed heavily during the night, and the storm ended in a watery sleet, which froze as soon as it fell, and in the morning the animals were covered with a sheet of ice. We ourselves suffered extremely, turning constantly, and rolling almost into the embers of the scanty fire; and toward daybreak I really thought I should have frozen bodily. My bedding consisted of two blankets—one of them a very thin one, which was all I had between my body and the snow; and the other, first soaked with the sleet and afterward frozen stiff and hard, was more like a board than a blanket, and was in that state no protection against the cold. It is well known that the coldest period of the twenty-four hours is that immediately preceding the dawn of day.

At this time one is generally awakened by the sensation of death-like chill, which penetrates into the very bones; and as the fire is by this time usually extinguished, or merely smouldering in the ashes, the duty of replenishing is a very trying process. To creep out of the blanket and face the cutting blast requires no little resolution; and, if there be more than one person in the camp, the horrible moment is put off by the first roused, in hopes that someone else will awaken and perform the duty.

However, should the coughs and hems succeed in rousing all, it is ten to one but that all with a blank look at the cheerless prospect, cover their heads with the blanket, and, with a groan, cuddling into a ball, resettle themselves to sleep, leaving the most chilly victim to perform the office.

The half-frozen animals, standing over their picket-pins and collapsed with cold, seem almost drawn within themselves, and occasionally approach the fire as close as their *lariats* will allow, bending down their noses to the feeble warmth, the breath in steaming volumes of cloud issuing from their nostrils, while their bodies are thickly chid with a coat of frozen snow or sleet.

Our next camp was on La Trinchera, or Bowl Creek. The country was barren and desolate, covered with sage, and with here and there a prairie with tolerable pasture. Antelope were abundant, and deer and turkeys were to be seen on the creeks. The trail passed, to the westward, a lofty peak resembling in outline that one known as James's or Pike's Peak, which is some two hundred and fifty miles to the north. The former is not laid down in any of the maps, although it is a well-known landmark to the Indians.

The creeks are timbered with cotton-woods, quaking-asp, dwarf-oak, cedar, and wild cherry, all of small growth and stunted, while the uplands are covered with a dwarfish growth of pines. From Rio Colorado we had been constantly followed by a large gray wolf. Every evening, as soon as we got into camp, he made his appearance, squatting quietly down at a little distance, and after we had turned in for the night helping himself to anything lying about.

Our first acquaintance commenced on the prairie where I had killed the two antelope, and the excellent dinner he then made, on the remains of the two carcasses, had, evidently attached him to our society. In the morning, as soon as we left the camp, he took possession, and quickly ate up the remnants of bur supper arid some little extras I always took care to leave for him. Shortly after he would trot after us, and, if we halted for a short time to adjust the mule-packs or water the animals, he sat down quietly until we resumed our march.

But when I killed an antelope, and was in the act of butchering it, he gravely looked on, or loped round and round, licking his jaws, and in a state of evident self-gratulation. I had him twenty times a-day within reach of my rifle, but he became such an old friend that I never dreamed of molesting him

Our day's travel was usually from twenty to thirty miles, for the days were very short, and we were obliged to be in camp an hour before sunset, in order to procure wood, and water the animals before dark. Before arriving at the creek where we purposed to camp, I rode ahead and selected a spot where was good grass and .convenient water.

We then unpacked the mules and horses, and immediately watered them, after which we allowed them to feed at large until dark. In the meantime we hunted for firewood, having sometimes to go half a mile from camp, packing it on our shoulders, to the spot we intended for our fire, the mule-packs and saddles, &c., being placed to windward of it, as a protection from the cold blasts. We then cooked supper, and at dark picketed the animals round the camp, their *lariats* (or skin-ropes) being attached to pegs driven in the ground.

After a smoke, we spread our blankets before the fire and turned in, rising once or twice in the night to see that all was safe, and remove the animals to fresh grass when they had cleared the circle round the pickets. Guard or watch we kept none, for after a long day's travel it was too much for two of us to take alternate sentry, thus having but half the night for sleep.

We were now approaching a part of the journey much dreaded by the Indians and New-Mexican buffalo-hunters, and which is quite another "*Jornada del Muerto*," or dead man's journey. A creek called Sangre Cristo—blood of Christ—winds through a deep canon, which opens out at one point into a small circular basin called El Vallecito—the little valley. It is quite embosomed in the mountains; and down their rugged sides, and through .the deep gorges, the wind rushes with tremendous fury, filling the valley with drifted snow, and depositing it in the numerous hollows with which it is intersected. This renders the passage of the Vallecito very dangerous, as animals are frequently buried in the snow, which is sometimes 15 or 20 feet deep in the hollows, and four or five on the level.

This valley is also called by the mountaineers the "Wind-trap;" a very appropriate name, as the wind seems to be caught and pent up here the year round, and, mad with the confinement, blows round and round, seeking for an escape.

Wishing to have my animals fresh for the passage of this dreaded spot, I this day made a short journey of fifteen miles, and camped in the *cañon* about three miles from the mouth of the wind-trap. The *cañon* was so precipitous, that the only place I could find for our camp was on the side of the mountain, where was tolerably good *gramma*-grass, but a wretched place for ourselves; and we had to burrow out a level spot in the snow before we could place the packs in a position where they would not roll down the hill.

The cedars were few and far between, and the snow covered everything in the shape of wood; and, as in our last camp my tomahawk had been lost in the snow, I was unable to procure a log, and was fain to set fire to a cedar near which we had laid our packs. The flame, licking the stringy and dry bark, quickly ran up the tree, blazed along the branches in a roar of fire, illuminating the rugged mountain, and throwing its light upon the thread of timber skirting the creek which wound along the bottom far beneath.

All night long the wind roared through the *cañon*, and at times swept the blankets from our chilled bodies. The mules and horses refused to feed after dark, and, as there was no spot near where we could picket them, the poor beasts sought shelter from the cruel blasts in the belt of dwarf-oak which fringed the creek.

We passed a ,miserable night, perched upon the mountainside in our lonely camp, and without a fire, for the tree was soon consumed. Our old friend the wolf, however, was still a companion, and sat all night within sight of the fire, howling piteously from cold and hunger. The next morning I allowed the animals, a couple of hours after sunrise, to feed and fill themselves; and then, descending from our camp, we entered the pass into the dreaded Vallecito. A few hundred yards from the entrance lay a frozen mule, half buried in the snow; and a little farther on another, close to the creek where the Mormons had evidently encamped not two days before.

The Vallecito was covered with snow to the depth of three feet, to all appearance perfectly level, but in fact full of hollows, with 15 or 20 feet of snow in them. With the greatest difficulty and labour we succeeded in crossing, having to dismount and beat a path through the drifts with our bodies. The pack-mules were continually falling, and were always obliged to be unpacked before they could rise. As this happened every score yards, much time was consumed in traversing the valley, which cannot exceed four miles in length.

The mountain rises directly from the north end of the Vallecito, and is the dividing ridge between the waters of the Del Norte and the Arkansas or Rio Napeste of the Mexicans. The ascent to the summit, from the western side, is short, but very steep; and the snow was of such a depth that the mules could hardly make their way to the top. Leading my horse by the bridle, I led the way, and at length, numbed with cold, I reached the summit, where is a level plateau of about a hundred square yards. Attaining this, and exposed to the full sweep of the wind, a blast struck me, carrying with it a perfect avalanche of snow and sleet, full in my front, and knocked me as clean off my legs as I could have been floored by a twenty-four pound shot.

The view from this point was wild and dismal in the extreme. Looking back, the whole country was covered with a thick carpet of snow, but eastward it was seen in patches only here and there. Before me lay the main chain of the Rocky Mountains, Pike's Peak lifting its snowy head far above the rest; and to the southeast the Spanish Peaks (*Cumbres Españolas*) towered like twin giants over the plains. Beneath the mountain on which I stood was a narrow valley, through which ran a streamlet bordered with dwarf-oak and pine, and looking like a thread of silver as it wound through the plain. Rugged peaks and ridges, snow-clad and covered with pine, and deep gorges filled with broken rocks, everywhere met the eye.

To the eastward the mountains gradually smoothed away into detached spurs and broken ground, until they met the vast prairies, which stretched far as the eye could reach, and hundreds of miles beyond—a sea of seeming barrenness, vast and dismal. A hurricane of wind was blowing at the time, and clouds of dust swept along the sandy prairies, like the smoke of a million bonfires.

On the mountaintop it roared and raved through the pines, filling the air with snow and broken branches, and piling it in huge drifts against the trees. The perfect solitude of this vast wildness was most appalling. From my position on the summit of the dividing ridge I had a bird's-eye view, as it were, over the rugged and chaotic masses of the stupendous chain of the Rocky Mountains, and the vast deserts which stretched away from their eastern bases; while, on all sides of me, broken ridges, and chasms and ravines, with masses of piled-up rocks and uprooted trees, with clouds of drifting snow flying through the air, and the hurricane's roar battling through the forest at my feet, added to the wildness of the scene, which was unrelieved by the slightest vestige of animal or human life. Not a sound, either of bird or beast, was heard—indeed, the hoarse and stunning rattle of the wind would have drowned them, so loud it roared and raved through the trees.

The animals strove in vain to face the storm, and, turning their sterns to the wind, shrunk into themselves, trembling with cold. Panchito, whom I was leading by the bridle, followed me to the edge of the plateau, but drew back, trembling, from the dismal scene which lay stretched below. With a neigh of fear he laid his cold nose against my cheek, seeming to say, "Come back, master: what can take you to such a wretched place as that, where not even a blade of grass meets the eye?"

The descent on the eastern side is steep and sudden, and through a thick forest of pines, to the valley beneath. Trail there was none to direct us, and my half-breed know nothing of the road, having passed but once before, and many years ago, but said it went somewhere down the pines. The evening was fast closing round us, and to remain where we were was certain death to our animals, if not to ourselves: I therefore determined to push for the valley, and accordingly struck at once down the pines.

Once among the trees, there was nothing to do but reach the bottom as fast as possible, as it was nearly dark, and nothing was to be seen at the distance of a dozen yards, so dense was the forest. Before we had proceeded as many paces from the edge of the plateau, and almost before I knew where I was, horses, mules, &c., were rolling down the mountain all together, and were at last brought up in a snow-drift some twelve feet deep.

There they all lay in a heap, the half-breed under one of the pack-mules, and his swarthy face just peering out of the snow. Before a mule would stir every pack had to be removed; and this, with a temperature some ten degrees below zero, was trying to the fingers, as may be imagined. As it was impossible to reach the bottom from this point, we struggled once more to the top through six feet of snow and an almost perpendicular ascent.

I had to beat a road for the animals, by throwing myself bodily on the snow, and pounding it down with all my weight. We were nearly frozen by this time, and my hands were perfectly useless—so much so that, when a large bird of the grouse species[1] flew up into a pine above my head, I was unable to cock my rifle to shoot at it. The mules were plunging into the snow at every step, and their packs were hanging under their bellies, but to attempt to adjust them was out of the question. It was nearly dark too, which made our situation anything but pleasant, and the mules were quite exhausted.

At last, however, we reached the top and struck down the mountain at another point, but it was with the greatest toil and difficulty that we reached the bottom long after dark, and camped shortly after near the creek which wound through the valley, or, rather, in its very bed. One of the mules had slipped its pack completely under the belly, and, the girth pinching her, she

---

1. Called by the hunters *le coq des bois* (Scotch capercailzie).

started off just before reaching the creek at full gallop, kicking everything the pack contained to the four winds of heaven.

This pack happened to contain all the provisions, and, as the search for them in the dark would have been useless, we this night had no supper. To shelter ourselves from the wind we camped in the bed of the creek, which was without water, but the wind howled down it as if it were a funnel, scattering our fire in every direction as soon as it was lighted, and tearing the blankets from our very bodies. The animals never moved from, the spot where they had been unpacked; even if there had been grass, they were too exhausted to feed, but stood shivering in the wind, collapsed with cold, and almost dead.

Such a night I never passed, and hope never to pass again. The hurricane never lulled for a single instant; all our efforts to build a fire were unavailing; and it was with no small delight that I hailed the break of day, when we immediately packed the mules and started on our journey.

The trail now led along the creek and through small broken prairies, with bluffs exhibiting a very curious formation of shale and sandstone. At one point the *cañon* opens out into a pretty open glade or park, in the middle of which is a large rock resembling a ruined castle: the little prairie is covered with fine grass, and a large herd of black-tailed deer were feeding in it. A little farther on we descried the timber on the Huerfano or Orphan Creek, so called from a remarkable isolated rock of sandstone which stands in a small prairie on its left bank, and is a well-known landmark to the Indians.

We camped on the Huerfano under some high cotton-woods, the wind blowing with unabated violence. The next morning all the animals were missing, and, following their trail, we found them on the other side of the creek, five or six miles from the camp, in a little prairie full of buffalo-grass. As it was late in the day when we returned to camp, we did not leave till next morning, when we crossed on to the Cuernaverde or Greenhorn Creek.

On a bluff overlooking the stream I had the satisfaction of

seeing two or three Indian lodges and one adobe hovel of a more aspiring order. As we crossed the creek a mountaineer on an active horse galloped up to us, his rifle over the horn of the saddle, and clad in hunting-shirt and pantaloons of deer-skin, with long fringes hanging down the arms and legs. As this was the first soul we had seen since leaving Red River, we were as delighted to meet a white man (and him an American) as he was to learn the news from the Mexican settlements.

We found here two or three hunters, French Canadians, with their Assinaboin and Sioux squaws, who have made the Greenhorn their headquarters; and game being abundant and the rich soil of the valley affording them a sufficiency of Indian corn, they lead a tolerably easy life, and certainly a lazy one, with no cares whatever to annoy them. This valley will, I have no doubt, become one day a thriving settlement, the soil being exceedingly rich and admirably adapted to the growth of all kinds of grain. The prairies afford abundant pasture of excellent quality, and stock might be raised upon them in any numbers.

The depreciation in the value of beaver-skies has thrown the great body of trappers out of employment, and there is a general tendency among the mountain-men to settle in the fruitful valleys of the Rocky Mountains. Already the plow has turned up the soil within sight of Pike's Peak, and a hardy pioneer, an Englishman, has led the way to the Great Salt Lake, where a settlement of mountaineers has even now been formed, three thousand miles from the frontier of the United States.

From the Greenhorn an easy day's travel brought us to the banks of the San Carlos, which, receiving the former creek, falls into the Arkansas about two hundred and fifty miles from its source. The San Carlos is well timbered with cotton-wood, cherry, quaking-asp, box, alder, and many varieties of shrubs, and many spots in the valley are admirably adapted for cultivation, with a rich loamy soil, and so situated as to be irrigated with great facility from the creek.

Irrigation is indispensable over the whole of this region, rain seldom falling in the spring and summer, which is one of the greatest drawbacks to the settlement of this country, the labour of irrigation being very great. The San Carlos heads in a lofty range of mountains about forty miles from its junction with the Arkansas. Near its upper waters is a circular valley inclosed by rugged highlands, through which the stream forces its way in a *cañon* whose precipitous sides overhang it to the height of three hundred feet. The face of the rock (of a dark limestone) is in many places perfectly vertical, and rises from the water's edge to a great elevation, *piñons* and small cedars growing out of crevices in the sides.

After leaving this creek we passed a barren rolling prairie with scanty herbage and covered with the *palmilla*[2] or soap-plant. A few antelope were its only tenants, and these so shy that I was unable to approach them. Fourteen miles from the San Carlos we struck the Arkansas at the little Indian trading-fort of *Pueblo*, which is situated on the left bank, a few hundred yards above the mouth of the *Fontaine-qui-bouille*, or Boiling Spring River, so called from two springs of mineral water near its head-waters under Pike's Peak, about sixty miles from its mouth.

Here I was hospitably entertained in the lodge of one John Hawkins, an ex-trapper and well-known mountaineer. I turned my animals loose, and allowed them to seek for themselves the best pastures, as in the vicinity of the fort the prairies were perfectly bare of grass, and it was only near the mountain that any of a good quality was to be found.

---

2. The *palmilla* or soap-plant is a species of cactus, the fibrous root of which the New Mexicans use as a substitute for soap. An abundant lather is obtained from it.

CHAPTER 26

Return to Arkansas

The Arkansas is here a clear, rapid river about a hundred yards in width. The bottom, which is inclosed on each side by high bluffs, is about a quarter of a mile across, and timbered with a heavy growth of cotton-wood, some of the trees being of great size. On each side fast, rolling prairies stretch away for hundreds of miles, gradually ascending on the side toward the mountains, and the highlands are there sparsely covered with *piñon* and cedar. The high banks through which the river occasionally passes are of shale and sandstone, and rise precipitously from the water.

Ascending the river the country is wild and broken until it enters the mountains, when the scenery is grand and imposing; but the prairies around it are arid and sterile, producing but little vegetation, and the grass, though of good quality, is thin and scarce. The *Pueblo* is a small square fort of adobe with circular bastions at the corners, no part of the walls being more than eight feet high, and round the inside of the yard or corral are built some half dozen little rooms inhabited by as many Indian traders, *coureurs des bois,* and mountain-men.

They live entirely upon game, and the greater part of the year without even bread, since but little maize is cultivated. As soon as their supply of meat is exhausted they start to the mountains with two or three pack-animals, and bring them back in two or three days loaded with buffalo or venison. In the immediate vicinity of the fort game is very scarce, and the buffalo have within a few years deserted the neighbouring prairies, but they are always found in the mountain- valleys, particularly in one called Bayou Salado, which abounds in every species of game, including elk, bears, deer, big-horn or Rocky Mountain sheep, buffalo, antelope, &c.

Hunting in the mountains round the head of *Fontaine-qui-bouille* and Bayou Salado I remained for the rest of the winter, which was unusually severe—so much so, that the hunters were not unfrequently afraid to venture with their animals into the mountains. Shortly after my arrival on Arkansas, and during a spell of fine sunny weather, I started with a Pueblo hunter for a load or two of buffalo meat, intending to hunt on the waters of the Platte and the Bayou, where bulls remain in good condition during the winter months, feeding on the rich grass of the mountain-valleys. I took with me my horse and three pack-mules, as it was our intention to return with a good supply of meat.

Our course lay up the Fontaine-qui-bouille, and on the third day we entered the pine-covered uplands at the foot of the mountain. Here we found deer so abundant that we determined to hunt here, rather than proceed across the ridge on to the waters of the Platte. We camped on a little mountain-stream running into the creek an hour or two before sunset, and, as we had no provisions, we sallied out to hunt as soon as we had unpacked the mules. We killed two deer almost immediately, and, returning to camp, made a good supper off some of the tit-bits.

The next morning at daybreak, as soon as I had risen from my blanket, I saw a herd of deer feeding within a few hundred yards of camp, and, seizing my rifle, I immediately took advantage of some broken ground to approach them. Before, however, I could get within shot they ascended the bluffs and moved across a prairie, feeding as they went.

I took a long circuit to get the wind of them, and, following a ravine, at length brought my rifle to bear, and knocked over a fine buck, the others running two or three hundred yards and then stooping to look round for their missing comrade. As I ran up to the dead one, and took out my knife to cut the throat, another deer ran past and stopped between me and the herd, and, taking a long shot, I dropped the animal, which however, rose again and limped slowly away. Leaving the dead one and my ramrod on its body, I followed the wounded deer, and, about half a mile from where I fired, found it lying dead.

The process of butchering occupied about twenty minutes, and, packing the hams and shoulders on my back, I trudged back to my first victim. As I was crossing a ravine and ascending the opposite bluff, I saw the figure of a man crawling along the bottom, evidently with the intention of approaching me. A close inspection assured me that it was an Indian; and as none but Arapahós were likely to be in the vicinity, and as these are the Indians most hostile to the white hunters, killing them whenever an opportunity offers, I made up my mind that a war party was about, and that myself and companion stood a very good chance of "losing our hair." As the Indian cautiously advanced, I perceived another was running round the prairie to cut me off from camp, and consequently I determined to make good my ground where I was, throwing down the meat and getting my rifle in readiness for work.

The only tribes of Indians who frequent this part of the mountains are the Yutas (or Eutaws) and the Arapahós, who are hereditary enemies, and constantly at deadly war .with each other. A large band of the Yutas had been wintering in the Bayou Salado, to which one trail leads by the Boiling Spring River (where I was hunting), and another by the Arkansas. The former is the trail followed by the Arapahó war-parties when on an expedition against the Yutas in the Bayou, and therefore I felt certain that none but the former. Indians would be met with in this vicinity.

However, as the Yutas are a very friendly tribe, I was loath to be the first to commence hostilities in case my antagonist might prove to belong to that nation, and, therefore, I awaited his approach, which he made stealthily, until he saw that I had discovered him, when, throwing himself erect, and gun in hand,

254

he made directly toward me. With rifle cocked I watched his eye until he came within fifty yards, when suddenly, seeing my hostile appearance, he stopped, and, striking his hand thrice on his brawny chest, exclaimed, in a loud voice.

"Arapahó, Arapahó!" and stood erect and still. This announcement was very nearly being fatal to him, for, on hearing him proclaim himself one of that hostile nation, my rifle was up to my shoulder in an instant, and covering his heart. As my finger was on the trigger, it flashed across my mind that I had heard that two Arapahós were among the hunters on the Arkansas, their sister being married to a mountaineer, and that probably the dusky gentleman at the end of my rifle was one of these, as indeed he proved to be. I accordingly made signals of peace, and he approached and shook me by the hand.

That his intentions were not altogether honest I have no doubt, but, finding me prepared, he thought it more advisable to remain "*en paz.*" What strengthened me in this belief was the. fact, which I shortly after discovered, that a war-party of his nation were at that moment camped within a few hundred yards of us, whose vicinity he never apprised me of, and who, if they had seen us, would not have hesitated an instant to secure our scalps and animals.

When I returned to the spot where I had left the first deer, not a particle was visible except some hair scattered on the ground, but a few hundred yards from the spot a dozen wolves were engaged in dining off a lump of something, which, on approach, I found to be the remains of my deer, leaving behind them, when dispersed, a handful of hair.

The sagacity of wolves is almost incredible. They will remain round a hunting-camp and follow the hunters the whole day, in bands of three and four, at less than a hundred yards' distance, stopping when they stop, and sitting down quietly when game is killed, rushing to devour the offal when the hunter retires, and then following until another feed is offered them. If a deer or antelope is wounded, they immediately pursue it, and not unfrequently pull the animal down in time for the hunter to come up and secure it from their ravenous clutches. However, they appear to know at once the nature of the wound, for if but slightly touched they never exert themselves to follow a deer, chasing those only which have received a mortal blow.

I one day killed an old buck which was so poor that I left the carcass on the ground untouched. Six coyotes, or small prairie wolves, were my attendants on that day, and of course, before I had left the deer twenty paces, had commenced their work of destruction. Certainly not ten minutes after I looked back and saw the same six loping after me, one of them not twenty yards behind me, with his nose and face all besmeared with blood, and his belly swelled almost to bursting.

Thinking it scarcely possible that they could have devoured the whole deer in so short a space, I had the curiosity to return, and, to my astonishment, found actually nothing left but a pile of bones and hair, the flesh being stripped from them as clean as if scraped with a knife. Half an hour after I killed a large black-tail deer, and, as it was also in miserable condition, I took merely the fleeces (as the meat on the back and ribs is called), leaving four fifths of the animal untouched.

I then retired a short distance, and, sitting down on a rock, lighted my pipe, mid watched the operations of the wolves. They sat perfectly still until I had withdrawn some threescore yards, when they scampered, with a flourish of their tails, straight to the deer. Then commenced such a tugging, and snarling, and biting, all squeaking and swallowing at the same moment. A skirmish of tails and flying hair was seen for five minutes, when the last of them, with slouching tail and evidently ashamed of himself, withdrew, and nothing remained on the ground but a well-picked skeleton. By sunset, when I returned to camp, they had swallowed as much as three entire deer.

We remained hunting in the mountains some days, and left the Boiling Spring River with our mules loaded with meat, having, almost by a miracle, been unmolested by the Arapahó war-party, some of whom I saw hunting nearly every day, without being myself discovered. Nothing occurred on our return until the night of the second day, when we camped on the creek in a spot destitute of grass, and our animals took themselves off in search of food during the night, where we knew not.

The next morning my companion, thinking to find them close at hand, left me in the camp cooking the breakfast while he went to bring in the animals, but presently returned, saying that he could find neither them nor their track, but he had discovered fresh Indian sign in the bottom, where several Indians had been but a few hours before, and that, doubtless, they had made "a raise."

I instantly seized my rifle, and, taking a circuit round the camp, came presently upon the track of horses and mules, and struck at once after them, thinking, of course, they were those made by our animals, as they tallied with the number, being two horses and three mules. I had followed up the track for ten miles, when, in crossing a piece of hard prairie which scarcely yielded to the impression of the hoofs, I, for the first time, observed that not one of the animals I was following was shod, and, knowing that most of my own were so, I began to think, and soon satisfied myself of the fact, that they were not those I was in search of.

As soon as I had made up my mind to this I retraced my steps to camp, and immediately started again with my companion in another direction. This time we came upon the right track, and found that it took an easterly direction, and that the animals were not in the possession of the Indians, as their ropes still dragged along the ground, making a broad trail. Finding this, we returned to camp and *"cachéd"* our meat and packs in the forks of a cotton-wood tree, out of reach of wolves; and without thinking of cooking anything, so anxious were we to find our animals, we started off at once in pursuit, carrying a *lariat* and saddle-blanket to ride back on in case we found the mules.

We followed the trail until midnight, by which time I felt not a little tired, as I had been on my legs since daybreak, and had not broken my fast since the preceding day. We therefore turned into the bottom, floundering through the bushes, and impaling ourselves at every step on the prickly pears which covered the ground, and made a fire near the stream, in a thicket which in some degree sheltered us from the cold.

We had scarcely, however, lighted a fire when the gale of wind burst upon us, and, scattering the burning brands in every direction, quickly set fire to the dry grass and bushes to leeward of the fire. All our efforts to prevent this were unavailing, and we were necessitated to put out our fire to prevent the whole bottom from being burned.

As the cold was intense, and I had no covering but a paltry saddle-blanket about four feet square, sleep was out of the question if I wished to keep unfrozen, so that, after an hour or two's rest and a good smoke, we again turned out, and by the light of the moon pursued the trail. As it passed over prairies entirely destitute of grass, the animals had never once stopped, but continued a straight course, without turning to the right or left, in search of pasture. We travelled on all night, and, halting for an hour's rest in the morning, about noon, looking ahead, I descried four objects feeding in the plain. I called out to my companion, who was a little in rear, that there they were.

"Elk," he answered, after a long look, "or Injuns. They're no mules, I'll lay a dollar: Arapahós, or I never see a redskin."

However, at that distance I recognized my mules, and, pushing on, I found them quietly feeding with Panchito, my companion's horse being alone missing, and they suffered me to catch them without difficulty. As we were now within twenty miles of the fort, Morgan, who had had enough of it, determined to return, and I agreed to go back with the animals to the *cache,* and bring in the meat and packs. I accordingly tied the blanket on a mule's back, and, leading the horse, trotted back at once to the grove of cotton-woods where we had before encamped.

The sky had been gradually overcast with leaden-coloured clouds, until, when near sunset, it was one huge inky mass of rolling darkness; the wind had suddenly lulled, and an unnatural calm, which so surely heralds a storm in these tempestuous regions, succeeded. The ravens were winging their way toward the shelter of the timber, and the coyote was seen trotting quickly to cover, conscious of the coming storm.

The black, threatening clouds seemed gradually to descend until they kissed the earth, and already the distant mountains were hidden to their very bases. A hollow murmuring swept through the bottom, but as yet not a branch was stirred by wind; and the huge cotton-woods, with their leafless limbs, loomed like a line of ghosts through the heavy gloom. Knowing but too well what was coming. I turned my animals toward the timber, which was about two miles distant.

With painted ears, and actually trembling with fright, they were as eager as myself to reach the shelter; but, before we had proceeded a third of the distance, with a deafening roar the tempest broke upon us. The clouds opened and drove right in our faces a storm of freezing sleet, which froze upon us as it fell. The first squall of wind carried away my cap, and the enormous hailstones, beating on my unprotected head and face, almost stunned me. In an instant my hunting-shirt was soaked, and as instantly frozen hard, and my horse was a mass of icicles.

Jumping off my mule—for to ride was impossible—I tore off the saddle-blanket and covered my head. The animals, blinded with the sleet, and their eyes actually coated with ice, turned their sterns to the storm, and blown before it, made for the open prairie. All my exertions to drive them to the shelter of the timber were useless. It was impossible to face the hurricane, which now brought with it clouds of driving snow; and perfect darkness soon set in. Still the animals kept on, and I determined not to leave them, following, or, rather, being blown, after them.

My blanket, frozen stiff like a board, required all the strength of my numbed fingers to prevent it being blown away, and, although it was no protection against the intense cold, I knew it would in some degree shelter me at night from the snow. In half an hour the ground was covered on the bare prairie to the depth of two feet, and through this I floundered for a long time before the animals stopped. The prairie was as bare as a lake; but one little tuft of grease-wood bushes presented itself, and here, turning from the storm, they suddenly stopped and remained perfectly still.

In vain I again attempted to turn them toward the direction of the timber; huddled together, they would not move an inch; and, exhausted myself, and seeing nothing before me but, as I thought, certain death, I sunk down immediately behind them, and, covering my head with the blanket, crouched like a ball in the snow. I would have started myself for the timber, but it was pitchy dark, the wind drove clouds of frozen snow into my face, and the animals had so turned about in the prairie that it was impossible to know the direction to take; and although I had a compass with me, my hands were so frozen that I was perfectly unable, after repeated attempts, to unscrew the box and consult it.

Even had I reached the timber, my situation would have been scarcely improved, for the trees were scattered wide about over a narrow space, and, consequently, afforded but little shelter; and if even I had succeeded in getting firewood—by no means an easy matter at any time, and still more difficult now that the ground was covered with three feet of snow—I was utterly unable to use my flint and steel to procure a light, since my fingers were like pieces of stone, and entirely without feeling.

The way the wind roared over the prairie that night—how the snow drove before it, covering me and the poor animals partly—and how I lay there, feeling the very blood freezing in my veins, and my bones petrifying with the icy blasts which seemed to penetrate them—how for hours I remained with my head on my knees, and the snow pressing it down like a weight of lead, expecting every instant to drop into a sleep from which I knew it was impossible I should ever awake—how every now and then the mules would groan aloud and fall down upon the snow, and then again struggle on their legs—how all night long the piercing howl of wolves was borne upon the wind, which never for an instant abated its violence during the night—I would not attempt to describe.

I have passed many nights alone in the wilderness, and in a solitary camp have listened to the roarings of the wind and the howling of wolves, and felt the rain or snow beating upon me, with perfect unconcern; but this night threw all my former experiences into the shade, and is marked with the blackest of stones in the memoranda of my journeyings.

Once, late in the night, by keeping my hands buried in the breast of my hunting-shirt, I succeeded in restoring sufficient feeling into them to enable me to strike a light. Luckily my pipe, which was made out of a huge piece of cotton-wood bark, and capable of containing at least twelve ordinary pipefuls, was filled with tobacco to the brim; and this, I do believe, kept me alive during the night, for I smoked and smoked until the pipe itself caught fire, and burned completely to the stem.

I was just sinking into a dreamy stupor, when the mules began to shake themselves, and sneeze and snort; which hailing as a good sign, and that they were still alive, I attempted to lift my head and take a view of the weather. When with great difficulty I raised my head, all appeared dark as pitch, and it did not at first occur to me that I was buried deep in snow; but when I thrust my arm above me, a hole was thus made, through which I saw the stars shining in the sky, and the clouds fast clearing away. Making a sudden attempt to straighten my almost petrified back and limbs, I rose, but, unable to stand, fell forward in the snow, frightening the animals, which immediately started away.

When I gained my legs I found that day was just breaking, a long, gray line of light appearing over the belt of timber on the creek, and the clouds gradually rising from the east, and allowing the stars to peep from patches of blue sky. Following the animals as soon as I gained the use of my limbs, and taking a last look at the perfect cave from which I had just risen, I found them in the timber, and, singular enough, under the very tree where we had *cachéd* our meat. However, I was unable to ascend the tree in my present state, and my frost-bitten fingers refused to perform their offices; so that I jumped upon my horse, and, followed by the mules, galloped back to the Arkansas, which I reached in the evening, half dead with hunger and cold.

The hunters had given me up for lost, as such a night even

the "oldest inhabitant" had never witnessed. My late companion had reached the Arkansas, and was safely housed before it broke, blessing his lucky stars that he had not gone back with me. The next morning he returned and brought in the meat: while I spent two days in nursing my frozen fingers and feet, and making up, in feasting mountain fashion, for the banyans I had suffered.

The morning after my arrival on Arkansas, two men, named Harwood and Markhead—the latter one of the most daring and successful trappers that ever followed this adventurous mountain-life, and whom I had intended to have hired as a guide to the valley of the Columbia the ensuing spring—started off to the settlement of New Mexico, with some packs of peltries, intending to bring back Taos whisky (a very profitable article of trade among the mountain-men) and some bags of flour and Indian meal.

I found, on returning from my hunt, that a man named John Albert had brought intelligence that the New Mexicans and Pueblo Indians had risen in the valley of Taos, and, as I have before mentioned, massacred Governor Bent and other Americans, and had also attacked and destroyed Turley's ranch on the Arroyo Hondo, killing himself and most of his men. Albert had escaped from the house, and, charging through the assailants, made for the mountains, and, travelling night and day, and without food, had reached the Greenhorn with the news, and, after recruiting for a couple of days, had come on to the Arkansas with the intelligence, which threw the fierce mountaineers into a perfect frenzy.

As Markhead and Harwood would have arrived in the settlements about the time of the rising, little doubt remained as to their fate, but it was not until nearly two months after that any intelligence was brought concerning them. It seemed that they arrived at the Rio Colorado, the first New Mexican settlement, on the seventh or eighth day, when the people had just received news of the massacre in Taos. These savages, after stripping them of their goods, and securing, by treachery, their arms, made them mount their mules under the pretence of conducting them to Taos, there to be given up to the chief of the insurrection. They had hardly, however, left the village when a Mexican, riding behind Harwood, discharged his gun into his back: Harwood, calling to Markhead that he was "finished;" fell dead to the ground.

Markhead, seeing that his own fate was sealed, made no struggle, and was likewise shot in the back by several balls. They were then stripped and scalped, and shockingly mutilated, and their bodies thrown into the bush by the side of the creek, to be devoured by the wolves. They were both remarkably fine young men. Markhead was celebrated in the mountains for his courage and reckless daring, having had many almost miraculous escapes when in the very hands of hostile Indians. He had, a few years ago, accompanied Sir W. Drummond Stewart in one of his expeditions across the mountains.

It happened that a half-breed of the company absconded one night with some animals belonging to Sir William, who, being annoyed at the circumstance, said, hastily, and never dreaming that his offer would be taken up, that he would give five hundred dollars for the scalp of the thief. The next day Markhead rode into camp with the scalp of the unfortunate horse-thief hanging at the end of his rifle, and I believe received the reward, at least so he himself declared to me, for this act of mountain law.

On one occasion, while trapping on the waters of the Yellow Stone, in the midst of the Blackfoot country, he came suddenly upon two or three lodges, from which the Indians happened to be absent. There was no doubt, from signs which he had previously discovered, that they were lying in wait for him somewhere on the stream, to attack him when examining his traps, the Blackfeet, moreover, being most bitterly hostile to the white trappers, and killing them without mercy whenever an occasion offered.

Notwithstanding the almost certainty that some of the Indians were close at hand, probably gone out for a supply of wood and would very soon return, Markhead resolved to visit the lodges and help himself to anything worth taking that he might find there. The fire was burning, and meat was actually cooking in a pot over it. To this he did ample justice, emptying the pot in a very satisfactory manner, after which he tied all the blankets, dressed skins, moccasins, &c., into a bundle, and, mounting his horse, got safely off with his prize.

It was not always, however, that he escaped scathless, for his body was riddled with balls received in many a bloody affray with Blackfeet and other Indians.

Laforey, the old Canadian trapper, with whom I stayed at Red River, was accused of having possessed himself of the property found on the two mountaineers, and afterward of having instigated the Mexicans to the barbarous murder. The hunters on Arkansas vowed vengeance against him, and swore to have his hair some day, as well as similar love-locks from the people of Red River. A war-expedition was also talked of to that settlement, to avenge the murder of their comrades, and ease the Mexicans of their mules and horses.

The massacre of Turley and his people, and the destruction of his mill, were not consummated without considerable loss to the barbarous and cowardly assailants. There were in the house, at the time of the attack, eight white men, including Americans, French Canadians, and one or two Englishmen, with plenty of arms and ammunition. Turley had been warned of the intended insurrection, but had treated the report with indifference and neglect, until one morning a man named Otterbees, in the employ of Turley, and who had been dispatched to Santa Fé with several mule loads of whisky a few days before, made his appearance at the gate on horseback, and, hastily informing the inmates of the mill that the New Mexicans had risen and massacred Governor Bent and other Americans, galloped off. Even then Turley felt assured that he would not be molested, but, at the solicitations of his men, agreed to close the gate of the yard round which were the buildings of a mill and distillery, and make preparations for defence.

A few hours after a large crowd of Mexicans and Pueblo Indians made their appearance, all armed with guns and bows and arrows, and, advancing with a white flag, summoned Turley to surrender his house and the Americans in it, guaranteeing that his own life should be saved, but that every .other American in the valley of Taos had to be destroyed; that the governor and all the Americans at Fernandez and the *rancho* had been killed, and that not one was to be left alive in all New Mexico.

To this summons Turley answered that he would never surrender his house nor his men, and that, if they wanted it or them, "they must take them."

The enemy then drew off, and, after a short consultation, commenced the attack. The first day they numbered about five hundred, but the crowd was hourly augmented by the arrival of parties of Indians from the more "distant pueblos, and of New Mexicans from Fernandez, La Canada, and other places.

The building lay at the foot of a gradual slope in the *sierra*, which was covered with cedar-bushes. In front ran the stream of the Arroyo Hondo, about twenty yards from one side of the square, and on the other side was broken ground, which rose abruptly and formed the bank of the ravine. In rear, and behind the still-house, was some garden-ground inclosed by a small fence, and into which a small wicket-gate opened from the corral.

As soon as the attack was determined upon, the assailants broke, and, scattering, concealed themselves under the cover of the rocks and bushes which surrounded the house.

From these they kept up an incessant fire upon every exposed portion of the building where they saw the Americans preparing for defence.

They, on their parts, were not idle; not a man but was an old mountaineer, and each had his trusty rifle, with good store of ammunition. Wherever one of the assailants exposed a hand's breadth of his person, there whistled a ball from an unerring barrel. The windows had been blockaded, loopholes being left to fire through, and through these a lively fire was maintained. Already several of the enemy had bitten the dust, and parties were constantly seen bearing off the wounded up the banks of the Cañada. Darkness came on, and during the night a continual fire was kept up on the mill, while its defenders, reserving their ammunition, kept their posts with stern and silent determination. The night was spent in running balls, cutting patches, and completing the defences of the building.

In the morning the fight was renewed, and it was found that the Mexicans had effected a lodgement in a part of the stables, which were separated from the other portions of the building, and between which was an open space of a few feet. The assailants, during the night, had sought to break down the wall, and thus enter the main building, but the strength of the adobes and logs .of which it was composed resisted effectually all their attempts.

Those in the stable seemed anxious to regain the outside, for their position was unavailable as a means of annoyance to the besieged, and several had darted across the narrow space which divided it from the other part of the building, arid which slightly projected, and behind which they were out of the line of fire. As soon, however, as the attention of the defenders was called to this point, the first man who attempted to cross, and who happened to be a Pueblo chief, was dropped on the instant, and fell dead in the centre of the intervening space.

It appeared an object to recover the body, for an Indian immediately dashed out to the fallen chief, and attempted to drag him within the cover of the wall. The rifle which covered the spot again poured forth its deadly contents, and the Indian, springing into the air, fell over the body of his chief, struck to the heart. Another and another met with a similar fate, and at last three rushed at once to the spot, and, seizing the body by the legs and head, had already lifted it from the ground, when three puffs of smoke blew from the barricaded window, followed by the sharp cracks of as many rifles, and the three daring Indians added their number to the pile of corpses which now covered the body of the dead chief.

As yet the besieged had met with no casualties; but after the fall of the seven Indians, in the manner above described, the whole body of assailants, with a shout of rage, poured in a rattling volley, and two of the defenders of the mill fell mortally wounded. One, shot through the loins, suffered great agony, and was removed to the still-house, where he was laid upon a large pile of grain, as being the softest bed to be found.

In the middle of the day the assailants renewed the attack more fiercely than before, their baffled attempts adding to their furious rage. The little garrison bravely stood to the defence of the mill, never throwing away a shot, but firing coolly, and only when a fair mark was presented to their unerring aim. Their ammunition, however, was fast failing, and, to add to the danger of the situation, the enemy set fire to the mill, which blazed fiercely, and threatened destruction to the whole building.

Twice they succeeded in overcoming the flames, and, taking advantage of their being thus occupied, the Mexicans and Indians charged into the corral, which was full of hogs and sheep, and vented their cowardly rage upon the animals, spearing and shooting all that came in their way. No sooner, however, were the flames extinguished in one place, than they broke out more fiercely in another; and as a successful defence was perfectly hopeless, and the numbers of the assailants increased every moment, a council of war was held by the survivors of the little garrison, when it was determined, as soon as night approached, that everyone should attempt to escape as best he might, and in the mean time the defence of the mill was to be continued.

Just at dusk, Albert and another man ran to the wicket-gate which opened into a kind of inclosed space, and in which was a number of armed Mexicans. They both rushed out at the same moment, discharging their rifles full in the faces of the crowd. Albert, in the confusion, threw himself under the fence, whence he saw his companion shot down immediately, and heard his cries for mercy, mingled with shrieks of pain and anguish, as the cowards pierced him with knives and lances.

Lying without motion under the fence, as soon as it was quite dark he crept over the logs and ran up the mountain, travelled day and night, and, scarcely stopping or resting, reached the Greenhorn, almost dead with hunger and fatigue. Turley himself succeeded in escaping from the mill and in reaching the mountain unseen. Here he met a Mexican, mounted on a horse, who had been a most intimate friend of the unfortunate man for many years.

To this man Turley offered his watch (which was treble its worth) for the use of his horse, but was refused. The inhuman wretch, however, affected pity and commiseration for the fugitive, and advised him to go to a certain place, where he would bring him or send him assistance; but on reaching the mill, which was now a mass of fire, he immediately informed the Mexicans of his place of concealment, whither a large party instantly proceeded and shot him to death.

Two others escaped and reached Santa Fé in safety. The mill and Turley's house were sacked and gutted, and all his hard-earned savings, which were considerable, and concealed in gold about the house, were discovered, and of course seized upon, by the victorious Mexicans.

The Indians, however, met a few days after with a severe retribution. The troops marched out of Santa Fé, attacked their *pueblo*, and levelled it to the ground, killing many hundreds of its defenders, and taking many prisoners, most of whom were hanged.

CHAPTER 27

Delicious Draught

Beaver has so depreciated in value within the last few years, that trapping has been almost abandoned; the price paid for the skin of this valuable animal having fallen from six and eight dollars per pound to one dollar, which hardly pays the expenses of traps, animals, and equipment for the hunt, and is certainly no adequate remuneration for the incredible hardships, toil, and danger, which are undergone by the hardy trappers in the course of their adventurous expeditions.

The cause of the great decrease in value of beaver-fur is the substitute which has been found for it in skins of the fur-seal and *nutria*—the improved preparation of other skins of little value, such as the hare and rabbit—and, more than all, in the use of silk in the manufacture of hats, which has in a great measure super-seded that of the beaver. Thus the curse of the trapper is levelled against all the new-fashioned mate*riales* of Paris hats; and the light and (h)airy gossamer of twelve-and-six is anathematized in the mountains in a way which would be highly distressing to the feelings of Messrs. Jupp and Johnson, and other artists in the ventilating-gossamer line.

Thanks to the innovation, however, a little breathing-time has been allowed the persecuted castor; and this valuable fur-bearing animal, which otherwise would, in the course of a few years, have become extinct, has now a chance of multiplying, and will in a short time again become abundant; for, although not a very prolific animal, the beaver has, perhaps, fewer natural enemies than any other of the *feræ naturæ,* and, being at the same time a wise and careful one, provides against all contingencies of cold and hunger, which in northern climates carry off so large a proportion of their brother beasts.

The beaver was once found in every part of North America from Canada to the Gulf of Mexico, but has now gradually retired from the encroachments and the persecutions of civilized man, and is met with only in the far, Far West, on. the tributaries of the great rivers, and the streams which water the mountain-valleys in the great chain of the Rocky Mountains. On the waters of the Platte and Arkansas they are still numerous, and within the last two years have increased considerably in numbers; but the best trapping-ground now is on the streams running through the Bayou Salado, and the Old and New Parks, all of which are elevated mountain-valleys.

The habits of the beaver present quite a study to the naturalist, and they are certainly the most sagaciously instinctive of all quadrupeds. Their dams afford a lesson to the engineer, their houses a study to the architect of comfortable abodes, while their unremitting labour and indefatigable industry are models to be followed by the working-man. The lodge of the beaver is generally excavated in the bank of the stream, the entrance being invariably under water; but not unfrequently, where the banks are flat, they construct lodges in the stream itself, of a conical form, of limbs and branches of trees woven together and cemented with mud.

For the purpose of forming dams, for the necessary timber for their lodges, or for the, bark which they store for their winter's supply of food, the beaver often fells a tree eight or ten inches in diameter, throwing it, with the skill of an expert woodsman, in any direction he pleases, always selecting a tree above stream, in order that the logs may be carried down with it to their destination. The log is then chopped into small lengths, and, pushing them into the water, the beaver steers them to the lodge or dam.

These trees are as cleanly cut as they could be by a sharp axe, the gouging furrows made by the animal's strong teeth cutting into the very centre of the trunk, the notch being as smooth as sawed wood.

With his broad tail, which is twelve or fourteen inches long, and about four in breadth, and covered with a thick scaly skin, the beaver plasters his lodge, thus making it perform all the offices of a hand. They say that, when the beaver's tail becomes dry, the animal dies, but, whether this is the case or not, I have myself seen the beaver when at work return to the water and plunge his tail into the stream, and then resume his labour with renewed vigour; and I have also seen them, with their bodies on the bank, thumping the water with their tails with a most comical perseverance.

The female seldom produces more than three kittens at a birth, but I know an instance where one was killed with young, having no less than eleven in her. They live to a considerable age, and I once ate the tail of an old "man" beaver whose head was perfectly gray with age, and his beard was of the same venerable hue, notwithstanding which his tail was as tender as a young racoon. The kittens are as playful as their namesakes of the feline race, and it is highly amusing to see an old one with grotesque gravity inciting her young to gambol about her, while she herself is engaged about some household work.

The *nutrias* of Mexico are identical with the beavers of the more northern parts of America; but in South America, and on some parts of the western coast of North America, a species of seal, or, ns I have heard it described, a hybrid between the seal and the beaver, is called *nutria*—quite a distinct animal, however, from the Mexican *nutria*.

The trappers of the Rocky Mountains belong to a *genus* more approximating to the primitive savage than perhaps any other class of civilized man. Their lives being spent in the remote wilderness of the mountains, with no other companion than Nature herself, their habits and character assume a most singular cast of simplicity mingled with ferocity, appearing to take their colouring from the scenes and objects which surround them. Knowing no wants save those of nature, their sole care is to procure sufficient food to support life, and the necessary clothing to protect them from the rigorous climate. This, with the assistance of their trusty rifles, they are generally able to effect, but sometimes at the expense of great peril and hardship. When engaged in their avocation, the natural instinct of primitive man is ever alive, for the purpose of guarding against danger and the provision of necessary food.

Keen observers of nature, they rival the beasts of prey in discovering the haunts and habits of game, and in their skill and cunning in capturing it. Constantly exposed to perils of all kinds, they become callous to any feeling of danger, and destroy human as well as animal life with as little scruple and as freely as they expose their own. Of laws, human or divine, they neither know nor care to know. Their wish is their law, and to attain it they do not scruple as to ways and means.

Firm friends and bitter enemies, with them it is "a word and blow," and the blow often first. They may have good qualities, but they are those of the animal; and people fond of giving hard names call them revengeful, bloodthirsty, drunkards (when the wherewithal is to be had), gamblers, regardless of the laws of *meum* and *tuum*—in fact, "White Indians." However, there are exceptions, and I have met honest mountain-men. Their animal qualities, however, are undeniable.

Strong, active, hardy as bears, daring, expert in the use of their weapons, they are just what uncivilized white man might be supposed to be in a brute state, depending upon his instinct for the support of life. Not a hole or corner in the vast wilderness of the "Far West" but has been ransacked by these hardy men. From the Mississippi to the mouth of the Colorado of the West, from the frozen regions of the North to the Gila in Mexico, the beaver-hunter has set his traps in every creek and stream.

All this vast country, but for the daring enterprise of these men, would be even now a *terra incognita* to geographers, as indeed a great portion still is; but there is not an acre that has not been passed and repassed by the trappers in their perilous excursions. The mountains and streams still retain the names assigned to them by the rude hunters; and these alone are the hardy pioneers who have paved the way for the settlement of the western country.

Trappers are of two kinds, the "hired hand" and the "free trapper:" the former hired for the hunt by the fur companies; the latter, supplied with animals and traps by the company, is paid a certain price for his furs and peltries.

There is also the trapper "on his own hook;" but this class is very small. He has his own animals and traps, hunts where he chooses, and sells his peltries to whom he pleases.

On starting for a hunt, the trapper fits himself out with the necessary equipment, either from the Indian trading-forts, or from some of the petty traders—*coureurs des bois*—who frequent the western country. This equipment consists usually of two or three horses or mules—one for saddle, the others for packs— and six traps, which are carried in a bag of leather called a trap-sack. Ammunition, a few pounds of tobacco, dressed deerskins for moccasins, &c., are carried in a wallet of dressed buffalo-skin, called a possible-sack.

His "possibles" and "trap-sack" are generally carried on the saddle-mule when hunting, the others being packed with the furs. The costume of the trapper is a hunting-shirt of dressed buckskin, ornamented with long fringes; pantaloons of the same material, and decorated with porcupine-quills and long fringes down the outside of the leg. A flexible felt hat and moccasins clothe his extremities. Over his left shoulder and under his right arm hang his powder-horn and bullet-pouch, in which he carries his balls, flint, and steel, and odds and ends of all kinds. Round the waist is a belt, in which is stuck a large butcher-knife in a sheath of buffalo-hide, made fast to the belt by a chain or guard of steel, which also supports a little buckskin case containing a whetstone.

A tomahawk is also often added; and of course, a long, heavy rifle is part and parcel of his equipment. I had nearly forgotten the pipe-holder, which hangs round his neck, and is generally *a gage d'amour*, and a triumph of squaw workmanship, in shape of a heart, garnished with beads and porcupine-quills.

Thus provided, and having determined the locality of his trapping-ground, he starts to the mountains, sometimes alone, sometimes with three or four in company, as soon as the breaking up of the ice allows him to commence operations. Arrived on his hunting-grounds, he follows the creeks and streams, keeping a sharp lookout for "sign."

If he sees a prostrate cotton-wood tree, he examines it to discover if it be the work of beaver—whether "thrown" for the purpose of food, or to dam the stream. The track of the beaver on the mud or sand under the bank is also examined; and if the "sign" be fresh, he sets his trap in the run of the animal, hiding it under water, and attaching it by a stout chain to a picket driven in the bank, or to a brush or tree.

A "float-stick" is made fast to the trap by a cord a few feet long, which, if the animal carry away the trap, floats on the water and points out its position. The trap is baited with the "medicine." an oily substance obtained from a gland in the scrotum of the beaver, but distinct from the testes. A stick is dipped into this and planted over the trap; and the beaver, attracted by the smell, and wishing a close inspection, very foolishly puts his leg into the trap, and is a "gone beaver."

When a lodge is discovered, the trap is set at the edge of the dam, at the point where the animal passes from deep to shoal water, and always under water. Early in the morning the hunter mounts his mule and examines the traps. The captured animals are skinned, and the tails, which are a great dainty, carefully packed into camp. The skin is then stretched over a hoop or framework of osier twigs, and is. allowed to dry, the flesh and fatty substance being carefully scraped (grained). When dry, it is folded into a square sheet, the fur turned inward, and the bundle, containing about ten to twenty skins, tightly pressed and corded, is ready for transportation.

During the hunt, regardless of Indian vicinity, the fearless trapper wanders far and near in search of "sign." His nerves must ever be in a state of tension, and his mind ever present at his call. His eagle eye sweeps round the country, and in an instant detects any foreign appearance. A turned leaf, a blade of grass pressed down, the uneasiness of the wild animals, the flight of birds, are all paragraphs to him written in nature's legible hand and plainest language.

All the wits of the subtile savage are called into play to gain an advantage over the wily woodsman; but with the natural instinct of primitive man, the white hunter has the advantages of a civilized mind, and, thus provided, seldom fails to outwit, under equal advantages, the cunning savage.

Sometimes, following on his trail, the Indian watches him set his traps on a shrub-belted stream, and, passing up the bed, like Bruce of old, so that he may leave no track, he lies in wait in the bushes until the hunter comes to examine his carefully set traps. Then, waiting until he approaches his ambushment within a few feet, whiz flies the home-drawn arrow; never failing at such close quarters to bring the victim to the ground. For one white scalp, however, that dangles in the smoke of an Indian's lodge, a dozen black ones, at the end of the hunt, ornament the campfires of the rendezvous.

At a certain time, when the hunt is over, or they have loaded their pack-animate, the trappers proceed to the "rendezvous," the locality of which has been previously agreed upon; and here the traders and agents of the fur companies await them, with such assortment of goods as their hardy customers may require, including generally a fair supply of alcohol. The trappers drop in singly and in small bands, bringing their packs of beaver to this mountain market, not unfrequently to the value of a thousand dollars each, the produce of one hunt.

The dissipation of the "rendezvous," however, soon turns the trapper's pocket inside out. The goods brought by the traders, although of the most inferior quality, are sold at enormous prices:—coffee, twenty and thirty shillings a pint-cup, which is the usual measure; tobacco fetches ten and fifteen shillings a plug; alcohol, from twenty to fifty shillings a pint; gunpowder, sixteen shillings a pint-cup; and all other articles at proportionably exorbitant prices.

The "beaver" is purchased at from two to eight dollars per pound; the Hudson's Bay Company alone buying it by the *pluie,* or "plew," that is, the whole skin, giving a certain price for skins, whether of old beaver or "kittens."

The rendezvous is one continued scene of drunkenness, gambling, and brawling and fighting, as long as the money and credit of the trappers last. Seated, Indian fashion, round the fires, with a blanket spread before them, groups are seen with their "decks" of cards, playing at "*euker,*" "poker," and "seven-up," the regular mountain-games. The stakes are "beaver," which here is current coin; and when the fur is gone, their horses, mules, rifles, and shirts, hunting-packs, and *breeches,* are staked.

Daring gamblers make the rounds of the camp, challenging each other to play for the trapper's highest stake—his horse, his squaw (if he have one), and, as once happened, his scalp. There goes "hos and beaver!" is the mountain expression when any great loss is sustained; and, sooner or later, "hos and beaver" invariably find their way into the insatiable pockets of the traders. A trapper often squanders the produce of his hunt, amounting to hundreds, of dollars, in a couple of hours; and, supplied on credit with another equipment, leaves the rendezvous for another expedition, which has the same result time after time, although one tolerably successful hunt would enable him to return to the settlements and civilized life, with an ample sum to purchase and stock a farm, and enjoy himself in ease and comfort the remainder of his days.

An old trapper, a French Canadian, assured me that he had received fifteen thousand dollars for beaver during a sojourn of twenty years in the mountains. Every year he resolved in his mind to return to Canada, and, with this object, always converted his fur into cash; but a fortnight at the "rendezvous" always cleaned him out, and at the end of twenty years, he had not even credit sufficient to buy a pound of powder.

These annual gatherings are often the scene of bloody duels, for over their cups and cards no men are more quarrelsome than your mountaineers. Rifles, at twenty paces, settle all differences, and, as may be imagined, the fall of one or other of the combatants is certain, or, as sometimes happens, both fall to the word "fire."

A day or two after my return from the mountain, I was out in search of my animals along the river-bottom, when I met a warparty of Arapahós loping along on foot in Indian file. It was the same party who had been in the vicinity of our camp on Fontaine-qui-bouille, and was led by a chief called *Coxo,* "the Game Leg." They were all painted and armed for war, carrying bows and well-filled quivers, war-clubs and lances, and some had guns in deerskin covers.

They were all naked to the waist, a single buffalo robe being thrown over them, and from his belt each one had a *lariat* or rope of hide to secure the animals stolen in the expedition. They were returning without a scalp, having found the Yutas "not at home;" and this was considered a sign by the hunters that they would not be scrupulous at "raising some hair," if they caught a straggler far from camp.

However, their present visit was for the purpose of procuring some meat, of which they stood in need, as to reach their village they had to cross a country destitute of game. They were all remarkably fine young men, and perfectly cleanly in their *persona;* indeed, when on the warpath, more than ordinary care is taken to adorn the body, and the process of painting occupies considerable time and attention. The Arapahós do not shave their heads, as do the Pawnees, Caws, and Osages, merely braiding the centre or scalp-lock, and decorating it with a gay ribbon or feather of the war-eagle.

This war-party was twenty-one in number, the oldest, with the exception of the chief, being under thirty, and not one of them was less than five feet eight inches in height. In this they differ from their neighbours the Yutas and Comanches, who are all of small stature; the latter especially, when off their horses, presenting small, ungainly figures, with legs crooked by constant riding, and limbs exhibiting but little muscular development. Not one of this Arapahó band but could have sat as a model for an Apollo. During their stay the animals were all collected and corralled, as their penchant for horseflesh, it was thought likely, might lead some of the young men to appropriate a horse or mule.

Each tribe of prairie Indians has a different method of making moccasins, so that anyone, acquainted with the various fashions, is at no loss to know the nation to which any particular one belongs whom he may happen to meet. The Arapahós and Cheyennes use a "shoe" moccasin, that is, one which reaches no higher than the instep, and wants the upper side-flaps which moccasins usually have. I always used Chippewa moccasins, which differ from those of the Prairie make, by the seam being made up the centre of the foot to the leg, and puckered into plaits. This, which is the true fashion of the "Forest Indian," who, by the by, is as distinct in character and appearance from him of the "plains" as a bear from a bluebottle, attracted the attention of the Arapahó warriors, and caused a lively discussion among themselves, owing to the novelty of the manufacture. They all surrounded me. and each examined and felt carefully the unusual *chaussure*.

"*Ti-yah!*" was the universal exclamation of astonishment. The old chief was the last to approach, and, after a minute examination, he drew himself up, and explained to them, as I perfectly understood by his gestures, "that the people who made those moccasins lived far, far away from the sun, where the snow lay deep on the ground, and where the night was illuminated by the mystery fire (the *aurora borealis*), which he had seen, years ago, far to the north."

The vicinity of the *pueblo* affording no pasture, my *cavallada* had undertaken a voyage of discovery in search of grass, and had found a small valley up the bed of a dry creek, in which grew an abundance of bunch-grass. As, however, the river was fast frozen, they were unable to find a watering-place themselves, and one day made their appearance in camp, evidently for the purpose of being conducted to water: I therefore led them to the river and broke a large hole, which they invariably resorted to every morning and evening at the same hour, although it was three or four miles from their feeding-place.

This enabled me to catch them whenever I required, for at a certain time I had only to go to this hole, and I never failed to see them approaching leisurely, the mules following the horse in Indian file, and always along the same trail which they had made in the snow.

The grass, although to all appearance perfectly withered, still retained considerable nourishment, and the mules improved fast in flesh. Panchito, however, fell off in condition as the others improved, more, I think, from the severity of the winter than the scarcity of grass. When they had cleared the valley they sought a pasture still farther off, and, after losing sight of them for fifteen days, I found them fifteen miles from the river, at the foot of the mountain, in a prairie in which was a pool of water (which prevented their having recourse to the water-hole I had made for them), and where was plenty of buffalo-grass.

It was now always a day's work for me to catch my hunting-mule, and the animals were becoming so wild that I often returned without effecting the capture at all, my only chance being to chase them on horseback and lasso the horse, when they all followed as quiet as lambs, never caring to forsake their old companion.

The weather in January, February, and March was exceedingly severe; storms of sleet and snow, invariably accompanied by hurricanes of wind, were of daily occurrence, but the snow rarely remained more than thirty hours on the ground, an hour or two of the meridian sun being sufficient to cause it to disappear.

On the 17th of March the ice in the Arkansas, "moved" for the first time, and the next day it was entirely broken up, and the arrival of spring weather was confidently expected. However, it froze once more in a few days as firm as ever, and the weather became colder than before, with heavy snow-storms and hard gales of wind.

After this succeeded a spell of fine weather, and about the 24th the ice moved bodily away, and the river was clear from that date, the edges of the water only being frozen in the morning. Geese now made their appearance in considerable numbers, and afforded an agreeable variety to our perpetual venison and tough bull-meat, as well as good sport in shooting them with rifles. The "blue-bird" followed the goose; and when the first robin was seen, the hunters pronounced the winter at an end.

When the river was clear of ice I tried my luck with the fish, and in ten minutes pulled out as many trout, hickory shad, and suckers, but from that time never succeeded in getting a nibble. The hunters accounted for this by saying that the fish migrate up the stream as soon as the ice breaks, seeking the deep holes and bends of its upper waters, and that my first piscatory attempt was in the very nick of time, when a shoal was passing up for the first time after the thaw.

Toward the latter end of March I removed my animals from their pasture, which was getting dry and rotten, and took them up Fontaine-qui-bouille into the mountains, where the grass is of better quality and more abundant. On the Arkansas and the neighbouring prairies not a vestige of spring vegetation yet presented itself, but nearer the mountains the grass was beginning to shoot. It is a curious fact that the young blade of the buffalo and bunch-grass pierces its way through the old one, which completely envelops and protects the tender blade from the nipping frosts of spring, and thus also the weakening effects of feeding on the young grass are rendered less injurious to horses and mules, since they are obliged to eat the old together with the young shoots.

The farther I advanced up the creek, and the nearer the mountains, the more forward was the vegetation, although even here in its earliest stage. The bunch-grass was getting green at the roots, and the absinthe and grease-wood were throwing out their buds. As yet, however, the cotton-woods and the larger trees in the bottom showed no signs of leaf, and the currant and cherry-bushes still looked dry and sapless. The thickets, however, were filled with birds, and resounded with their songs, and the plains were alive with prairie-dogs, busy in repairing their houses and barking lustily as I rode through their towns.

Turkeys, too, were calling in the timber, and the boom of the prairie-fowl, at rise and set of sun, was heard on every side. The snow had entirely disappeared from the plains, but Pike's Peak and the mountains were still clad in white; the latter, being sometimes clear of snow and looking dark and sombre, would for an hour or two be hidden by a curtain of clouds, which rising displayed the mountains, before black and furrowed, now white and smooth with their snowy mantle.

On my way I met a band of hunters who had been driven in by a war-party of Arapahós. who were encamped on the eastern fork of the Fontaine-qui-bouille. They strongly urged me to return, as, being alone, I could not fail to be robbed of my animals, if not killed myself. However, in pursuance of my fixed rule, never to stop on account of Indians, I proceeded up the river, and about fifty miles from the mouth encamped on the first fork, where was an abundance of deer and antelope.

In the timber on the banks of the creek I erected a little shanty, covering it with the bark of the prostrate trees which strewed the ground, and picketing my animals at night in a little prairie within sight, where they luxuriated on plenty of buffalo- grass. Here I remained for a day or two hunting in the mountain,

leaving my *cavallada* to take care of themselves, and at the mercy of the Arapahós should they discover them. At night I returned to camp, made a fire, and cooked an *appola* of antelope-meat, and enjoyed my solitary pipe after supper with as much relish as if I was in a divan, and lay down on my blanket, serenaded by packs of hungry wolves, and sleeping as soundly as if there were no such people in existence as Arapahós, merely waking now and then and raising my hand to the top of my head to assure myself that my top-knot was in its place.

The next day I moved up the main fork, on which I had been directed by the hunters to proceed, in order to visit the far-famed springs from which the creek takes its name. The valley of the upper waters is very picturesque: many mountain-streams course through it, a narrow line of timber skirting their banks.

On the western side the rugged mountains frown overhead, and rugged *cañons* filled with pine and cedar gape into the plain. At the head of the valley, the ground is. much broken up into gullies and ravines where it enters the mountain-spurs, with topes of pine and cedar scattered here and there, and masses of rock tossed about in wild confusion. On entering the broken ground the creek turns more to the westward, and passes by two remarkable *buttes*[1] of a red conglomerate, which appear at a distance like tablets cut in the mountainside.

The eastern fork skirts the base of the range, coming from the ridge called "The Divide," which separates the waters of the Platte and Arkansas; and between the main stream and this branch, running north and south, is a limestone ledge which forms the western wall of the lateral valley running at right angles from that of the Fontaine-qui-bouille. The uplands are clothed with cedar and dwarf-oak, the bottoms of the river with cotton-wood, quaking-asp, oak, ash, and box-alder, and a thick undergrowth of cherry and currant-bushes.

I followed a very good lodge pole-trail, which struck the creek before entering the broken ground, being that used by the Yutas and Arapahós on their way to the Bayou Salado. Here the valley narrowed considerably, and, turning an angle with the creek, I was at once shut in by mountains and elevated ridges, which rose on each side the stream. This was now a rapid torrent, tumbling over rocks and stones, and fringed with oak and a shrubbery of brush.

A. few miles on, the *cañon* opened out into a little shelving glade; and on the right bank of the stream, and raised several feet above it, was a flat white rock in which was a round hole, where one of the celebrated springs hissed and bubbled with its escaping gas. I had been cautioned against drinking this, being

---

1. Any prominent rock or bluff is called a *butte* (pronounced biute) by the hunters and trappers.

directed to follow the stream a few yards to another, which is the true soda-spring.

Before doing this, however, I unpacked the mule and took the saddle from Panchito, piling my saddle and meat on the rock. The animals, as soon as I left them free, smelled the white rock, and instantly commenced licking and scraping with their teeth with the greatest eagerness. At last the horse approached the spring, and, burying his nose deep in the clear water, drank greedily. The mules appeared at first to fear the bubbling of the gas, and smelled and retreated two or three times before they mustered courage to take a draught; but when they had once tasted the water I thought they would have burst themselves.

For hours they paid no attention to the grass, continuing to lick the rock and constantly returning to the spring to drink. For myself, I had not only abstained from drinking that day, but, with the aid of a handful of salt which I had brought with me for the purpose, had so highly seasoned my breakfast of venison, that I was in a most satisfactory state of thirst. I therefore at once proceeded to the other spring, and found it about forty yards from the first, but immediately above the river, issuing from a little basin in the flat white rock, and trickling over the edge into the stream. The escape of gas in this was much stronger than in the other, and was similar to water boiling smartly.

I had provided myself with a tin cup holding about a pint; but, before dipping it in, I divested myself of my pouch and belt, and sat down in order to enjoy the draught at my leisure. I was half dead with thirst; and, tucking up the sleeves of my hunting-shirt, I dipped the cup into the midst of the bubbles, and raised it hissing and sparkling to my lips. Such a draught! Three times, without drawing a breath, was it replenished and emptied, al-most blowing up the roof of my mouth with its effervescence. It was equal to the very best soda-water, but possesses that fresh, natural flavour which manufactured water cannot impart.

CHAPTER 28

Mountain on Fire

The Indians regard with awe the "medicine" waters of these fountains, as being the abode of a spirit who breathes through the transparent water, and thus, by his exhalations, causes the perturbation of its surface. The Arapahós, especially, attribute to this water-god the power of ordaining the success or miscarriage of their war-expeditions; and as their braves pass often by the mysterious springs, when in search of their hereditary enemies the Yutas, in the "Valley of Salt," they never fail to bestow their votive offerings upon the water-sprite, in order to propitiate the "Manitou" of the fountain, and insure a fortunate issue to their "path of war."

Thus at the time of my visit the basin of the spring was filled with beads and *wampum*, and pieces of red cloth and knives, while the surrounding trees were hung with strips of deerskin, cloth, and moccasins, to which, had they been serviceable, I would most sacrilegiously have helped myself. The "sign," too, round the spring, plainly showed that here a wardance had been executed by the braves; and I was not a little pleased to find that they had already been here, and were not likely to return the same way; but in this supposition I was quite astray.

This country was once possessed by the Shos-shone or Snake Indians, of whom the Comanches of the plains are a branch; and although many hundred miles now divide their hunting-grounds, they were once, if not the same people, tribes of the same grand nation. They still, however, retain a common language; and there is great analogy in many of their religious rites and legendary tales, which proves that at least a very close alliance must at one period have bound the two tribes together.

They are even now the two most powerful nations, in point of numbers, of all the tribes of western Indians; the Comanches ruling supreme on the eastern plains, as the Shos-shones are the dominant power in the country west of the Rocky Mountains, and in the mountains themselves. A branch of the latter is the tribe of Tlamath Indians, the most warlike of the western tribes; as also the Yutas, who may be said to connect them with the nation of Comanche.

Numerically, the Snakes are supposed to be the most powerful of any Indian nation in existence.

The Snakes, who, in common with all Indians, possess hereditary legends to account for all natural phenomena, or any extraordinary occurrences which are beyond their ken or comprehension, have, of course, their legendary version of the causes which created, in the midst of their hunting-grounds, these two springs of sweet and bitter water; which are also intimately connected with the cause of separation between the tribes of "Comanche" and the "Snake." Thus runs the legend :

Many hundreds of winters ago, when the cotton-woods on the Big River were no higher than an arrow, and the red men, who hunted the buffalo on the plains, all spoke the same language, and the pipe of peace breathed its social cloud of *kinnik-kinnek* whenever two parties of hunters met on the boundless plains—when, with hunting-grounds and game of every kind in the greatest abundance, no nation dug up the hatchet with another because one of its hunters followed the game into their bounds, but, on the contrary, loaded for him his back with choice and fattest meat, and ever proffered the soothing pipe before the stranger, with well-filled belly, left the village—it happened that two hunters of different nations met one day on a small rivulet, where both had repaired to quench their thirst.

A little stream of water, rising from a spring on a rock within a few feet of the bank, trickled over it, and fell splashing into the river. To this the hunters repaired; and while one sought the spring itself, where the water, cold and clear, reflected on its surface the image of the surrounding scenery, the other, tired by his exertions in the chase, threw himself at once to the ground, and plunged his face into the running stream.

The latter had been unsuccessful in the chase., and perhaps his bad fortune, and the sight of the fat deer which the other hunter threw from his back before he drank at the crystal spring, caused a feeling of jealousy and ill-humour to take possession of his mind. The other, on the contrary, before he satisfied his thirst, raised in the hollow of his hand a portion of the water, and, lifting it toward the sun, reversed his hand, and allowed it to fall upon the ground —a libation to the Great Spirit who had vouchsafed him a successful hunt, and the blessing of the refreshing water with which he was about to quench his thirst.

Seeing this, and being reminded that he had neglected the usual offering, only increased the feeling of envy and annoyance which the unsuccessful hunter permitted to get the mastery of his heart; and the Evil Spirit at that moment entering his body, his temper fairly flew away, and he sought some pretence by which to provoke a quarrel with the stranger Indian at the spring.

"Why does a stranger," he asked, rising from the stream at the same time, "drink at the spring-head, when one to whom the fountain belongs contents himself with the water that runs from it?"

"The Great Spirit places the cool water at the spring," answered the other hunter, "that his children may drink it pure and undented. The running water is for the beasts which scour the plains. Au-sa-qua is a chief of the Shos-shone: he drinks at the head-water."

"The Shos-shone is .but a tribe of the Comanche," returned the other: "Waco-mish leads the grand nation. Why does a Shos-shone dare to drink above him?"

"He has said it. The Shos-shone drinks at the spring head; other nations of the stream which runs into the fields. Au-sa-qua is chief of his nation. The Comanche are brothers. Let them both drink of the same water."

"The Shos-shone pays tribute to the Comanche. Waco-mish leads that nation to war. Waco-mish is chief of the Shos-shone, as he is of his own people."

"Waco-mish lies; his tongue is forked like the rattlesnake's; his heart is black as the *Misho-tunga* (bad spirit). When the Manitou made his children, whether Shos-shone or Comanche, Arapahó, Shi-an, or Painé, he gave them buffalo to eat, and the pure water of the fountain to quench their thirst. He said not to one, drink here, and to another, drink there; but gave the crystal spring to all, that all might drink."

Waco-mish almost burst with rage as the other spoke; but his coward heart alone prevented him from provoking an encounter with the calm Shos-shone. He, made thirsty by the words he had spoken—for the red man is ever sparing of his tongue—again stooped down to the spring to quench his thirst, when the subtile warrior of the Comanche suddenly threw himself upon the kneeling hunter, and, forcing his head into the bubbling water, held him down with all his strength, until his victim no longer struggled, his stiffened limbs relaxed, and he fell forward over the spring, drowned and dead.

Over the body stood the murderer, and no sooner was the deed of blood consummated than bitter remorse took possession of his mind, where before had reigned the fiercest passion and vindictive hate. With hands clasped to his forehead, he stood transfixed with horror, intently gazing on his victim, whose head still remained immersed in the fountain. Mechanically he dragged the body a few paces from the water, which, as soon as the head of the dead Indian was withdrawn, the Comanche saw suddenly and strangely disturbed.

Bubbles sprung up from the bottom, and, rising to the surface, escaped in hissing gas. A thin, vapoury cloud arose, and, gradually dissolving, displayed to the eyes of the trembling murderer the figure of an aged Indian, whose long, snowy hair and venerable beard, blown aside by a gentle air from his breast, discovered the well-known *totem* of the great Wan-kan-aga, the father of the Comanche and Shos-shone nation, whom the tradition of the tribe, handed down by skilful hieroglyphics, almost deified for the good actions and deeds of bravery, this famous warrior had performed when on earth.

Stretching out a war-club toward the affrighted murderer, the figure thus addressed him:

"Accursed of my tribe! this day thou hast severed the link between the mightiest nations of the world, while the blood of the brave Shos-shone cries to the Maniton for vengeance. May the water of thy tribe be rank and bitter in their throats!"

Thus saying, and swinging his ponderous war-club (made from the elk's horn) round his head, he dashed out the brains of the Comanche, who fell headlong into the spring, which, from that day to the present moment, remains rank and nauseous, so that, not even when half dead with thirst, can one drink the foul water of that spring.

The good Wan-kan-aga, however, to perpetuate the memory of the Shos-shone warrior, who was renowned in his tribe for valour and nobleness of heart, struck with the same avenging club a hard flat rock, which overhung the rivulet, just out of sight of this scene of blood; and forthwith the rock opened into a round, clear basin, which instantly filled with bubbling sparkling water, than which no thirsty hunter even drank a sweeter or a cooler draught.

Thus the two springs remain, an everlasting memento of the foul murder of the brave Shos-shone, and the stern justice of the good Wan-kan-aga; and from that day the two mighty tribes of the Shos-shone and Comanche have remained severed and apart; although a long and bloody war followed the treacherous murder of the Shos-shone chief, and many a scalp torn from the head of the Comanche paid the penalty of his death.

The American and Canadian trappers assert that the numerous springs which, under the head of Beer, Soda, Steamboat springs, &c., abound in the Rocky Mountains, are the spots where his satanic majesty comes up from his kitchen to breathe

the sweet fresh air, which must doubtless be refreshing to his worship after a few hours spent in superintending the culinary process going on below.

Never was there such a paradise for hunters as this lone and solitary spot. The shelving prairie, at the bottom of which the springs are situated, is entirely surrounded by rugged mountains, and, containing perhaps two or three acres of excellent grass, affords a safe pasture to their animals, which would hardly care to wander from such feeding and the salitrose rocks they love so well to lick.

Immediately overhead Pike's Peak, at an elevation of twelve thousand feet above the level of the sea, towers high into the clouds; while from the fountain, like a granitic amphitheatre, ridge after ridge, clothed with pine and cedar, rises and meets the stupendous mass of mountains, well called "Rocky," which stretches far away north and southward, their gigantic peaks being visible above the strata of clouds which hide their rugged bases.

This first day the sun shone out bright and warm, and not a breath of wind ruffled the ever-green foliage of the cedar-groves. Gay-plumaged birds were twittering in the shrubs, and ravens and magpies were chattering overhead, attracted by the meat I had hung upon a tree; the mules, having quickly filled themselves, were lying round the spring, basking lazily in the sun; and myself, seated on a pack, and pipe in mouth, with rifle ready at my side, indolently enjoyed the rays which, reverberated from the white rock on which I was lying, were deliciously warm and soothing.

A piece of rock, detached from the mountainside and tumbling noisily down, caused me to look up in the direction whence it came. Half a dozen big-horns, or Rocky Mountain sheep, perched on the pinnacle of a rock, were gazing wonderingly upon the prairie, where the mules were rolling enveloped in clouds of dust. The enormous horns of the mountain sheep appeared so disproportionably heavy, that I every moment expected to see them lose their balance and topple over the giddy height. My motions frightened them, and, jumping from rock to rock, they quickly disappeared up the steepest part of the mountain.

At the same moment a herd of black-tail deer crossed the corner of the glade within rifle-shot of me, but, fearing the vicinity of Indians, I refrained from firing before I had reconnoitred the vicinity for sighs of their recent presence.

Immediately over me, on the left bank of the stream, and high above the springs, was a small plateau, one of many which are seen on the mountainsides. Three buffalo-bulls were here quietly feeding, and remained the whole afternoon undisturbed. I saw from the sign that they had very recently drank at the springs, and that the little prairie where my animals were feeding was a frequent resort of solitary bulls.

Perceiving that the game, which was in sight on every side of me, was unwarily tame, I judged from this fact that no Indians were in the immediate vicinity, and therefore I resolved to camp where I was. Ascending a bluff where had been an old Indian camp, I found a number of old lodge-poles, and packed them down to the springs, near which I made my fire, but out of arrow-shot of the shrubbery which lines the stream. Instead of permitting the animals to run loose, I picketed them close to and round the camp, in order that they might act as sentinels during the night, for no man or dog can so soon discover the presence or approach of an Indian as a mule.

The organ and sense of smelling in these animals are so acute that they at once detect the scent peculiar to the natives, and, snorting loud with fear, and by turning their heads with ears pointed to the spot whence the danger is approaching, wake, and warn at the same moment, their sleeping masters of the impending peril.

However, this night I was undisturbed, and slept soundly until the chattering of a magpie overhead awoke me, just as Pike's Peak was being tinged with the first gray streak of dawn.

Daybreak in this wild spot was beautiful in the extreme. While the deep gorge in which I lay was still buried in perfect gloom, the mountain-tops loomed gray and indistinct from out the morning mist. A faint glow of light broke over the ridge which shut out the valley from the east, and, spreading over the sky, first displayed the snow-covered peak, a wreath of vapoury mist encircling it, which gradually rose and disappeared.

Suddenly the dull white of its summit glowed with light like burnished silver; and at the same moment the whole eastern sky blazed, as it were in gold, and ridge and peak, catching the refulgence, glittered with the beams of the rising sun, which at length, peeping over the crest, flooded at once the valley with its dazzling light.

Blowing the ashes of the slumbering fire, I placed upon it the little pot containing a piece of venison for my breakfast, and, relieving my four-footed sentries from their picket-guard, sallied down to the stream, the edges of which were still thickly crusted with ice, for the purpose of taking a luxuriously cold bath; and cold enough it was in all conscience. After my frugal breakfast, unseasoned by bread or salt, or by any other beverage than the refreshing soda-water, I took my rifle and sallied up the mountain to hunt, consigning my faithful animals to the protection of the Dryad of the fountain, offering to that potent sprite the never-failing "medicine" of the first whiff of my pipe before starting from the spot.

Climbing up the mountainside, I reached a level plateau, interspersed with clumps of pine and cedar, where a herd of black-tail deer were quietly feeding. As I had the "wind" I approached under cover of a cedar whose branches feathered to the ground, and, resting my rifle in a forked limb, I selected the plumpest-looking of the band, a young buck, and "let him have it," as the hunters say. Struck through the heart, the deer for an instant stretched out its limbs convulsively, and then bounded away with the band, but in a zig-zag course; and, unlike the rest, whose tails were lifted high, his black-tufted appendage was fast "shut up."

While I, certain of his speedy fall, reloaded my rifle, the band, seeing their comrade staggering behind, suddenly stopped. The wounded animal, with outstretched neck, ran round and round for a few seconds in a giddy circle, and dropped dead within fifty yards of where I stood. The others, like sheep, walked slowly up to the dead animal, and again my rifle gave out its sharp crack from the screen of branches, and another of the hand, jumping high in air, bit the dust. They were both miserably poor, so much so that I left all but the hind quarters and fleece, and, hanging them upon a tree, I returned to camp for a mule to pack in the meat.

The mountains are full of grizzly bears, but, whether they had not yet left their winter-quarters thus early in the season, I saw but one or two tracks, one of which I followed unsuccessfully for many miles over the wildest part of the mountains, into the Bayou Salado. While intent upon the trail, a clattering as of a regiment of cavalry immediately behind me made me bring my rifle to the ready, thinking that a whole nation of mounted Indians were upon me; but, looking back, a band of upward of a hundred elk wore dashing past, looking like a herd of mules, and in their passage down the mountain carrying with them a perfect avalanche of rocks and stones. I killed another deer on my return close to camp, which I reached, packing in the meat on my back, long after dark, and found the animals, which received me with loud neighs of recognition and welcome, with well-filled bellies, taking their evening drink at the springs.

I spent here a very pleasant time, and my animals began soon to improve upon the mountain-grass. Game was very abundant; indeed, I had far more meat than I possibly required; but the surplus I hung up to jerk, as now the sun was getting powerful enough for that process.

I explored all the valleys and canons of the mountains, and even meditated an expedition to the summit of Pike's Peak, where mortal foot has never yet trod. No dread of Indians crossed my mind, probably because I had remained so long unmolested; and I was so perfectly contented that I had even selected a camping-ground where I intended to remain two or three months, and probably should be at the present moment, if I had not got into a "scrape."

The bears latterly began to move, and their tracks became more frequent. One day I was hunting just at the foot of the Peak, when a large she-bear jumped out of a patch of cedars where she had been lying, and, with a loud grunt, charged up the mountain, and, dodging among the rocks, prevented my getting a crack at her. She was very old, and the grizzliest of the grizzly. She was within a few feet of me when I first saw her. It was unluckily nearly dark, or I should have followed and probably killed her, for they seldom run far, particularly at this season, when they are lank and weak.

One day, as I was following a band of deer over the broken ground to the eastward of the mountain, I came suddenly upon an Indian camp, with the fire still smouldering, and dried meat hanging on the trees. Robinson Crusoe could not have been more thoroughly disgusted at the sight of the "footprint in the sand," than was I at this inopportune discovery. I had anticipated a month or two's undisturbed hunting in this remote spot, and now it was out of the question to imagine that the Indians would leave me unmolested. I presently saw two Indians, carrying a deer between them, emerge from the timber bordering the creek, whom I knew at once by their dress to be Arapahós. As, however, my camp was several miles distant, I still hoped that they had not yet discovered its locality, and continued my hunt that day, returning late in the evening to my solitary encampment.

The next morning I removed the animals and packs to a prairie a little lower down the stream, which, although nearer the Indian camp, was almost hidden from view, being inclosed by pine-ridges and ragged buttes, and entered by a narrow gap filled with a dense growth of brush. When I had placed them in security, and taken the precaution to fasten them all to strong picket-pins, with a sufficient length of rope to enable them to feed at ease, and at the same time prevent them straying back to the springs, I again sallied out to hunt.

A little before sunrise I descended the mountain to the

springs, and, being very tired, after taking a refreshing draught of the cold water, I lay down on the rock by the side of the water and fell fast asleep. When I awoke the sun had already set; but, although darkness was fast gathering over the mountain, I was surprised to see a bright light flickering against its sides.

A glance assured me that the mountain was on fire, and, starting up, I saw at once the danger of my position. The bottom had been fired about a mile below the springs, and but a short distance from where I had secured my animals. A dense cloud of smoke was hanging over the gorge, and presently, a light air springing up from the east, a mass of flame shot up into the sky and rolled fiercely-up the stream, the belt of dry brush on its banks catching fire and burning like tinder.

The mountain was already invaded by the devouring element, and two wings of flame spread out from the main stream, which, roaring along the bottom with the speed of a racehorse, licked the mountainside, extending its long line as it advanced. The dry pines and cedars hissed and cracked, as the flame, reaching them, ran up their trunks and spread among the limbs, while the long, waving grass underneath was a sea of fire. From the rapidity with which the fire advanced I feared that it would already have reached my animals, and hurried at once to the spot as fast as I could run.

The prairie itself was as yet untouched, but the surrounding ridges were clothed in fire, and the mules, with stretched ropes, were trembling with fear. Throwing the saddle on my horse, and. the pack on the steadiest mule, I quickly mounted, leaving on the ground a pile of meat, which I had not time to carry with me. The fire had already gained the prairie, and its long, dry grass was soon a sheet of flame, but, worse than all, the gap through which I had to retreat was burning.

Setting spurs into Panchito's sides, I dashed him at the burning bush, and, though his mane and tail were singed in the attempt, he gallantly charged through it. Looking back, I saw the mules huddled together on the other side, and evidently fearing to pass the blazing barrier. As, however, to stop would have been fatal, I dashed on, but, before I had proceeded twenty yards, my old hunting-mule, singed and smoking, was at my side, and the others close behind it.

On all sides I was surrounded by fire. The whole scenery was illuminated, the peaks and distant ridges being as plainly visible as at noonday. The bottom was a roaring mass of flame, but on the other side, the prairie being more bare of cedar-bushes, the fire was less fierce and presented the only way of escape.

To reach it, however, the creek had to be crossed, and the bushes on the banks were burning fiercely, which rendered it no easy matter; moreover, the edges were coated above the water with thick ice, which rendered it still more difficult. I succeeded in pushing Panchito into the stream, but, in attempting to climb the opposite bank, a blaze of fire was puffed into his face, which caused him to rear on end, and, his hind feet flying away from him at the same moment on the ice, he fell backward into the middle of the stream, and rolled over me in the deepest water. Panchito rose on his legs and stood trembling with affright in the middle of the stream, while I dived and groped for my rifle, which had slipped from my hands, and of course sunk to the bottom.

After a search of some minutes I found it, and, again mounting, made another attempt to cross a little further down, in which I succeeded, and, followed by the mules, dashed through the fire and got safely through the line of blazing brush.

Once in safety, I turned in my saddle and had leisure to survey the magnificent spectacle. The fire had extended, at least three miles on each side of the stream, and the mountain was one sheet of flame. A comparatively thin line marked the progress of the devouring element, which, as there was no wind to direct its course, burned on all sides, actually roaring as it went.

I had from the first no doubt but that the fire was caused by the Indians, who had probably discovered my animals, but, thinking that a large party of hunters might be out, had taken advantage of a favourable wind to set fire to the bottom, hoping to secure the horse and mules fn the confusion, without the

295

risk of attacking the camp. Once or twice I felt sure that I saw dark figures running about near where I had seen the Indian camp the previous day, and just as I had charged through the gap I heard a loud yell, which was answered by another at a little distance.

Singularly enough, just as I had got through the blazing line, a breeze sprung up from the westward and drove the fire after me, and I had again to beat a hasty retreat before it.[1]

I encamped six or seven miles from the springs, and, while proceeding down the creek, deer and antelope continually crossed and recrossed the trail, some in their affright running back into the very jaws of the fire. As soon as I had secured the animals I endeavoured to get my rifle into shooting order, but the water had so thoroughly penetrated and swelled the patching round the balls, that it was a long time before I succeeded in cleaning one barrel, the other defying all my attempts. This was a serious accident, as I could not but anticipate a visit from the Indians if they discovered the camp.

All this time the fire was spreading out into the prairies, and, creeping up the "divide," was already advancing upon me. It extended at least five miles on the left bank of the creek, and on the right was more slowly creeping up the mountainside, while the brush and timber in the bottom was one body of flame. Besides the long sweeping line of the advancing flame, the plateaus on the mountainside, and within the line, were burning in every direction, as the squalls and eddies down the gullies drove the fire to all points.

The mountains themselves being invisible, the air, from the low ground where I then was, appeared a mass of fire, and huge crescents of flame danced as it were in the very sky, until a mass of timber blazing at once exhibited the sombre background of the stupendous mountains.

I had scarcely slept an hour when huge clouds of smoke rolling down the bottom frightened the animals, whose loud hin-

1. This fire extended into the prairie, toward the waters of the Platte, upward of forty miles, and for fourteen days its glare was visible on the Arkansas, fifty miles distant.

296

nying awoke me, and, half suffocated by the dense smoke which hung heavily in the atmosphere, I again retreated before the fire, which was rapidly advancing: and this time I did not stop until I had placed thirty or forty miles between me and the enemy. I then encamped in a thickly-timbered bottom on the Fontaine-qui-bouille, where the ground, which had been burned by the hunters in the winter, was studded like a wheat-field with green grass.

On this the animals fared sumptuously for several days—better, indeed, than I did myself, for game was very scarce, and in such poor condition as to be almost uneatable. While encamped on this stream, the wolves infested the camp to that degree, that I could scarcely leave my saddles for a few minutes on the ground without finding the straps of raw hide gnawed to pieces; and one night the hungry brutes ate up all the ropes which were tied on the necks of the animals and trailed along on the ground: they were actually devoured to within a yard of the mules' throats.

One evening a wolf came into camp as I was engaged cleaning my rifle, one barrel of which was still unserviceable, and a long hickory wiping-stick in it at the time. As I was hidden by a tree, the wolf approached the fire within a few feet, and was soon tugging away at an *apishamore* or saddle-cloth of buffalo calfskin which lay on the ground. Without dreaming that the rifle would go off, I put a cap on the useless barrel, and holding it out across my knee in a line with the wolf, snap—ph-i-zz—bang—went the charge of damp powder, much to my astonishment, igniting the stick which remained in the barrel, and driving it like a fiery comet against the ribs of the beast, who, yelling with pain, darted into the prairie at the top of his speed, his singed hair smoking as he ran.

Chapter 29

Buffalo Hunting

It is a singular fact that within the last two years the prairies, extending from the mountains to a hundred miles or more down the Arkansas, have been entirely abandoned by the buffalo. Indeed, in crossing from the settlements of New Mexico, the boundary of their former range is marked by skulls and bones, which appear fresher as the traveller advances westward and toward the waters of the Platte. As the skulls are said to last only three years on the surface of the ground, that period has consequently seen the gradual disappearance of the buffalo from their former haunts.

With the exception of the Bayou Salado, one of their favourite pastures, they are now rarely met with in large bands on the upper waters of the Arkansas; but straggling bulls pass occasionally the foot of the mountain, seeking wintering-places on the elevated plateaus, which are generally more free from snow than the lowland prairies, by reason of the high winds. The bulls separate from the cows about the month of September, and scatter over the prairies and into the mountains, where they recruit themselves during the winter. A few males, however, always accompany the cows, to act as guides and defenders of the herd, on the outskirts of which they are always stationed. The countless bands which are seen together at all seasons are generally composed of cows alone; the bulls congregating in smaller herds, and on the flanks of the main body.

The meat of the cow is infinitely preferable to that of the

male buffalo; but that of the bull, particularly if killed in the mountains, is in better condition during the winter months. From the end of June to September bull-meat is rank and tough, and almost uneatable; while the cows are in perfection, and as fat as stall-fed oxen, the *dépouillé* or fleece exhibiting frequently four inches and more of solid fat.

Whether it is that the meat itself (which, by the way, is certainly the most delicious of flesh) is most easy of digestion, or whether the digestive organs of hunters are "ostrichified" by the severity of exercise, and the bracing, wholesome climate of the mountains and plains, it is a fact that most prodigious quantities of "fat cow" may be swallowed with the greatest impunity, and not the slightest inconvenience ever follows the mammoth feasts of the gourmands of the Far West. The powers of the Canadian voyageurs and hunters in the consumption of meat strike the greenhorn with wonder and astonishment, and are only equalled by the gastronomical capabilities exhibited by the Indian dogs, both following the same plan in their epicurean gorgings.

On slaughtering a fat cow, the hunter carefully lays by, as a titbit for himself, the "boudins" and medullary intestine, which are prepared by being inverted and partially cleaned (this, however, is not thought indispensable). The *dépouillé* or fleece, the short and delicious hump-rib and "tender-loin," are then carefully stowed away, and with these the rough edge of the appetite is removed. But the course is, *par excellence,* the sundry yards of "boudin," which, lightly browned over the embers of the fire, slide down the well-lubricated throat of the hungry mountaineer, yard after yard disappearing in quick succession.

I once saw two Canadians[2] commence at either end of such a coil of grease, the mass lying between them on a dirty *apishamore*[3] like the coil of a huge snake. As yard after yard glided glibly down their throats, and the serpent on the saddle-cloth was dwindling from an anaconda to a moderate-sized rattlesnake, it became a

2. The majority of the trappers and mountain-hunters are French Canadians and Saint-Louis French Creoles.
3. Skin of the buffalo-calf, dressed soft, of which a saddle-cloth is made.

great point with each of the feasters to hurry his operation, so as to gain a march upon his neighbour, and improve the opportunity by swallowing more than his just proportion; each, at the same time, exhorting the other, whatever he did, to feed fair, and every now and then, overcome by the unblushing attempts of his partner to bolt a vigorous mouthful, would suddenly jerk back his head, drawing out at the same moment, by the retreating motion, several yards of boudin from his neighbour's mouth and stomach (for the greasy *viand* required no mastication, and was bolted whole), and, snapping up himself the ravished portions, greedily swallowed them, to be in turn again withdrawn and subjected to a similar process by the other.

No animal requires so much killing as a buffalo. Unless shot through the lungs or spine, they invariably escape; and, even when thus mortally wounded, or even struck through the very heart, they will frequently run a considerable distance before falling to the ground, particularly if they see the hunter after the wound is given. If, however, he keeps himself concealed after firing, the animal will remain still, if it does not immediately fall. It is a most painful sight to witness the dying struggles of the huge beast.

The buffalo invariably evinces the greatest repugnance to lie down when mortally wounded, apparently conscious that, when once touching mother earth, there is no hope left him. A bull, shot through the heart or lungs, with blood streaming from his mouth, and protruding tongue, his eyes rolling, bloodshot, and glazed with death, braces himself on his legs, swaying from side to side, stamps impatiently at his growing weakness, or lifts his rugged and matted head and helplessly bellows out his conscious impotence.

To the last, however, he endeavours to stand upright, and plants his limbs farther apart, but to no purpose. As the body rolls like a ship at sea, his head slowly turns from side to side, looking about, as it were, for the unseen and treacherous enemy who has brought him, the lord of the plains, to such a pass. Gouts of purple blood spurt from his mouth and nostrils, and gradually the failing limbs refuse longer to support the ponderous carcass; more heavily rolls the body from side to side, until suddenly, for a brief instant, it becomes rigid and still; a convulsive tremor seizes it, and, with a low, sobbing gasp, the huge animal falls over on his side, the limbs extended stark and stiff, and the mountain of flesh without life or motion.

The first attempts of a "greenhorn" to kill a buffalo are invariably unsuccessful. He sees before him a mass of flesh, nearly five feet in depth from the top of the hump to the brisket, and consequently imagines that, by planting his ball midway between these points, it must surely reach the vitals. Nothing, however, is more erroneous than the impression; for to "throw a buffalo in his tracks," which is the phrase for making a clean shot, he must be struck but a few inches above the brisket, behind the shoulder, where alone, unless the spine be divided, a death-shot will reach the vitals.

I once shot a bull, the ball passing directly through the very centre of the heart and tearing a hole sufficiently large to insert the finger, which ran upward of half a mile before it fell, and yet the ball had passed completely through the animal, cutting its heart almost in two. I also saw eighteen shots, the half of them muskets, deliberately fired into an old bull, at six paces, and some of them passing through the body, the poor animal standing the whole time, and making feeble attempts to charge. The nineteenth shot, with the muzzle touching his body, brought him to the ground. The head of the buffalo-bull is so thickly covered with coarse matted hair, that a ball fired at half a dozen paces will not penetrate the skull through the shaggy front-lock. I have frequently attempted this with a rifle carrying twenty-five balls to the pound, but never once succeeded.

Notwithstanding the great and wanton destruction of the buffalo, many years must elapse before this lordly animal becomes extinct. In spite of their numerous enemies, they still exist in countless numbers, and, could any steps be taken to protect them; as is done in respect of other game, they would ever remain the life and ornament of the boundless prairies, and afford ample and never-failing provision to the travellers over these otherwise desert plains. Some idea of the prodigious slaughter of these animals may be formed, by mentioning the fact that upward of one hundred thousand buffalo robes find their way annually into the United States and Canada: and these are the skins of cows alone, the bull's hide being so thick that it is never dressed.

Besides this, the Indians kill a certain number for their own use, exclusive of those whose meat they require; and the reckless slaughter of buffalo by parties of white men, emigrants to the Columbia, California, and elsewhere, leaving, as they proceed on their journey, thousands of untouched carcasses on the trail, swells the aggregate of this wholesale destruction to an enormous amount.

CHAPTER 30

Grizzly Bears

The grizzly bear is the fiercest of the *feræ naturæ* of the mountains. His great strength and wonderful tenacity of life render an encounter with him anything but desirable, and therefore it is a rule with the Indians and white hunters never to attack him unless backed by a strong party. Although, like every other wild animal, he usually flees from man, yet at certain seasons, when maddened by love or hunger, he not unfrequently charges at first sight of a foe; when, unless killed dead, a hug at close quarters is anything but a pleasant embrace, his strong hooked claws stripping the flesh from the bones as easily as a cook peels an onion. Many are the tales of bloody encounters with these animals which the trappers delight to recount to the "greenhorn," to enforce their caution as to the foolhardiness of ever attacking the grizzly bear.

Some years ago a trapping party was on their way to the mountains, led, I believe, by old Sublette, a well-known captain of the West. Among the band was one John Glass, a trapper who had been all his life in the mountains, and had seen, probably, more exciting adventures, and had had more wonderful and hairbreadth escapes, than any of the rough and hardy fellows who make the West their home, and whose lives are spent in a succession of perils and privations.

On one of the streams running from the "Black Hills," a range of mountains northward of the Platte, Glass and a companion were one day setting their traps, when, on passing through a cherry-thicket which skirted the stream, the former, who was in advance, descried a large grizzly bear quietly turning up the turf with his nose, searching for *yampa*-roots or pig-nuts, which there abounded.

Glass immediately called his companion, and both, proceeding cautiously, crept to the skirt of the thicket, and, taking steady aim at the animal, whose broadside was fairly exposed at the distance of twenty yards, discharged their rifles at the same instant, both balls taking effect, but not inflicting a mortal wound. The bear, giving a groan of pain, jumped with all four legs from the ground, and, seeing the wreaths of smoke hanging at the edge of the brush, charged at once in that direction, snorting with pain and fury.

"Hurraw, Bill!" roared out Glass, as he saw the animal rushing toward them, "we'll be made 'meat' of as sure as shootin'!" and, leaving the tree behind which he had concealed himself, he bolted through the thicket, followed closely by his companion. The brush was so thick, that they could scarcely make their way through, whereas the weight and strength of the bear carried him through all obstructions, and he was soon close upon them.

About a hundred yards from the thicket was a steep bluff, and between these points was a level piece of prairie; Glass saw that his only chance was to reach this bluff, and shouting to his companion to make for it, they both broke from the cover and flew like lightning across the open space. When more than half way across, the bear being about fifty yards behind them, Glass, who was leading, tripped over a stone, and fell to the ground, and just as he rose to his feet, the beast, rising on his hind feet, confronted him.

As he closed, Glass, never losing his presence of mind, cried to his companion to load up quickly, and discharged his pistol full into the body of the animal, at the same moment that the bear, with blood streaming from its nose and mouth, knocked the pistol from his hand with one blow of its paw, and, fixing its claws deep into his flesh, rolled with him to the ground.

The hunter, notwithstanding his hopeless situation, struggled manfully, drawing his knife and plunging it several times into the body of the beast, which, furious with pain, tore with tooth and claw the body of the wretched victim, actually baring the ribs of flesh, and exposing the very bones. Weak with loss of blood, and with eyes blinded with the blood which streamed from his lacerated scalp, the knife at length fell from his hand, and Glass sunk down insensible, and to all appearance dead.

His companion, who, up to this moment, had watched the conflict, which, however, lasted but a few seconds, thinking that his turn would come next, and not having had presence of mind even to load his rifle, fled with might and main back to camp, where he narrated the miserable fate of poor Glass. The captain of the band of trappers, however, dispatched the man with a companion back to the spot where he lay, with instructions to remain by him if still alive, or to bury him if, as all supposed he was, defunct, promising them at the same time a sum of money for so doing.

On reaching the spot, which was red with blood, they found Glass still breathing, and the bear, dead and stiff, actually lying upon his body. Poor Glass presented a horrifying spectacle; the flesh was torn in strips from his chest and limbs, and large flaps strewed the ground; his scalp hung bleeding over his face, which was also lacerated in a shocking manner.

The bear, beside the three bullets which had pierced its body; bore the marks of the fierce nature of Glass's final struggle, no less than twenty gaping wounds in the breast and belly testifying to the gallant defence of the mountaineer.

Imagining that, if not already dead, the poor fellow could not possibly survive more than a few moments, the men collected his arms, stripped him even of his hunting-shirt and moccasins, and, merely pulling the dead bear off the body, mounted their horses, and slowly followed the remainder of the party, saying, when they reached it, that Glass was dead, as probably they thought, and that they had buried him.

In a few days the gloom which pervaded the trappers' camp,

occasioned by the loss of a favourite companion, disappeared, and Glass's misfortune, although frequently mentioned over the campfire, at length was almost entirely forgotten in the excitement of the hunt and Indian perils which surrounded them. Months elapsed, the hunt was over, and the party of trappers were on their way to the trading-fort with their packs of beaver.

It was nearly sundown, and the round adobe bastions of the mud-built fort were just in sight, when a horseman was seen slowly approaching them along the banks of the river. When near enough to discern his figure, they saw a lank, cadaverous form with a face so scarred and disfigured that scarcely a feature was discernible. Approaching the leading horsemen, one of whom happened to be the companion of the defunct Glass in his memorable bear scrape, the stranger, in a hollow voice, reining in his horse before them, exclaimed, "Hurraw, Bill, my boy! you thought I was 'gone under' that time, did you? but hand me over my horse and gun, my lad; I ain't dead yet by a dam sight!"

What was the astonishment of the whole party, and the genuine horror of Bill and his worthy companion in the burial story, to hear the well-known, though now much altered, voice of John Glass, who had been killed by a grizzly bear months before, and comfortably interred, as the two men had reported, and all had believed!

There he was, however, and no mistake about it; and all crowded round to hear from his lips, how, after the lapse of he knew not how long, he had gradually recovered, and being without anus, or even a butcher-knife, he had fed upon the almost putrid carcass of the bear for several days, until he had regained sufficient strength to crawl, when, tearing off as much of the bear's-meat as he could carry in his enfeebled state, he crept down the river; and suffering excessive torture from his wounds, and hunger, and cold, he made the best of his way to the fort, which was some eighty or ninety miles from the place of his encounter with the bear, and, living the greater part of the way upon roots and berries, he after many, many days, arrived in a pitiable state, from which he had now recovered, and was, to use his own expression, "as slick as a peeled onion."

A trapper on Arkansas, named Valentine Herring, but better known as "Old Rube," told me that once, when visiting his traps one morning on a stream beyond the mountains, he found one missing, at the same time that he discovered fresh bear "sign" about the banks. Proceeding down the river in search of the lost trap, he heard the noise of some large body breaking through the thicket of plum-bushes which belted the stream. Ensconcing himself behind a rock, he presently observed a huge grizzly bear emerge from the bush and limp on three legs to a flat rock, which he mounted, and then, quietly seating himself, he raised one of his fore paws, on which Rube, to his amazement, discovered his trap tight and fast.

The bear, lifting his iron-gloved foot close to his face, gravely examined it, turning his paw round and round, and quaintly bending his head from side to side, looking, at the trap from the corners of his eyes, and with an air of mystery and puzzled curiosity, for he evidently could not make out what the novel and painful appendage could be; and every now and then smelled it and tapped it lightly on the rock. This, however, only paining the animal the more, he would lick the trap, as if deprecating its anger, and wishing to conciliate it.

After watching these curious antics for some time, as the bear seemed inclined to resume his travels, Rube, to regain his trap, was necessitated to bring the bear's cogitations to a close, and, levelling his rifle, shot him dead, cutting off his paw and returning with it to camp, where the trappers were highly amused at the idea of trapping a b'ar.

Near the same spot where Glass encountered his "scrape," some score of Sioux squaws were one day engaged in gathering cherries in the thicket near their village, and had already nearly filled their baskets, when a bear suddenly appeared in the midst, and, with a savage growl, charged among them. Away ran the terrified squaws, yelling and shrieking, out of the shrubbery, nor stopped until safely ensconced within their lodges. Bruin, however, preferring fruit to meat, albeit of tender squaws, after routing the petticoats, quietly betook himself to the baskets, which he quickly emptied, and then quietly retired.

Bears are exceedingly fond of plums and cherries, and a thicket of this fruit in the vicinity of the mountains is, at the season when they are ripe, a sure "find" for Mr. Bruin. When they can get fruit they prefer such food to meat, but are, nevertheless, carnivorous animals.

The game, *par excellence,* of the Rocky Mountains, and that which takes precedence in a comestible point of view, is the *carnero cimmaron* of the Mexicans, the big-horn or mountain-sheep of the Canadian hunters. This animal, which partakes both of the nature of the deer and goat, resembles the latter more particularly in its habits, and its characteristic liking to lofty, inaccessible points of the mountains, whence it seldom descends to the upland valleys excepting in very severe weather. In size the mountain-sheep is between the domestic animal and the common red deer of America, but more strongly made than the latter.

Its colour is a brownish dun (the hair being tipped with a darker tinge as the animal's age increases), with a whitish streak on the hind quarters, the tail being shorter than a deer's, and tipped with black. The horns of the male are enormous, curved backward, and often three feet in length with a circumference of twenty inches near the head. The hunters assert that, in descending the precipitous sides of the mountains, the sheep frequently leap from a height of twenty or thirty feet, invariably alighting on their horns, and thereby saving their bones from certain dislocation.

They are even more acute in the organs of sight and smell than the deer; and as they love to resort to the highest and most inaccessible spots, whence a view can readily be had of approaching danger, and particularly as one of the band is always stationed on the most commanding pinnacle of rock as sentinel, while the others are feeding, it is no easy matter to get within rifle-shot of the cautious animals. When alarmed they ascend still higher up the mountain: halting now and then on some overhanging crag, and looking down at the object which may have frightened them, they again commence their ascent, leaping from point to point, and throwing down an avalanche of rocks and stones as they bound up the steep sides of the mountain.

They are generally very abundant in all parts of the main chain of the Rocky Mountains, but particularly so in the vicinity of the "Parks" and the Bayou Salado, as well as in the range between the upper waters of the Del Norte and Arkansas, Called the. "Wet Mountain" by the trappers. On the Sierra Madre, or Cordillera of New Mexico and Chihuahua, they are also numerous.

The first mountain-sheep I killed, I got within shot of in rather a curious manner. I had undertaken several unsuccessful hunts for the purpose of procuring a pair of horns of this animal, as well as some skins, which are of excellent quality when dressed, but had almost given up any hope of approaching them, when one day, having killed and butchered a black-tail deer in the mountains, I sat down, with my back to a small rock, and fell asleep.

On awaking, feeling inclined for a smoke, I drew from my pouch a pipe, and flint and steel, and began leisurely to cut a charge of tobacco. While thus engaged I became sensible of a peculiar odour which was wafted right into my face by the breeze, and which, on snuffing it once or twice, I immediately recognized as that which emanates from sheep and goats. Still I never thought that one of the former animals could be in the neighbourhood, for my mule was picketed on the little plateau where I sat, and was leisurely cropping the buffalo-grass which thickly covered it.

Looking up carelessly from my work, as a whiff stronger than before reached my nose, what was my astonishment at seeing five mountain-sheep within ten paces, and regarding me with a curious and astonished gaze! Without drawing a breath, I put out my hand and grasped the rifle, which was lying within reach;

but the motion, slight as it was, sufficed to alarm them, and with a loud bleat the old ram bounded up the mountain, followed by the band, and at so rapid a pace that all my attempts to "draw a bead" upon them were ineffectual.

When, however, they reached a little plateau about one hundred and fifty yards from where I stood, they suddenly stopped, and, approaching the edge, looked down at me, shaking their heads, and bleating their displeasure at the intrusion. No sooner did I see them stop than my rifle was at my shoulder, and covering the broadside of the one nearest to me. An instant after and I pulled the trigger, and at the report the sheep jumped convulsively from the rock, and made one attempt to follow its flying companions; but its strength failed, and, circling round once or twice at the edge of the plateau, it fell over on its side, and, rolling down the steep rock, tumbled dead very near me.

My prize proved a very fine young male, but had not a large pair of horns. It was, however, "seal" fat, and afforded me a choice supply of meat, which was certainly the best I had eaten in the mountains, being fat and juicy, and in flavour somewhat partaking both of the domestic sheep and buffalo.

Several attempts have been made to secure the young of these animals and transport them to the States; and, for this purpose, an old mountaineer, one Billy Williams, took with him a troop of milch-goats, by which to bring up the young sheep; but although he managed to take several fine lambs, I believe that he did not succeed in reaching the frontier with one living specimen out of some half-score. The banters frequently rear them in the mountains; and they become greatly attached to their masters, enlivening the camp with their merry gambols.

The elk, in point of size, ranks next to the buffalo. It is found in all parts of the mountains, and descends not unfrequently far down into the plains in the vicinity of the larger streams. A full-grown elk is as large as a mule, with rather a heavy neck and body, and stout limbs, its feet leaving a track as large as that of a two-year-old steer. They are dull, sluggish animals, at least in comparison with others of the deer tribe, and are easily approached and killed. In winter they congregate in large herds, often numbering several hundreds; and at that season are fond of travelling, their track through the snow having the appearance of a broad beaten road.

The elk requires less killing than any other of the deer tribe (whose tenacity of life is remarkable); a shot anywhere in the fore part of the animal brings it to the ground. On one occasion I killed two with one ball, which passed through the neck of the first, and struck the second, which was standing a few paces distant, through the heart: both fell dead. A deer, on the contrary, often runs a considerable distance, strike it where you will. The meat of the elk is strong-flavoured, and more like "poor bull" than venison: it is only eatable when the animal is fat and in good condition; at other times it is strong-tasted and stringy.

The antelope, the smallest of the deer tribe, affords the hunter a sweet and nutritious meat, when that of nearly every other description of game, from the poorness and scarcity of the grass during winter, is barely eatable. They are seldom seen now in very large bands on the grand prairies, having been driven from the old pastures by the Indians and white hunters. The former, by means of "surrounds," an inclosed space formed in one of the passes used by these animals, very often drive into the toils an entire band of antelope of several hundreds, when not one escapes slaughter.

I have seen them on the western sides of the mountains, and in the mountain valleys, in herds of several thousands. They are exceedingly timid animals, but at the same time wonderfully curious; and their curiosity very often proves their death, for the hunter, taking advantage of this weakness, plants his wiping-stick in the ground, with a cap or red handkerchief on the point, and concealing himself in the long grass, waits, rifle in hand, the approach of the inquisitive antelope, who, seeing an unusual object in the plain, trots up to it, and, coming within range of the deadly tube, pays dearly for his temerity.

An antelope, when alone, is one of the stupidest of beasts, and becomes so confused and frightened at sight of a travelling party, that it frequently runs right into the midst of the danger it seeks to avoid.

I had heard most wonderful accounts from the trappers of an animal, the existence of which was beyond all doubt, which, although exceedingly rare, was occasionally met with in the mountains, but, from its supposed dangerous ferocity, and the fact of its being a cross between the devil and a bear, was never molested by the Indians or white hunters, and a wide berth given whenever the animal made its dreaded appearance.

Most wonderful stories were told of its audacity and fearlessness; how it sometimes jumps from an overhanging rock on a deer or buffalo, and, fastening on its neck, soon brings it to the ground; how it has been known to leap upon a hunter when passing near its place of concealment, and devour him in a twinkling—often charging furiously into a camp, and playing all sorts of pranks on the goods and chattels of the mountaineers. The general belief was that the animal owes its paternity to the old gentleman himself; but the most reasonable declare it to be a cross between the bear and wolf.

Hunting one day with an old Canadian trapper, he told me that, in a part of the mountains which we were about to visit on the morrow, he once had a battle with a "*carcagieu*," which lasted upward of two hours, during which he fired a pouchful of balls into the animal's body, which spat them out as fast as they were shot in. To the truth of this improbable story he called all the saints to bear witness.

Two days after, as we were toiling up a steep ridge after a band of mountain-sheep, my companion, who was in advance, suddenly threw himself flat behind a rock, and exclaimed, in a smothered tone, signalling me with his hand to keep down and conceal myself, "*Sacré enfant de Gârce, mais* here's von dam *carcagieu!*"

I immediately cocked my rifle, and, advancing to the rock, and peeping over it, saw an animal, about the size of a large badger, engaged in scraping up the earth about a dozen paces from where we were concealed. Its colour was dark, almost black;

312

its body long, and apparently tailless; and I at once recognized the mysterious beast to be a "glutton." After I had sufficiently examined the animal, I raised my rifle to shoot, when a louder than common "*Enfant de Gârce*" from my companion alarmed the animal, and it immediately ran off, when I stood up and fired both barrels after it, but without effect; the attempt exciting a derisive laugh from the Canadian, who exclaimed, "*Pe gar*, may be you got fifty balls; vel, shoot 'em all at *de* dam *carcagieu*, and he not care a dam!"

The skins of these animals are considered "great medicine" by the Indians, and will fetch almost any price. They are very rarely met with on the plains, preferring the upland valleys and broken ground of the mountains, which afford them a better field for their method of securing game, which is by lying in wait behind a rock, or on the steep bank of a ravine, concealed by a tree or shrub, until a deer or antelope passes underneath, when they spring upon the animal's back, and, holding on with their strong and sharp claws, which they bury in the flesh, soon bring it bleeding to the ground. The Indians say they are purely carnivorous; but I imagine that, like the bear, they not unfrequently eat fruit and roots, when animal food is not to be had.

I have said that the mountain wolves, and, still more so, the coyote of the plains, are less frightened at the sight of man than any other beast. One night, when encamped on an affluent of the Platte, a heavy snow-storm falling at the time, I lay down in my blanket, after first heaping on the fire a vast pile of wood, to burn till morning. In the middle of the night I was awakened by the excessive cold, and, turning toward the fire, which was burning bright and cheerfully, what was my astonishment to see a large gray wolf sitting quietly before it, his eyes closed, and his head nodding in sheer drowsiness!

Although I had frequently seen wolves evince their disregard to fires, by coming within a few feet of them to seize upon any scraps of meat which might be left exposed, I had never seen or heard of one approaching so close as to warm his body, and for that purpose alone. However, I looked at him for some moments

313

without disturbing the beast, and closed my eyes and went to sleep, leaving him to the quiet enjoyment of the blaze.

This is not very wonderful when I mention that it is a very common thing for these animals to gnaw the straps of a saddle on which your head is reposing for a pillow.

When I turned my horse's head from Pike's Peak I quite regretted the abandonment of my mountain life, solitary as it was, and more than once thought of again taking the trail to the Bayou Salado, where I had enjoyed such good sport.

Apart from the feeling of loneliness which any one in my situation must naturally have experienced, surrounded by stupendous works of nature, which in all their solitary grandeur frowned upon me, and sinking into utter insignificance the miserable mortal who crept beneath their shadow, still there was something inexpressibly exhilarating in the sensation of positive freedom from all worldly care, and a consequent expansion of the sinews, as it were, of mind and body, which made me feel elastic as a ball of Indian rubber, and in a state of such perfect *insouciance* that no more dread of scalping Indians entered my mind than if I had been sitting in Broadway, in one of the windows of Astor House.

A citizen of the world, I never found any difficulty in investing my resting-place, wherever it might be, with all the attributes of a home; and hailed, with delight equal to that which the artificial comforts of a civilized home would have caused, the, to me, domestic appearance of my hobbled animals, as they grazed around the camp, when I returned after a hard day's hunt. By the way, I may here remark that my sporting feeling underwent a great change when I was necessitated to follow and kill game for the support of life, and as a means of subsistence; and the slaughter of deer and buffalo no longer became sport when the object was to fill the larder, and the excitement of the hunt was occasioned by the alternative of a plentiful feast or a *banyan*; and, although ranking under the head of the most red-hot of sportsmen, I can safely acquit myself of ever wantonly destroying a deer or buffalo unless I was in need of meat; and such consideration for the *feræ naturæ* is common to all the mountaineers who look to game alone for their support.

Although liable to an accusation of barbarism, I must confess that the very happiest moments of my life have been spent in the wilderness of the Far West; and I never recall but with pleasure the remembrance of my solitary camp in the Bayou Salado, with no friend near me more faithful than my rifle, and no companions more sociable than my good horse and mules, or the attendant coyote which nightly serenaded us. With a plentiful supply of dry pine-logs on the fire, and its cheerful blaze streaming far up into the sky, illuminating the valley far and near, and exhibiting the animals, with well-filled bellies, standing contentedly at rest over their picket-pins, I would sit cross-legged enjoying the genial warmth, and, pipe in mouth, watch the blue smoke as it curled upward, building castles in its vapoury wreaths, and, in the fantastic shapes it assumed, peopling the solitude with figures of those far away.

Scarcely, however, did I ever wish to change such hours of freedom for all the luxuries of civilized life, and, unnatural and extraordinary as it may appear, yet such is the fascination of the life of the mountain hunter, that I believe not one instance could be adduced of even the most polished and civilized of men, who had once tasted the sweets of its attendant liberty and freedom from every worldly care, not regretting the moment when he exchanged it for the monotonous life of the settlements, nor sighing, and sighing again, once more to partake of its pleasures and allurements.

Nothing can be more social and cheering than the welcome blaze of the camp fire on a cold winter's night, and nothing more amusing or entertaining, if not instructive, than the rough conversation of the single-minded mountaineers, whose simple daily talk is all of exciting adventure, since their whole existence is spent in scenes of peril and privation; and consequently the narration of their everyday life is a tale of thrilling accidents and hairbreadth 'scapes, which, though simple matter-of-fact to them, appear a startling romance to those who are not

315

acquainted with the nature of the lives led by these men, who, with the sky for a roof and their rifles to supply them with food and clothing, call no man lord or master, and are as free as the game they follow.

A hunter's camp in the Rocky Mountains is quite a picture. He does not always take the trouble to build any shelter unless it is in the snow season, when a couple of deerskins stretched over a willow frame shelter him from the storm. At other seasons he is content with a mere break-wind. Near at hand are two upright poles, with another supported on the top of these, on which is displayed, out of reach of hungry wolf or coyote, meat of every variety the mountains afford. Buffalo *dépouillés*, hams of deer and mountain- sheep, beaver-tails, &c., stock the larder.

Under the shelter of the skins hang his powder-horn and bullet-pouch; while his rifle, carefully defended from the damp, is always within reach of his arm. Round the blazing fire the hunters congregate at night, and while cleaning their rifles, making or mending moccasins, or running bullets, spin long yarns of their hunting exploits, &c.

Some hunters, who have married Indian squaws, carry about with them the Indian lodge of buffalo-skins, which are stretched in a conical form round a frame of poles. Near the camp is always seen the graining-block, a log of wood with the bark stripped and perfectly smooth, which is planted obliquely in the ground, and on which the hair is removed from the skins to prepare them for being dressed. There are also "stretching-frames," on which the skins are placed to undergo the process of dubbing, which is the removal of the flesh and fatty particles adhering to the skin, by means of the *dubber*, an instrument made of the stock of an elk's horn.

The last process is the "smoking," which is effected by digging a round hole in the ground and lighting in it an armful of rotten wood or punk. Three sticks are then planted round the hole, and their tops brought together and tied. The skin is then placed on this frame, and all the holes by which the smoke might escape carefully stopped: in ten or twelve hours the skin is thoroughly smoked and ready for immediate use.

The camp is invariably made in a picturesque locality, for, like the Indian, the white hunter has ever an eye to the beautiful. The broken ground of the mountains, with their numerous tumbling and babbling rivulets, and groves and thickets of shrubs and timber, always afford shelter from the boisterous winds of winter, and abundance of fuel and water. Facing the rising sun the hunter invariably erects his shanty, with a wall of precipitous rock in rear to defend it from the gusts which often sweep down the gorges of the mountains. Round the camp his animals, well hobbled at night, feed within sight, for nothing does a hunter dread more than a visit from the horse-stealing Indians; and to be "afoot" is the acme of his misery.

CHAPTER 31

Return to Arkansas

When I returned to the Arkansas I found a small party were making preparations to cross the grand prairie to the United States, intending to start on the 1st of May, before which time there would not be a sufficiency of grass to support the animals on the way. With these men I determined to travel, and in the mean time employed myself in hunting on the "Wet Mountain," and Fisher's Hole, a valley at the head of St. Charles, as well as up the Arkansas itself. I observed in these excursions that vegetation was in a much more forward state in the mountain valleys and the prairies contiguous to their bases than on the open plains, and that in the vicinity of the *pueblo* it was still more backward than in any other spot; on the 15th of April not a blade of green grass having as yet made its appearance round the fort.

This was not from the effects of drought, for several refreshing showers had fallen since the disappearance of the snow; neither was there any apparent difference in the soil, which is a rich loam, and in the river-bottom, an equally rich vegetable mould. At this time, when the young grass had not yet appeared here, it was several inches high on the mountains and upland prairies, and the cherry and currant-bushes on the creeks were bursting into leaf.

Among the wives of the mountaineers in the fort was one Mexican woman from the state of Durango, who had been carried off by the Comanches in one of their raids into that department. Remaining with them several years, she eventually accompanied a party of Kioways (allies of the Comanche) to Bent's Fort on the Arkansas. Here she was purchased from them and became the wife of Hawkens, who afterward removed from Bent's and took up his abode at the *pueblo*, and was my hospitable host while on the Arkansas.

It appeared that her Mexican husband, by some means or another, heard that she had reached Bent's Fort, and, impelled by affection, undertook the long journey of upward of fifteen hundred miles to recover his lost wife. In the mean time, however, she had borne her American husband a daughter, and when her first spouse claimed her as his own, and wished her to accompany him back to her own country, she only consented on condition that she might carry with her the child, from which she steadily refused to be separated. The father, however, turned a deaf ear to this request, and eventually the poor Durangueño returned to his home alone, his spouse preferring to share the buffalo-rib and venison with her mountaineer before the *frijole* and *chile colorado* of the bereaved *ranchero*.

Three or four Taos women, and as many squaws of every nation, comprised the "female society" on the Upper Arkansas, giving good promise of peopling the river with a sturdy race of half-breeds, if all the little dusky buffalo-fed urchins who played about the corral of the fort arrived scathless at maturity.

Among the hunters on the Upper Arkansas were four Delaware Indians, the remnant of a band who had been trapping for several years in the mountains, and many of whom had been killed by hostile Indians, or in warfare with the Apaches while in the employ of the states of New Mexico and Chihuahua. Their names were Jim Dicky, Jim Swannick, Little Beaver, and Big Nigger. The last had married a squaw from the Taos *pueblo*, and, happening to be in New Mexico with his spouse at the time of the late rising against the Americans, he very naturally took part with the people by whom he had been adopted.

In the attack on the Indian *pueblo* it was said that Big Nigger particularly distinguished himself, calling by name to several of the mountain-men who were among the attacking party, and inviting them to come near enough for him, the Big Nigger, to "throw them in their tracks." And this feat he effected more than once, to the cost of the assailants, for it was said that the Delaware killed nearly all who fell on the side of the Americans, his squaw loading his rifle and encouraging him in the fight.

By some means or another he escaped after the capture of the *pueblo*, and made his way to the mountains on the Arkansas; but as it was reported that a price was put upon his head, he retired, in company with the other Delawares, to the mountains, where they all lay *perdus* for a time; and it was pretty well understood that any one feeling inclined to reap the reward by the capture of Big Nigger would be under the necessity of "taking him," and with every probability of catching a *Tartar* at the same time, the three other Delawares having taken the delinquent under the protection of their rifles. Although companions of the American and Canadian hunters for many years, anything but an *entente cordiale* existed toward their white *confrères* on the part of the Delawares, who knew very well that anything in the shape of Indian blood is looked upon with distrust and contempt by the white hunters.

Tharpe, an Indian trader, who had just returned from the Cheyenne village at the "Big Timber" on the Arkansas, had purchased from some Kioways two prisoners, a Mexican and an American negro. The former had been carried off by the Comanche from Durango when about seven years old, had almost entirely forgotten his own tongue, and neither knew his own age nor what length of time he had been a captive among the Indians. The degraded and miserable existence led by this poor creature had almost obliterated all traces of humanity from his character and appearance.

Probably not more than twenty-five years of age, he was already wrinkled and haggard in his face, which was that of a man of threescore years. Wrapped in a dirty blanket, with his long hair streaming over his shoulders, he skulked, like some savage animal, in holes and corners of the fort, seeming to shun his fellow-men, in a consciousness of his abject and degraded condition. At night he would be seen with his face close to the rough doors of the rooms, peering through the cracks, and envying the (to him) unusual luxury within. When he observed anyone approach the door, he instantly withdrew and concealed himself in the darkness until he passed. A present of tobacco, now and then, won for me the confidence of the poor fellow, and I gathered from him, in broken Spanish mixed with Indian, an account of his miseries.

I sat with him one night on a log in the corral, as he strove to make me understand that once, long, long ago, he had been *muy rico*"—very rich; that he lived in a house where was always a fire like that burning within, and where he used to sit on his mother's lap; and this fact he repeated over and over again, thinking that to show that once affectionate regard had been bestowed upon him, was to prove that he had been at one time an important personage. "*Me quiso mucho, mucho*," he said, speaking of his mother—"she loved me very, very much; and I had good clothes and plenty to eat; but that was many, many moons ago."

"*Mire*," he continued, "from this size," putting his hand out about three feet from the ground—"*ni padre, ni madre, ni amigos he tenido yo*"—neither father, mother, nor friends have I had; "*pero patadas, bastante*"—but plenty of kicks, "*ypoca carne*"—and very little meat.

I asked him if he had no wish to return to his own country. His haggard face lighted, up for an instant, as the dim memory of his childhood's home returned to his callous mind. "*Ay, Dios mio!*" he exclaimed, "*si fuera posible*"—Ah, my God, if it were possible! "but no," he continued, after a pause, "*estoy ahora muy bruto, y asi no me quadrara à ver mi madre*"—I am now no more than a brute, and in this state would not like to see my mother.

"*Y de mas*"—and moreover—"my *compadre*," as he called the man who had purchased him, "is going to give me a shirt and a *sombrero*; what can I want more? *Vaya, es-mejor asi*"—it is better as it is. One night he accosted me in the corral in an unusual degree of excitement.

"*Mire!*" he exclaimed, seizing me by the arm, "look here!

321

estoy boracho"—I am drunk! "*Me dio mi compadre un pedazo de aguardiente*"—my godfather has given me a bit of brandy. "*Y estoy tan feliz, y ligero! como paxaro, eomo pa-x-ar-o*"—he hiccupped— and I am as happy and as light as a bird. "*Me vuelo*"—I am flying. "*Me dicen que estoy boracho: ay que palabra bonita!*" —they tell me I am drunk: drunk—what a beautiful word is this! "*En mi vida, nunca he sentido como ahora*"—never in my life have I felt as I do now. And the poor wretch covered his head with a blanket, and laughed long and loud at the trick he had played his old friend misery.

The negro, on the contrary, was a characteristic specimen of his race, always laughing, singing, and dancing, and cutting uncouth capers. He had been a slave in the semi-civilized Cherokee nation, and had been captured by the Comanches, as he himself declared, but most probably had run away from his master, and joined them voluntarily. He was a musician, and of course could play the fiddle; and having discovered an old weather-beaten instrument in the fort, Lucy Neal, Old Dan Tucker, and Buffalo Gals, were heard at all hours of the day and night; and he was, moreover, installed into the Weippert of the *fandangos* which frequently took place in the fort, when the hunters with their squaws were at the rendezvous.

Toward the latter part of April green grass began to show itself in the bottoms, and myself and two others, who had been wintering in the mountains for the benefit of their health, made preparations for our departure to the United States. Packsaddles were inspected and repaired, *apishamores* made, *lariats* and lassos greased and stretched, mules and horses collected from their feeding-grounds, and their forefeet shod. A small supply of meat was "made" (*i.e.*, cut into thin flaps and dried in the sun), to last until we reached the buffalo-range; rifles put in order, and balls run; hobbles cut out of raw hide, *parflêche* moccasins cobbled up, deerskin hunting-shirts and pantaloons patched, and all our very primitive "kit" overhauled to render it serviceable for the journey across the grand prairies, while the "possible-sack" was lightened of all superfluities—an easy task by the way. When everything was ready I was delayed several days in hunting up my animals. The Indian traders having arrived, bringing with them large herds of mules and horses, my mules had become separated from the horse and from one another, and it was with no small difficulty that I succeeded in finding and securing them. Having once tasted the green grass, they became so wild, that, at my appearance, lasso in hand, the cunning animals, knowing full well what was in store for them, threw up their heels and scampered away, defying for a long time all my efforts to catch them.

My two companions had left the United States the preceding year, having been recommended to try the effect of change of climate on a severe pulmonary disease under which both laboured. Indeed, they were both apparently in a rapid consumption, and their medical advisers had given up any hope of seeing them restored to health. They had remained in the mountains during one of the severest winters ever known, had lived upon game, and frequently suffered the privations attendant upon a mountain life, and were returning perfectly restored, and in robust health and spirits.

It is an extraordinary fact that the air of the mountains has a wonderfully restorative effect upon constitutions enfeebled by pulmonary disease; and of my own knowledge I could mention a hundred instances where persons, whose cases have been pronounced by eminent practitioners as perfectly hopeless, have been restored to comparatively sound health by a *sojourn* in the pure and bracing air of the Rocky Mountains, and are now alive to testify to the effects of the revigorating climate.

That the lungs are most powerfully acted upon by the rarefied air of these elevated regions, I myself, in common with the acclimated hunters, who experience the same effects, can bear witness, as it is almost impossible to take violent exercise on foot, the lungs feeling as if they were bursting in the act of breathing, and consequently the hunters invariably follow game on horseback, although, from being inured to the climate, they might be supposed to experience these symptoms in a lesser degree.

Whatever may be urged against such a climate, the fact nevertheless remains, that the lungs are thus powerfully affected, and that the violent action has a most beneficial effect upon these organs when in a highly diseased state.'

The elevation above the level of the sea, of the plains at the foot of the mountains, is about four thousand feet, while the mountain valley of the Bayou Salado must reach an elevation of at least eight or nine thousand, and Pike's Peak has been estimated to exceed twelve thousand.

CHAPTER 32

Cheyenne Village

On the 30th of April, having the day before succeeded in collecting my truant *mulada*, I proceeded alone to the forks of the Arkansas and St. Charles, where I had observed, when hunting, that the grass was in better condition than near the pueblo, and here I remained two or three days, the animals faring well on the young grass, waiting for my two companions, who were to proceed with me across the grand prairies.

As, however, the trail was infested by the Pawnees and Comanche, who had attacked every party which had attempted to cross from Santa Fé during the last six months, and carried off all their animals, it was deemed prudent to wait for the escort of Tharpe, the Indian trader, who was about to proceed to St. Louis with the peltries, the produce of his winter trade; and as he would be accompanied by a large escort of mountain-men, we resolved to remain and accompany his party for the security it afforded.

The night I encamped on the St. Charles the rain poured down in torrents, accompanied by a storm of thunder and lightning, and the next morning I was comfortably lying in a pool of water, having been exposed to the full force of the storm. This was, however, merely a breaking in for a continuation of wet weather, which lasted fifteen days without intermission, and at short intervals followed us to the Missouri, during which time I had the pleasure of diurnal and nocturnal shower-baths, and was for thirty days undergoing a natural hydropathic course of wet clothes and blankets, my bed being the bare prairie, and nothing between me and the reservoir above but a single *sarape*.

On the 2nd of May my two fellow-travellers arrived with the intelligence that Tharpe could not leave until a trading party from the north fork of the Platte came in to Arkansas, and consequently we started the next day alone. I may here mention that Tharpe started two days after us, and was killed on Walnut Creek by the Pawnees, while hunting buffalo at a little distance from camp. He was scalped and horribly mutilated.

The night before our departure the wolves ate up all the *riatas* by which our mules and horses were picketed: and in the morning all the animals had disappeared but one. We saw by the tracks that they had been stampeded; and, as a very suspicious moccasin-track was discovered near the river, we feared that the Arapahós had paid a visit to the *mulada*. One of my mules, however, was picketed very near the camp, and was safe; and, mounting it, I followed the tracks of the others across the river, and had the good fortune to find them all quietly feeding in the prairie, with the ropes eaten to their very throats. This day we proceeded about twenty-five miles down the river, camping in the bottom in a tope of cotton-woods, the rain pouring upon us all night.

The next day we still followed the stream, and encamped about four miles above Bent's Fort, which we reached the next morning, and most opportunely, as a company of wagons belonging to the United States commissariat were at the very moment getting under way for the Missouri. They had brought out provisions for the troops forming the Santa Fe division of the army of invasion, and were now on their return, empty, to Fort Leavenworth, under the charge of Captain ——, of the quartermaster-general's department, who at once gave us permission to join his company, which consisted of twenty wagons, and as many teamsters, well armed.

A government train of wagons had been attacked, on their way to Santa Fé, the preceding winter by the Pawnees, and the whole party—men, mules, and wagons—captured; the men, however, being allowed to continue their journey, without wagons or animals. They had likewise lately attacked a party under Kit Carson, the celebrated mountaineer, who was carrying dispatches from Colonel Fremont, in California, to the government of the United States, and, in fact, every party who had passed the plains; therefore, as a large number of loose stock was also to be carried in with the wagons, an attack was more than probable during the journey to the frontier.

Bent's Fort is a square building of adobe, flanked by circular bastions loopholed for musketry, and entered by a large gateway leading into the corral or yard. Round this are the rooms inhabited by the people engaged in the Indian trade; but at this time the Messrs. Bent themselves were absent in Santa Fé, the eldest brother, as I have before mentioned, having been killed in Taos during the insurrection of the Pueblo Indians. We here procured a small supply of dried buffalo-meat, which would suffice until we came to the buffalo-range, when sufficient meat might be procured to carry us into the States.

We started about noon, proceeding the first day about ten miles, and camped at sundown opposite the mouth of the Purgatoire—the Pickatwaire of the mountaineers, and "Las Animas" of the New Mexicans—an affluent of the Arkansas, rising in the mountains in the vicinity of the Spanish Peaks. The timber on the Arkansas becomes scarcer as we proceed down the river, the cotton-wood groves being scattered wide apart at some distance from each other; and the stream itself widens out into sandy shallows, dotted with small islands covered with brush.

At this camp we were joined by six or seven of Fremont's men, who had accompanied Kit Carson from California; but their animals "giving out" here, had remained behind to recruit them. They were all fine, hardy-looking young fellows, with their faces browned by two years' constant exposure to the sun and wind, and were fine specimens of mountaineers. They were accompanied by a Californian Indian, a young centaur, who handled his lasso with a dexterity which threw all the Mexican exploits I had previously seen into the shade, and was the means of bereaving several cows of their calves when we were in the buffalo-range.

Our next camping-place was the "Big Timber," a large grove of cotton-woods on the left bank of the river, and a favourite wintering place of the Cheyennes. Their camp was now broken up, and the village had removed to the Platte for their summer hunt. The debris of their fires and lodges were plentifully scattered about, and some stray horses were running about the bottom. On the 5th and 6th we moved leisurely down the river, camping at Sandy Creek, and in the "Salt Bottom," a large plain covered with salitrose efflorescences.

Here we proceeded more cautiously, as we were now in the outskirt of the Pawnee and Comanche country. The wagons at night were drawn up into a square, and the mules inclosed after sunset within the corral. Mine, however, took their chance outside, being always picketed near my sleeping-place, which I invariably selected in the middle of a good patch of grass, in order that they might feed well during the night. A guard was also placed over the corral, and every one slept with his rifle at his side.

Near the Salt Bottom, but on the opposite side of the river, I this day saw seven bulls, the advanced party of the innumerable bands of buffalo we shortly passed through.

On the 7th, as I rode two or three miles in advance of the party, followed by my mules, I came upon fresh Indian sign, where a village had just passed, with their lodge-poles trailing on the ground; and presently, in a level bottom on the river, the white conical lodges of the village presented themselves a short distance on the right of the trail. I at once struck off and entered it, and was soon surrounded by the idlers of the place.

It was a Cheyenne village; and the young men were out, an old chief informed me, after buffalo, and that they would return an hour before sunset, measuring the hour with his hand on the western horizon. He also pointed out a place a little below for the wagons to encamp, where he said was plenty of wood and grass. The lodges, about fifty in number, were all regularly planted in rows of ten, the chief's lodge being in the centre, and the skins of it being dyed a conspicuous red. Before the lodges of each of the principal chiefs and warriors was a stack of spears, from which hung his shield and arms; while the skins of the lodge itself were covered with devices and hieroglyphics, describing his warlike achievements. Before one was a painted pole supporting several smoke-dried scalps, which dangled in the wind, rattling against the pole like bags of peas.

The language of signs is so perfectly understood in the western country, and the Indians themselves are such admirable pantomimists, that, after a little use no difficulty whatever exists in carrying on a conversation by such a channel; and there are few mountain-men who are at a loss in thoroughly understanding and making themselves intelligible by signs alone, although they neither speak nor understand a word of the Indian tongue.

The wagons shortly after coming up, we proceeded to the spot indicated by the chief, which is a camping-place well known to the Santa Fé traders by the name of the "Pretty Encampment." Here we were soon surrounded by men, women, and children from the village, who arrived in horse-loads of five or six mounted on the same animal, and, begging and stealing everything they could lay their hands upon, soon became a perfect nuisance.

An hour before sundown the hunting-party came in, their animals tottering under heavy loads of buffalo-meat. Twenty-one had gone out, and in the chase had killed twenty-one bulls, which were portioned out, half the animal to each lodge. During the night a huge cotton-wood, which had been thoughtlessly set on fire, fell, a towering mass of flame, to the ground, and nearly in the midst of my animals, who, frightened by the thundering crash, and the showers of sparks and fire, broke their ropes and ran off. In the morning, however, they returned to camp at daybreak, and allowed me to catch them without difficulty.

The next night we encamped on a bare prairie, without wood, having recourse to the *bois de vâches,* or buffalo-chips, which strewed the ground to make a fire. This fuel was so wet, that nothing but a stifling smoke rewarded our attempts. During the day an invalid died in one of the wagons, in which upward of twenty poor wretches were being conveyed, all suffering from most malignant scurvy. The first wagon which arrived in camp sent a man to dig a hole in the prairie; and on the wagon containing the dead man coming up, it stopped a minute to throw the body into the hole, where, lightly covered with earth, it was left, without a prayer, to the mercies of the wolves and birds of prey.

Bent's Fort had been made a depot of provisions for the supply of the government trains passing the grand prairies on their way to New Mexico, and the wagons now returning were filled with sick men suffering from attacks of scurvy.[1] The want of fresh provisions and neglect of personal cleanliness, together with the effects of the rigorous climate, and the intemperate and indolent habits of the men, rendered them proper subjects for this horrible scourge. In Santa Fé, and wherever the volunteer troops were congregated, the disease made rapid progress, and proved fatal in an extraordinary number of cases.

As I was riding with some of the Californians in advance of the train, a large white wolf limped out of the bottom, and, giving chase, we soon came up to the beast, which on our approach crouched to the ground, and awaited its death-stroke with cowardly sullenness. It was miserably poor, with its bones almost protruding from the skin, and one of its forelegs had been broken, probably by a buffalo, and trailed along the ground as it ran snarling and chopping its jaws with its sharp teeth.

On the 9th, as I rode along ahead, I perceived some dark objects in the prairie, which, refracted by the sun striking the sandy ground, appeared enormous masses, without form, moving slowly along. Riding toward them on my mule, I soon made them out to be buffalo, seventeen bulls, which were coming toward me. Jumping off the mule, I thrust the picket at the end of its *lariat* into the ground, and, advancing cautiously a few paces,

1. Called "Black Leg" in Missouri.

as the prairie was entirely bare, and afforded not even the cover of a prairie-dog mound to approach under, I lay down on the ground to await their coming.

As they drew near, the huge beasts, unconscious of danger, picked a bunch of grass here and there, sometimes kicking up the dust with their forefeet, and, moving at the slowest walk, seemed in no hurry to offer me a shot. Just, however, as they were within a hundred paces, and I was already squinting along the barrel of my rifle, a greenhorn from the wagons, who had caught a glimpse of the game, galloped headlong down the bluff, and before the wind. He was a quarter of a mile off when the leading bull, raising his head, snuffed the tainted air, and with tail erect scampered off with his companions, leaving me showering imprecations on the head of the "muff" who had spoiled my sport and supper.

While I was lying on the ground three wolves, which were following the buffalo, caught sight of me, and seemed instantly to divine my intentions, for they drew near, and, sitting within a few yards of me, anxiously gazed upon me and the approaching bulls, thinking no doubt that their persevering attendance upon them was now about to be rewarded. They were doubtless disgusted, when, as soon as I perceived the bulls disappear, I turned my rifle upon one cur, which sat licking his chops, and knocked him over, giving the others the benefit of the remaining barrel as they scampered away from their fallen comrade. I now rode on far ahead determined not to be disturbed; and by the time the wagons came into camp I had already arrived there with the choice portions of two bulls which I had killed near the river.

We encamped on the 9th at Choteau's Island, called after an Indian trader named Choteau, who was here beleaguered by the Pawnees for several weeks, but eventually made his escape in safety. Every mile we advanced the buffalo became more plentiful, and the camp was soon overflowing with fresh meat.

The country was literally black with immense herds, and they were continually crossing and recrossing the trail during the day, giving us great trouble to prevent the loose animals from break-

331

ing away and following the bands.

On the 12th a man was found dead in one of the wagons on arriving in camp, and was buried in the same unceremonious style as the first. In the evening I left the camp for a load of meat, and approached an immense herd of buffalo under cover of a prairie-dog town, much to the indignation of the villagers, who resented the intrusion with an incessant chattering. The buffalo passed right through the town, and at one time I am sure that I could have touched many with the end of my rifle, and thousands were passing almost over me; but, as I lay perfectly still, they only looked at me from under their shaggy brows, and passed on.

One huge bull, and the most ferocious-looking animal I ever encountered, came to a dead stop within a yard of my head, and steadily examined me with his glaring eyes, snorting loudly his ignorance of what the curious object could be which riveted his attention. Once he approached so close that I actually felt his breath on my face, and, smelling me, he retreated a pace or two, and dashed up the sand furiously with his feet, lashing his tail at the same time about his dun sides with the noise of a carter's whip, throwing down his ponderous head, and shaking his horns angrily at me.

This old fellow was shedding his hair, and his sleek skin, now bare as one's hand in many parts, was here and there dotted with tufts of his long winter-coat. From the shoulder backward the body was, with these exceptions, perfectly smooth, but his head, neck, and breast were covered with long, shaggy hair, his glowing eyes being almost hidden in a matted mass, while his coal-black beard swept his knees. His whole appearance reminded me strongly of a lion, and the motion of the buffalo when running exactly resembles the canter of the king of beasts.

At last my friend began to work himself up into such a fury that I began to feel rather uncomfortable at my position, and, as he backed himself and bent his head for a rush, I cocked my rifle, and rose partly from the ground to take a surer aim, when the cowardly old rascal, with a roar of affright, took to his heels, followed by the whole band; but as one sleek, well-conditioned bull passed me within half a dozen yards, I took a flying shot, and rolled him over and over in a cloud of dust, levelling to the ground, as he fell, a well-built dog-house.

No animals in these western regions interested me so much as the prairie-dogs. These lively little fellows select for the site of their towns a level piece of prairie with a sandy or gravelly soil, out of which they can excavate their dwellings with great facility. Being of a merry, sociable disposition, they, unlike the bear or wolf, choose to live in a large community, where laws exist for the public good, and there is less danger to be apprehended from the attacks of their numerous and crafty enemies.

Their towns equal in extent and population the largest cities of Europe, some extending many miles in length, with considerable regularity in their streets, and the houses of a uniform style of architecture. Although their form of government may be styled republican, yet great respect is paid to their chief magistrate, who, generally a dog of large dimensions and imposing appearance, resides in a house conspicuous for size in the centre of the town, where he may always be seen on his housetop, regarding with dignified complaisancy the various occupations of the busy population—some industriously bearing to the granaries the winter supply of roots, others building or repairing their houses; while many, their work being over, sit chatting on their housetops, watching the gambols of the juveniles as they play around them.

Their hospitality to strangers is unbounded. The owl, who on the bare prairie is unable to find a tree or rock in which to build her nest, is provided with a comfortable lodging, where she may in security rear her round-eyed progeny; and the rattlesnake, in spite of his bad character, is likewise entertained with similar hospitality, although it is very doubtful if it is not sometimes grossly abused; and many a childless dog may perhaps justly attribute his calamity to the partiality of the epicurean snake for the tender meat of the delicate prairie-pup.

However, it is certain that the snake is a constant guest; and, whether admitted into the domestic circle of the dog family, or living in separate apartments, or in co-partnership with the owl, is an acknowledged member of the community at large.

The prairie-dog (a species of marmot) is somewhat longer than a guinea-pig, of a light brown or sandy colour, and with a head resembling that of a young terrier pup. It is also furnished with a little stumpy tail, which, when its owner is excited, is in a perpetual jerk and flutter. Frequently, when hunting, I have amused myself for hours in watching their frolicsome motions, lying concealed behind one of their conical houses.

These are raised in the form of a cone, two or three feet above the ground, and at the apex is a hole, vertical to the depth of three feet, and then descending obliquely into the interior. Of course, on the first approach of such a monster as man, all the dogs which have been scattered over the town scamper to their holes as fast as their little legs will admit, and, concealing nil but their heads and tails, bark lustily their displeasure at the intrusion. When they have sufficiently exhibited their daring, every dog dives into his burrow, but two or three who remain as sentinels, chattering in high dudgeon, until the enemy is within a few paces of them, when they take the usual summerset, and the town is silent and deserted.

Lying perfectly still for several minutes, I could observe an old fellow raise his head cautiously above his hole and reconnoitre; and if satisfied that the coast was clear, he would commence a short bark. This bark, by the way, from its resemblance to that of a dog, has given that name to this little animal, but it is more like that of a wooden toy-dog, which is made to bark by raising and depressing the bellows under the figure. When this warning has been given, others are soon seen to emerge from their houses, and, assured of their security, play and frisk about.

After a longer delay, rattlesnakes issue from the holes, and coil themselves in the sunny side of the hillock, erecting their treacherous heads, and rattling an angry note of warning if, in his play, a thoughtless pup approaches too near; and, lastly, a sober owl appears, and, if the sun be low, hops through the town, picking up the lizards and chameleons, which every where abound. At the first intimation of danger given by the sentinels, all the stragglers hasten to their holes, tumbling over owls and rattlesnakes, who hiss and rattle angrily at being disturbed.

Everyone scrambles off to his own *domicile*, and if, in his hurry, he should mistake his dwelling, or rush for safety into any other than his own, he is quickly made sensible of his error, and, without ceremony, ejected. Then, every house occupied, commences such a volley of barking, and such a twinkling of little heads and fails, which alone appear above the holes, as to defy description. The lazy snakes, regardless of danger, remain coiled up, and only evince their consciousness by an occasional rattle; while the owls, in the hurry and confusion, betake themselves, with sluggish wing, to wherever a bush of sage or grease- wood affords them temporary concealment.

'The prairie-dog leads a life of constant alarm, and numerous enemies are ever on the watch to surprise him. The hawk and the eagle, hovering high in air, watch their towns, and pounce suddenly upon them, never failing to carry off in their cruel talons some unhappy member of the community. The coyote, too, an hereditary foe, lurks behind a hillock, watching patiently for hours until an unlucky straggler approaches within reach of this murderous spring. In the winter, when the prairie-dog, snug in his subterranean abode, and with granaries well filled, never cares to expose his little nose to the icy blasts which sweep across the plains, but, between eating and sleeping, passes merrily the long, frozen winter, he is often roused from his warm bed, and almost congealed with terror by hearing the snorting yelp of the half-famished wolf, who, mad with hunger, assaults, with tooth and claw, the frost-bound roof of his house, and, with almost super *lupine* strength, hurls down the well-cemented walls, tears up the passages, plunges his cold nose into the very chambers, snorting into them with his earth-stuffed nose, in ravenous anxiety, and drives the poor little trembling inmate into the most remote corners, too often to be dragged forth, and unhesitatingly devoured.

The rattlesnake, too, I fear, is not the welcome guest he reports himself to be; for often I have slain the wily serpent, with a belly too much protuberant to be either healthy or natural, and bearing, in its outline, a very strong resemblance to the figure of a prairie-dog.

A few miles beyond a point on the river known as the Câches, and so called from the fact that a party of traders, having lost their animals, had here *cachéd,* or concealed, their packs, we passed a little log fort, built by the government *employés,* for the purpose of erecting here a forge to repair the commissariat wagons on their way to Santa Fé. We found the fort beleaguered by the Pawnees, who killed every one who showed his nose outside the gate. They had carried off all their stock of mules and oxen, and in the vicinity had, two or three days before, attacked a company under an officer of the United States Engineers, running off with all the mules belonging to it.

We were now, day after day, passing through countless herds of buffalo. I could scarcely form an estimate of the numbers within the range of sight at the same instant, but some idea may be formed of them by mentioning, that one day, passing along a ridge of upland prairie at least thirty miles in length, and from which a view extended about eight miles on each side of a slightly rolling plain, not a patch of grass ten yards square could be seen, so dense was the living mass that covered the country in every direction.

On leaving the Câches, the trail, to avoid a bend in the Arkansas, strikes to the northeast over a tract of rolling prairie, intersected by many ravines, full of water at certain seasons, known as the Coon Creeks. On this route there is no other fuel than *bois de vâches,* and the camps are made on naked bluffs, exposed, with the slightest shelter, to the chilling winds that sweep continually over the bare plains. I scarcely remember to have suffered more from cold than in passing these abominable Coon Creeks.

With hunting-shirt saturated with the rain, the icy blast penetrated to my very bones, and, night after night, lying on the wet ground and in wet clothes, after successive days of pouring rain

I felt my very blood running cold in my vein's, and as if I never could again imbibe heat sufficient to warm me thoroughly.

One night, while standing guard round the camp, which was about two miles-from the river, I heard an inexplicable noise, like distant thunder, but too continuous to proceed from that source, which gradually increased, and drew nearer to the camp. Placing my ear to the ground, I distinguished the roaring tramp of buffalo thundering on the plain; and as the moon for a moment burst from a cloud, I saw the prairie was covered by a dark mass, which undulated, in the uncertain light, like the waves of the sea.

I at once became sensible of the imminent danger we were in; for when thousands and hundreds of thousands of these animals are pouring in a resistless torrent over the plains, it is almost impossible to change their course, particularly at night, the myriads in the rear pushing on those in front, who, spite of themselves, continue on their course, trampling down all opposition to their advance. Even if we ourselves were not crushed by the mass of beasts, our animals would most certainly be borne away bodily with the herd, and irrecoverably lost.

I at once alarmed the camp, and all hands turned out, and, advancing toward the buffalo, which were coming straight upon us, by shouting and continued firing of guns we succeeded in turning them, the wind being, luckily, in our favour; and the main body branching in two, one division made off into the prairie, while the other crossed the river, where for hours we heard their splashing, sounding like the noise of a thousand cataracts. In the daytime even our *cavallada* was in continual danger, for immense bands of buffalo dashed repeatedly through the wagons, scarcely giving us time to secure the animals before they were upon us; and on one occasion, when I very foolishly dismounted from Panchito to fire at a band passing within a few yards, the horse, becoming alarmed, started off into the herd, and, followed by the mules, was soon lost to sight among the buffalo, and it was some time before I succeeded in recovering them.

As might be inferred, such gigantic sporting soon degenerates into mere butchery. Indeed, setting aside the excitement of a chase on horseback, buffalo-hunting is too wholesale a business to afford much sport—that is, on the prairies; but in the mountains, where they are met with in small bands, and require no little trouble and expertness to find and kill, and where one may hunt for days without discovering more than one band of half a dozen, it is then an exciting and noble sport.

There are two methods of hunting buffalo—one on horseback, by chasing them at full speed, and shooting when alongside; the other by "still hunting," that is, "approaching," or stalking, by taking advantage of the wind and any cover the ground affords, and crawling to within distance of the feeding herd. The latter method exhibits in a higher degree the qualities of the hunter, the former those of the horseman. The buffalo's head is so thickly thatched with long, shaggy hair that the animal is almost precluded from seeing an object directly in its front; and if the wind be against the hunter he can approach, with a little caution, a buffalo feeding on a prairie as level and bare as a billiard-table.

Their sense of smelling, however, is so acute, that it is impossible to get within shot when to the windward, as, at the distance of nearly half a mile, the animal will be seen to snuff the tainted air, and quickly satisfy himself of the vicinity of danger. At any other than the season of gallantry, when the males are, like all other animals, disposed to be pugnacious, the buffalo is a quiet, harmless animal, and will never attack unless goaded to madness by wounds, or, if a cow, in sometimes defending its calf when pursued by a horseman; but even then it is seldom that they make any strong effort to protect their young.

When gorged with water, after a long fast, they become so lethargic they sometimes are too careless to run and avoid danger. One evening, just before camping, I was, as usual, in advance of the train, when I saw three bulls come out of the river and walk leisurely across the trail, stopping occasionally, and one, more indolent than the rest, lying down whenever the others halted. Being on my hunting-mule, I rode slowly after them, the lazy one stopping behind the others, and allowing me to ride within a dozen paces, when he would slowly follow the rest. Wishing to see how near I could get, I dismounted, and, rifle in hand, approached the bull, who at last stopped short, and never even looked round, so that I walked up to the animal and placed my hand on his quarter. Taking no notice of me, the huge beast lay down, and while on the ground I shot him dead. On butchering the carcass I found the stomach so greatly distended, that another pint would have burst it. In other respects the animal was perfectly healthy and in good condition.

One of the greatest enemies to the buffalo is the white wolf. These persevering brutes follow the herds from pasture to pasture, preying upon the bulls enfeebled by wounds, the cows when weak at the time of calving, and the young calves whenever they straggle from their mothers. In bands of twenty and thirty they attack a wounded bull, separate him from the herd, and worry the poor animal until, weak with loss of blood and the ceaseless assaults of his active foes, he falls hamstrung, a victim to their ravenous hunger.

On one of the Coon Creeks I was witness to an attack of this kind by three wolves on a cow and calf, or, rather, on the latter alone, which by some accident had got separated from the herd. My attention was first called to the extraordinary motions of the cow (for I could neither see the calf nor the wolves on account of the high grass), which was running here and there, jumping high in the air and bellowing lustily.

On approaching the spot I saw that she was accompanied by a calf about a month old, and all the efforts of three wolves were directed to get between it and the cow, who, on her part, used all her generalship to prevent it. While one executed a diversion in the shape of a false attack on the cow, the others ran at the calf, which sought shelter under the very belly of its mother. She, poor animal! regardless of the wounds inflicted on herself, sought only to face the more open attack; and the wolf in rear, taking advantage of this, made a bolder onslaught, and fastened upon her hams, getting, however, for his pains, such a well-delivered kick in his stomach as threw him a summerset in the air.

The poor cow was getting the worst of it; and the calf would certainly have fallen a victim to the ravenous beasts, if I had not most opportunely come to the rescue; and, waiting until the battle rolled near the place of my concealment, I took advantage of a temporary pause in the combat, when two of the wolves were sitting in a line, with their tongues out and panting for breath, to level my rifle at them, knocking over one dead as a stone, and giving the other a pill to be carried with him to the day of his death, which, if I am any judge of gunshot wounds, would not be very distant.

The third took the hint and scampered off, a ball from my second barrel whistling after him as he ran; and I had the satisfaction of seeing the cow cross the river with her calf, and join in safety the herd, which was feeding on the other side.

CHAPTER 33

A Storm at Night

We reached Pawnee Fork of the Arkansas without any "*nove-dad*," but found this creek so swelled with the rains that we feared we should experience no little trouble in crossing. We here met a train of wagons detained by the above cause on their way to Santa Fé, and we learned from them that a party of Mexican traders had been attacked by the Pawnees at this very spot a few days before, losing one hundred and fifty mules, one Indian having been killed in the fight, whose well-picked skeleton lay a few yards from our camp.

Pawnee Fork being considered the most dangerous spot on the trail, extraordinary precautions were taken in guarding against surprise, and the animals belonging to the train were safely corralled before sundown, and a strong guard posted round them. Mine, however, were picketed, as usual, round my sleeping-place, which was on a bare prairie at some distance from the timber of the creek. Such a storm as poured upon our devoted heads that night I have seldom had the misfortune to be exposed to.

The rain, in bucketsful, Niagara'd down as if a twenty-years' supply was being emptied from the heavens on that one night; vivid forked lightning, in continuous flashes, lighted up the flooded prairie with its glare; and the thunder, which on these plains is thunder indeed, kept up an incessant and mammoth cannonade. My frightened mules crept as near my bed as their *lariats* would allow them, and, with water streaming from every extremity, trembled with the chilling rain.

In the early part of the night, when the storm was at its height, I was attracted to a fire at the edge of the encampment by the sound of a man's voice perpetrating a song. Drawing near, I found a fire, or, rather, a few embers and an extinguished log, over which cowered a man sitting cross-legged in Indian fashion, holding his attenuated hands over the expiring ashes. His features, pinched with the cold, and lank and thin with disease, wore a comically serious expression, as the electric flashes lighted them up, the rain streaming off his nose and prominent chin, and his hunting-shirt hanging about him in a flabby and soaking embrace.

He was quite alone, and sat watching a little pot, doubtless containing his supper, which refused to boil on the miserable fire. Spite of such a situation, which could be termed anything but cheering, he, like Mark Tapley, evidently thought that now was the very moment to be jolly, and was rapping out at the top of his voice a ditty, the chorus of which was, and which he gave with peculiar emphasis,

How happy am I!
From care I'm free:
Oh, why are not all
Contented like me?—

Not for an instant intending it as a satire upon himself, but singing away with perfect seriousness, raising his voice at the third line, *Oh, why are not all*, particularly at the *Oh*, in a most serio-comical manner. During the night I occasionally shook the water out of my blanket, and raised my head to assure myself that the animals were safe, lying down to sleep again, perfectly satisfied that not even a Pawnee would face such a storm, even to steal horses. But I did that celebrated thieving nation gross injustice; for they, on that very night, carried off several mules belonging to the other train of wagons, notwithstanding that a strict guard was kept up all the night.

The next day, as there was no probability of the creek subsiding, it was determined to cross the wagons at any risk; and they were accordingly, one after the other, let down the steep bank of the stream, and, several yokes of oxen (which had first been swum over) being attached, were hauled bodily through the water, some swimming, and others, if heavily laden, diving across.

I myself crossed on Panchito, whose natatory attempt, probably his first, was anything but first-rate; for on plunging in, and at once, into deep water, instead of settling himself down to a quiet swim, he jumped up into the air, and, sinking to the bottom, and thus gaining a fresh impetus, away he went again, carrying me, rifle, and ammunition under water at every plunge, and holding on by his neck like grim death. All my kit was contained in a pair of mule-packs, which I had had made of waterproof material.

Unfortunately, one had a hole in the top, which had escaped my notice. This admitted the water, which remained in the pack, several inches deep, for a fortnight. This pack contained all my papers, notes, and several manuscripts and documents relative to the history of New Mexico and its Indian tribes, which I had collected with considerable trouble and expense. On opening the trunk, I found all the papers completely destroyed, and the old manuscripts, written on bad paper, and with worse ink, reduced to a pulpy mass—every scrap of writing being perfectly illegible.

At length all the wagons were got safely over, with the exception of having everything well soaked; and as the process had occupied the whole day, we camped on the other side of the creek. Every day we found greater difficulty in procuring fuel; for, as we were now on the regular Santa Fé trail, the creeks had been almost entirely stripped of firewood, and it was the work of hours to collect a sufficiency of brush to make a small fire to boil a pot of water. On arriving at camp, and having unpacked the mules, the first thing was to sally forth in quest of wood; an expedition of no little danger, for it was always more than probable that Indians were lurking in the neighbourhood, and therefore the rifle always accompanied the fuel-hunter.

Between Pawnee Fork and Cow Creek all our former experiences of buffalo-seeing were thrown into the shade, for here they literally formed the whole scenery, and nothing but dense masses of these animals was to be seen in every direction, covering valley and bluff, and actually blocking up the trail. Nothing was heard along the line of march but pop—bang—pop—bang every minute; and the Californian Indian lassoed the calves and brought them in in such numbers, that many were again set free.

I had hitherto refrained from "chasing," in order to save my poor horse; but this day, a fine band of cows crossing the trail on a splendid piece of level prairie, I determined to try Panchito's mettle. Cantering up to the herd, I singled out a wiry-looking cow (which sex is the fleetest), and, dashing at her, soon succeeded in separating her from the rest. As I steered Panchito right into the midst of a thousand of these animals, he became half mad with terror, plunging and snorting, and kicking right and left; but he soon became tamer and more reconciled when the chase was a trial of speed between him and the flying cow, and he then was as much excited as his rider.

The cow held her ground wonderfully well, and for a quarter of a mile kept us a couple of lengths astern, which distance my horse seemed hardly to wish to decrease. As he became warm, however, I pushed him up to her just as she entered a large band, where she doubtless thought to have found refuge; but, running through it, she again made for the open prairie, and here, after a burst of a few hundred yards, I again came up with her; but Panchito refused to lay me alongside, darting wildly on one side if I attempted to pass the animal.

At last, pushing him with spur and leg, I brought him to the top of his speed, and, shooting past the flying cow in his stride, and with too much headway on him to swerve, I brushed the ribs of the buffalo with my moccasin, and, edging off a little to avoid her horns, discharged my rifle into her side, behind the shoulder. Carried forward a few paces in her onward course, she fell headlong to the ground, burying her horns deep into the soil, and, turning over on her side, was dead. She was so poor that I contented myself with the tongue, leaving the remainder of the carcass to the wolves and ravens.

We continued to find the buffalo in similar abundance as far as Cow Creek, a little beyond which we saw the last band; and on Turkey Creek the last straggler, an old grizzly bull, which I killed for a last supply of meat.

After passing the Little Arkansas, the prairie began to change its character; the surface became more broken, the streams more frequent, and fringed with better timber, and of a greater variety; the eternal cotton-wood now giving place to aspen, walnut, and hickory, and the short curly buffalo-grass to a more luxuriant growth of a coarser quality, interspersed with numerous plants and gay flowers. The dog-towns, too, disappeared; and, in lieu of these little animals, the prairie-hen boomed at rise and set of sun, and, running through the high grass, furnished ample work for the rifle. Large game was becoming scarcer; and but few antelopes were now to be seen, and still fewer deer.

No scenery in nature is more dreary and monotonous than the aspect of the "grand prairies" through which we had been passing. Nothing meets the eye but a vast undulating expanse of arid waste; for the buffalo-grass, although excellent in quality, never grows higher than two or three inches, and is seldom green in colour: and, being but thinly planted, the prairie never looks green and turf-like.

Not a tree or shrub is to be seen, except on the creeks, where a narrow strip of unpicturesque cotton-wood only occasionally relieves the eye with its verdant foliage. The sky, too, is generally overcast, and storms sweep incessantly over the bare plains during all seasons of the year; boisterous winds prevailing at all times, carrying with them a chilling sleet or clouds of driving snow. It was therefore a great relief to look upon the long green waving grass, and the pretty groves on the streams: although our animals soon exhibited the consequences of the change of diet, between the rich and fattening buffalo-grass, and the rank, although more luxuriant herbage they now fed upon.

On approaching Council Grove the scenery became very

345

picturesque: the prairie lost its flat and monotonous character, and was broken into hills and valleys, with well-timbered knolls scattered here and there, intersected by clear and babbling streams, and covered with gaudy flowers, whose bright colours contrasted with the vivid green of the luxuriant grass.

My eye, so long accustomed to the burned and withered vegetation of the mountains, revelled in this refreshing scenery, and never tired of gazing upon the novel view. Council Grove is one of the most beautiful spots in the western country. A clear, rapid stream runs through the valley, bordered by a broad belt of timber, which embraces all the varieties of forest-trees common to the West. Oak, beech, elm, maple, hickory, ash, walnut, &c., here presented themselves like old friends; squirrels jumped from branch to branch, the hum of the honey-bee sounded sweet and homelike, the well-known chatter of the blue jay and cat-bird resounded through the grove; and in the evening the whip-poor-will serenaded us with its familiar tongue, and the drumming of the ruffled grouse boomed through the grove.

The delight of the teamsters on first hearing these well-known sounds knew no bounds whatever. They danced, and sang, and hurrahed, as, one after the other, some familiar note caught their ear. Poor fellows! they had been suffering a severe time of it, and many hardships and privations, and doubtless snuffed in the air the Johnny-cakes and hominy of their Missouri homes.

"Wagh!" exclaimed one raw-boned young giant, as a bee flew past; "this feels like the old 'ooman, and mush and molasses at that! if it don't, I'll be dog-gone!"

"Hurroo for old Missouri!" roared another; "h'yar's a hos as will knock the hind sights off the corn-doins. Darn my old heart if thar arn't a reg'lar-built hickory—makes my eyes sweat to look at it! This child will have no more 'mountains;' hurroo for old Missouri! Wagh!" .

A trader among the Caw Indians had erected himself a log-house at the grove, which appeared to us a magnificent palace. Himself, his cows and horses, looked so fat and sleek, that we really thought them unnaturally so; and so long had I been used

346

to see the raw-boned animals of Mexico and the mountains, that I gravely asked him what he gave them, and why he made them so unwieldy.

When he told me that his stock were all very poor, and nothing to what they were when they left the States a month before, I thought the man was taking a "rise" out of me; and when I showed him my travel-worn animals, and bragged of their, to me, plump condition, he told me that where he came from it would be thought cruel to work such starved-looking beasts. There was one lodge of Caw Indians at the grove, the big village being out on the prairie, hunting buffalo.

On the opposite side of the stream was a party of Americans from Louisiana, who had been out for the purpose of catching calves; and round their camp some thirty were feeding, all they had been able to keep alive out of upward of a hundred.

From Council Grove to Caw, or Kansas, River, the country increases in beauty, and presents many most admirable spots for a settlement; but as it is guaranteed by treaty to the Caw and Osage Indians, no white man is allowed by the United States government to settle on their lands.

The night before reaching Caw River we encamped on a bare prairie, through which ran a small creek, fringed with timber. At sundown the wind, which had blown smartly the whole day, suddenly fell, and one of those unnatural calms succeeded, which so surely herald a storm in these regions. The sky became overcast with heavy inky clouds, and an intolerably sultry and oppressive heat pervaded the atmosphere.

Myriads of fire-flies darted about, and legions of bugs and beetles, and invading hosts of sand-flies and mosquitoes droned and hummed in the air, swooping like charging Cossacks on my unfortunate body. Beetles and bugs of easy squeezability, Brobdingnag proportions, and intolerable odour, darted into my mouth as I gasped for breath; while sand-flies with their atomic stings probed my nose and ears, and mosquitoes thrust their poisoned lances into every part of my body.

Hoping for the coming storm, I lay without covering, exposed to all their attacks; but the agony of this merciless persecution was nothing to the thrill of horror which pervaded my very bones when a cold, clammy rattlesnake crawled over my naked ankles; a flash of lightning at the moment revealing to me the reptile, as with raised head it dragged its scaly belly across my skin, during which time, to me an age, I feared to draw a breath lest the snake should strike me.

Presently the storm broke upon us; a hurricane of wind squalled over the prairie, a flash of vivid lightning, followed by a clap of deafening thunder, and then down came the rain in torrents. I actually revelled in the shower-bath; for away on the instant were washed bugs and beetles; mosquitoes were drowned in millions; and the rattlesnakes I knew would now retire to their holes, and leave me in peace and quiet.

We now passed through a fine country, partially cultivated by the Caw Indians, whose log-shanties were seen scattered among the timbered knolls.

Caw River itself is the headquarters of the nation, and we halted that night in the village, where, in the house of a white farmer, I ate the first civilized meal I had tasted for many months, and enjoyed the unusual luxury of eating at a table with knife and fork; moreover sitting on a chair, which, however, I would gladly have dispensed with, for I had so long been accustomed to sit Indian fashion on the ground, that a chair was at first both unpleasant and awkward.

The meal consisted of hot cakes and honey, delicious butter, and lettuce and radishes. My animals fared well too, on Indian corn, and oats in the straw; and the whole expense, eleven horses and mules having been fed the better part of a day and one night, amounted to one dollar and a half, or six shillings sterling.

A troop of dragoons from St. Louis to Fort Leavenworth met us on the road, on their way to the latter station, from whence they were about to escort a train of wagons, containing specie, to Santa Fé. They were superbly mounted: the horses, uniting plenty of blood with bone, so great a *desideratum* for cavalry, were about fifteen hands high, and in excellent condition.

The dragoons themselves were all recruits, and neither soldier-like in dress nor appearance.

Chapter 24

Miseries of Civilized Life

We passed the Kansas or Caw River by a ferry worked by Indians, and, striking into a most picturesque country of hill and dale, well timbered and watered, entered the valley of the great Missouri. A short distance from the river, on the left of the trail, is a tabular bluff of most extraordinary formation, being the exact and accurately- outlined figure of a large fortification, with escarpments, counterscarps, glacis, and all details, perfectly delineated.

A little farther on we came in sight of the garrison of Fort Leavenworth, the most western military station of the United States, and situated on the right bank of the Missouri, in the Indian territory. The fort is built on an eminence overhanging the river, but, although called a fort, has no pretensions to be a military work, the only defence to the garrison being four wooden block-houses, loopholed for musketry, placed at each corner of the square of buildings. The barracks, stables, and officers' quarters surrounded this square, which is planted with trees and covered with luxuriant grass.

The accommodation for the men and officers is excellent; the houses of the latter being large and commodious, and quite unlike the dirty pigsties which are thought good enough for the accommodation of British officers. The soldiers' barrack-rooms are large and airy, but no attention appears to be paid to cleanliness, and the floors, walls, and windows were dirty in the extreme.

The beds are all double, or, rather, the bedsteads, for the bedding is separate, but in close contact. What struck me more than anything was the admirable condition of the horses, and their serviceable appearance: I did not see a single troop-horse in the squadron which would not have sold in England for eighty guineas; the price paid for them here, that is, the government contract price, being from fifty to eighty dollars, or from ten to twenty pounds.

The garrison constitutes the whole population of the place. With the exception of the sutler's store for the use of the soldiers, there are neither shops, taverns, nor private buildings of any description; and I should have fared but badly if it had not been for the hospitality of Captain Enos, of the quartermaster-general's department, who most kindly assigned to me a room in his own quarters in the garrison, and made me a member of his mess.

The officers of the dragoons, who may be said to be buried for life in this wilderness, are mostly married, and their families constitute the only society the place affords. I remember to have been not a little struck at the first sight of many very pretty, well-dressed ladies, who, after my long *sojourn* among the dusky squaws, appeared to me like the *houris* of paradise; and I have no doubt that I myself came in for a share of "staring," for I was dressed in complete "mountain costume," with my mahogany-coloured face shaded by a crimson turban, *à la Indien,* and in all the pride of fringed deerskin and porcupine-quills; and I was paid the compliment of being more than once mistaken for an Indian chief; and on one occasion I was appealed to by two of the dragoons to decide a bet as to whether I was a white man or a redskin. One day I was passing through the dragoons' stables when the men were cleaning their horses, and my appearance created no little difference of opinion among the troopers as to what tribe of Indians I belonged.

"That's a Pottowatomie," said one, "by his red turban."

"How long have you been in the West," cried another, "not to know a Kickapoo when you see him?"

"Pshaw !" exclaimed a third; "that's a white trapper from the mountains. A regular mountain-boy that, I'll bet a dollar!"

One smart-looking dragoon, however, looked into my face, and, turning round to his comrades, said, "Well, boys, I'll just bet you a dollar all round that that Injun's no other than a British officer. Wagh! And what's more, I can tell you his name." And, sure enough, my acquaintance proved to be one of the many deserters from the British army belonging to the dragoons, and one who had known me when in the service myself.

After a few days' stay at Fort Leavenworth, I made preparations for my departure to St. Louis, getting rid of my mountain-traps, and, what caused me no little sorrow, parting with my faithful animals, who had been my companions in a long and wearisome journey of more than three thousand miles, during the greater part of which they had been almost my only friends and companions. I had, however, the satisfaction of knowing that, while with me, they had never experienced a blow or an angry word from me, and had always fared of the very best— when procurable; and many a mile I had trudged on foot to save them the labour of carrying me.

For Panchito I found a kind master—exacting, in return for the present, a promise that he should not be worked for the next three months; and, before leaving, I had the satisfaction of knowing that, in company with three old acquaintances who had pastured with him in the mountains, he was enjoying himself in veritable "clover," and corn unlimited, where, I doubt not, he soon regained his *quondam* beauty and condition.

The disposal of the mules gave me greater anxiety, as there was such a demand for these animals at the moment to send with the government trains to New Mexico, that I knew to give them away would only be to put their value in the pocket of a stranger, and the animals themselves into the first wagon which crossed the plains. I therefore sold them to the commissary at the fort, and paid them daily visits at the government stables, where they revelled in the good things of this life, and had, moreover, a kind-hearted master in the shape of the Missourian teamster who had the charge of them, and who, on my giving him a history of their adventures, and a good and true account of their dispositions and qualities, promised to take every care of the poor beasts; and, indeed, was quite proud of having under his charge such a travelled team.

The parting between Panchito and the mules was heart-rending, and for two or three days they all refused to eat and be comforted; but at the end of that time their violent grief softened down into a chastened melancholy, which gradually merged into n steady appetite for the "corn-*doins*" of the liberal master of the mules; and before leaving I felt assured, from their sleek and well-filled appearance, that they were quite able to start on another expedition across the plains.

A steamboat touching at the fort, bound for the Mississippi and St. Louis, I availed myself of the opportunity, and secured myself a berth for the latter city. After running upon sand-bars every half-hour, about thirty miles below Independence we at last stuck hard and fast, and, spite of the panting efforts of the engine, there we remained during the night, and until noon the next day.

A steamboat then made its appearance, bound, like ourselves, down the river, and, coming up alongside, the two captains held a consultation, which ended in ours recommending his passengers to "make tracks" into the other boat, as he did not expect to get off: which interchange being effected, and our fares paid to the other boat, a hawser was attached to the one aground, and she was readily hauled off—we, the passengers, having been done pretty considerably brown in the transaction. However, such rascalities as these, on the western waters, are considered no more than "smart," and are taken quite as a matter of course by the free and enlightened citizens of the model republic.

I must say that since a former visit to the States, made three years ago, I perceived a decided improvement, thanks to the Trollope and Boz castigations, in the manners and conduct of steamboat travellers, and in the accommodations of the boats themselves. With the exception of the expectorating nuisance, which still flourishes in all its disgusting "monstrosity," a stranger's sense of decency and decorum is not more shocked than it would be in travelling down the Thames in a Gravesend or Herne-Bay steamer. There is even quite an arbitrary censorship established on the subject of dress and dirty linen, which is, since it is passively submitted to by the citizens, an unmistakable sign of the times. As a proof of this, one evening, as I sat outside the cabin, reading, a young man, slightly "corned," or overtaken in his drink, accosted me abruptly:

"Stranger, you haven't are a clean shirt to part with, have you? The darned [hiccup] capen says I must go ashore bekase my 'tarnal shirt ain't clean."

And this I found to be the fact, for the man was actually ejected from the saloon at dinner-time, on his attempting to take his seat at the table in a shirt which bore the stains of *julep* and cocktail.

The miserable scenery of the muddy Missouri has been too often described to require any additional remarks. The steamboat touched occasionally at a wood-pile, to take in fuel; and sallow, aguish faces peered from the log-shanties as we passed. We had the usual amount of groundings on sand-bars, and thumping against snags and sawyers; passed the muddy line of demarcation between the waters of the Missouri and the "Father of Streams," and, in due course, on the fourth day ran alongside the outer edge of three tiers of huge steamboats which lined the wharf at St. Louis.

We had but one exciting episode during the voyage in the shape of a combat between one of the "hands" of the boat (a diabolical-looking Mexican) and the mate. The latter, at a wooding station, thinking that the man was not sufficiently "spry," administered a *palthogue*, which not meeting the approbation of the *Mejicano*, that worthy immediately drew his knife and challenged the aggressor. The mate, seizing a log from the pile, advanced toward him, and the Mexican, likewise, dropping his knife, took up a similar weapon, and rushed to the attack.

After a return of blows they came to close quarters, hugged, and fell, the Yankee uppermost, whose every energy was now directed to gouge out the eye of the prostrate foe, while he on his part, seizing the eye-scooper by his long hair, tugged, with might and main, to pull him to the ground. With a commendable spirit of fair play, the other "hands" danced round the combatants, administering well-directed kicks on the unfortunate Mexican's head and body, in all the excitement of unrestrained valour.

The captain, however, interfered, and secured a fair field for the gallant pair; but at length, tired of the bungling attempts of his mate to screw his antagonist's eye out of its socket, pulled him off, and, giving the Mexican a friendly kick in the ribs, desired him to get up. That worthy rose undismayed, and, ramming the end of his thumb into his eye, to drive that organ into its proper place, exclaimed, "*Que carajo es este, qui no sabe pelear!*"— what a cur is this, who does not know how to fight?—and, shaking himself, sat upon a log, and proceeded coolly to make himself a shuck-cigar.

A negro came up to me at Fort Leavenworth, and asked me to allow him to accompany me down to St. Louis. On my saying that I did not require a servant for so short a distance, he told me that, although himself a free negro, yet no black was allowed to travel without a master, and that if he attempted it he would, in probability, be seized and imprisoned as a runaway slave.

This reminded me that I was in that transcendently free country, ever boasting of its liberty and equality, which possesses, in a population of some eighteen millions, upward of three millions of fellow-men in most abject yet lawful slavery—a foul blot upon humanity, which has every appearance of being perpetuated until the evil grows to such a height as will end in curing itself.

This subject, which necessarily forces itself upon the mind of all travellers in the Slave States, is one which, having received the attention of the most enlightened philanthropists of both hemispheres, it would scarcely become me to dilate upon, or even notice, did I not feel that every one, however humble, should raise his voice in condemnation of that disgraceful and inhuman *institution,* which, in a civilized country and an enlightened age, condemns to a social death, and degrades (by law) to the level of the beasts of the field, our fellow-men; subjecting them to a moral as well as a physical slavery, and removing from them every possible advantage of intellectual culture or education, by which they might attain any position a grade higher than they now possess—the human beasts of burden of inhuman masters.

It is adduced as an argument against the abolition of slavery, of course by those whose interest it is to uphold the evil, that the emancipation of the slaves would, in the present state of feeling against the negro race, be productive of effects which would convulse the whole social state of the country, or, in other words, that the whites would never rest until the whole race was exterminated in the United States. That there is a physical impossibility to any amalgamation in the southern states is as certain as that, year by year, the difficulty of removing the evil is surely increasing; and its very magnitude and the moral coward-ice of the American people prevent this evil being grappled with at once, and some steps taken to oppose its perpetuation.

The three arguments brought forward by those who endeav-our to palliate or uphold slavery, in feeble sophistry, plainly ex-hibit the weakness of the cause.

First, they say, We admit the evil, but the cure will be worse than the disease. We have inherited it: the blame rests not upon us, but our fathers. If the negroes be emancipated, what is to become of them? They cannot, and shall not, remain in our community, on an equality with us and our children, and enjoy-ing the privileges of white men. This cannot be. Moreover, the burden of supporting them will fall upon us, for they will not work unless compelled.

Secondly: We deny the sinfulness of the institution. Negroes are not men, but were sent into the world to be slaves to the white man. To support this they are ready with quotations from Scripture, and I blush to say that I have heard well-educated and liberal-minded men take no other ground than this to support the cause.

And, thirdly, they say no legislation can reach the evil. Law cannot deprive a citizen of his property: if so, away with liberty at once, if one act confirms rights and another removes them.

The abolitionist of the North raves at the slave-owner of the South; but let a foreigner converse with the former, and he will at once turn round and take the part of the slave-owner. It is like a third person interfering in the quarrels of man and wife. "No, no, my good sir," they say, "let us settle this question among ourselves; this is a family affair." No one could deny the justice of this, if they really made a *bonâ fide* attempt to grapple the evil; but I must confess that abolitionism in the United States appears to me to be anything but genuine and honest, and that, if left to themselves, the question is very, very far from any chance of settlement, unless, as I believe will be the result, the slaves themselves cut the Gordian knot of the difficulty.

The great difficulty to be combated in America, in freeing the country from the curse of slavery, is prejudice. The negro is not recognized (startling as this assertion may be) as a fellow-creature—I mean by the .mass of the people. This anomaly, in a country where the very first principle of their social organism is the axiom, the incontrovertible truth, that *all men are born equal*, is the more palpable, since the popular and universal outcry is, and ever has been, the same sentiment which animated the Fathers of the Revolution, when they offered to the world, as a palliation for the crime of rebellion, the same watchword which is now so prodigally used by every American tongue, and so basely and universally prostituted. *All men are born equal. Liberty, therefore, and equal rights to all*—except to those whose skins are black !

I have heard clergymen of the American church affirm their belief that the negro was placed on earth by God to be the white man's slave. I have heard many educated, and in every other respect moral and conscientious, Americans assert that negroes were not made in God's image, but were created as a link between man and the beast, to minister to the former's wants, and to support him by the toil of their hands and the sweat of their brows.

And when I add that by law it is felony to teach a negro to read or write, what argument can be offered to combat such unnatural prejudices? I believe that slaves are generally well treated in the United States, although many instances could be adduced where the very reverse is the fact, particularly on the western frontier. But this good treatment is on the same grounds that we take care of our horses, and cows, and pigs, because it is the owner's interest to do so; and the well-being—that is, the physical healthiness—of slaves is attended to in the same degree that we feed and clothe our horses, in order that they may be in condition to work for us, and thereby bring in a return for the care we have bestowed upon them.

That this question will one day shake to its very centre, if it does not completely annihilate, the union of the American States, is as palpable as the result is certain. This belief is very generally entertained by both parties, and yet in spite of it the evil is allowed to increase, although its removal or cure thereby becomes hourly more difficult.

Hundreds of plans have been suggested for the abolition of slavery, but all have been found to be impracticable, if not impossible to be carried out. Perhaps the most feasible and practicable was that proposed by the late Mr. King, many years ago, and which at the time met with the fate of every other suggestion on the same subject. Mr. King, as sound and practical a statesman as the country ever produced, proposed that a certain yearly sum should be laid aside out of the revenue derived from the sale of the public lands, to be devoted to the emancipation of slaves, by the purchase of their freedom.

This process, however slow, at the same time that it would effect the gradual abolition of slavery, and at all events effectually prevent its increase and perpetuation, and offer a final, although distant termination to the evil, was at the same time less calculated to alarm the interested minds of the slave-owners; since, as the emancipation would be gradual, and the compensation proportionable to the loss sustained, their interests were not so materially affected as they would be by the entire removal, at one swoop, of their vested rights of property and possessions. As it is, however, there is no evidence of any positive action being taken by the legislature to effect the removal of this disgraceful stain on the national character.

So rabid and intolerant is the temper of the southern people when this question is mooted, and so fraught with danger to the Union is the agitation even of the subject, that all discussion is shunned and avoided, and the evil hour protracted and put off, which will, as surely as that the sun shines in the heavens, one day plunge the country into a convulsion dreadful to think of or anticipate. Meanwhile the plague-spot remains; the foul cancer is eating its way; and only by its extirpation can the body it disfigures regain its healthfulness and beauty, and take its place in the scale of humanity and civilization, from which the loathsome pestilence has out-paled it.

As I have said, I notice the subject merely to add my humble voice to the cry for humanity's sake, which should never cease to stun the ears of the unholy men who, in spite of every law, both human and divine, use their talents, and the intellect which God has given them, to uphold and perpetuate the curse of slavery.

CHAPTER 35

St. Louis—The Mexican War

Proceeding, on my arrival at St. Louis, to an excellent hotel called the "Planter's House," I that night, for the first time for nearly ten months, slept upon a bed, much to the astonishment of my limbs and body, which, long accustomed to no softer mattress than mother earth, tossed about all night, unable to appreciate the unusual luxury. I found chairs a positive nuisance, and in my own room caught myself in the act, more than once, of squatting cross-legged on the floor.

The greatest treat to me was bread; I thought it the best part of the profuse dinners of the Planter's House, and consumed prodigious quantities of the staff of life, to the astonishment of the waiters. Forks, too, I thought were most useless superfluities, and more than once I found myself on the point of grabbing a tempting leg of mutton mountain fashion, and butchering off a hunter's mouthful. But what words can describe the agony of squeezing my feet into boots, after nearly a year of moccasins, or discarding my turban for a great boardy hat, which seemed to crush my temples? The miseries of getting into a horrible coat—of braces, waistcoats, gloves, and all such implements of torture—were too acute to be described, and therefore I draw a veil over them.

Apart from the bustle attendant upon loading and unloading thousands and thousands of barrels of grain upon the wharf, St. Louis appeared to me one of the dullest and most commonplace cities of the Union. A great proportion of the population consists of French and Germans; the former congregating in a suburb called Vide Pôche, where they retain a few of the characteristics of their light-hearted nation, and the sounds of the fiddle and tambourine may be nightly heard, making the old-fashioned, tumble-down tenements shake with the tread of the merry dancers. The Dutch and Germans have their beer-gardens, where they imbibe huge quantities of malt and honey-dew tobacco; and the Irish their shebeen-shops, where *monongahela* is quaffed in lieu of the "rale crather."

The town was full of returned volunteers from the wars. The twelvemonth's campaign they had been engaged in, and the brilliant victories achieved by them, which, according to the American newspapers, are unparalleled in the annals of the world's history, have converted these rowdy and vermin-covered veterans into perfect heroes; and every batch on arriving is feasted by the public, addresses are offered to them, the officers presented with swords and snuff-boxes, and honours of all kinds lavished upon them in every direction.

The intense glorifications at St. Louis, and in every other part of the United States, on the recent successes of their troops over the miserable Mexicans, which were so absurd as to cause a broad grin on the face of an unexcited neutral, make me recur to the subject of this war, which hitherto I have avoided mentioning in the body of this little narrative.

It is scarcely necessary to trace the causes of the war at present raging between the two republics of North America. The fable of the wolf and lamb drinking at the same stream may be quoted, to explain to the world the reason why the *soi-disant* champion of liberty has quarrelled with its sister state for "muddying the water" which the model republic uses to quench its thirst.

A lesson has been read to the citizens of the United States which ought to open their eyes to the palpable dishonesty of their government, their unblushing selfishness, and total disregard to the interests of their country, when those of themselves or of their party are at stake; and although in the present instance President Polk has overreached himself, and raised a storm which he would be only too glad to lay at any cost, yet, in the whole history of the Mexican war, the violence of party and political feeling is evident, from the 9th of May, 1846, when the first shot was fired at Palo Alto, to the date of the last half-score dispatches which inform the world that General Scott "still remained at Puebla," waiting re-enforcements.

It is enough to observe that the immediate cause of hostilities was the unjustifiable invasion of Mexican territory by the army of the United States, to take possession of a tract of country of which the boundary-line had been disputed between the Mexican government and one of its revolted states, and which had been annexed to the American Union before its recognition as an independent state by the country from which it had seceded.

There can be no question but that the United States had deep cause of complaint against Mexico, in the total disregard evinced by the latter to the spirit of international treaties and the injuries inflicted upon the persons and property of American citizens: all redress of which grievances was either totally refused, or procrastinated until the parties gave up every hope of ultimate compensation.

The acquisition of Texas, however, was in any case a balancing injustice, and should have wiped out all old grievances, at least those of a pecuniary nature; while, if a proper spirit of conciliation had been evinced on the part of the Americans, at the period when the question of annexation was being mooted, all danger of a rupture would have been removed; and Mexico would have yielded her claims to Texas with a better grace, if taken as a receipt in full for all obligations, than in suffering a large portion of her territory to be torn from her, against all laws held sacred by civilized nations.

It is certain that such consequences, as have resulted from the advance of the American troops from the Nueces to the Rio Grande, were never anticipated by the President of the United States, whose policy in bringing on a quasi crisis of the state affairs on the Mexican frontier, and provoking the Mexicans to overt acts which could at any moment be converted into a casus belli, was not for the sake of territorial aggrandizement, but for a purpose which, it is known to those in the secret of his policy, had an object more remote, and infinitely more important, than a rupture with the Mexican government.

At that time the position taken up by Mr. Polk and his party with regard to the Oregon question involved, as a natural consequence, the probability of a war with England; nay, more, if such position were persisted in, the certainty of a war with that power. That a majority of the people, and all the right-thinking and influential classes, were opposed to such measures as would hazard or produce such a rupture, was so palpable, that the government was conscious that any proposal for making preparations for a war with England, which they knew a perseverance in their policy would assuredly bring about, would not be favourably received, or even tolerated, and therefore they looked about them for means of attaining their object, by blinding the eyes of the people as to their ulterior designs. Mexico was made the scape-goat.

A war with that weak and powerless state would be popular, since its duration, it was supposed, could be but for. a very brief period, the government having no resources whatever, and being sadly deficient in any of the sinews of war; and moreover such a war would be likely to flatter the national pride and conceit of the American people.

To bring, therefore, affairs to such a critical position on the Texan frontier, that a "state of war" could at any moment be assumed, and its imminence be actually very apparent, was the stroke of policy by which Polk and his party hoped to blind the people, and, profiting by it, make such preparations as would enable them to carry out their plans in connection with the Oregon question and the probable war with England. They thought that, even if hostilities broke out with Mexico, that power would at once succumb; and, in the mean time, that the war-fever in the United States would spread, and that the people would sanction an increase in the army and navy in such a case, which could at any time be. made available for another purpose.

The first shot fired on the Rio Grande changed their views. Until then the Americans were in utter ignorance of the state of Mexico and the Mexicans. They never anticipated such resistance as they have met with; but, judging, from the moral and physical inferiority of the people, at once concluded that all they had to do was *venire, videre, et vincere.* Children in the art of war, they imagined that personal bravery and physical strength were the only requisites for a military people; and that, possessing these qualities in as great a degree as the Mexicans were deficient in them, the operations in Mexico would amount to nothing more arduous than a promenade through the table-lands of Annhuac—the "Halls of Montezuma," in which it was the popular belief that they were destined "to revel," being the goal of their military *paseo* of six weeks.

As soon, however, as the list of killed and wounded on the fields of Palo Alto and Resaca de la Palma reached Washington, President Polk saw at once the error into which he had fallen. It became evident to him that all the resources of the country would be required to carry on the war with one of the most feeble powers in the world, and that the sooner he pulled his foot out of the hot water, which at the temperature of 54° 40' was likely to scald him, the better for him and his country; for it naturally occurred to him that, if such a scrimmage as the Mexican war gave him considerable trouble, an affair with such a respectable enemy as England was likely to prove anything but an agreeable pastime: and hence the very speedy acceptance of Lord Aberdeen's ultimatum, and the sudden settlement of the Oregon question.

As affairs now stand, and unless the United States very materially modify the conditions under which they signify their willingness to withdraw from the Mexican territory, and notwithstanding the avowedly pacific proposals of Commissioner Trist, it is difficult to assign any probable period for the termination of the war; and it is certain that, as the Mexican armies, one after the other, dissolve before the American attacks, and the farther the latter penetrate into the country, the greater are the difficulties which they will have to surmount. Harassed by hordes of guerrillas, with a long line of country in their rear admirably adapted by nature for the system of warfare pursued by irregular troops, and through which all supplies have to pass, to defeat an army is but to increase the conquerors' difficulties, since, while before they had one tangible enemy in their front, now they are surrounded by swarms of hornets, who never risk defeat by standing the brunt of a regular engagement.

Neither have the invariable and signal defeats the Mexicans have met with the same moral effect which such reverses have among more civilized nations. They take them as matters of course, and are not dispirited; while, on the other hand, the slightest success instils new life and energy into their hearts.

Until the whole country is occupied by American troops, the war, unless immediately concluded, will be carried on, and will eventually become one of conquest. But, in the mean time, the expenses it entails upon the treasury of the United States are enormous, and hourly increasing; and it would seem that the amount of compensation for the expenses of the war, which, in money or territory, is a *sine quâ non* in the peace proposals of the American commissioner, is consequently increasing *pari passu,* and therefore the settlement of the question becomes more difficult and uncertain.

It is extremely doubtful if the Mexican people will consent to a surrender of nearly one third of their territory, which will most probably be required as compensation for the expenses of the war, or, what is the same thing, be demanded as a security for the payment of a certain sum of money; and whether they will not rather prefer war to the knife to the alternative of losing their nationality. In reality, this war does them little harm. They were in such a state of misery and anarchy before it commenced, and have been for so long a period tyrannized over by the republican despots who have respectively held the reins of power, that no change could possibly make their condition more degraded; and the state of confusion and misrule attendant upon the war in such a country as Mexico is so congenial to the people, that, from my own observations, I believe them to be adverse, even on this account alone, to the termination of hostilities.

Moreover, the feeling against the Americans, which was at first mere apathy, has increased to the bitterest hatred and animosity, and is sufficient in itself to secure the popular support to the energetic prosecution of the war: and the consciousness of the justice of their cause, and the injustice of the unprovoked aggression on the part of the United States, ought, and I have no doubt will, keep alive one spark of that honour, which prompts a people to resent and oppose a wilful and wanton attack on their liberties and nationality.

CHAPTER 36

The End

After a stay of a few days in St. Louis, in order to rig myself out in civilized attire, I went on board a steamboat bound for the Illinois River and Peoria, intending to cross the prairies of Illinois to Chicago, and thence down the Canadian lakes to New York.

This river is more picturesque than the Missouri or Mississippi; the banks higher, the water clearer, and the channel dotted with pretty islands, between which the steam-boat passes, almost brushing the timber on the banks. At Peoria we were transferred to stagecoaches, and, suffering a martyrdom of shaking and bad living on the road—if road it can be called—we arrived at last at Chicago—the city, that is to be, of the Lakes, and which may be termed the City of Magnificent Intentions.

Chigago, or Chicago, is situated at the southwestern corner of Lake Michigan, and on the lake-shore. In spite of the pasteboard appearance of its houses, churches, and public edifices, all of wood, it is a remarkably pretty town, its streets wide and well laid out, and it will, doubtless, after it has been burned down once or twice, and rebuilt of stone or brick, be one of the finest of the western cities. It has several excellent hotels, some of which are of gigantic dimensions, a theatre, courthouse, and an artificial harbour, constructed at the expense of the city.

An American stagecoach has often been described: it is a huge lumbering affair with leathern springs, and it creaks and groans over the corduroy roads and unmacadamized causeways, thumping, bumping, and dislocating the limbs of its "insides," whose smothered shrieks and exclamations of despair often cause the woodsman to pause from his work, and, leaning upon his axe, listen with astonishment to the din which proceeds from its convulsed interior.

The coach contains three seats, each of which accommodates three passengers; those on the centre, and the three with their backs to the horses, face each other, and, from the confined space, the arrangement and mutual convenience of leg-placing not unfrequently leads to fierce outbreaks of ire. A fat old lady got into the coach at Peoria, whose uncompromising rotundity and snappishness of temper, combined with a most unaccommodating pair of "limbs" (legs, on this side the Atlantic), rendered her the most undesirable *vis-à-vis* that a traveller could possibly be inflicted with.

The victim happened to be an exceedingly mild Hoosier, whose modest bashfulness prevented his remonstrating against the injustice of the proceeding; but, after unmitigated sufferings for fifty miles, borne with Christian resignation, he disappeared from the scene of his martyrdom, and his place was occupied by a hard-featured New Yorker, the captain of one of the Lake steamboats, whose sternness of feature and apparent determination of purpose assured us that he had been warned of the purgatory in store for him, and was resolved to grapple gallantly with the difficulty.

As he took his seat, and bent his head to the right and left over his knees, looking, as it were, for some place to bestow his legs, an ominous silence prevailed in the rocking coach, and we all anxiously awaited the result of the attack which this bold man was evidently meditating; the speculations being as to whether the assault would be made in the shape of a mild rebuke, or a softly-spoken remonstrance and request for a change of posture.

Our skipper evidently imagined that his pantomimic indications of discomfort would have had a slight effect, but when the contrary was the result, and the uncompromising knees wedged him into the corner, his face turned purple with emotion, and, bending toward his tormentor, he solemnly exclaimed—"I guess, marm, it's got to be done anyhow sooner or later, so you and I, marm, must jist 'dovetail.'"

The lady bounded from her seat, aghast at the mysterious proposal.

"Must what, sir-r?"

"Dovetail, marm; you and I have got to dovetail, and no two ways about it."

"Dovetail me, you inhuman savage!" she roared out, shaking her fist in the face of the skipper, who shrunk, alarmed, into his corner; "dovetail a lone woman in a Christian country! if thar's law on airth, sir-r, and in the state of Illinoy, I'll have you hanged!"

"Driver, stop the coach," she shrieked from the window; "I go no farther with this man. I believe I ar' a free 'ooman, and my name is Peck. Young man," she pathetically exclaimed to the driver, who sought to explain matters, while we, inside, were literally convulsed with laughter, "my husband shall larn of this, as shiure as shiooting. Open the door, I say, and let me out!"

And, spite of all our expostulations, she actually left the coach and sought shelter in a house at the roadside; and we heard her, as we drove off, muttering, "Dovetail me, will they? the Injine savages! if thar's law in Illinoy, I'll have him hanged!"

It is unnecessary to say that "dovetailing" is the process of mutually accommodating each other's legs followed by stagecoach and omnibus passengers; but the term—certainly the first time I had ever heard it used in that sense—shocked and alarmed the modesty of the worthy Mrs. Peck of Illinoy.

A canal is in course of construction in the State of Illinois, to connect the waters of the lakes with the Mississippi—a gigantic undertaking, but one which will be of the greatest benefit to the western country. When this canal is completed, the waters of Lake Superior will, therefore, communicate with the Gulf of Mexico by way of the Mississippi, as they do already with the North Atlantic by means of the Welland and Rideau canals, which pass through Canada; and, even already, vessels have been spoken in mid-ocean, built on Lakes Michigan and Huron, cleared from Chicago, and bound for England, passing an inland navigation of upward of three thousand miles.

Leaving Chicago, I crossed the lake to Kalamazoo, whence I "railed" across the Michigan peninsula to Detroit, the chief city of the State of Michigan. This railroad was a very primitive affair, with but one line of rails, which, in very many places, were entirely divested of the iron, and in these spots the passengers were requested to "assist" the locomotive over the "bad places." However, after killing several hogs and cows, we arrived safe enough at Detroit.

I remarked that, since a former visit to the United States, three or four years ago, there had been a very palpable increase in the feeling of jealousy and dislike to England and everything British which has very generally characterized the free and enlightened citizens from the affair of Lexington to the present time. I must, however, do them the justice to declare, that in no one instance have I ever perceived that feeling evinced toward an individual; but it exists, most assuredly, as a national feeling, and is exhibited in the bitterest and most uncompromising spirit in all their journals, and the sayings and doings of their public men.

Thus, in travelling through the United States, an Englishman is perpetually hearing his country and its institutions abused. Everything he admires is at once seized upon, to be tortured into a comparison with the same thing in England. But what is more amusing is, that it is a very general belief that, from the Queen down to the gruel-stirrer in Marylebone workhouse, everybody's time is occupied with the affairs of the United States, and all their pleasures turned to gall and wormwood by the bitter envy they feel at her well-being and prosperity.

In passing down the lakes, I took a passage from Detroit to Buffalo in a Canadian steamer, which, by-the-by, was the most tastefully decorated and best-managed boat on the lake. As we passed through the Detroit River, which connects Lakes Erie and St. Clair, we had a fine view of the Canadian as well as the American shore; and the contrast between the flourishing settlements and busy cities of the latter, and the quaint, old-fashioned villages of the French Canadians was certainly sufficiently striking.

As the boat passed Malden, celebrated as being the scene of stirring events in the Indian wars, and the more recent one of 1812, I ascended, spite of the burning sun, to the upper deck, in order to obtain a view of the shore, which at this point, where the river enters the lake, is very picturesque and beautiful. I found a solitary passenger seated on the roof, which was red-hot with the burning rays of the sun, squirting his tobacco-juice fast and furiously, and with his eyes bent on the shore, and a facetious and self-satisfied grin on his lank, sallow countenance. His broad-brimmed brown beaver hat, with dishevelled nap, suit of glossy black, including a shining black satin waistcoat, of course proclaimed him to be a citizen. Waving his hand toward the Canada shore, he asked me, in a severe tone,

"What do you call this, sir? Is this the land of the Queen of England, sir?"

"Well, I guess it ain't nothing else," answered, for me, the pilot of the boat. "But," he continued, "it ain't a going to be so much longer."

"Longer, sir!" quoth my severe interrogator; "too long by half has that unfortunate country been oppressed by British tyrants. Look thar, sir," waving his arm toward the opposite shore; "thar's a sight, sir, where a man can look up to G— A'mighty's heavens, and bless him for having made him a citizen of the United States!"

"A fine country," I observed; "there's no doubt of it."

"A fine country, sir! the first country in the world, sir; and feeds the starving English with what it can't consume itself, sir. The philanthropy of our country" (he took me for a citizen) "flies on the wings of the wind, sir, and bears to the hungry slaves of the Queen of England corn, air, and bread-doins of every description. Yes, sir! and to show them, sir, that we can feed 'em with one band and whip 'em with the other, we send it over in a ship of war, which once carried their flag, until it was lowered to the flag of freedom. I allude, sir" (turning to me), "to the frigate *Macedonian*, and the stars and stripes of our national banner."

This speech, delivered in the most pompous manner, and with exuberant gesture, was too much for my gravity, and I exploded in an immoderate fit of laughter.

"Laugh, sir," he resumed, "pray laugh. I perceive you are not a native, and your countrymen had ort to laugh without loss of time; for soon, sir, will their smile of triumph be turned to a howl of despair, when Liberty treads to the earth your aristocracy—your titled lords—and the star-spangled banner waves over Windsor Palace." Saying which, and squirting over the deck a shower of tobacco-spray, he turned magnificently away.

"A smart man that, stranger," said the pilot to me, giving the wheel a spoke to port—"one of the smartest men in these parts." This I easily believed.

We had the misfortune to damage a part of the machinery just after entering Lake Erie, and were compelled to wait until another steamboat made her appearance, and towed us back to Detroit, where it took twenty-four hours to repair damages.

From Buffalo I travelled by railroad to Albany, on the Hudson, and, descending that magnificent river, reached New York early in July, in eight travelling days from St. Louis, a distance of—I am afraid to say how many thousand miles.

From New York the good ship *New World* carried myself and a dozen fellow-passengers, spite of contrary winds, in thirty days to Liverpool, where I arrived, *sin novedad,* sometime in the middle of August, 1847.

LEONAUR

ALSO FROM LEONAUR
AVAILABLE IN SOFTCOVER OR HARDCOVER WITH DUST JACKET

WAR BEYOND THE DRAGON PAGODA by *J. J. Snodgrass*—A Personal Narrative of the First Anglo-Burmese War 1824 - 1826.

ALL FOR A SHILLING A DAY by *Donald F. Featherstone*—The story of H.M. 16th, the Queen's Lancers During the first Sikh War 1845-1846.

AT THEM WITH THE BAYONET by *Donald F. Featherstone*—The first Anglo-Sikh War 1845-1846.

A LEONAUR ORIGINAL

THE HERO OF ALIWAL by *James Humphries*—The days when young Harry Smith wore the green jacket of the 95th-Wellington's famous riflemen-campaigning in Spain against Napoleon's French with his beautiful young bride Juana have long gone. Now, Sir Harry Smith is in his fifties approaching the end of a long career. His position in the Cape colony ends with an appointment as Deputy Adjutant-General to the army in India. There he joins the staff of Sir Hugh Gough to experience an Indian battlefield in the Gwalior War of 1843 as the power of the Marathas is finally crushed. Smith has little time for his superior's 'bull at a gate' style of battlefield tactics, but independent command is denied him. Little does he realise that the greatest opportunity of his military life is close at hand.

THE GURKHA WAR by *H. T. Prinsep*—The Anglo-Nepalese Conflict in North East India 1814-1816.

SOUND ADVANCE! by *Joseph Anderson*—Experiences of an officer of HM 50th regiment in Australia, Burma & the Gwalior war.

THE CAMPAIGN OF THE INDUS by *Thomas Holdsworth*—Experiences of a British Officer of the 2nd (Queen's Royal) Regiment in the Campaign to Place Shah Shuja on the Throne of Afghanistan 1838 - 1840.

WITH THE MADRAS EUROPEAN REGIMENT IN BURMA by *John Butler*—The Experiences of an Officer of the Honourable East India Company's Army During the First Anglo-Burmese War 1824 - 1826.

BESIEGED IN LUCKNOW by *Martin Richard Gubbins*—The Experiences of the Defender of 'Gubbins Post' before & during the sige of the residency at Lucknow, Indian Mutiny, 1857.

THE STORY OF THE GUIDES by *G.J. Younghusband*—The Exploits of the famous Indian Army Regiment from the northwest frontier 1847 - 1900.